ANTICIPATING CHINA

ANTICIPATING CHINA

*Thinking through the Narratives
of Chinese and Western Culture*

DAVID L. HALL
and
ROGER T. AMES

STATE UNIVERSITY OF NEW YORK PRESS

Published by
State University of New York Press, Albany

©1995 State University of New York

For information, address State University of New York Press,
State University Plaza, Albany, N.Y., 12246

Production by Cathleen Collins
Marketing by Theresa Abad Swierzowski

Library of Congress Cataloging in Publication Data

Hall, David L. and Roger T. Ames
    Anticipating China : thinking through the narratives of Chinese and
Western culture / David L. Hall and Roger T. Ames.
        p.   cm.
    ISBN 0-7914-2477-4. — ISBN 0-7914-2478-2
    1. China—Civilization.   2. Civilization, Western.   I. Ames,
Roger T., 1947–   . II. Title.
DS721.H24   1995
303.48'21921051—dc20   94-29157
                                                          CIP

10 9 8 7 6 5 4 3 2 1

For Angus

I settle my body like a rooted tree stump,
I hold my arm like the branch of a withered tree;
out of the vastness of heaven and earth,
the multitude of the myriad things,
it is only the wings of the cicada that I know.
I don't let my gaze wander or waver,
I would not take all the myriad things in exchange for the
  wings of a cicada.

Zhuangzi

Contents

Acknowledgements

This present work contains some material adapted from the following publications: David Hall's "Reason and it's Rhyme," first published in *Journal of the Indian Council of Philosophical Research* [Vol. IX (2), Sept.–Dec. 1992, pp. 25–46]; our joint publication, "Rationality, Correlativity and the Language of Process" [*The Journal of Speculative Philosophy*. [Vol 5 (2), 1991, pp. 85–106]; Roger Ames' "The Focus-Field Self in Classical Confucianism" in *Self as Person in Asian Theory and Practice* [ed. Roger T. Ames with Thomas Kasulis and Wimal Dissanayake, SUNY Press, 1993], and "Chinese Rationality: An Oxymoron?" in *Journal of the Indian Council of Philosophical Research* [Vol. IX (2) Sept.–Dec. 1992, pp. 95–119].

In the course of our own collaborative efforts, which began more than ten years ago, we have become increasingly aware of the manner in which all responsible scholarship is the product of collaboration. We are pleased, therefore, to acknowledge here some of those individuals who, often without knowing how significant was their contribution, have participated with us in the activities which have resulted in this book.

As with our *Thinking Through Confucius*, we were able to rehearse the argument of this present work in a number of venues which included locations in Europe, Russia, India, China, and Australia, as well as our home country. The most sustained of such efforts involved a tour of various American colleges and universities in the Fall of 1992. To our hosts and audiences at The University of Southern Maine, Boston University, Harvard University, Brown University,

Dickinson College, Ohio State University, DuPage Community College, Trinity University of San Antonio, Rice University, The University of California at Berkeley, The University of California at Davis, and Stanford University, we offer our gratitude along with the expectation that many who engaged our work at these locations will find in our book, and in the sequel volume which will follow shortly upon the publication of this one, tangible evidence of their positive contributions.

We are pleased to be able to thank the principal administrators at our two institutions who were sympathetic to the difficulties of long-distance collaboration and were willing to underwrite our efforts to get together, often for extended periods, in various parts of the world.

Five readers for SUNY Press—Joseph Grange, Randy Peerenboom, Lisa Raphals, John Rothfork, and Jim Tiles—read our work with varying degrees of sympathy but with a consistent regard for its improvement. This book, and its future readers, have certainly benefitted from their critiques.

Our relationship with Bill Eastman, editor of SUNY Press, has deepened over the years. One could hardly imagine an editor so inclined to nurture and support his authors' best efforts. Beginning with the splendid lunch in Albany which launched the formal publication of this book, and proceeding to the final phases of its production, Bill has expressed his belief in the work's importance and has maintained a consistent and creative oversight of the many details which attended its publication.

The quiet competence of our production editor, Cathleen Collins, has served throughout both to challenge and to reassure us. We are aware that the production of a book of this sort involves more than the average allotment of problems and of complexities, and are most appreciative of the sensitive and professional manner in which Cathleen has managed to guide our book into print.

Normally, there would be some hesitation in offering thanks to one who is, by all accounts, deceased. But Angus Graham, to whom this book is dedicated, clearly calls for an exception. Angus' presence throughout the preparation of this work has been both palpable, and vital. It would have been impossible for us to think through these issues without including him in our dialogue.

Finally, as is our custom, each of us wishes to thank the other for his supererogatory dedication, hard work, and enthusiasm. Mutual friends, recognizing that both parties to this collaboration may be said to own more than his share of *hubris*, often wonder how we manage to maintain such a harmonious working relationship. Sometimes, on reflection, we wonder about that ourselves. Perhaps the secret lies in the fact that, *hubris* aside, each of us also owns a profound appreciation of difference.

David L. Hall
The University of Texas
at El Paso

Roger T. Ames
The University of Hawai'i

Introduction:
Anticipating the Argument

1. CLEARING A PATH TO CHINA

Some years ago, Karl Jaspers forwarded his concept of the "Axial Age"—the period between roughly 800 and 200 B.C.E. in which all major cultures presumably had their most creative development. This was an age, according to Jaspers, in which individuals began "to experience the absolute through the heights of transcendence and the depths of subjectivity."[1]

If comparative philosophy has anything to say about Chinese culture during the so-called Axial Age, it is certainly this: notions of "absoluteness," "transcendence," and "subjectivity" were of doubtful significance. Absolute and transcendent Beings such as Aristotle's God or Plato's Forms, or absolute and transcendent principles such as the Principle of Sufficient Reason, would be difficult to find in China—as would the celebration of the autonomous, meditative, subjective individual who emerges as a principal character in developing Western cultures. Indeed, the philosopher of culture is likely to find that not only such ideas as "absoluteness," "transcendence," and "subjectivity," but any number of other notions essential to the development of Western intellectual traditions, were broadly irrelevant to the origins and development of the Chinese cultural milieu.

In a most important sense, it does appear that divergent paths were taken at a number of crucial moments in the development of Chinese and Western cultures. The consequence of this divergence is that the problematics of Anglo-European culture and that of China are really quite distinct. That is to say, the art, politics, and religion; the scientific and moral sensibilities; and the senses of chronology embodied in history are distinct enough between China and the West so as to make the task of translating issues and meanings from one culture to another extremely challenging.

One of the principal barriers precluding the Westerner from understanding China on its own terms involves the persistence in Western cultures of what Robert Solomon has so aptly termed the "transcendental pretense."[2] In part, this term refers to the paradoxical shape taken by Western ethnocentrism. Central to our beliefs as Anglo-European heirs of the Enlightenment is the conviction that the scientific rationality emergent at the beginnings of the sixteenth century names a universal norm for assessing the value of cultural activity everywhere on the planet. This expression of our provincialism has arguably been more harmful than those insular attitudes that harbor less evangelical motives.

Late-nineteenth-and early-twentieth-century translations of classical Chinese texts, made by missionizing Christians, introduced terms such as "Heaven," "Truth," and "Self" as translations for terms which bear little resemblance to these concepts. More recently, there have been psychologists, both Western and Chinese, who have significantly distorted the Chinese world by presupposing that notions such as Freud's "Oedipal situation" or Jung's "archetypes" are relevant to the interpretation of Chinese sensibilities. Historians of science and political theorists have at times conspired to insure a misunderstanding of Chinese concepts of law by assuming the validity of transcendent forms of natural law, on the one hand, or positivist forms of imposed law, on the other. And there are both sociologists and political theorists who perpetuate flawed understandings of the Chinese political process by failing to note shifts in the meanings of power and authority as we move from West to East, or by presupposing the traditional Western distinction of private and public spheres of social existence where no such distinction obtains, or by assuming that the absence of a tradition of natural rights in China is necessarily a function of authoritarian or even totalitarian motivations. Some Western historians have insisted upon exporting to China irrelevant historiographical models that make the Chinese appear to be naive and irresponsible caretakers of their own past.

These distortions arise from a failure to give adequate notice to the contrasting assumptions that shape the cultural milieux of China and the West. This failing is itself encouraged by the universalist impulse associated with Western rationality and the "transcendental pretense."

At least one miscalculation made in approaching China is more a consequence of insensitivity to the nuances of the Chinese tradition than to transcendental pretense. This is the questionable assumption that Karl Marx is more important than Confucius—or Zhuangzi—in understanding contemporary China. Doctrinaire Marxism is effectively moribund as a political philosophy. Indeed, for much of its life in China, as elsewhere, Marxism was reshaped by its proponents into a seedy, effete, ideology which rationalized elitist, top-down forms of revolution. In instance after instance in recent Chinese history, the rhetoric has been Marxist while the motivation and sentiment has, in the broadest sense, been more traditional and "Confucian." And we, to our detriment, have been inclined to listen to China's rhetoric, thus misconstruing its sentiment and motivation.

While attempting to maintain a real sensitivity to the nuances of the Chinese experience, we must not become lost in the details. As important as such details are when performing analyses of this or that aspect of a society or culture, comparativists will be prevented from making sense of a culture if they do not diligently avoid the Fallacy of the Counterexample. After all, generalizations concerning cultural importances are often vindicated, not falsified, by resort to counter-examples precisely to the extent that such examples suggest the relative absence of a particular belief or doctrine. For to determine whether a concept or theory or thematic is *in* a culture in the strong sense that assessments of cultural determinants require, we must ask: Is it *importantly* present? Has it contributed significantly to the shaping of a cultural milieu. Therefore, as a means of maintaining our focus upon the truly important ideas and issues, we will do our best to respect the following principle:

> *The mere presence of an idea or doctrine in a particular cultural matrix does not permit us to claim that the doctrine or idea is importantly present—that is, present in such a way that it significantly qualifies, defines, or otherwise shapes the culture.*[3]

An employment of the Principle of Mere Presence, where relevant, allows the comparativist to remain focused upon what is truly important in shaping cultural sensibilities.

The difficulty of intercultural translation can be illustrated by recourse to Ludwig Wittgenstein's familiar figure of the Duck-Rabbit. The Chinese have drawn a duck in instances where we should expect to see a rabbit. The failure to appreciate this difference and its implications can lead us into some discomfiting confusions. Thus we may be led to ask: Are the cultural assumptions of mainstream Western culture *in* China if we are able to make out the outlines of a rabbit only over against the insistence of the artist that the figure is a duck?

The problem may become even more perplexing if our Chinese and Western interlocutors have learned of one another's worlds, as intellectuals most often do, principally through textual media. More often than not, the filter of one's own language serves to make otherwise alien ways of thinking seem almost familiar. For example, when Western students of Chinese culture see *tian* 天 translated as "Heaven," they may naturally assume that connotations of transcendence and spirituality attaching to the notion of "heaven" in their tradition apply to *tian*. And when Chinese students of Western culture see "God" translated as *tianzhu* 天主, "the Master of *tian*," or as *shangdi* 上帝, "the ancestral lord," they contextualize this term by appealing to an ancestral continuum analogous to our family structure. In instances such as this, the Westerner is inclined to believe that the Chinese, too, see a rabbit, just as the Chinese individual is persuaded that we are all looking at a duck.

In the process of completing our *Thinking Through Confucius*,[4] we realized the need for a sequel which would provide the broadest of contexts for the sorts of claims we were making there. Most of the comparative essays we have produced since 1987, both jointly and independently, have been written with that aim in mind. *Anticipating China*, and a second volume which will follow soon after the publication of this work,[5] are meant to realize that aim. We hope that this present work, and its sequel, will serve to clarify and develop many lines of argument we have heretofore only sketchily presented.

The argument of our essay may be summarized as follows: In chapter 1 we will defend the claim that the shape of our intellectual culture has been importantly determined by ideas invented or discovered in the period culminating with the work of Augustine in the fifth century of our Common Era. This defense will take the form of a narrative of the development of Western philosophical culture from its beginnings to the Augustinian age.

Our motivation in making such a broad claim is heuristic and pragmatic. The import of our claim is simply this: (a) the period we shall be detailing is a source of truly important interpretive constructs, (b) these constructs are contingent products of particular historical and cultural circumstances, and (c) they continue to qualify our cultural and intercultural understandings in significant manners.

If we can sustain these three assertions we shall be in a position to approach the ultimate aim of our study, which is to promote intercultural understanding between China and the West. For our argument will be that awareness of at least some of the important ideas and beliefs that have shaped us, and of their cultural contingency, will prevent us from too easily resorting to "transcendental pretense" in our approach to alternative cultures.

While the broad assumptions we shall outline have dominated our societies well into the Modern period, and remain obvious to most of us, every one of them is the consequence of the often tacit rejection of alternative beliefs. In the narrative of chapter 1, we shall provide a sense of the evolution of these commonly held notions from a context that includes some of their more controversial alternatives. Along the way we shall elaborate a contrast between *first* and *second problematic thinking* as a means of providing a language with which to articulate the relationship between the dominant and recessive modes of thinking within our Western tradition.[6]

Second problematic thinking, which we shall also term *causal thinking*, is the mode which comes to dominate the classical West. Its presuppositions are (1) the construal of the beginning of things in terms of "chaos" as either emptiness, separation, or confusion; (2) the understanding of "cosmos" as a single-ordered world; (3) the assertion of the priority of rest over change and motion (alternately expressed as the preference for "being" over "becoming"); (4) the belief that the order of the cosmos is a consequence of some agency of construal such as *Nous* (Νοῦς), the *Demiourgos* (Δημιουργός), the Unmoved Mover, the Will of God, and so on; and, finally, (5) the tacit or explicit claim that the states of affairs comprising "the world" are grounded in, and ultimately determined by, these agencies of construal.

Alongside the development of rational, causal thinking we shall consider the importance of what we will term *first problematic*, or alternatively, *analogical* or *correlative* thinking. First problematic thinking is neither strictly cosmogonical nor cosmological in the sense that there is the presumption neither of an initial beginning nor of the existence of a single-ordered world. This mode of thinking accepts the priority of change or process over rest and permanence, presumes no ultimate agency responsible for the general order of things, and seeks to account for states of affairs by appeal to correlative procedures rather than by determining agencies or principles.

Our comparative exercise would be philosophically empty were it not for the fact that, as we shall attempt to demonstrate, comparisons between classical Chinese and Western culture turn out to be comparisons of contexts shaped by alternative problematics *analogous* to the two just described: A form of first problematic thinking, while recessive in the West, dominates classical Chinese culture. Likewise, the cultural dominant of the West, which we are calling second problematic or causal thinking, is recessive within classical Chinese culture.

We shall argue that the respective values of analogical and causal thinking, as two contingent strategies human beings employ to accommodate themselves to their surroundings, should be assessed solely on pragmatic terms. Such a claim challenges the viability of the Enlightenment reading of cultural development, which argues that the movement from *mythos* to *logos* or "from religion to philosophy,"[7] or from analogical to causal thinking, ought to serve as the norm for the civilizing of human experience.

Our claim is hardly as controversial as it once might have been. "Postmodern" sensibilities, associated with individuals such as Heidegger, Foucault, and Derrida, along with the new pragmatism of Donald Davidson and Richard Rorty, carry forward (in a variety of ways) the critique of the Enlightenment project begun by Friedrich Nietzsche in the nineteenth century. The relevance of this critique to the argument of our present work is that it constitutes a sustained assault upon the dominance of rational and casual thinking, and a stimulus to return to the analogical procedures of first problematic thought. And though our primary concern is to illumine the contrasting assumptions shaping classical Chinese and Western cultures, we shall not be disappointed if a side effect of our discussion is to add some plausibility to the various intellectual movements which are attempting to reformulate important aspects of our own cultural sensibility.

After rehearsing in the broadest of strokes what we take to be a plausible narrative of our cultural development, we move on in chapter 2 to a consideration of the value, for comparative understandings of Chinese and Western culture, of the existence of an interpretive strand alternative to that of the rational problematic. Our argument here is essentially that we set aside the inventory of interpretive concepts drawn from the rational problematic and interpret Chinese culture by appealing to the inspiration of the aesthetic problematic. Given our historicist assumptions, we cannot support any final dependence upon the specific content of ideas and doctrines developing from first problematic thinking in the West. Rather we shall argue that comparativists must, insofar as is possible, attempt to understand Chinese culture on its own terms. This means that we must take our cues from the manner in which the intellectual activity in classical China *most analagous to* our first problematic has been articulated.

Chapter 3 attempts to illustrate how this might be done by providing an account of the congealing of classical Chinese culture in the Han dynasty. Having identified and set aside the dominant, but extraneous, interpretive notions from the Western inventory, we attempt to provide a less freighted understanding of "the people of the Han." This understanding is informed by the dominance of notions of process and particularity, and the preference for "correlative" over "causal" thinking.

The main title of our work is purposefully ambiguous. The locution "anticipating China" carries a number of allied meanings. In the first sense, we shall anticipate an understanding of China by reconstituting the elements of classical Western culture in a manner that will provide us a better set of tools for assaying the Chinese sensibility. In a second sense, aided by these new tools, we shall attempt at least to *adumbrate* a fresh account of the development of Chinese culture. This account, in turn, is meant to anticipate a more elaborate interpretation in a second book to follow. Thus, both in this volume and its sequel, we wish to argue for a "deferred understanding." An immediate consequence of surrendering the transcendental pretense is that ambitious, globalizing assertions which essentialize cultural experience and interpretation must give way to more modest and localized understandings. Theoretical structures must ultimately be replaced by more tentative and provisional narratives. Our project is

XX   INTRODUCTION

not at all to *tell it like it is*; we merely wish to present a narrative
which is interesting enough and plausible enough to engage those
inclined to join the conversation.

A third use of the term "anticipation" is specifically relevant to the
admittedly unusual organization of our work. A reader, anticipating a
book about China, may wonder why we have begun our work with a
lengthy narrative of the development of classical Western culture. The
answer to this question lies in the fact that we believe comparative
discussions cannot usefully depend upon dialectical argumentation.
The most fruitful method for the comparative philosopher is one
which provides accounts that contextualize alternative arguments in
such a manner as to highlight their practical strengths and weaknesses
as interpretive devices. This is done, not through logical analysis, but
through a simple juxtaposition which seeks to identify those contexts
within which one's arguments, as well as the proposed alternatives,
are relevant. Our construction of a narrative of the development of
classical Western culture as a means of contextualizing our subsequent discussion of classical China is a consequence of having chosen
this method.

Our comparative method, which we have in other contexts termed
ars contextualis,[8] presumes that it is often impossible to clarify what
something is without saying a great deal about what it is not. This is
particularly true when, as in the present situation, the otherwise most
useful interpretive ideas turn out to be real barriers to understanding.
In his efforts at reconstructing philosophy, John Dewey asserted his
aim to be that of "removing the useless lumber blocking our highways of thought." This well defines the task we have set for ourselves.
We wish primarily to clear away the useless lumber blocking the path
to China. Paradoxically, that useless lumber turns out to include
many of the concepts and doctrines that came to comprise the dominant intellectual inventory of Western culture.

Our account of the rise of the Western cultural dominant during
the classical period is meant to raise to consciousness those assumptions which hinder members of Western culture from understanding
China on its own terms, and to provide those alternative categories
more likely to allow access to Chinese culture. To the extent that we
are successful, we hope not only to convince some individuals of the
irrelevance of interpretive notions to which they may have formerly
appealed in their accounts of Chinese culture, but also to persuade

other more empirically minded thinkers who believed themselves to have avoided resort to philosophical interpretation, that they too are burdened by these same assumptions.

In fact we are less concerned with the tender-minded theoreticians than with the tough-minded social scientists. For the turn toward pragmatism and historicism endorsed by this work has as a basic implication an ultimate devaluation of the cultural role of philosophy. An underlying assumption of this work is that, in the area of comparative studies, philosophical theorizing should be replaced by more concrete, praxis-oriented endeavors. But, though we do believe that anthropologists, ethnographers, and others will *eventually* be prepared to tell us more of what we need to know about alternative cultural sensibilities, this will not come about until they are first persuaded that they, too, are unknowing carriers of extraneous interpretive constructs.

A further word concerning the rationale behind including a detailed account of the development of classical Western culture in a book about China: This book has been self-consciously written for both Chinese and Western audiences. The narrative of the development of the Western cultural sensibility from the Greeks to Augustine will offer our Chinese readers a foothold for further comparative reflection, if only by offering an account of that development that highlights an alternative to the exclusionary Enlightenment narrative, one which is much better disposed toward those elements in Western culture which resonate with the Chinese sensibilities. It is also the case that those Western sinologists trained primarily in Chinese language and culture, and less so in Greek philosophy, might find our account of the beginnings of Western culture useful. Finally, by virtue of its concern to parallel two distinct cultural developments, our work might serve as a useful introduction to comparative philosophy.

2. CIRCLES AND SQUARES

One manner of evoking a sense of the differences between China and the West is through a meditation on the figures of the circle and the square.

For example, the primordial importance of the image of "circularity" in both cultures may belie the distinct manners in which the two cultures have dealt with this image. In the Western world, defined ultimately in terms of Being and Permanence, the perfection of circularity has been used to challenge the imperfections of motion and change. That which exists was seen as "the body of a well-rounded sphere." The bounded cosmos was itself most often construed as spherical.

But the acknowledged perfection of the circle has not prevented certain modern heirs of Pythagoras from lamenting the incommensurability of mathematical expressions (such as that irrational π) that try to express its nature. Thus, we in the West have tended to rationalize the circle, rendering it in some formulaic manner that more closely approximates the demands of exactness and certitude. In fact, one of the romantic ideals of Western thinkers was for a long time "squaring the circle."

The theme of squaring the circle found in the West has its functional counterpart in China in the effort to envision the square, like the circle, as ultimately unbounded and incomplete. The Han dynasty tables which provide ordered columns of correlations, matching the various seasons with the principal directions, the processes of nature, classes of animals, and so forth, offer no suggestion of exhaustiveness. Like the circle, these modes of organization are open and indefinitely extensible.

Among the Chinese, circles and squares have been dominated not by their peripheries but by their centers. It is not the bounded circle or square one is apt to meet in Chinese art, literature, or philosophy, but the "radial" circle and the "nested" square which extend themselves ever outward from their centers.[9] The Chinese claim that the world is but "the ten thousand things" bears little suggestion that it is a bounded or a boundable whole. Such a world is a set of foci from which relatedness to what at the moment is deemed "center" may be negotiated.

The differing understandings of circles and squares in Chinese and Western cultures is more suggestive than might first appear to be the case. The importance of the development of formal concepts in the Western tradition, born with the Socratic quest for "definitions," illustrates the significance of knowledge as a function of *enclosure*. To "de-fine" is to set finite boundaries. On the other hand, the Chinese depend, for the most part, upon exemplary models or instances rather than strict definitions to evoke understanding. Knowledge under these conditions has an element of rich, unbounded vagueness which contrasts rather starkly with the Western "quest for certainty."

We shall elaborate upon these contrasting interpretations of circles and squares in the latter part of this work specifically with respect to the question of the acquisition and organization of knowledge. We mention this contrast here as a means of offering a set of guiding metaphors which will allow our readers to anticipate the most general features of our argument.

Our book is really about the activity of intercultural philosophy, and its ultimate aim is to encourage strategic and tactical reflections that serve to abet intercultural conversations. We hope, as well, that our work will help to recover novel elements within our own cultural resources that resonate with aspects of the classical Chinese sensibility. For it is only when we become sensitive to indigenous elements that resonate with the important Chinese values and doctrines that we will be able to appropriate elements of that alien culture to enrich our own experience. Alternatively, we would hope that our work will facilitate the complementary operations on the part of Chinese translators of Western concepts.

In sum: the path we are endeavoring to clear to China should encourage traffic in both directions.

CHAPTER ONE

Squaring the Circle

There is reason to believe that human genius reached
its culmination in the twelve hundred years preceding
and including the initiation of the Christian Epoch. . . .
Of course, since then there has been progress in
knowledge and technique. But it has been along lines
laid down by the activities of that golden age.

A.N. Whitehead

A chief task of those who call themselves philosophers
is to help get rid of the useless lumber that blocks our
highways of thought, and strive to make straight and
open the paths that lead to the future.

John Dewey

Western culture in its broadest, most effective sense was formed
in two separate phases: first, in the period prior to the collapse
of the Athenian city-states in the fourth century before the Common
Era; and second, in that period characterized by the convergence of
Hellenic, Hebraic, and Roman values and institutions. This latter
phase effectively culminated in the fifth century in the work of
St. Augustine. By that time we had come to hold as self-evident a
number of significant propositions that have shaped and continue to
shape our cultural reasonings and practice with respect to our
aesthetic, moral, religious, scientific, philosophic, and historical sensibilities.

Such a stark assertion as the above, which does in fact entail the
claim that the present status of our culture is in some sense a projection of its temporal origins, may suggest to some that we have con-

fused the logical and temporal orders and have fallen into the "genetic fallacy." But such a suggestion would be plausible only if we were to claim that the present status of our intellectual culture is either *exhaustively* isomorphic with its beginnings, or in some important senses *inevitably* so. The dominant features of our culture, expressed in the form of broad doctrinal traditions which contextualize the most important meanings for our concepts and beliefs, exist alongside an inexhaustibly complex set of alternative ideas and practices the attentuation of which is, though partly the result of limitations of creativity and imagination, largely a function of the rise to dominance of an objectivist bias which leads us, above all, to search out "the truth of the matter," and to exclude what does not conform to that truth.

Thus, the lack of subtlety and nuance characterizing our inventory of interpretive tools, and the heavy-handedness with which they have so often been employed, is little more than the ideological consequence of that intellectual inertia which so often accompanies objectivist and dogmatic sensibilities. Far from supporting this consequence by seeking any transcendental rationale for our cultural development, we shall be arguing that this objectivist bias is in the truest sense a product of our peculiar history.

In what follows we shall dismiss any attempt to tell the story of classical Western culture *als zwar gewesen ist*, believing that to be the most fanciful of projects. A chief purpose of historical narratives is, after all, to make some sense of one's presented locus by responsible appeals to the past. In providing a narrative of the development of our classical cultural sensibility which is a distinct alternative to that offered by the familiar Enlightenment account of the movement from *mythos* to *logos*, we are, of course, claiming that our present is a post-Enlightenment present, one which is no longer informed by the assumptions that characterize our so-called modern age.[1]

Our claim is that there are as many distinctive and important accounts of the past as there are significant perspectives offered by the present. That we shall be offering a story of the rise and fall of second problematic, causal thinking is solely due to the fact that one of the most important perspectives currently offered us is that of a present characterized by a powerful, sustained, and thus far largely successful critique of second problematic assumptions.

1. FROM CHAOS TO COSMOS

In characterizing the shape of our intellectual culture we should like to begin at the beginning. But if our discussion must presuppose a world—that is, a cosmos as an ordered whole—we are hardly able to do so. As reasoning creatures, we seem forced to cut short any return to the origins and "begin" *in medias res*. Celebrating the truth of Virgil's advice in the words of Robert Frost, we feel constrained to say:

Ends and beginnings—there are no such things.
There are only middles.[2]

Reasonable words, certainly: the end hasn't come, and the beginning is lost in the obscurity of chaos. Were we to stalk the time of beginnings before there was order or harmony, we could find only irrationality, since reason as the means by which we grasp first principles would take us only as far as that moment after the illumining of chaos. Reason and reasoning are tied to the notion of primordial beginnings. Cosmologies are the groundworks of rational order. Cosmogonies, by presupposing a "time" characterized by a basic irrationality, or nonrationality, remind us that beyond the conception of an ordered and harmonious universe lies emptiness, alienation, confusion. Pursued to their ground, therefore, all theories, principles, laws, and valuations characteristic of our Anglo-European culture dissolve into the yawning gap, the emptiness, the confusion, of our chaotic beginnings.

The *Oxford English Dictionary* tells us that "beginning" refers to "the action or process of entering upon existence," "that out of which anything has its rise." The source of this arising is chaos ($\chi\acute{\alpha}o\varsigma$)—"the elemental," "the first state of the universe," "the great deep or abyss." Further: "principle" (*arche ἀρχή*) is directly related to *archon* ($\check{\alpha}\rho\chi\omega\nu$), one authorized to *give orders*. Principles are beginning points of thought and action. But "beginning" itself is a richly poetic term carrying, through primary associations with the Old English *gínan*, the meaning of "the yawning gap," or "gaping void" of chaos. Principles and beginnings dissolve, at their roots, into arbitrariness and confusion.

Thus, *arche, principium*, beginning, all refer to the *origin*, "the first state of the universe"—namely, chaos. We contrast chaos with "cosmos" as the ordered or harmonious world. The idea of bringing cosmos out of chaos is at the very root of our conception of beginnings. But "cosmos" as applied to the external surround is a relatively late notion. The presumption of a single-ordered world was by no means authorized by empirical or logical generative criteria. "Cosmos" comes from the verb *kosmeo* (κοσμέω), which means "to set in order." This word carries primary associations of housekeeping, military organization, or cosmetic adornment. Thus *kosmos* describes a state of being ordered, arranged, or adorned. The term was long in such ordinary use before it came to be applied, ostensibly by Pythagoras (?582–?500), as a means of describing the external surround:

> Pythagoras was the first to call what surrounds us a cosmos, because of the order in it.[3]

Anaximander (?611–?547) believed that all things arose out of "the boundless (τὸ ἄπειρων)." He thus replaced the more materialistic sounding imagery of Thales ("Everything is water") with something without qualities or shape or structure, but from out of which all things with qualities, shape, and structure arose. For Anaximander, qualities were conceived to exist in pairs, as contraries, "hot and cold," "moist and dry." The indeterminate "boundless" could thus be determined in relation to a balance or conflict of opposite qualities:

> And the source of coming to be for existing things is that into which destruction, too, happens, "according to necessity"; for they pay penalty and retribution to each other for their injustice according to the assessment of Time.[4]

What is striking about this citation from Anaximander is that the world-order is analogized from the order of the law court.[5] Since, as we have seen, the ordering function associated with the Greek *kosmeo* was originally used to designate man-made orders, the analogy suggested here supports the notion that the very idea of cosmos was an invention.[6]

Not only is the status of the notion of cosmos as an ordered whole called into question; of equal significance is the fact that the singularity of world-order is itself controversial. Xenophanes believed that

> there are innumerable world-orders, but that they do not overlap.[7]

Indeed, it was commonly accepted by the early chroniclers of philosophy that Anaximander believed in an infinite number of worlds which succeeded one another in time. This is an implication of his vision of the harmony of opposites. All things that come into being from the boundless must return to it. This includes any given world-order:

These world-orders, Anaximander supposed, are dissolved and born again according to the age which each is capable of attaining.[8]

Democritus, too, believed in the existence of a plurality of worlds:

In some worlds there is no sun and moon, in others they are larger than in our world, and in others more numerous. The intervals between the worlds are unequal; in some parts there are more worlds, in others fewer; some are increasing, some at their height, some decreasing; in some parts they are arising, in others failing. They are destroyed by collision one with another. There are some worlds devoid of living creatures or plants or any moisture.[9]

Democritus' view that a plurality of world-orders coexist in space is a consequence of his assumption of an infinite number of eternally existing atoms randomly colliding in infinite space. The likely combinations of atoms into elements, compounds, planets, star systems, and so forth would be infinite, and over an infinite amount of time these combinations would be realized, but it is also true that in infinite space an indefinitely large number of world-orders would coexist.

One of the valuable lessons of returning to the origins of philosophic speculation is we thereby discover that many of our more obvious commonsense beliefs are the result of choices made at the beginning of reflective thought. Order is not presupposed, but constructed by analogy to the artificial order of human society. That there is a single world is not a given but is something that comes to be believed.[10]

One interesting bit of evidence about the early controversy concerning the question of one or many worlds comes from Plato's writings. In the *Philebus*, Plato has Socrates enjoin censure against the "blasphemy" that "the sum of things or what we call this universe is controlled by a power that is irrational and blind," and is "devoid of order."[11] And in the *Timaeus* there is the claim that "the creator made not two worlds or an infinite number of them, but there is and ever will be one only-begotten and created heaven."[12] That the order of the world, particularly in its character as a single-ordered universe, should be in question might seem rather odd to us moderns, but the struggle suggested by the discussions of order in Plato was a real one. Many of the earliest thinkers believed in a plurality of worlds. These worlds were thought either to succeed one another in time, or to coexist in the vastness of unlimited space.[13]

Plato's struggle with "blasphemy" and "impiety" throughout his writings culminates in the *Laws*, wherein the penalties for those who assert that the world is "devoid of order"—that it is not ordered according to "what is best"—are set out as five years imprisonment for an initial offense, followed by execution and burial outside the gates of the city for a second act of impiety.[14]

On the principle that it is unlikely that such a fuss would be made over an issue unless the issue were of practical importance, we can plausibly speculate that the debate over the existence of a unitary cosmos was one of the significant debates in the ancient world. And, as we shall see, the fact that proponents of a single-ordered world won the argument in the West is truly a consequence of this view being more "reasonable." The irony, of course, is that this fact in turn is a consequence of the interdependence of the notions of "reason" and the belief in a single-ordered world. Thus, it is not just the contingency of the latter belief we are focusing upon; we mean to call attention to the contingency of the notion of rationality as well.

"Cosmos" is a metaphor, applied analogically to the world about us. Our ambiance was thought to be a complex manyness before it was held to be "one, single, and unitary." Indeed, quite apart from the explicitly Greek context, the Germanic-based English word, "world" (*wer* + *ald*, Ger. *Welt*) means the "age or life of man." Any association of orderedness besides that relevant to the arbitrary, contingent, human order is absent from this notion. In the beginning was chaos.

Three primitive conceptions of chaos have taken on importance in our cultural self-understanding. The Semitic myth of *Genesis*, related to the Babylonian creation myth, *Enuma elish*, tells us:

In the beginning the earth was without form, and void, and darkness was upon the face of the waters.[15]

The description of the source or origin as a formless, dark, void is similar to the characterizations of chaos in terms of the "primordial waters" in Egyptian and Mesopotamian creation myths. Such a cosmogonic process tells of a victory over the forces of chaos. God's command in *Genesis*, "Let there be light," establishes order by a command.

Besides the vision of chaos as formless nonbeing,[16] there is the position of the Orphic cosmologies of the fifth- and sixth-century B.C.E. which interprets chaos as "separation," reflecting one of the root meanings of chaos—namely, "yawning gap." In these myths, chaos is often associated with the gap between heaven and earth. Eros, as specifically sexual or procreative love, serves as the means of unifying the two and overcoming chaos.

Hesiod's *Theogony* tells of the coming into being of earth and sky and of the region in between. The union of earth and sky achieves unity at the cosmological level.[17] This myth may have been influenced by the Babylonian creation epic, *Enuma elish*, with its division of Tiamat into sky and earth, as well as by *Genesis*, which tells of God's division of the waters below and above the firmament. Of course, the specific senses of chaos in the two myths are distinct.

The sexual imagery in Hesiod (Earth = Female, Heaven = Male) suggests that opposition is at the root of generation but that differentiation of this sort entails distance, a gap, chaos. Aristophanes' myth of the round men in Plato's *Symposium* rings a variation on this theme. Individuals, split in two by Zeus, seek though the agency of eros to reestablish their original wholeness. The separation, the chaos, that came into being with sexual differentiation is to be overcome by love.

A third type of cosmogonic myth is illustrated by Plato's *Timaeus*. Here the imposition of order through persuasion leads to the creation of an ordered cosmos:

> Desiring, then, that all things should be good and, so far as might be, nothing imperfect, the god took over all that is visible—*not at rest but in discordant and unordered motion*—and brought it from disorder into order. . . . Reason overruled Necessity by persuading her to guide *the greatest part of things that become* towards what is best; in that way and on that principle this universe was fashioned in the beginning by the victory of reasonable persuasion over Necessity.[18]

There is no concern in Plato's myth for supporting a preexistent chaos; the only important consideration is that the divine persuasive agency reduces the threat of chaotic disorder (though, as the text suggests, not completely).

The reference to "rest" is interesting in that it advertises the view of the majority of the Greeks (Plato and Aristotle were chief protagonists of such a vision) that rest is the more perfect state, and that motion, therefore, requires explanation. Plato's version of this belief is, as we have seen, connected with the view that chaos is disordered motion, and any explanation of such motion must take into account that its origin is to be found in the disordered and the irrational.

In the *Genesis* myth, the origin of light from darkness, and the consequent creation of an ordered universe, consequences of *creatio ex nihilo*, are accomplished by a command, an *order*. Plato's cosmogony promotes an alternative explanation: Whereas power creates something from nothing, reason brings order from discord. Hesiod's *Theogony* describes the conquest of chaos by eros as a drive toward primordial unity. Thus, in all the senses of chaos rehearsed so far, the beginning of things involves an act of construal. Whether as nonbeing, as disorder, or as a separating gap, chaos is *overcome*.

There are certain Gnostic cosmogonies of the early Christian era which provide a radical alternative to the dominant cosmogonic myths. Many of the gnostics believed that the world is the product of a demiurge identified with the Old Testament God who is evil, not good:

> Whoever has created the world, man does not owe him allegiance. . . . Since not the true God can be the creator of that to which selfhood feels so utterly a stranger, nature merely manifests its lowly demiurge: as a power deep beneath the Supreme God, upon which every man can look down from the height of his god-kindred spirit, this perversion of the Divine has retained of it only the power to act, but to act blindly, without knowledge and benevolence.[19]

In the three types of myth rehearsed above, the ordering element was described as thought, action, or passion. Gnostic cosmogonies merely invert these alternatives by claiming that the creator's power is the blind and reckless power of an ignorant being with distorted emotion. Chaos is the consequence of an abortive attempt at creation.

As regards the question of origins, Gnostic myths share the same attitude toward chaos.

We do find interpretations of chaos which are not wholly negative. According to Werner Jaeger,

> The common idea of chaos as something in which all things are wildly confused is quite mistaken; and the antithesis between Chaos and Cosmos, which rests on this incorrect view, is a purely modern invention. Possibly the idea of *tohu wa bohu* has inadvertently been read into the Greek conception from the biblical account of creation in *Genesis*.[20]

It is true that, for Aristotle, chaos meant merely "empty space."[21] But then Aristotle's use of the term was itself quite modern compared to that of the Orphics and Hesiod. Already Aristotle has demythologized the concept of beginnings by employing the notion of "principle" (ἀρχή) in a nontheological context. Aristotle is part of a tradition that has begun to forget the presence of the chaotic that lies directly beneath the surface of a no-longer-mythologized language.

The effect of the cosmogonic tradition, nonetheless, remains powerful. Jaeger is doubtless correct, as well, when he notes that the Semitic *tohu wa bohu* has been read into the Greek meanings of chaos. But it was not only the Semitic, but the Orphic and Platonic versions of chaos as well, that have reinforced the negative sense of the term.

As the etymology of "chaos" suggests, the construal of reason in terms of *arche* or *principium* is dependent upon mythical sources. Aristotle's avoidance of mythopoetic language and his rejection of the need to posit any initial creative act did not prevent him from serving as the primary source of our understanding of principles as determining sources of order.

According to Aristotle, a principle, is "that from which a thing can be known, that from which a thing first comes to be, or that at whose will that which is moved is moved and that which changes changes."[22] As such, principles of knowledge and of being are the origins of thought and sources of origination per se. In the political realm, an *archon* or *princeps* is one who gives orders.

Any who doubt the negative characteristic of chaos have only to reflect upon the traditional Western attitudes toward political anarchy. Anarchy is feared as much as it is because, at the most general philosophical level, anarchy denotes the absence of principles as determining sources. In other words, anarchy bespeaks the absence of a cosmos, the denial of a cosmogonic act.

Chaos is nonrational, unprincipled, anarchic; it is the indefinite in need of definition; it is the lawless, the anomic; it is the unlimited begging limitation. Though we have secularized and demythologized the mythic themes that hide us from direct contact with the awe-ful character of chaos, we have only to look to our poets to recognize the fundamental attitude toward confusion, separation, and emptiness which we variously describe by the term "chaos."

For Ovid, Chaos is "all rude and lumpy matter."[23] Milton calls it a "wild Abyss, the Womb of nature and perhaps her Grave."[24] He explicitly identifies chaos as evil by making it subject to Satan's will:

> Chaos Umpire sits,
> And by decision more embroils
> the fray by which he Reigns.[25]

We celebrate "the great morning of the world when first God dawned on Chaos,"[26] but nonetheless cannot but fear that chaos may return:

> Lo! thy dread empire, Chaos! is restor'd
> Light dies before thy uncreating word
> Thy hand, great Anarch, lets the curtain fall,
> And universal darkness buries all.[27]

Cosmogonic myths all seem to share a negative appraisal of chaos, either as "yawning gap," "confusion," or "formlessness." The importance of this fact in shaping our cultural consciousness can only be assessed after we have traced at greater length the cultural developments beyond the strictly mythopoetic age.

The most important conclusion one may wish to draw from this brief meditation upon mythopoetic language relates to the special character of cosmogonic myths. Mircea Eliade, one of our century's most prolific mythographers and philosophers of religion, thought all myths to be ultimately cosmogonic. Myths, according to Eliade are "etiological tales," "stories of origins."[28]

One can certainly challenge such an interpretation of myth, but, nonetheless, it is cosmogonic myths which are deemed most important in our tradition. Further, if stories of the origin are stories of the overcoming of chaos, one can immediately see how the sense of *agency* creeps into these early myths. It is from this sense of agency directed toward the construal of order that both the notions of rationality and causality emerge. To reason is to construe or uncover order; it is to think *causally*.

It is important to make this point now since the account of our cultural development found in the following pages will articulate the persistence of a tradition of thinking alternative to that of the rational and the causal. This tradition, associated with what we are calling "first problematic thinking," seeks understanding through the employment of informal analogies based upon meanings associated with images and image clusters. What we shall call "second problematic thinking," on the other hand, is privileged in our tradition in large measure because of the sense of chaos as the absence of order which must be somehow brought into an ordered state.

——— FIRST ANTICIPATION ———

Cosmogonic speculation of the kind described above was a fundamental element in the process of cultural self-articulation in the West. Notions of "Being" and "Not-Being," of "Cosmos" as a single-ordered whole, of "principles" as the origins of order and, specifically, of "causal agency" as an important explanatory principle—in short the central components of the concept of "rationality"—are grounded in the myths of origins to which the founders of the Hellenic and Hebraic traditions appealed. The account of the development of the classical Chinese cultural sensibilities in chapter 3 will demonstrate that the sort of cosmogonic speculations central to the Western tradition were of no great importance to the Chinese. When accounts of the origins of things do appear with regularity in the Chinese tradition in the Han dynasty, they are genealogical narratives which tell, not of the creation of a "cosmos," but of the emergence of the "ten thousand things." The Chinese tradition, therefore, is "acosmotic" in the sense that it does not depend upon the belief that the totality of things constitutes a single-ordered world. Employing Western cosmogonic assumptions in the interpretation of the classical Chinese tradition can only result in an expectation that the modes of reflection and argumentation undergirded by these cosmogonic assumptions are shared by the Chinese. Such a resort to the "transcendental pretense" would lead, as it has often in the past, to a skewed understanding of classical China. [See chapter 3, sections 1, 5.3.]

2. REST AND PERMANENCE

Though we shall be able to offer no final wisdom concerning the question why chaos comes to be construed negatively and why, therefore, beginnings come to be associated with victory over chaos, it is clear that the chaos/cosmos dialectic disposes our tradition toward what we shall call the "second problematic." Significant for the development of our traditional understandings of reason and rationality is the fact that this problematic urges us to accept the priority of rest and permanence over motion and change.

The ancient Greek preference for rest and permanence is best illustrated by appealing to the development of those mathematical and metaphysical speculations which led to the formalization of the idea of *quantity*. Enlightenment interpretations of Greek thought have underwritten this preference by providing a narrative of the progressive growth of rationality couched in terms of the presumed transition from *mythos* to *logos*. This narrative tells the story of how the Greeks came to provide responsible *accounts* (*logoi* λόγοι) of the world.

Three principal modes of "accounting" have been available to us from the beginning. These are *mythos* (μῦθος), *logos* (λόγος), and *historia* (ἰστορία). The privileged status of *logos* in our tradition has largely determined the manner in which we understand both *mythos* and *historia*. Further, when later in the tradition, mythical, rational, and historical accounts hardened into the disciplinary divisions of literature, philosophy (and science), and history, it was the rational mode of accounting which determined the relative degrees of respectability of the other modes.

In spite of the eventual privileging of *logos* as "rational account," *mythos* was the source of all modes of accounting. Indeed, an implication of our argument that second problematic thinking is but an elaboration of the agencies of construal associated with cosmogonic myths is that rationality per se emerges from a mythical ground which it never succeeds in surmounting. Thus the presumed rationalization of mythical thought associated with the rise of philosophy and science, history, and secular literature, is nothing more or less than the perfecting of that *mythos* constituted by accounts which tell of the overcoming of chaos. Reason is the elaboration and ramification of the cosmogonic impulse.

This is but to say that *mythos* grounds *logos* and *historia*. But the earliest ramifications of *mythos* involved the emergence of the genres of epic, lyric, and tragic poetry. These developed as three principal media of mythical expression. In the Homeric epic, mythic themes are employed as a means of setting up structural analogies expressing similarities between the human and the mythic realms. These structural analogies help to meet "our need for establishing our place in the world order by means of comparisons, in order to arrive at a tolerable degree of certainty and stability."[29] Likewise, the judgments of the gods, and their mutual conflicts and transactions, form the mythical matrix in terms of which events in the human world are played out. Direct interventions of the gods and goddesses account for significant actions and events in the human realm. *Ate* "strikes Agamemnon in the breast"; Zeus induces in him a false dream—in such manners are the events of the *Iliad* directed. Again, once the gods, after some debate, decide that Odysseus will be allowed to return home safely, a significant amount of divine intervention is required to bring this about.

With respect to the lyric, myth serves a more personal, self-creating, function. When Sappho sang

Once more Eros, looser of limbs, drives me about,
a bitter-sweet creature which puts me at a loss[30]

she told, as did Homer, of divine intervention. But the effects of the two sorts of intervention are quite different. *Ate*'s intervention occasions the action that calls for the wrath of Achilles, thus serving as a primary motor of the events recounted in the *Iliad*. The intervention of Eros brings the mixed pain and joy of love to the individual, Sappho. Of course, in both the epic and the lyric there is a reflection of the cosmogonic activity involving the construal of order from chaos. But through the epic, one is aided in finding one's place in the wider world of human action, while in the lyric, *mythos* offers a means of self-articulation, an ordering of affect.

With the tragic poets, who were able to draw upon both epic and lyric resources, the function of myth was both broadened and deepened. This took place by virtue of the addition of a *reflective* dimension. Models of actions and passions began increasingly to be resourced in the individual rather than the gods. With the increased sense of responsibility, one was urged to reflect upon one's actions and their consequences. Both Antigone and Creon, though from different perspectives, face conflicting obligations—toward the state, on the one hand, and toward their relative, Polyneices, on the other. And the fact that they resolve this conflict in different manners meant that they, too, are at odds with one another. The modes of deliberation that emerge throughout the *Antigone* are functions of the desire to resolve these conflicts.[31] Though the deliberations taking place within Greek tragedies do indeed take place in a world largely determined by *Moira* (Destiny)—a world wherein individuals may still be hounded by the Furies, unable to escape the evils sent by the gods—nonetheless, by the end of the epoch of Greek tragedy, mythical constructs had receded into the background.

> In tragedy myth severed its connection with the particular concrete situation. The human situations which it expresses are no longer, as in the archaic lyric, fixed in time and place by victory, marriage, or cult; they are universal situations. It is evident that this broadening of the situation marks a tendency toward philosophical generalization. Before long the problem of human action which is the concern of tragedy was to become a matter of intellectual cognition. . . . Where a divine world had endowed the human world with meaning, we now find the universal determining the particular.[32]

This backgrounding of *mythos* might better be termed a forgetting of the mythical sources of rational speculation. Philosophers, after all, have not really separated themselves from *mythos*. They do not simply implicate mythical structures into their thinking as necessary appeals to "likely stories" when reason has reached the end of its tether, nor do they simply affix them as metaphorical accouterments meant to add depth to their speculations. Simply by appealing to principles as determining sources of order, by pressing for univocal definitions that bring order into thinking through the process of wringing clarity from vagueness, and by the ordering of concepts in a coherent theoretical frame, philosophical speculation—indeed, rational speculation of any kind—advertises its embodiment of the cosmogonic impulse from which reason was born. Even in its most immediate forms—as epic, lyric, and tragic poetry—*mythos* serves as a securing, stabilizing, *rationalizing*, medium, bringing order into the otherwise chaotic actions, emotions, and deliberations of human beings.

Turning to the development of *logos* and *historia* as modes of accounting, we should note that both the disciplines of history and of philosophy have their prominent origins among the Milesian Greeks. "Historians," particularly the Milesian, Herodotus, were greatly influenced by the materialism of the *physiologoi* (φυσιολόγοι). The first philosophers wished to provide an account of the *physis* (φύσις) of things. The marriage of the terms *physis* and *logos* shaped the philosophical preference for permanence over process and change.

The term *physis* has come into our tradition through the Latin, *natura*, both terms being translated as "the nature of things." But it is clear that both *physis* and *natura* have roots suggesting "birth" and "growth," associations which were progressively lost with the increasing dominance of substantialist and causal interpretations in later Greek philosophy.

Philosophy provides an account of the *physis* of things—the way things are. But the search for this *physis* involves *logos*. It is a structured accounting that is sought. History, thus, has the sense of "enquiry," but this enquiry was itself initially characterized as involving *logoi*, "accounts." By offering an account of important public events, the historian provided for the world of human affairs what the *physiologoi* provided for the natural world.

Herodotus and Thucydides in their activity as historians provided accounts (*logoi*). It would be mistaken to think of history as something like a chronicle of the past.[33] The first historians were closer to ethnographers (Herodotus) and war correspondents (Thucydides). The first mythographers, the *philomythoi* (φιλομῦθοι), were those who sought to account for past and present time in terms of the time of beginnings.

Philosophia (φιλοσοφία) and *historia* were closely related in the beginning. What Pythagoras later came to call "philosophy" was itself enquiry, *historia*. For example, Pythagoras called his mathematical investigations "*historia*." Aristotle's *History of Animals* employs the term *historia* in this sense.

According to the received interpretation of Greek thought, the purpose of the intellect is seen to be that of giving accounts. These may be the sort of accounts that appeal to the *logos* of *physis*, the meaning of natural phenomena, or they may be the *historical* accountings associated with the realm of human action and public events. Behind both of these accounts lie those of the *philomythoi* who tell of the origins of order from chaos, and those of the tragic, epic, and lyric poets who implicate these cosmogonic accounts into their creations as means of bringing order into human thought, action, and passion. Each of these types of accounting—*mythos, logos, historia*—privilege the notion of permanence, structure, stability, and law over that of process and change.

In her *The Fragility of Goodness*, Martha Nussbaum has significantly broadened the traditional understanding of Greek rationality by taking a chronological step backward and examining the work of the tragic poets. Her argument, briefly put, is this: In addition to the conception of rationality which envisions the intellect as "pure sunlight," stresses activity and control, places trust solely in the immutable, and defines the good life in terms of solitariness, there is an alternative conception which sees the intellect as "flowing water, given and received," stresses both activity and receptivity, is satisfied with limited control, trusts the mutable and unstable, and defines the good life as one lived among "friends, loved ones, and community."[34] Tragedy includes both norms of rationality, "criticizing (the former) with reference to the specifically human value contained only in (the latter)."[35] Plato offers a version of the former and Aristotle a version of the latter.

Nussbaum moves Aristotle rather far in the direction of the first problematic. Judged simply as an important alternative interpretation, her reading seems both viable and of real benefit for those who are engaged in the reconstruction of more standard treatments of ethical issues. It is essential to our task, however, that we first invoke the Principle of Mere Presence introduced in the first pages of this work, for this revised Aristotle is precisely *not* the one who has shaped our cultural self-consciousness. It is Aristotle as arch-patron of the second problematic who has owned the most powerful cultural import.

Moreover, as our brief discussion of the function of *mythos* in epic, lyric, and tragic poetry has suggested, the sort of understanding Nussbaum identifies is presented within the context of the "fragile" and "vulnerable" character of the good life. Fragility and vulnerability are shadows, echoes, of that sense of chaos which underlies second problematic thinking.

Our point is simply this: Second problematic thinking is deeply embedded in our culture, and there are real constraints placed upon the possibilities of historical reconstruction. In this present instance, accepting Nussbaum's non-Platonic version of rationality—a vision which, as we shall discover in chapter 3, in many ways resonates well with Confucian or Daoist understandings—would urge us, as well, to import the tragic vision of the Greeks, shaped by responses to vulnerability and fragility. And to do this would mean that we had imported the cosmogonic mechanisms undergirding second problematic thinking into a context largely alien to them.

There is no question that reflections such as those Nussbaum and others[36] have provided can be valuable in suggesting interpretive strategies which will serve us better than those alternatives that have so clouded our understandings of classical Chinese culture. But we must be cautious in any attempt to employ theoretical constructs directly from one culture to another.

There is a larger point to be made: What we are calling second problematic thinking, at its maturity, will be forwarded by its advocates as a transcultural, universal sensibility. Proponents of rational, causal thinking will not be constrained by any presumed culture-specificity from applying rational methods in interpreting alternative cultures. On the other hand, first problematic thinking *is* culturally specific, and the shape of first problematic activities vary from one culture to the next. What this means is that even the purest examples of first problematic thinking in our culture may be used only suggestively, and by analogy, to interpret an alternative sensibility. It is for this reason that we are performing the negative task of indicating what amounts to "useless lumber," rather than elaborating in any detail the specific content of our first problematic thinking as a means of attempting to identify transcultural constructs. While we wholeheartedly endorse the historical reconstructions of the sort represented by Nussbaum's work insofar as they enrich our own cultural self-consciousness, we are purposefully avoiding too much dependence on these constructions as material with which to pave a way to China.

The Enlightenment bias of the transition from *mythos* to *logos* involves the assumption, then, that the sorts of accounting which are to be privileged will be those which concern the *logos* of *physis*, on the one hand, or those that provide a structured narrative of human events, on the other. In either case, rational accounting comes to be associated with the essential, the universal, and the permanent rather than with the idiosyncratic, the particular, and the transitory character of things and events.

This fact is attested to at the very beginnings of what came to be called philosophic speculation in the sixth century B.C.E. Thales claimed everything to be *hydor* (ὕδωρ)—"water." What does it mean to say that everything is water? Perhaps nothing more than that since there must be (such is the intuition of those who seek a single principle of explanation for things) only one basic "stuff," the best candidate among the observable items of our world is a fluid medium that seems to be the most capable of taking on different forms (water, vapor, ice) and which appears to be the essential factor in maintaining the viability of living things. It is not so much Thales' own account which leads us to believe in his substantialist bias. It is rather the fact that his account will be increasingly understood in static, materialistic terms by later interpreters of his thought.

Anaximenes (fl. 545 B.C.E.) held that the basic stuff of which things are made is *aer* (ἀήρ), which carries something like our own common sense meaning of "air." Anaximenes introduced the concept of the "vortex," together with the notions of condensation and rarefaction, to account for the origins of things. Air compressed will solidify, and, when dilated, will rarefy. Heavy, dense matter is drawn toward the center of the vortex, while lighter matter drifts to the outside.

Aristotle, whose thinking serves as such a prominent source of our knowledge of the Presocratics, termed the Milesians the first "materialists." On his authority, generations of historians have repeated that judgment. But we should be cautious here. Aristotle's reference to the materialism of the Milesians was based upon his own doctrine of the four causes, which, by dividing matter and form, and activity and aim, managed to slice the pie in such manner as to make "matter" (*hyle* ὕλη), a term perhaps first used stipulatively by Aristotle, into something inert and formless. This matter was, of course, something quite distinct from the *physis* of Thales, Anaximander, and Anaximenes, who, if we were to recall the connotations of "growth" and "originating power" carried by the term *physis*, could be more faithfully categorized than has traditionally been the case.

It is much better to belay any recourse to the term "materialist" to apply to the Milesian thinkers since we are tempted thereby to misconstrue them in two ways: (1) as thinkers believing in an inert world of matter, and (2) as thinkers reflecting upon cause and effect in the "efficient cause" sense entailed by later understandings of materialism. This latter misunderstanding is particularly damaging since it was Aristotle who, by organizing explanatory *logoi* into four "causes," in effect, invented the concept of efficient cause as a separate agency.

However much one may stress the dynamic character of *physis* in the first *physiologoi*, it is clear that the dominance of substance over process and growth was guaranteed in the first centuries of philosophic speculation. *Physis* was to be accounted for by recourse to *logos*. In addition to the fact that the preferred means of "giving an account" privileged substantialist interpretations of *physis*, there are two other fundamental turnings which helped to guarantee the preference for permanence over the flux of human experience. The first is the dualism of soul and body, most prominently expressed by Pythagoras (and, later, Plato), and the second, of course, the ontological dualism introduced by Parmenides, which received its paradigmatic synthesis, again, in Platonic thinking.

The dualism of soul and body, familiar to us from Christian theology (which inherited it from Plato and Pythagoras), presents a new problem for philosophers. With the development among the Greeks of self-conscious concepts of "personality," we begin to encounter a basic sort of ethical or religious problem focused upon the tensions between mind and materiality. Heretofore the assumption had been that the person was one with his body, but more and more as reason and thought came to be identified with the guiding and directing agency of the world, a distinction between "that which orders" and "that which requires ordering" was needed.

Pythagoras conceived the nature of things as number and the relations among things to be the sort of relations numbers have. And as he conceived the world to be a harmonious order, the relations among things (numbers) were such as to establish harmonies. This means that numerical relationships could be expressed as mathematical ratios:

> The so-called Pythagoreans . . . thought that the principles of mathematics were the principles of all things. Since of these principles numbers are by nature first, they thought they saw many similarities to things which exist and come into being in numbers rather than in fire and earth and water—justice being such and such a modification of numbers, soul and reason being another, opportunity still another, and so with the rest, each being expressible numerically. Seeing, further, that the properties and ratios of the musical consonances were expressible in numbers, and indeed that all other things seemed to be wholly modeled in their nature upon numbers, they took numbers to be the whole of reality.[37]

This citation from Aristotle is interesting because it focuses Pythagoras' discovery of the abstract quantitative character of mathematics. Thus when we count to ten, we do so without the necessity of fingers or toes, since we have "numbers" which serve to measure all quantifiable things. In the sums of ten apples or ten fingers or ten minutes, the quality of the apples or the fingers or the minutes does not affect the meaning of the number ten. Since mathematics is a quantitative science, we are able to add five hungry elephants and five bales of freshly mown hay and arrive at ten objects rather than five (reasonably) satisfied elephants.

Of course, it is possible to misinterpret this original interest in purely quantitative considerations. If numbers are things and their relationships form patterns by virtue of proportions and ratios, then we have a geometrical vision of number. It is this conception that underwrites the perfection of the soul vis-à-vis the body. Materiality is ultimately dissolved into the formal structure or pattern established by numerical order. Still, quantitative exactness is assured. Even, and especially, musical harmonies are consequences of reliably exact ratios.

We should stress that the Pythagoreans—and Plato, who will be greatly influenced by them—were always concerned to maintain the connection between quantity and quality, between numerical order and the harmonies or values that promoted normative human life. Indeed, the fact that Pythagoreans were a religious community and were concerned with the ordering of the relationships of soul and body are fair indications that this was the case.

One of the important themes of later intellectual culture, continuing into our contemporary technological age, will be the effects of an increasing separation of quantitative and qualitative considerations on the part of scientists, technicians, politicians, and educators. And one of the perennial questions asked by at least a significant minority of philosophers has always been: How, in the present social and cultural situation, may we insure the appropriate relationship between order and value?

Pythagoras' dualism of body and soul, interpreted in terms of his understanding of the numerical character of all things, places his thinking on the side of permanence over change. Parmenides' ontological dualism will lend added plausibility to that preference. Parmenides (b. 515 B.C.E.) lived in Elea in southern Italy. He wrote a treatise composed of two parts, "The Way of Truth" and "The Way of Opinion." While most of the "Way of Truth" has survived, we have only a small portion of the "Way of Opinion." The latter is concerned with a world of becoming, flux and change, the world admixed of Being and Not-Being. It is the world of sensible objects in which opposites are said to coexist and interdepend.

But it is "The Way of Truth" that has had by far the greater influence. Here Parmenides examines the implications of an intuition of the nature of things which is asserted in this form: "Only Being is; Not-being cannot be." This Being is one, eternal and indivisible. Parmenides' explicit claim that thought and being are the same[38] is the doctrine of strict rationalism against which most of subsequent Greek philosophy gauges itself:

> But motionless in the limits of mighty bonds, it is without beginning or end, since coming into being and passing away have been driven far off, cast out by true belief. Remaining the same, and in the same place, it lies in itself, and so abides firmly where it is. For strong Necessity holds it in the bonds of the limit which shuts it in on every side, because it is not right for what is to be incomplete. For it is not in need of anything, but not-being would stand in need of everything.[39]

Being can have no beginning since that would require that it came into being. But it could not have come into being since only Being is, and there can be no "nothing" from which Being could have come. Further, if Being had parts or elements, if more than a single Being existed, they would have to be separated by Not-being—a void, nothing. But if nothing separated beings then nothing would *be*, and Not-being cannot be. Further, if there are no parts, then there can be no moving elements. And Being itself cannot move since motion requires space, or "nothing," to traverse.

What Parmenides attempts to show is that any belief that would challenge the unity of Being would lead one into contradiction. Now, a logical contradiction can be expressed in the form "*x* is both *F* and not *F*." Parmenides argues that any employment of the idea of Not-being as existing would lead one into this sort of contradiction: the nothing from which Being might be said to come or which would be claimed to separate beings would be said both to be and not-be.

> But since there is a furthest limit, it is complete on every side, like the body of a well-rounded sphere, evenly balanced in every direction from the middle; for it cannot be any greater or any less in one place than another. For neither is there what is not, which would stop it from reaching its like, nor could what is possibly be more in one place and less in another, since it is all inviolable. For being equal to itself in every direction it nevertheless meets with its limits.[40]

In these doctrines, we can see the use of logical distinctions, probably derived in part from the mathematical speculations and constructions of the Pythagoreans, employed in the defense of a fundamental intuition concerning the nature of things. We do well, however, not to attempt too literal an interpretation of Parmenides' positive descriptions of Being. It is "like" the body of a well-rounded sphere. It is clear that resort to a positive description of what is entailed by the intuition of the unity of Being would get Parmenides into linguistic difficulties.

Some modern critics of Parmenides' "Way of Truth" have attempted to use logical arguments to overturn the conviction that "Only Being is." These critics claim that Parmenides has confused the existential and the predicative sense of the verb, "to be." To say that something is or is not round, is qualitatively distinct from saying that it is or is not "in existence." The predicative sense of "is" must be followed by a predicate—"red," "round," "silly," or "sad." To say "The ball is round" entails the claim that "The ball is not square." But would Parmenides claim that a round ball cannot be not-square on the ground that Not-being cannot be?

Much has been made of this sort of critique of Parmenides, but it hardly touches the insight of Parmenides at all. Parmenides' intuition is of the unity of Being. He employs logic to defend that intuition. Logically, there can be no distinction between existential and predicative senses of the verb, "to be," if one affirms the unity of Being. For if we accept the unity of Being, there would be no beings about which we might predicate this or that. This does not, of course, logically justify Parmenides' use of predicates such as "oneness," "indivisibility," "motionlessness," and "eternality," with respect to Being, and doubtless Parmenides was mildly uncomfortable, or could be made so, by virtue of this fact. But this does not seem to be a difficulty that could be overcome without ruling out altogether any discussion of the strong sense of the concept of unity—and that would be already to beg the question. The distinction between predicative and existential uses of "to be" is a mainstay of our World of Seeming or Opinion, but cannot be applied to discussions of the Way of Truth. We are forced to accept, as all mystical intuitions require, the limitations of ordinary language.

———— SECOND ANTICIPATION ————

The Western preference of rest and permanence over becoming and process is well-nigh reversed in Chinese culture. There are at least three important reasons for this. First, there was the separation of *mythos*, *logos*, and *historia* as modes of accounting, and the subsequent priority given to the notion of *logos* as "rational account" to provide the primary means of explaining things. This way of thinking then combined with the search for the *physis* or objective "nature" of things to privilege formal, static, structural understandings of the way things are. Second, the mind/body dualism associated with the Pythagorean/Platonic tradition offered additional support for the primacy of the ideational and conceptual meanings associated with mind, which would continue to be influential even in those systems that did not stress such a dualism, such as Aristotelian naturalism. Third, the Parmenidean claim that "Only Being is" set up a dialectic between Being and Not-Being, and Being and Becoming, which privileged the notion of permanence.

None of these three developments had an important counterpart in the Chinese tradition. Chinese conceptions of "nature" (*xing* 性) are to be interpreted in dynamic terms which suggest a preference for processive over substantial understanding. Terms such as *xin* 心, usually rendered "heart-and-mind," indicate the absence of any mind/body dualism. This means that mentalist conceptions of the human being are not effectively present. And metaphorical and imagistic language is stressed over concepts which fix meanings, and in so doing privilege a static and unchanging sense of things. Finally, there was no Chinese Parmenides to set the dialectic between Being, Not-Being, and Becoming.

Specifically with regard to this last point, we should be alerted to the fact that differences between the Chinese and Indo-European senses of the verb "to be" will make for significant differences between the two traditions. It is clear that Parminides, among other Greek thinkers (Aristotle is the great exception), conflated existential and copulative senses of "being." Whether this is to be counted as a confusion, as is often said, is a matter of dispute. At the very least this conflation contributed to the tendency to think of Chaos (as "nonbeing") in a negative manner, investing it with suggestions of the Nihil, the Void, the Naught. By contrast, the absence of this kind of cosmogonic tradition in China may be considered both cause and consequence of the fact that the verb, *you* 有, "being," overlaps with the sense of "having" rather than "existing." If *wu* 無, "not to be," means only "not to be present," there is certainly less *mysterium* and *tremendum* attaching to the notion of Not-being. [See chapter 3, sections 1, 4.1.]

3. THE WATERSHED: ZENO AND THE POWER OF PARADOX

It is doubtful that the highly paradoxical doctrines of Parmenides would have had the influence they did in fact have upon subsequent Greek thinkers, and thereby upon the modern world as well, had it not been for Parmenides' famous disciple, Zeno (?490–?430). By appealing to a set of disarming logical conundrums, Zeno articulated the consequences of denying the truth of Parmenides' conviction that "Only Being is."

None of the Presocratics is more controversial than Zeno. The controversial character of his thinking is doubtless due to the fact that, in defense of Parmenidean rationalism, he forwarded a series of arguments that, perhaps against his own wishes, threatened to reduce second problematic thinking to absurdity. By employing the tools of logic and dialectic in the service of the Parmenidean doctrine, "Only Being is," Zeno managed to drive a wedge between the claims of reason and those of sense experience that even the most subtle of his opponents has not been able to remove. In general, the responses of later philosophers to Zeno's arguments effectively moved philosophy away from the immediacies of experience and toward abstract speculation.

Zeno used his arguments to demonstrate the absurd consequences attending a belief in the rationality of change and motion. Until one examines these puzzles rather carefully, it may be difficult to understand how they came to exert such influence on the theoretical development of philosophy, science, and mathematics.

Some introductory remarks are in order. First, in terms of the specific occasion of their construction, the arguments of Zeno, like the discussions of Parmenides, are best understood as a sustained effort to counter the influence of Pythagorean cosmology, which was the most influential doctrine of the times. Second, the power of the arguments as philosophic statements that transcend their historical locus may be understood only if the four principal paradoxes of motion are taken as a set.

The principal paradoxes deal with the concept of motion in terms of the relations of space and time. Since the seventeenth century, we have expressed these relations in the following way: $v = s/t$, which expresses the relationships of velocity, space (or distance), and time.

Thus, we are allowed to see that Zeno's four paradoxes permit us to examine the consequences of believing in the reality of motion, given four different sets of assumptions about the character of space and time, the relations between which (s/t) provide our understanding of motion.

The four possible assumptions are:

1. Both points and moments are infinitely divisible.
2. Neither points nor moments are infinitely divisible.
3. Points are infinitely divisible, but moments are not.
4. Moments are infinitely divisible, but points are not.[41]

Infinite divisibility means there are no least units of space or time. Finite divisibility requires that some least unit be reached which is extended, but which cannot be further divided. Options 3 and 4 above require rather modern assumptions. The views against which Zeno intended to argue were likely those involving the assumptions of 1 and 2. The point to emphasize, however, is that Zeno provided a logically exhaustive set of arguments with regard to theories of motion involving the use of concepts of points and moments.

The simplest of the paradoxes is known as "The Bisection." The argument involves the simple claim that motion is impossible because to move one must move from one point to another, and to do that requires one to traverse half the distance between those points, and to do that one must traverse half of that half, and so on. If space is infinitely divisible then one cannot reach any point to which one wishes to move in a finite time. Just how one gets to the doorway seconds after hearing the shout, "Fire!" is something of a puzzle.

The second of the paradoxes is called "The Achilles." By tradition Achilles is placed in a race with a tortoise who has been given a slight head start. Achilles will never overtake the tortoise since *by the time that* Achilles has reached the point from which the tortoise began, the beast will have advanced some distance, and *by the time that* Achilles reaches the second point to which the tortoise has advanced, the tortoise will have advanced again (a smaller distance, of course, but some distance). This argument depends upon the assumption that time is infinitely divisible, but spatial units are extended.

A third paradox, historically the most influential, is called "The Arrow." Again, it is simply stated. One of the early recorders of the Greek tradition gives it this form:

Zeno argues thus. Either the moving object moves in the place where it is, or in the place where it is not. And it does not move in the place where it is [since at each present moment it is at rest in a place equal to itself], nor in the place where it is not; therefore, nothing moves.[42]

If, at each of the instants in the flight of an arrow it will be found at rest, when does it move? If one assumes that both space and time are infinitely divisible, then the claim is that at each of an infinitely large number of moments, the arrow will occupy an infinite number of distinct places without ever once moving from one place to another.

Finally, there is "The Stadium" paradox. Consider the following figure:

$$/=/\ /=/\ /=/\ /=/$$
$$/=/\ /=/\ /=/\ /=/$$
$$/=/\ /=/\ /=/\ /=/$$

There are three rows of objects containing four elements each. If the top row remains stationary and rows two and three move at the same velocity in opposite directions until the three rows are precisely aligned,

$$/=/\ /=/\ /=/\ /=/$$
$$/=/\ /=/\ /=/\ /=/$$
$$/=/\ /=/\ /=/\ /=/$$

then one may claim with Zeno that half of a given time is equal to the whole of that time. This is so since with respect to the top row the other rows have traversed two unit distances, but with respect to one another each has traversed four.

This argument is interesting only if it is assumed that space and time are made of extended, indivisible minima. That is to say, if, in our analysis of the "relative motion" of the second and third rows vis-à-vis one another and the stationary row, we concern ourselves with the manner in which the least spatial units which comprise elements of the rows pass one another, we must conclude that these discrete, spatial minima can only pass one another in discrete infinitesimal units of time. But, if the speed of the second and third rows are equal and opposite, it would be impossible to explain how the alignment takes place without assuming that one-half of an indivisible unit had been traversed in a unit of time, or, alternatively, that it had taken one-half of an indivisible moment to move through some unit of space. But discrete units of space and time are by definition incapable of being physically divided.[43]

Zeno provided a number of puzzles other than those associated with the denial of motion. We might just mention his argument against place: If everything that exists has a place then it is clear that place too will have a place, and so on without limit. This argument is aimed at supporting Parmenides' notion of Being as placeless, since if Being had a place then "place" would either be, in which case more than one being would exist, or it would not-be, and we would be forced to admit that Not-being exists.

A later follower of Parmenides, Melissus, provided a series of arguments defending the Parmenidean position, but one of the ironies of the history of philosophy is that his argument against plurality contained within it the seeds of the doctrine of material atomism which will later emerge in direct response to Parmenides. Melissus attempted to refute the notion of a plurality of beings by the reductio ad absurdum argument, establishing that

> If there were a plurality, things would have to be of the same kind as I say the one is.[44]

Melissus thought such a conclusion absurd, but to Leucippus, the founder of atomic theory, it seemed a perfectly plausible doctrine and he proceeded to build the atomic theory on precisely that assumption.

The arguments of Parmenides and Zeno were to shape the character of the subsequent history of Greek philosophy in a most dramatic fashion. Three sorts of approaches to the problems posed by Eleatic philosophy will be tried by thinkers prior to Plato and Aristotle. One group of thinkers—Empedocles, Anaxagoras, and the Atomists, Leucippus and Democritus—will continue the Ionian tradition of natural philosophy by seeking to demonstrate that a consistent pluralism is possible. Each of these philosophers will respond to the Eleatic philosophy in a self-conscious manner.[45]

A large and divergent group of thinkers known as Sophists, for the most part rejecting speculations about the natural world, often in direct response to Zeno, will yield themselves up to varying degrees of skepticism about the power of reason to penetrate to the nature of things, and will examine the consequences of a relativist approach to the practical problems of human beings in society. Finally, the philosopher, Socrates, teacher of Plato, will offer the method of open-ended enquiry as a means of withholding judgments of truth or falsity until certainty is attained. The Socratic claim will be that reason in principle can discern the character of the world, but we should not claim success too soon.

The net effect of the fact that none of these responses met with consensual agreement was that the Parmenidean philosophy was never successfully refuted. And the split between reason and the world of immediate experience has persisted down to the present day. We shall pause long enough to illustrate this latter point by recourse to some contemporary treatments of Zeno.

In an oft-quoted statement, Bertrand Russell claimed that "Zeno's arguments, in some form, have afforded grounds for almost all the theories of space and time and infinity which have been constructed from his day to our own."[46] In his justly famous treatment of the paradoxes, Russell accepts the validity of the third and fourth arguments insofar as they refute the assumption that points and moments are extended, and argues that the first two arguments are fallacious if taken as attempts to refute visions of space and time which presume that points and moments are unextended.

Russell claims that rather than seeking to overcome the strictures of Zeno's arguments by denying the reality of space and time (as did Parmenides), or by arguing, as did Henri Bergson, that space and time constitute a continuous flow which our rational minds may only understand by resort to static, falsifying abstractions, we should deal with Zeno's challenge by developing an adequate theory of infinite numbers. This would permit us to resolve the more troublesome of the paradoxes. Unfortunately, the paradoxes involved in theories of infinite numbers (for example, the implication that adding a number to an infinite number does not increase its sum) are at least as daunting as are those which Zeno's arguments require us to accept. They certainly do nothing to heal the breach between rational and experiential approaches to understanding.[47]

Zeno's contemporary influence is most obviously present in speculations surrounding the attempts to correlate our descriptions of the macrocosmic world ruled by relativity theory and the microcosmic world in which quantum theory reigns. It is in the former, of course, that the problem of "motion" is most prominent. A typical discussion of "velocity" in a physics textbook would yield a formula such as the following:

$$v = \lim_{t \to 0} \frac{\Delta s}{\Delta t}$$

Clearly the ghost of Zeno haunts such formulaic "explanations." Not only, out of deference to Zeno, are we forced to define velocity at an instant (that is, we must express it in terms of rest), we can do this only by recourse to the ad hoc assumption that the changes in time (the time interval) will only *approach* zero. That is, of course, the assumption of temporal continuity. It is precisely the dependence upon spatial and temporal continuity in relativity physics that is called into question by phenomena at the level of quantum physics. And though many quantum thinkers continue to affirm the continuity of space and time, the assumption is an ad hoc one, broadly inconsistent with much of the experimental evidence upon which their theories rest. For a theory which atomizes the apparent motions and other changes of microphysical phenomena would realize greater parsimony, not to mention coherence, if it acceded to the atomization of space and time, as well.

Such atomization was in fact an implication of A. N. Whitehead's mathematical interpretation of the physical world. Whitehead, Russell's mentor and sometime colleague, was led by his own philosophic intuitions to accept Zeno's arrow paradox as persuasive, with truly remarkable consequences. Whitehead quotes with approval William James' commentary on Zeno's arrow paradox:

> Either your experience is of no content, of no change, or it is of a perceptible amount of content or change. Your acquaintance with reality grows literally by buds or drops of perception. Intellectually and reflectively you can divide these into components, but as immediately given, they come totally or not at all.[48]

Whitehead agrees with James that (after removing those elements of Zeno's arguments which are the product of inadequate mathematical knowledge), Zeno presents a valid argument. Noting that the introduction of motion into the arrow paradox brings in "irrelevant details," Whitehead claims that "the true difficulty is to understand how the arrow survives the lapse of time."[49]

To overcome this difficulty, Whitehead developed his theory of "actual occasions" as the final real things of which the world is constituted. These occasions are acts of becoming. Thus Whitehead's "philosophy of process" is characterized by occasions of experience which achieved the status of "entities" by coming into being. The paradoxical nature of process philosophy is due to the fact that actual occasions come into being *outside of time*.

> The conclusion is that in every act of becoming there is the becoming of something with temporal extension; but that the act itself is not extensive, in the sense that it is divisible into earlier and later acts of becoming which correspond to the extensive divisibility of what has become.[50]

Whitehead's view, like that of Anaxagoras, is that all change must be qualitative. One implication of this view is that there is no motion in the sense of local motion—that is, the movement of an entity from one place to another. The appearance of motion is explained by the fact that the actual entities comprising some physical object passed away at one point in the continuum which constitutes space and time and their relations, and new entities maintaining that same structure through time came into being at another point in that continuum. Thus, as I move my hand, there is $hand_1$ (at s_1, t_1), $hand_2$ (at s_2, t_2), and so forth.

A considerable number of philosophical thinkers belonging to the process tradition founded by Whitehead maintain their discipleship to Zeno through a defense of change that entails a denial of motion. Other contemporary process thinkers, equally attentive to the seriousness of Zeno's challenge, follow Henri Bergson, affirming that there is a fatal flaw in rational, second problematic assumptions. Faced with the necessity to inform us of a world of change and becoming, the message of reason is: "You can't get there from here."

The effect of Zeno's paradoxes in shaping the character of intellectual culture simply cannot be overstressed. Though Whitehead claimed that "all of Western philosophy is a series of footnotes to Plato," it was in fact Whitehead's footnote to Zeno that decisively determined the character of his philosophic speculations. Further, since the philosophy inherited by Socrates and Plato was one whose problems and issues were largely constructed as counter-ripostes to Zeno, Whitehead might have said with equal validity that the most telling glosses on Plato, down to the present day, were occasioned by his failure to meet the principal challenge arising from Zeno's conundrums—namely, the challenge to accommodate the conflicting demands of reason and of sense experience.

One of the profoundest scandals of Western intellectual culture is the manner in which so many of our otherwise intelligent contemporaries have sought to discount the seriousness of Zeno's challenge. Ignored by many unable to understand the subtle problems his paradoxes entail, impatiently dismissed by others whose bad faith permits them to dodge the unresolved difficulties, Zeno's Cheshire smile continues to mock the entire subsequent history of Western philosophic speculation:

> It would, of course, be rash to conclude that we had actually arrived at a complete resolution of all the problems that come out of Zeno's paradoxes. Each age, from Aristotle on down, seems to find in the paradoxes difficulties that are roughly commensurate with the mathematical, logical, and philosophical resources then available. When more powerful tools emerge, philosophers seem willing to acknowledge deeper difficulties that would have proved insurmountable for more primitive methods.[51]

—— THIRD ANTICIPATION ——

The effect of Parmenides' and Zeno's speculations was to drive a wedge between reason and sense experience that even the cleverest efforts of subsequent thinkers could not remove. The effects of such speculations are unsurpassed in importance in the Western tradition. Almost all of the philosophical speculations and constructions of subsequent Presocratics were shaped by the need to resolve Zeno's paradoxes. Most importantly, the dichotomy between the realms of Being and Becoming was ramified by the Zenonian paradoxes.

Partly because there was no functional equivalent of Parmenides or Zeno effectively present in the Chinese tradition, classical culture in China developed without these hard and fast dualisms. A consequence of the absence of such historical determinants is that "thinking," unbeset by the conflicting claims of sense experience and of reason, may best be interpreted without resort to this specifically Western problematic. We shall see that the sort of thinking which is associated with the Chinese version of the first problematic is closer to the activity of the creation and correlation of images than to that of providing accounts of the evidences of reason or of the senses. As a consequence, Chinese thinkers were not forced to become obsessed with the goal of providing a rational account of motion and change. [See chapter 3, section 4.1.]

4. COUNTERDISCOURSE: HERACLITUS AND ANAXAGORAS

The march toward the dominance of substance thinking did not go totally unchecked. There was a counterdiscourse which promoted the reality of change over permanence. Heraclitus (ca. 544–484) was, doubtless, the greatest proponent of process thinking remembered from the ancient Greek world. One reason for this is that he developed his ideas before the challenge of Parmenides and Zeno, and thus was able to express his primary intuition, "All things flow," unburdened by attempts to address the Parmenidean strictures.

The first thing to be said about Heraclitus is that he presents us with a rather challenging problem of style. The mixing of image and metaphor with seemingly literal statements, a feature we have noted in other of the earliest philosophers as a sign of the residue of mythopoetic language, is in Heraclitus an apparently self-conscious attempt to express his peculiar intuition about the nature of things:

Thunderbolt steers all things.[52]

All things come into being through opposition, and all are in flux like a river.[53]

War is the father of all and the king of all.[54]

The path up and down is one and the same.[55]

The soul has a *logos* which increases itself.[56]

Changing it rests.[57]

Literal or scientific language and the language of common sense are particularly adapted to rational discourse. Words may be construed primarily as names which tag objects in the world, so that words and the material objects named by them are seen to be in productive association. Likewise, if one believes with Pythagoras that forms, or pattern regularities, constitute the nature of things, then a discursive language of logic is well suited to explain the structure and character of the world-order. But if one were to agree with Heraclitus that reality is in flux, and that the world is "an everliving fire" in a continual state of change, it would be necessary to refrain from anything like univocal language in order to influence one's communicants to sense and feel the world as a process. As Whitehead has suggested, "That 'all things flow' is the first vague generalization which the unsystematized, barely analyzed, intuition of men has produced."[58]

The attempt to systematize or analyze that intuition leads to stasis, for words as names and propositions tend to function as snapshots. And while metaphorical, parabolic, and paradoxical language leads us to resonate with the world of flux and becoming, this resonance is possible only if we employ language as a medium through which to *experience*, rather than to *understand*, the world.[59]

We would do well not to attempt too discursive a commentary on Heraclitus' reflections. They are purposefully paradoxical in order to evoke a sense of change. In fact, Heraclitus' attempt to communicate his belief that the world is in flux led him to be dubbed "the Obscure One" by his contemporaries.

If some "thing" changes into some other "thing," there either must be some constant substrate that remains unaltered throughout the process, or not. If there is, and this is what in essence the Milesian philosophers were looking for in the their various concepts of *physis*, then there is in reality no radical change at all. But if reality is in its essence changing, then for something A to become B it must first be A-but-not-B, then it must be no-longer-A-but-not-yet-B (or both-A-and-B), then it must be B. The difficulty of change is that the intermediate state in which it is "neither" or "both" seems to confound rational explanation. It was likely this consequence that led Heraclitus seemingly to affirm the identity of opposites:

> Things taken together are whole and not whole, something which is being brought together and brought apart, which is in tune and out of tune; out of all things there comes a unity, and out of a unity all things.[60]

Heraclitus is not saying *p* and *not-p* are literally the same. But neither is he simply saying that contrasts imply one another in some vague sense. Rather, he is saying that one cannot separate the qualitative aspect of change from its quantitative character. Changes are always qualitative: health and disease, cold and hot, wet and dry, youth and old-age, night and day, up and down. Since change is pervasive, there is no discrete, substantive, quantitative *p* that changes into *not-p*.

This view of Heraclitus is perhaps better understood if one recalls some of the contemporary existential criticisms of scientific objectification. The world of science and of the *lebenswelt*, the human world, are distinct. The quantification of life has limits. Qualitative considerations must always be taken into account. If change and becoming are stressed, then this must lead to an emphasis upon novelty and uniqueness. Process requires particularity if we are to make sense of it. The same old sorts of thing becoming the same old sorts of thing again would not lead to an interest in process and change, but would more likely influence one to yield to Pythagoras' intoxicated longing for an eternal, unchanging world-order. But things do change—in fact, *must* change—in order to make way for the novel, the particular, the unique.

Even in Heraclitus, the most radical of our process philosophers, there seems to be an element of permanence stressed. It is the *logos* which provides the "measure" for change. But it would be incorrect to translate *logos* in this context as "rational account." More consistent with Heraclitus' principal utterances is something like "narrative" which was one of the many senses of the term available to him.

The soul's *logos* "increases itself." Thus for Heraclitus, all things change according to a measure, *including this measure itself*. If it were the regularities resident in change that Heraclitus wished to stress, he would have spoken of changing things as if they were merely apparent—as did Parmenides, and as will Plato. However, the testimony of this obscure thinker is that, yes, things change according to a measure, but the important point is that *things change*.

Some might see Heraclitus' preference for change and becoming as in tension with his insistence upon the order of the cosmos:

> This world-order [the same of all] did none of gods or men make, but it always was and is and shall be: an everliving fire, kindling in measures and going out in measures.[61]

There is a disagreement among interpreters of Heraclitus as to the authenticity of the interpolation "the same of all." Some, with Gregory Vlastos, believe that Heraclitus is speaking of the single, unitary cosmos, the natural world experienced in common by all "waking men," as opposed to the private worlds into which one enters while sleeping.[62] Others, with G. S. Kirk, hold that the subject of these remarks is this present world-order.[63]

The important consideration, we believe, is to be found in the absence of cosmogonic speculation in Heraclitus and his stress upon the dynamic temporal changes associated with the oppositional alterations in the "everliving fire." These conditions strongly suggest that Heraclitus would be among those who believed in a plurality of worlds succeeding one another in time. For only by excepting the world order in its totality from these oppositional alterations could Heraclitus maintain that there is but one world.

But there is no reason to believe that Heraclitus would have made this exception, given his belief in the reality of change. After all, the preference for permanence and rest is allied with the affirmation of an ordering agency associated, in the beginning of Greek speculation, with cosmogonic acts. By describing the world in terms of an immanent dynamism requiring no transcendent agency, Heraclitus insures that his counterdiscourse of becoming is relevant not only to changes within the world but the change of one world into another.

Other proponents of process thinking, particularly those who expressed their ideas in reaction to Parmenides, never reached the level of Heraclitus' speculations. Anaxagoras, for example, sought to answer Zeno, and in the course of his attempt produced a rather compromised understanding of process and change.

Anaxagoras (500–428) was a protégé of Pericles, who brought him to Athens while he was still in his twenties. For thirty years he resided in Athens, where he fulfilled the role of what we would today call a "research scientist." Anaxagoras explained the dynamic aspect of the processes of nature—that is, the reason for the changes taking place—by recourse to the notion of *Nous* or Mind. Mind remains pure and unmixed with other qualities and serves as the initiator and sustainer of qualitative changes in nature. In this regard, Anaxagoras is developing an insight of Xenophanes who, as we will see, claimed that the mind of god is the chief ordering agency.

Anaxagoras' chief philosophic contribution was his notion of the continuity of matter and the assumption of an indefinite number of qualitative elements expressed in terms of opposites such as hot and cold, wet and dry, white and black, and so forth. In everything there is everything, so all of the qualities are contained in each discriminable entity. This does not mean, as Anaxagoras' language sometimes seems to suggest, that there are physical parts like flesh and bone and blood and hair in everything, but that the *qualities* in accordance with which these elements are constituted are in everything. The preponderance of qualities defines the nature of a thing. Fire has more of the hot and the dry than does, say, a laurel tree or a lamp post, but all extant qualities that we can name are contained in each of the objects of our world. Anaxagoras assumes that space and time are infinitely divisible and that they, therefore, form a continuum. Thus change is to be understood as alterations in the proportions of qualitative mixtures of an indefinite number of contrasting qualities. This is a theory of *qualitative materialism.*

We might note, however, that there is perhaps some cost to common sense required by this view. Zeno's "Arrow Paradox" sought to refute the possibility of motion on the assumption of the infinite divisibility of space and time. It is difficult to see how Anaxagoras' views avoided that particular paradox. Change involves alterations in the presence of qualities, and this understanding of change could never serve as an explanation of the common sense notion of movement in or through space.

It is interesting to see how far in the direction of traditional Ionian cosmology Anaxagoras' presumption of a qualitative atomism permits him to move. The concept of a vortex originally set in motion by Mind is employed essentially intact from his predecessors. The many-worlds view of several of the earlier Ionian thinkers also seems to be affirmed by Anaxagoras.

The mechanistic cosmology which Anaxagoras accepted included views that were expressed in ways which, in the second quarter of the fifth century B.C.E., offended his Athenian audiences. Anaxagoras thought the heavenly bodies to be stones maintained in space by the velocity of their circular "motion." This view, of course, challenged the popular belief that they were, in fact, gods. As a result of theories such as this, formal charges of impiety were eventually brought against Anaxagoras, and he was forced to withdraw to the city of Lampsacus where he died, still a much honored man, at the age of seventy-two.

Not until the twentieth century will the intuitions of Heraclitus and Anaxagoras receive an extended treatment. Henri Bergson and, with some qualifications, William James will follow the Heraclitean path, while A. N. Whitehead, a professional logician and mathematician, will address the Zenonian paradoxes in something like the manner adumbrated by Anaxagoras. By far the majority of thinkers until then will opt for the view that the world is substantial and that there is some underlying substrate in accordance with which we must give our accounts of the world.

After the elaboration of the Eleatic philosophy, the primary problem inherited by later philosophers will be that of accounting for the complex relationships between the worlds of Being and Becoming. This will involve attempts to reconcile the competing realities of body and soul, and the conflicting claims of perception and of reason. For the most part, the conflict will be resolved by the presumption of permanence and the acceptance, therefore, of an underlying reality amidst the illusory character or penultimacy of change.

It is important to realize that this decision effectively closes the traditional philosophic canon to process understandings. This means, of course, that there will be less need for recourse to poetic or metaphorical discourse—which is, effectively, the language of process and change. For Heraclitus had shown that the distinction between mythical and philosophic thinking is not primarily a distinction between rational and irrational thought but between the claims of reason, on the one hand, and those of imaginative generalization grounded in the immediate experience of the world, on the other.

Though there are two strains of thinking in the Greek tradition, one espousing the reality of permanence, the other the fundamental character of change, it is clear that very early on, the substance thinkers came to dominate. One way of explaining this dominance is simply to recall how the notion of rational, causal accounts came to dominate both mythological accountings and pure historical narratives.

In the interrelations among *mythos*, *logos*, and *historia*, the dominance of *logos* was significantly underwritten by the pluralism of the Greek world. Mythologies, and the literature they generate, are specific to a particular people; so, to a large degree, are historical narratives. In the search for a shared public discourse or practices which would achieve the social harmony essential for survival, Greek society was inevitably drawn to abstract conceptualization. Here, and only here, are there to be found those ideas and principles which diverse peoples may share. "You may be Persian, and I Greek, but we are both *men*." "Your gods may be different from mine, but surely we may find in the concept of 'God' qualities shared by all beings worthy of worship." "You may hold to the reality of matter, and I of mind, but surely we can both appeal to rules of logic and dialectic to settle our disagreements."

Ideas of permanence, rest, eternality, and Being came to dominate the sensibilities of the Greeks in the most natural of manners. Thinking, insofar as it is a dodge for survival, has as its most practical of ends the realization of that degree of social harmony which permits the pursuit of other ends promoting life and well-being.

The paradox of the transcendental adventure upon which the Greeks embarked, and which we only now seem close to abandoning, is that, though it seeks unity and harmony, it thrives on difference. The story of Greek philosophy to this point has been one of the development of distinctively different accounts of the way of things. Arguments begin to be mounted for the most varied of understandings. The plurality of divergent views provides the greatest motivation for the transcendental appeals to "laws of thought" and "rules of logical discourse" in order to settle disputes. It is on behalf of such transcendental appeals that intuitions of change and becoming, rooted in the mythopoetic and metaphorical expression of the Greeks, are to be suppressed.

As we shall see, it is the press toward "definition"—a primary means of concept-formation—which further articulates the rational, causal assumptions of the second problematic. For example, asked to say what you *mean* by "motion" rather than simply providing an example of it, leads inevitably away from the world of process and particularity and toward "ideal" and "formal" realms. We shall see next how this process of rationalization led to the rejection of more informal modes of analogical explanation in favor of the formalized methods of analysis and dialectic.

—— **FOURTH ANTICIPATION** ——

The dominance of "substance" over "process" understandings in the Western tradition entailed the devaluation of the metaphoric and imagistic language in which "Heraclitian" intuitions perforce must be expressed. There is no more important development than this for our coming to understand the differences between Chinese and Western sensibilities. *Mutatis mutandis*, China is characteristically "Heraclitian." Correlative thinking in China is not dominated by the demands of rational or empirical "objectivity." "Han thinking," as we shall refer to the specifically Chinese mode of thinking, depends upon the acceptance of "images" and "metaphors" as the primary means of expressing the becoming of things. Marginalizing the language of process and change has led to a situation in which Western interpreters of Chinese culture either condescend to Chinese thinkers because they have not matured past a "protorational" level of discourse, or find their attempts to engage the Chinese sympathetically frustrated by the fact that the Western philosophic inventory is, with respect to methods of addressing the reality of process and change, seriously impoverished. [See chapter 3, sections 1, 4.1, 4.2, 5.3, 5.4.]

5. FROM *THEORIA* TO THEORY

5.1. The Fate of Analogy

The movement from *mythos* to *logos* which undergirds the Enlightenment understanding of the development of Greek thought depends upon a reconstruction of analogical thinking such that the subjective, human focus is disciplined, if not altogether omitted.

The use of analogical thinking marked the very beginnings of Greek thought. Homeric similes, and the structural analogies associated with the mythic superstructure of Homeric epic which brought the human and divine realms into relative harmony, are illustrations of the analogizing mentality. Philosophers bring about a revolution in thinking by drawing direct analogies from the sphere of living creatures to that of the world-order. Anaximander, as we have seen, analogized from the law courts to the external surround as a means of accounting for the order of things.

In the case of Anaximenes, *aer* was explicitly associated with the principle of animation.

> As our soul . . . being air holds us together and controls us, so does wind [or breath] and air enclose the whole world.[64]

Here the analogy is employed in a depersonalized manner in the service of more comprehensive understanding.

The Pythagorean invention of the cosmos by reading the human social order into the heavens was perhaps the supreme example of how subsequent rational speculation depends upon rather sweeping analogical operations. This reconstruction of the analogical mode continues with Xenophanes (c. 570–475), who helped to carry out the implications of the new secular view of the nature of things that was beginning to qualify Greek intellectual culture in the sixth century B.C.E.:

> But if cattle and horses or lions had hands, and were able to draw with their hands and do the works that men can do, horses would draw the forms of the gods like horses, and cattle like cattle, and they would make their bodies such as they each had themselves.[65]

In place of an anthropomorphic god or gods, Xenophanes offers:

> One god, greatest among gods and men, in no way similar to mortals either in body or in thought.[66]

Xenophanes' attempt to avoid all anthropocentric references to the divine introduces a major theme in Western philosophy and science. But avoidance of anthropocentrism is not as easy as it might at first appear. Xenophanes speaks of his God as operating with "the thought of his mind."[67] And "All of him sees, all thinks, all hears."[68]

Though this is certainly not Xenophanes' intent, the claim that God "senses" and is "rational" is unavoidably anthropomorphic, since reason at least is likely a characteristic peculiar to the human species which may be applied only analogically outside the human realm.

Ironically, the term "analogy" (ἀναλογία) originates in mathematics as "identity of proportionality," though it is already used by Plato in an altered sense of "conformability," "similarity." The principal sense of analogy was that of *ratio* or proportionality. Logic is itself rooted in analogies: Resemblance of relations or attributes forms the ground of reasoning. Argument by analogy receives wide support from mathematical operations. On the other hand, causal arguments are in the early stages quite obviously related to anthropic (the law courts) and anthropomorphic (the gods) contexts. Nonetheless, causal thinking soon comes to assume objective, rational status.

Though stipulated first, as in the case of Pythagoras, in mathematical terms, the mystical and aesthetic appreciation of number by Pythagoras and his followers suggests that there was something more than a strictly objective or detached vision underlying mathematical analogies. It is argument based upon meaningful relationships aesthetically construed that gives rise in both classical Greece and China to the mode of thinking we shall be considering under the rubric "analogical thinking."

The rationalization of analogy occurred rather quickly in mathematics, since the ratios and proportions assigned are, from the beginning, quantitative in character. But even with the more qualitative analogies, this movement is easily seen to be taking place. The suspicion of anthropomorphism evidenced in Xenophanes moves as far as possible in the direction of canceling the similarity relation purported to exist between the human and divine realms. Homer, and to a lesser extent the tragic poets, had depended upon this correlation to provide meaningful paradigms allowing for deliberation with respect to both action and self-articulation. Xenophanes' spare, faceless deity reflects not human passions and actions but the emerging rational intellect intoxicated with universality and oneness.

Both Xenophanes and Empedocles (fl. 440 B.C.E.) employed the Homeric meter. In addition, Empedocles seems even to have imitated the pattern of Homeric simile in formulating his analogies. As is often noted, Homer appeals to natural things—animals and plants—to illumine the specific actions of men and gods:

Like a lion who pounces on cattle feeding in a glade . . . the son of Tydeus tumbled them rudely out of their chariot[69]

As fig juice quickly curdles milk, swiftly Apollo cured the wound of Ares.[70]

Compare these "slice of life" similes to the more convoluted constructions of Empedocles:

As when someone planning a journey prepared a lamp, the gleam of blazing fire through the wintry night, and fastened linen screens against all kinds of breezes, which scatter the wind of the blowing breezes but the light leapt outwards, as much of it was finer, and shone with its tireless beams across the threshold; in this way [Aphropdite] gave birth to the rounded pupil, primeval fire crowded in the membranes and in the fine linens. And they covered over the depths of the circumfluent water and sent forth fire, as much of it was finer.[71]

As when painters . . . take in their hands many colored pigments, mixing them in harmony, some more, others less . . . prepare forms resembling all things. . . . In this way let not deception overcome your thought organ, [by convincing you] that the source of mortal things . . . is anything else.[72]

The poetry of Empedocles has moved analogical operations rather far in the direction of a deanthropomorphized rationality. This is done, as is the case in every rationalized analogy, by introducing primary analogates which ground all analogical operations. These analogates are, in Empedocles' case, the four fundamental elements of earth, air, fire, and water, and the principles of Love and Strife. All comparisons are adjudicated by these elements and principles.

Homer's concern for ensconcing the human being in the world of living things through concrete similes, and then appealing to the analogical structures of myth to stabilize the human being within the supernatural scheme, readily contrasts with the tendencies of philosophers such as Anaximander, Anaximenes, Xenophanes, and Empedocles to rationalize the cosmos. Increasingly the world is losing its sacred aura, and with that loss, value recedes from the cosmos.

We moderns, of course, are tempted to justify the rationalizing of analogical operations in philosophy while admiring their richer form in Homer by insisting that Homer is creating poetry while the philosophers are doing protoscience. But, of course, such a claim would merely enforce the point we are trying to make. We moderns are products of the *mythos*-to-*logos* dynamic. Viewed honestly, there can be no doubt but that Homer and Empedocles were both attempting to present the way of things.

We would, perhaps, benefit from these words of a contemporary philosopher:

> For my part I do, qua lay physicist, believe in physical objects and not in Homer's gods; and I consider it to be a scientific error to believe otherwise. But in point of epistemological footing the physical objects and the gods differ only in degree and not in kind. Both sorts of entities enter our conception only as cultural posits. The myth of physical objects is epistemologically superior to most in that it has proved more efficacious than other myths as a device for working a manageable structure into the flux of experience.[73]

The antagonism to anthropocentrism will be softened somewhat with the eventual introduction of the Hebraic understanding of God as "Father" into Western culture. But classical science more and more will develop around the assumption that to provide the most accurate account of the world requires that one characterize it as it would be if the observer were not present. Likewise, speculative philosophy or metaphysics, presumably the most general science of order, will also attempt to avoid the sort of special pleading involved in arguing about the nature of things from a specifically human perspective.

Increasingly, however, critics of late twentieth-century science and philosophy endeavor to point out the anthropomorphic character of rational thinking. Thinking per se may turn out to be a form of special pleading in which cosmological and ethical visions are shown to be ways of entertaining a world presumed to be the sort of world it is because of the epistemological, ethical, and aesthetic requirements of the sort of beings we presume ourselves to be.[74] The issue is an important one, if only because it is the tension between anthropomorphic, and presumably "objective," accounts, which raises the question of the viability of analogical versus causal thinking.

Analogical thinking usually involves characterizing relations deemed meaningful from the perspective of the individual constructing the analogy. Anthropomorphism is often perfectly appropriate in such procedures.[75] Our conclusion must be that the suspicion of anthropomorphism, so well illustrated in the arguments of Xenophanes, will militate against the full acceptance of informal analogical thinking.

The character of the contrast between causal and analogical thinking is shaped by the different histories of the terms *cause* and *analogy*, respectively. Each concept is rooted in both the logical and rhetorical traditions, but the usurpation of the term *cause* by the natural sciences has led to its immediate "efficient" and "material" associations. The term *analogy*, on the other hand, with the demise of the theological traditions, has taken its associations primarily from the tropic analyses associated with literature and literary criticism.

The increased concern with the effects of anthropocentric and anthropomorphic thinking affected adversely the employment of analogical thinking. A second equally important event shaped the increasing objectivity of Greek rationality. In tracing the remainder of the history of Greek philosophy after the shock of Parmenides and Zeno, we must take some care to note the manner in which our philosophers construct theoretical visions of the world. For what is different now is that philosophy is conscious of its past.

5.2 Philosophy Discovers Its Past

After Parmenides and Zeno, the history of Western philosophy comes to be a history of unanswered questions and unresolved problems. All of the important issues that interest philosophers will remain unsettled. Whereas it is at least possible to think of the history of science and technology as cumulative, and to believe, therefore, in the growth at least of technical knowledge, in philosophy we tend to think in terms of perennial issues and problems which resist final resolution. What this means is that the discipline of philosophy is so conditioned by its past that philosophers cannot generally think of the past of their discipline as *past* in the sense of something that has been surpassed. Philosophy does not seem to outgrow its past.

The first implication of the fact that philosophy has become aware of its past is that philosophers will be inclined to employ the vocabulary of their tradition to meet the difficulties set for them by previous philosophers. This will lead to the articulation of a mode of engagement among thinkers and their tradition predicated upon the attempt to clarify, modify, or refute positions within that tradition. The dialogical or dialectical method that emerges from this process, and which will receive its most subtle expression in Plato's early dialogues, is developed from the mode of dialectic introduced by reflections of Parmenides on "Being" and "Not-Being," and refined by Zeno in his presentation of his paradoxes.[76] The *dialogical* method is a species of the *logical* method.

Unfortunately, one effect of conversation with the tradition is that overall there is less resort to constructive imagination. In our consideration of Heraclitus we claimed that the distinction between mythical and philosophic thinking is primarily a distinction not between rational and irrational thought but between the claims of reason on the one hand and those of imaginative generalization on the other. The resort to metaphor and imagery as constructive components of one's philosophic descriptions is threatened through the use of dialectical engagement which urges one to begin with the language of one's opponent. After philosophy becomes aware of its past, the constructive employment of imagination becomes questionable as a legitimate method of coming to understand the world. Henceforth, most claims to respectability will be made largely on behalf of a rational engagement with the doctrines and issues generated by the discourse of prior thinkers.

But as we said with regard to the thinking of Heraclitus, some sorts of experience of the world may in fact require the use of imagistic and metaphorical language. If such language is thought to be inappropriate in itself, apart from the specific things said by recourse to that language, then we have excluded possible types of experience from our field of speculation.

In the preceding section we saw how Empedocles added his weight to the rationalizing of analogical operations. The other side of the coin is that Empedocles was one of the last defenders of imaginative construction in ancient Greek philosophy. That Empedocles' imagination was fettered by rational constraints is in large measure the consequence of his having believed it necessary to engage the thought of his predecessors.

With Empedocles, philosophy becomes a self-conscious discipline. It seems clear that this thinker was consciously influenced by each of his principal precursors: Anaximander, Xenophanes, the Pythagoreans, and Parmenides. The vision of Empedocles could be described as one in which the insight of the Pythagoreans concerning the relationship of things and numbers is preserved, together with the Parmenidean denial of empty space and of the existence of Not-being, all in a manner that permitted the defense of change.

If change is to be defended without the introduction of empty space or Not-being, then, so Empedocles thought, more than a single substance was necessary. He posited the four elements—air, fire, water, and earth—as basic substances and characterized change in terms of the mutual displacement of these elements. This still leaves the reality of *motion* in doubt, of course, but there is now at least a consistent way of defining change. The four elements have specific shapes and sizes, so the quantitative aspect of Pythagorean philosophy is supported. In addition to the four physical elements, there are the principles of Love and Strife, attraction and repulsion, which account for the dynamism of change.

The doctrines that entail elements of specific shapes and sizes, and principles of attraction and repulsion, together yield a primitive understanding of physical phenomena as modern chemistry has described them. The quantitative ratios established by attractions among elements constitute the various material compounds. Nothing can come from nothing, so the elements are eternal; and the things that come into being from out of the various combinations of the elements are real in only a secondary sense.

Empedocles is in direct contradiction with Parmenides on the question of the legitimacy of sense experience:

> But come consider with all thy powers how each thing is manifest, neither holding sight in greater trust as compared with hearing, nor loud-sounding hearing above the clear evidence of thy tongue, nor withhold thy trust from any of the other limbs, wheresoever there is a path for understanding, but think on each thing in the way by which it is manifest.[77]

Empedocles' defense of sense experience is not simply a claim on behalf of the five senses. Love and Strife are themselves ways of sensing. The principles of Love and Strife are analogized from human experience and elaborated into cosmological principles. This is the basis of mythopoetic thought which presumes a resonance between *psyche* and its environs.

In his *On the Nature of Things*, Empedocles provided a cyclical theory of the origins and demise of the human world in four distinct stages. The specific application Empedocles made to human history is still debated, but the principles are clear enough: A primordial unity in which Love reigns yields itself at the extreme to a condition of total Strife, a complete separation of the basic elements. Out of this dispersed condition emerges again the reign of Love. The human world falls in the two stages between the extremes of complete unity and complete dispersion:

> And these things never cease from continual shifting, at one time all coming together, through Love, into one, at another each borne apart from the others through Strife.[78]

Empedocles' stage of complete unity is of course a stage of harmonious plurality in which all four of the physical elements are balanced and united by Love. The primordial sphere is a Unity but not a One.

Empedocles' principles of Love and Strife were, as we have indicated, analogized from human experience. It was doubtless his view that the experience of the senses, including the actual feelings of love and strife, augmented by the imagination, provide a less restricted understanding of the world. The importance of imagination in Empedocles is to be found here: The imagination permits the breaking down and recombination of the evidences of the senses. For most of us, given to the acceptance of the five senses and of reason as the arbiters of evidence, we would find in the imagination an arbitrary activity divorced from any hard-nosed experience of the world. For Empedocles, however, imagination was a source of extended knowledge because he believed the world to be a dynamic interchange of the basic elements limited only by the possible combinations of these elements. Immediate sense experience must be augmented by imagination if we are to appreciate the vast complexity of things that come into being with the cosmic cycle determined by the interactions of Love and Strife.

The active resorts to imaginative speculation of the sort represented by Empedocles become rare in philosophical discourse as the self-consciousness of the philosophic enterprise increases. As thinkers increasingly depend upon the assumptions of other thinkers as places from which to begin, and increasingly depend upon the tools of dia-

lectical analysis and construction, the openness of speculative wonder—the sense of *theoria*—yields itself to the activity of theory construction.

When Montaigne, the sixteenth-century humanist and essayist,
complained that "We have more books on books than we have on
things," he called attention to the fact that the past often burdens us
with predigested perspectives and problems, tempting us away from
the more open and naive approach to thinking for its own sake.

Once the philosophic tradition begins to develop, philosophers will
more and more develop their various theories in response to the theories of others rather than by beginning with the data of experience
and/or reason. For philosophers, the effect of poring over alternative
philosophic visions rather than over the data of immediate experience
is that the ad hoc solution is overused.

By ad hoc solution, we usually mean something like this: A thinker
may replace the question "What kinds of things are there?" with a
less naive query such as "What kind of world would there have to be
if we are to avoid the undesirable consequences of X's vision?"
Rather than looking for evidence through the senses, or by logical or
imaginative extrapolations from what must rationally follow from this
or that presumed experience of the world, one can simply critique an
alternative theory about the world.

Perhaps the most productive illustration of the appeal to ad hoc
theorizing is to be found in the development of Greek atomism.
Atomism originates with the fifth-century thinker, Leucippus, but we
have lost almost all of his doctrines. It is Democritus (?470–?366), the
follower and elaborator of Leucippus' thought, from whom we learn
of the first atomic theory.

Democritus, following Leucippus, began by asking: "What kind of
world must there be if we are to save the world from the strictures of
Eleatic philosophy?" He then answered this question by saying that
there must be a world in which physical and mathematical divisibility
are distinguished. This permits us to envision a world comprised by
material atoms which are physically indivisible minima, but which
may, perhaps, be passive to mathematical division.

The important point here is that atomic theory was largely ad hoc
in the sense that it was constructed in response to another theory
rather than by resort to experience, experiment, or imaginative construction occasioned by an encounter with the world of things.

Though strictly speaking the ad hoc resolution of a problem involves dialogue or dialectic, the ad hoc method seriously truncates dialectical enquiry by simply refuting or rejecting one or more of the premisses of an argument or theory. A theory is developed which excludes the alternative and, therefore, forces a choice between views.

Atoms and the void are eternal. Motion produced by the collisions of atoms in the void is itself without beginning; there is no explanation of the vortex motion apart from the motion of atoms, which is produced by collisions. The point here is subtle but important: There is no explanation of any original motion. Anaxagoras had resort to the principle of *Nous* to explain the presumed motions of things. Democritus refers to the vortex as "necessity" since it is this motion, a consequence of the collisions of atoms, which determines all physical states of affairs.

Motion is a consequence of the random collisions of the atoms. Infinite numbers of atoms colliding at random create a vortex motion in which separation takes place "like to like," in accordance with what we would term centrifugal and centripetal forces produced by the resulting whirl.

Aristotle faulted Democritus for his failure to distinguish motion "natural" to the atoms from "unnatural" motions resulting from their mutual collisions:

> Leucippus and Democritus, who say that the primary bodies are in perpetual movement in the void or infinite, may be asked to explain the manner of their motion and the kind of movement which is natural to them. For if the various elements are constrained by one another to move as they do, each must still have a natural movement which the constrained contravenes, and the prime mover must cause motions not by constraint but naturally. If there is no ultimate natural cause of movement and each preceding term in the series is always moved by constraint, we shall have an infinite process.[79]

Here we see Aristotle summing up the general tendency of Greek thought which required recourse to agency (*Nous*, Prime Mover, God) to explain the motions of and changes in things. The priority of rest and the consequent need to explain motion is, as we have said, one of the primary determinants of the articulation of causal theories.

Aristotle's criticism of Democritus is hardly just if viewed on Democritus' own terms, however, since the eternality of atoms and space entails the eternality of the sort of motion which Aristotle terms "unnatural" or "constrained." Atoms have *always* been colliding with one another as a result of collisions from other atoms, which in turn have been given their motions from yet other collisions, and so on. Democritus was not inclined to find this "infinite regress" unacceptable; it is an implication of the idea that the world is without a beginning.

Later theological arguments which attempt to show that reason ultimately requires a first principle are simply dealing with a meaning of reason distinct from that Democritus entertained. Is it more irrational to say that all motion is due to the collision of atoms, refusing to assign any beginning to those collisions, than to say that the universe originates from a big bang which had antecedent to it the condensation of matter and energy, which presupposed a still earlier big bang, and so on?

Thinking in terms of models, such as is involved in the development and application of atomic theory, involves a form of reductionism which employs *hypothesized* analogies. Models are ad hoc devices aimed at explicating or justifying a belief, doctrine or principle. As such, they are suppressed metaphors which are thought to have been rendered objective by virtue of their seeming detachment from the immediate aesthetic interest of the theorist.

Democritus carries the reductive mode of thinking to its farthest extreme:

At first men were begotten from water and slime. [They] emerged from the ground like worms, without a maker and for no reason.[80]

Atoms and the void, as first principles, provide no manner of explaining the development of complex physical things other than by appeal to simpler physical things. Further, since there is no purpose, end, or aim in the real world of the atomic swirl, there can be nothing of the sort in the world of human organisms.

The consequences of reductionism are best seen with regard to the Democritean explanation of the human experience of free action. In Democritus' world, everything occurs by necessity. There is no freedom. This simply means that everything is caused by the interactions of atoms and compounds. There is no reason why this or that occurs, except that associated with the causal factors in the immediate past. In order to explain the natural world it has been necessary to account for human beings in terms of atoms moving in empty space.

Democritus has defended our experience of motion and change adequately, but what of our equally profound sense of free action? That turns out to be as illusory as Parmenides claimed motion and change to be. Further, to be consistent, Democritus must claim that all knowledge comes from contact between atoms and compounds. Reason, of the type that allows him to make the claim that atoms and the void exist, must ultimately be explicable in terms of such interactions. That Democritus held to something like the possibility of rational access to the objective world of things is most likely; otherwise, he would be trapped in a rather significant inconsistency.

One might recall the similar problems often associated with other materialist explanations. Sigmund Freud in our century has been criticized for making knowledge the consequence of sublimated libidinal motivations, and then of attempting to except his theory from such an explanation. B. F. Skinner's claims concerning the origins of knowledge in contingencies of reinforcement in local environments provides no satisfactory explanation as to why his theory about such reinforcements, itself born of such contingencies, ought be accepted as "true."

The problem we confront in the analysis of ad hoc theorizing involves the basic issue of the function of first principles. An explanatory principle can potentially explain anything but itself. If we say, for example, as the Principle of Sufficient Reason holds that there is a sufficient reason to explain any given state of affairs, how are we to invoke that principle to explain the presumed fact that the world is such that this principle obtains without simply taking that principle for granted? Apparently, we cannot but beg the question with regard to first principles. Thus, if Democritus wishes to claim that all things come from necessity, he is not required (since it would not be possible) to explain the origin of necessity.

Nonetheless, the weight of the later tradition will connect reason and the "first principles" explanatory of motion. This requires resort to agency, which in turn privileges what Aristotle will term "efficient" and "final" causes. Thus "rational" thinking, as "causal" thinking, is primarily construed in terms either of physical agencies associated with the atomistic vision, or of teleological agencies associated with *Nous* or the Prime Mover as repositories of ends. Since the sixteenth century, of course, it is the former model, that of efficient causality, that has been most prominent.

The principal discovery of the atomists, paradoxically, has no material basis; it is the logical insight that physical and mathematical divisibility may be distinguished. This insight does not, of course, derive from sense experience, nor does it come from a reflection upon the nature of material atoms antecedently entertained. On the contrary, we must assume that the insight was not born of the question, "What kinds of things are there?" but was the consequence of asking (in much the same manner that Anaxagoras had asked), "What sort of world would there have to be if (a) we are to meet the strictures of Zeno's arguments as best we can, and (b) we are to accept the evidence for motion and change?"

The extent to which the philosophy of Democritus is similar to that of Parmenides is quite impressive. Not only does he posit his atoms as instances of the indivisible, homogeneous, Parmenidean Being, he also seems to have maintained something like the Eleatic form of rationalism that requires reality be accessible solely to reason. The attempt on the part of Democritus to maintain these notions within a consistently quantitative, materialistic framework of explanation provides us with one of the most subtle and profound theories to date.

The atomism of Democritus and the Roman, Lucretius (99–?55),[81] will be revived in the seventeenth and eighteenth centuries by Pierre Gassendi, Descartes, and others, in order to serve as the model for the articulation of the quantitative construal of the natural world in terms of matter and motion. Not, however, until Bertrand Russell's arguments in the early part of the twentieth century will any serious attempt be made to ground this vision empirically.[82] By that time, the theory will effectively have passed from the physical sciences and will have but a brief career remaining before the majority of philosophers reject it as well.

In Democritus' thinking, we have an explicit illustration of the consequences of the movement from *theoria* (θεωρία), with its original associations of open speculation, to *theory*. This is a movement from the openness of analogical understandings to the systematic, axiomatic closure based upon the need to confront one theoretical vision with another.

When Aristotle claimed that philosophy begins in wonder (*thauma* θαῦμα),[83] his words were perhaps more descriptive of the brief history of philosophical thinking to which he was heir than of the activities of the majority of later thinkers. For as we shall continue to note, the movement of Greek thought was away from the wonder associated with the original attitude of *theoria*, which involved the desire to celebrate the splendors of the world, and toward what we shall later associate with formal, theoretical understandings motivated by the desire for internal coherence, rigor, and consistency.

We often fail to realize that beginning one's thinking with *wonder* involves the thinker's senses, emotions, and imagination in such a manner as to ensure that he or she is the focus from which the speculative adventure begins. This is the primary source of that analogical thinking which accedes to the personal, subjective perspective. The quest for objectivity and certainty leads one to deny the importance of the personal and the human and, instead, to characterize the way of things by appeal to the apparently impersonal demands of reason. And though we have suggested that reason itself implicitly commits the thinker to a highly anthropocentric perspective, the history of rational speculation in the West is largely a story of attempts to deny that fact.

When, finally, we begin to discuss the Chinese sensibility, we shall find that something like the opposite development took place in classical China. Though there were numerous experiments in the development of logic and rational thinking, these were soon effectively abandoned in favor of concretely interpersonal exercises in analogical thinking.

——— **FIFTH ANTICIPATION** ———

The complete expression of second problematic thinking requires the presumption of an objectivity untainted by anthropomorphic and anthropocentric modes of thinking. In the West this led to the suppression of the origins of concepts formed by analogy from the human realm, and indeed, to a deemphasis upon the uses of analogy per se, and to a dependence instead, upon the privileging of analytic and dialectical modes of argumentation. The shift away from analogy was supported by the fact that philosophers began to develop their understandings increasingly by recourse to the speculations of other thinkers rather than by appeal to the immediacies of experience and imagination. This fact, in turn, promoted the development of theories as increasingly formalized systems which may be logically and dialectically defensible. The history of philosophy among the Greeks from this time forward will be determined in large measure by the dialectical interactions among alternative theories aiming at a single, objective truth.

Here there are two significant contrasts with the development of classical Chinese culture. First, neither Confucianism nor Daoism will condemn analogies rooted in personal and particular perspectives. The Confucian will insist that the anthropocentric perspective be maintained. The Daoist, though not anthropocentric, will seek to avoid any notion of objective truth which would presuppose a "God's-eye view," finding that each of the myriad things of the world offers a perspective from which "the ten thousand things" might be construed. As a consequence, first problematic, correlative thinking will involve the resort to analogies rooted either in the immediate perspective of the agent of understanding or in that which is to be understood. Further, this deferential mode of understanding accounts in part for the fact that interactions among various thinkers will emphasize accommodation over dialectical disputation. In fact, we shall see that the aim at social harmony, realized in the West by appeal to very general principles abstracted from the differences dialectically realized, was finally achieved in China through the rejection of dialectical disputation in favor of the "aesthetic" accommodation of alternative views. [See chapter 3, sections 2, 4.2, 5.1.]

6. COUNTERDISCOURSE: THE SOPHISTS

As a model of high culture, Athens holds perhaps an unparalleled position in Western history. Art, drama, science, and technology provided thinkers a cultural context within which to expand and deepen both their constructive and critical insights. The commercial vitality of the Athenian city-state, and the fact that it was a meeting place for travellers from a variety of distant places, insured the exchange of ideas essential to valuable speculations. Thus, beginning with the second quarter of the fifth century B.C.E., politics and commerce combined to provide freedom of thought and action unprecedented within the Athenian society for that admittedly small percentage of the occupants of Athens who were designated citizens.

From the time of Anaxagoras, therefore, the story of Greek philosophy is essentially the story of Athens. Though it is said that Democritus complained that he travelled to Athens, but no one recognized him,[84] his thought, along with that of all the other important intellectuals, was examined and debated at length by prominent Athenian thinkers.

The character of Athens shaped the direction of philosophic thinking, as much as it was shaped by it. The persecution of Anaxagoras by the Athenians illustrated the continued influence of conservative opinion, a factor which is often an essential part of the tension involved in creative thought. It is with respect to the Sophistic movement, however, that we can best see how the cosmopolitan character of Athenian society served as both partial cause and partial consequence of a distinctive manner of thinking.

Two principal factors are usually cited as accounting for the rise of the Sophistic movement. The first concerns the changing social order of the Greek city-states. The second has to do with a crisis of reason associated with the failure of the philosophical elite to arrive at any sort of theoretical consensus regarding the important theoretical and practical issues of the day.

In the sixth and fifth centuries B.C.E. there was an emergence of new democracies in many of the traditionally aristocratic and oligarchic cities of the Greek world. As in any democratic society, status and privilege were not inheritable; they had to be earned. When status and power are functions of the desires of the majority, this situation inevitably leads to the development of the art of political persuasion. In a democracy, those who were most persuasive attained the greatest political privilege and status. This is but to say that in the Greek world, as in modern democracies, the power to shape opinion was a most useful ability to possess.

In early democracies, the ability to shape opinion depended upon one's capacity to *speak* persuasively. Enter the Sophists, a class of itinerant teachers who, for a fee, would teach the art of citizenship, which was primarily construed as the art of persuasive speech. Thus the Sophists were masters of the emerging art of *rhetoric*.

In part, the development of rhetoric was independent of the story of philosophic development we have been tracing to this point. The art of persuasive speech which prepares one to make his way in the political arena is not in the least grounded in the same sort of interests that lead one to ask, "What kinds of things are there?" But not all of the Sophists articulated their principal doctrines independently of the philosophers. Some of the Sophists, in fact, may be thought to have developed their thinking in reaction to what they perceived to be the failures of philosophy, particularly the failure to meet the strictures of Zeno's paradoxes.

If one looks at the history of philosophy from the Milesian thinkers to Anaxagoras and Democritus, it is quite possible to think that little has been accomplished. Where, after all, have we come? There is little by way of consensus. We have *this* theory and *that* one, but no generally accepted answer to our philosophic questions. Especially after Parmenides and Zeno, when all of the philosophers seemed to be scurrying this way and that, in order to discover a way out of the impasse Parmenidean philosophy created for philosophic speculation, it was tempting for a number of intellectuals to believe that theoretical speculations should be abandoned because they effectively led nowhere. Thus, many Sophists believed that the only conclusion one might draw from the conflicting claims of the various philosophers is that "truth is relative." According to the famous maxim that is said to have begun Protagoras' (ca. 480–410) work *On Truth*, "Man is the measure of all things—alike of the being of things that are, and of the not-being of things that are not."[85]

Both of the presumed causes for the rise of the Sophistic movement are distinctly related to the character of Athenian society. The new democracy was itself predicated upon an attempt to deal with the plurality of beliefs and practices that characterized everyday life in Athens. At the level of the intellectual elites the same intense pluralism reigned. Athens was the marketplace at which all the principal ideas and theories were exchanged.

At both the theoretical and practical levels of Athenian society, the plurality of opinion and action threatened civic harmony. The attempt to confront the disequilibrizing consequences of a plurality of customs, beliefs, and theoretical visions provided the impetus for the development of one of the most crucial of all the intellectual controversies that occurred in the ancient Greek world. This was the debate over the priority of *physis* or *nomos*.

We have argued that the *physiologoi*—those who asked after the "nature" of things—were divided into those who tacitly or explicitly accepted the existence of multiple world-orders and those who affirmed the existence of a single–ordered world. All *physiologoi* agreed, however, that the question of the *physis* of things was the fundamental question one ought to ask. As Gregory Vlastos has said of the *physiologoi*, "The cosmos they had to invent. *Physis* they found ready-made in the inherited conceptual scheme."[86] This is why, says Vlastos, they came to be called *physiologoi* rather than *kosmologoi*.

Another technical term which is well represented in the inherited conceptual scheme of the sixth and fifth centuries B.C.E. is *nomos* (νόμος). Its early meaning is something like "custom," but very soon it takes on the slightly more formal senses of "convention" and "law." When the more practical Sophists and the speculative *physiologoi* begin self-consciously to diverge from one another, the debate about the distinction between that which exists "by nature" and "by convention" emerged as one of the most significant of intellectual disagreements. In many ways this dispute represents a contest between causal and analogical thinking.

The *physiologoi* would couch this debate in terms of the contrast of "convention" (or "appearance") and "reality." When Democritus said

> by convention are sweet and bitter, hot and cold, by convention is colour; in truth are atoms and the void . . .[87]

he was contrasting the world of senses, which gives rise to convention, with the world of reality. We have already rehearsed Democritus' naturalistic explanation of the origin of human beings who emerged solely by physical necessity, "without a maker and for no reason." These first men

> led an undisciplined and a bestial life. . . . Then, since they were attacked by the wild beasts, they came to each other's aid, being instructed by expediency, and when they gathered together in this way by reason of their fear, they gradually came to recognize their mutual characteristics. . . .
>
> Now the first men, since none of the things useful for life had yet been discovered, led a wretched existence. . . . Little by little, however, experience taught them both to take to the caves in winter and to store such fruits as could be preserved. And when they had become acquainted with fire and other useful things, the arts also and whatever else is capable of furthering man's social life were gradually discovered. Indeed, speaking generally, in all things it was necessity itself that became man's teacher, supplying in appropriate fashion instruction in every matter to a creature which was well endowed by nature and had, as its assistants for every purpose, hands and speech and sagacity of mind.[88]

Fear and expediency are the modalities of necessity from which men learn to be civilized beings. For Democritus, necessity is the mother of convention.

The Sophists provided the counterdiscourse to this manner of interpreting the relations of *physis* and *nomos*. Within the community of Sophists, there were many distinctive opinions over the relative value of *nomos* vis-à-vis *physis*, but a most significant result of their debates was that of raising to consciousness the power of *nomos* in both its informal and formal senses to shape our understandings of the world.

Faced with the theoretical pluralism of Athenian society, the Sophists were stimulated to argue in this manner: Many explanations of the origin and character of our world exist; these are often vastly different one from another and, as often, contradictory. If we ask which of these theories accurately describes the reality of things, we can only say that the meaning of the phrase, "the reality (*physis*) of things," alters as one moves from one theory to another. Now, whatever else a theory is, it is a linguistic product. The manner in which the Greeks and Persians understand the world differ greatly, in large measure because of the different customs and beliefs that shape their languages. Could it not be that the differences among individual understandings within the Greek world are themselves the consequences of distinctive beliefs and customs that have influenced the development of these theoretical modes of expression? And aren't the theories of the sort expressed so freely by the *physiologoi* nothing more or less than *nomoi*—conventional products of human beings attempting to express themselves in their most persuasive manner? And, could it not be that when Democritus says that, in reality, "there are only atoms and the void," he is agreeing that all theories, like language itself, are but conventional expressions since, if our thoughts are capable of reaching to the nature of things, they must not be altogether reducible to atoms? And if this is so, is not the "reality" Democritus describes in his theory itself but a product of convention?

The upshot of this way of thinking is that many of the Sophists came to believe that both what we as individuals and societies will find persuasive, as well as the arguments we will attempt to construct in order to persuade others, are matters of convention. There is no such thing as an absolute or final truth. It is society, and its most persuasive members, who decide what is true. This denial of any sort of objective standard by which something could be judged true or false, right or wrong, made of all of the important values, matters of convention. Those things which the customs and laws of a particular society dictate are to be accepted as correct. Issues which become controversial in a society, such as certain questions concerning the justice of this or that law, or questions of the guilt and innocence of an individual pleading his case before a jury, are decided by the courts.

The Sophistic view that "justice is what the courts decide" was responsible for the creation of a class of "lawyers" among the early Sophists. Indeed, the Sophists (Protagoras himself is credited with the invention of this technique) provided the basis for the adversarial system of justice which requires that a lawyer be trained to argue both sides of a case.

It is, of course, a short step from the claim that "justice is what the courts decide" to the rather cynical view expressed by Thrasymachus: "Justice is the interest of the stronger." For the power of persuasion may often be less a function of persuasive rhetoric and more that of the power of economic wealth or military might. Those among the Sophists, like Protagoras, who seemed to value the consensual norms of a given society or culture were hardly destabilizing forces in the Greek world. But Sophists such as Thrasymachus and Critias (known for his tenure as an unscrupulous member of the Thirty Tyrants who governed Athens at the close of the Peloponnesian War) were persuaded that it was powerful *individuals* and not society that decided what was right or true or just. This sort of Sophist could only add to the disorder of the Greek world in the turbulent fifth century B.C.E.

One of the characteristics of the Sophistic movement was the concern of its principal members for the study of language as a tool of persuasion. One aspect of this study led to the development of complex sorts of grammars, the invention of rhetorical figures, and so forth. Such a movement paralleled developments in the science of logic, a discipline that will achieve its most mature expression in the work of Aristotle. Nothing attests to the likelihood of the claim that the Sophists were at best on the fringes of the mainstream philosophic tradition than the fact that the tools of rhetoric and of logic, the paradigmatic tools of the Sophist and of the philosophers, respectively, are predicated on conflicting and often contradictory principles.

The aim of rhetoric at persuasion entails the consequence that, in the production of a good speech, one must always keep one's audience in mind. This, of course, is one of the first things a contemporary student of composition will be told by his or her professor. There are different ways of presenting one's arguments, depending upon the character and background of one's audience. On the other hand, philosophers who employ logic are writing or speaking for the "Mind of God," attempting to tell the truth in the most profound manner of which they are capable. The burden of understanding is placed upon the reader or listener, and few concessions will be made to one's audience, lest the truth be watered down or otherwise distorted.

The tension between philosophy and rhetoric is, thus, in part a tension between those who would address the "Mind of God" and those who seek to communicate with their peers. The universalism of the philosopher is to be contrasted with the community-based interests of the rhetorician. Borrowing terms from the contemporary pragmatist, Richard Rorty: At their respective bests, the philosopher strives for "objectivity" while the Sophist seeks "solidarity."[89]

It is important to note that standard interpretations of the Sophists often perpetuate the idea of causal thinking by substituting the causal efficacy of the human agent for that of natural agency. This individualistic interpretation is less representative of the actual character of the Sophistic movement than we have been led to believe. It is, perhaps, to be expected that those searching for the objective truth concerning the reality of things would be tempted to emphasize the potential arbitrariness and capriciousness of those who believe in the priority of *nomos* over *physis*.

It is more plausible to read the Sophists, as we are reading them, in a less dialectical manner. The chastening of rationality in the face of the intransigent variety of theoretical perspectives, not to mention the permanent embarrassment occasioned by Zeno's arguments, need not have led to the substitution of individual human action for the dynamism of nature as the foundation of "causality." We may as readily interpret the bulk of the Sophistic understandings as a return to the analogical activities of the first problematic thinkers. The aim of the most representative Sophists was, essentially, the same as that of all responsible intellectuals: to understand things in such a manner as to place oneself and one's peers within the world of nature and society in as harmonious a way as is possible.

When we approach the thought of Socrates next, we will see a shift of emphasis in his thinking away from the apparently unsuccessful attempts of the natural philosophers to answer questions about the nature of the physical world, and a turning toward the specifically human concerns associated with the discovery of those truths most relevant to the human situation. This response allies Socrates with the Sophistic movement.

This story of the emergence of the Sophistic movement is, admittedly, rather simplistic. It is essential that we note that the rhetorical and pragmatic character expressed by the Sophists is not only predicated upon a sense of the failure of reason, but continues an older tradition characterized by the poets and physicians.

The tension between the more experience-minded thinkers who maintain their roots in analogical thinking and the emerging philosophical rationalizers is captured in these words from the treatise, *Ancient Medicine*, presumably directed against Empedocles:

I am at a loss to understand how those who . . . abandon the old method in order to rest their art on a postulate treat their patients on the lines of that postulate. For they have not discovered, I think, an absolute hot or cold, dry or moist, that participates in no other form. But I think that they have at their disposal the same foods and the same drinks as we all use. . . . It would be futile to order a patient to take something hot, as he would at once ask, "What hot thing?"[90]

Empedocles' notion that health involves a balance of the four elements does not impress the physician who is concerned with exactly what must be done to achieve that balance.

In chapter 20, the author of *Ancient Medicine* objects to "certain physicians and philosophers [who] assert that nobody can know medicine who is ignorant [as to] what man is."[91] His claim is that what is needed is the knowledge of "what man is in relation to foods and drinks, and to habits generally, and what will be the effects of each on each individual."[92]

Analogical thinking of the sort that depends upon concrete comparisons made with respect to the furniture of the human world becomes increasingly suspect with the dominance of the mode of speculation which grounds comparisons in totally quantitative relations, and/or which depends upon a primary analogate which will ground and discipline all comparisons.

Homer and the Greek dramatists provided the most concrete and specific demonstrations of those striking human actions and responses which, beginning in earnest with Socrates, will receive formal definitions as virtues and vices. So influential will these definitions become that Homer and his poetic colleagues will increasingly be interpreted by recourse to such formal concepts. This anachronistic reading makes it difficult for we who view epic and lyric poetry from the vantage of modern culture to find in them the fruitful images and analogies they in fact contain.

Likewise with the digests of disease symptoms and cures in Hippocrates, or the advices on the art of good citizenship offered by Protagoras and his colleagues. In these instances the appeal was always to the concrete example or model. To treat these examples as "instances" or "applications" of a general concept or principle is to fall victim to the *mythos*-to-*logos* bias which traces but one strand, albeit the dominant one, of ancient Greek thought.

The standard reading of the Sophists gives altogether too much weight to the dialectic between Plato's refined version of Socrates and selected members of the Sophistic community.[93] This cannot but make the majority of them look as if they were theoretical relativists rather than individuals whose greatest concern was with the sphere of public praxis. The Sophists were practical thinkers in a way difficult for us to understand. We are accustomed to seeing philosophers involved in theorizing *about* praxis, but we seldom think of the truly pragmatic technicians of language and communication as philosophers. The Sophists must be seen as practitioners of an art of communication rather than as thinkers who sought understanding apart from relevance or applicability. They were among the first truly pragmatic thinkers.

Protagoras' "Man is the measure" (however one interprets that dictum) identifies thinking with analogical procedures that seek comparisons whose meaningfulness is a function of the perspective of the individual making the comparison, or the solidarity grouping from out of which the comparison is made. Thus, the human perspective, largely abandoned by the natural philosophers, is returned to a place of prominence.

The charges of relativity directed against the natural philosophers by their Sophistic colleagues required a renewed, if chastened, desire to attain truth in some more objective mode than that recognized by the Sophists. It is clear that with Socrates there begins the endeavor to counter the effects of Sophistic relativism by enquiring after objective truths concerning the nature of virtue. This is accomplished by seeking abstract definitions of terms.

A major consequence of this Socratic response, as we shall see, is that the rational, theoretical interests associated with the analytic and dialectical modes of thinking will come to reshape the area of intellectual activity which had formerly been the preserve of analogical activity. With the displacement of analogical thinking from those areas concerned with issues of value, the triumph of second problematic causal thinking was assured.

——— SIXTH ANTICIPATION ———

Unlike the counterdiscourse of the Heraclitian "process" tradition—effectively moribund until revived in the twentieth century by thinkers such as Bergson and Whitehead —the counterdiscourse of the Sophists has remained a self-conscious element in our tradition from its inception to the present. This is true, however, only insofar as it is interpreted in its dialectical relations with rational thinking. Distinctions such as those of reason and rhetoric, and of *physis* and *nomos*, which play about in our tradition depend in part upon the Sophistic arguments establishing the respectability of persuasive activity and of appeals to convention. Though marginalized by the insistence upon rational objectivity as the model for responsible thinking, the Sophistic tradition maintains a place in law and politics, and in the promotion and analysis of literary style. However, in its most concrete and practical form, the form which expresses its most distinctive character and its true genius, there is little left of the original Sophistic movement.

In classical China, appeals similar to those we associate with conventional appeals, and the cultivation of rhetorical styles, serve to define the principal discourse. The relevant counterdiscourse is constituted by something similar to the sorts of arguments we would call "logical" or "rational." Experiments with rationalism in classical China were not long-lived. As a consequence, there is no crucial reflection of the *physis/nomos* and reason/rhetoric dialectics in the Chinese tradition. The Chinese equivalent of *nomos* is not as seriously challenged as was its Western counterpart. This means that analogical or correlative arguments are not in effective tension with what we have discussed as rational, causal arguments. Metaphorical thinking is not articulated over against literal thinking. There is no determinative contrast between the "personal" and "objective" perspectives, or between "theoretical" and "practical" pursuits. Largely because the interactions among alternative views in China are most often shaped in an essentially nondialectical manner, appeals to metaphors or images, resorts to analogical operations, the belief in the creative function of language and ritual, the essentially pragmatic aims of "philosophic" thinking, the appeal to models or examples rather than abstract nouns to characterize "virtues" and "vices," and so on, all exist without effective challenge from any dialectical alter. It is important that we recognize this fact when attempting to understand the Chinese in terms of concepts and principles drawn from the Western Sophistic tradition. Otherwise, we are certain to import both the relevant concept *and* its dialectical "other," thereby disposing us to see the sorts of dialectical tensions and contradictions extant within Western culture reflected in the Chinese sensibility. For, though the Chinese intellectual tradition is shaped more by "rhetorical" than by "logical" operations, the contextualization of these operations in each of the two cultures is distinctive enough to provide different shapes to these operations. [See chapter 2, section 3.2; and chapter 3, sections 3, 4.1, 5.2, 5.3.]

7. SOCRATES AND PLATO: EROS AND ITS IRONIES

The contribution of Platonic thought to the culture of causal thinking begins with the concern of Plato's (429–347) teacher, Socrates (469–399), for the definition of terms. Socrates was notorious for asking after the meaning of "courage," "temperance," "justice," and so on. And his interlocutors are equally notorious for not giving him what he wanted—namely (in our contemporary language), connotative definitions which cite the properties common to all members of the class designated denotatively by the term. More often than not he was given examples, or lists which designated courageous actions or individuals rather than delimiting the essential properties of "courage."

If we are not cautious in our reading, we are apt to believe that in the early Socratic dialogues, Plato has set up some rather loosely packed straw men merely for the purpose of illustrating his argument. In these dialogues we continually confront what appear to be some rather slow-witted thinkers who experience supreme difficulty responding to Socrates' perfectly straightforward request for univocity. But this is to fail to recognize that, at the time of Socrates, saying what something is by giving an instance or instances of it was the accepted manner of proceeding. Resort to abstract nouns which serve to "define" concepts is, after all, precisely what Plato helped to introduce into our culture. Before the development of logical enquiry in Plato and Aristotle, what we would now term rhetorical thinking and expression was the more common exercise.

Take, for example, the following definition: "*Tree* n. perennial plant with self-supporting woody main stem (usually developing branches at some distance from the ground)." Provided one has some reasonable sense of the meaning of the key terms "woody," "stem," "perennial," and so on (that is, provided one has connotative definitions of these terms), one has a fair sense of the concept *tree*. A second sense of the term "connotation," the rhetorical sense which involves the emotional associations of the term, is not involved in the concept.

"Tree," defined denotatively, names all of the items that would be included in the class named *tree*—that is, all of the items that one could identify ostensively as trees by pointing to them and saying "tree." Defined connotatively, "treeness" consists in all of the *properties* that the members of the class *tree* (denotatively defined) contains. The connotative definition, therefore, provides us with a class of *properties*; the denotative definition with a class of *particular items*.

Rhetorical definitions omit the consideration of objective connotations, identifying the term *connotation* with "the emotional baggage carried by a word." Rhetorical definitions emphasize *subjective* connotations. One can easily confront this distinction today by comparing standard logic texts with textbooks used to teach composition. It is rare to find a composition text which even alludes to connotation in any other than its subjective sense.

As a consequence of this treatment of connotation by rhetoricians, denotation is forced to serve the function of objective connotation in logic. Rhetorical definitions identify *denotation* with "the dictionary sense of a word." That dictionary sense is often (in the case of formal or technical definitions) precisely what the logician means by the (objective) connotative definition. Little wonder that confusion results when shifting (often unconsciously) between the rhetorical and logical meanings of *connotation* and *denotation*.

One can surely see that the rhetorical tradition, eschewing the value of objective connotation (by virtue of holding onto the local, culture-specific nature of truth), would employ distinct sorts of moral argument. The use of heroic models from Homeric epic, conflictual situations in tragic poetry, the case studies of the physicians, and ethnographical accounts of the sort Herodotus often provided, suggests that one learns about the meaning of virtuous conduct, or health, or what it means to be a human being, by appeal to models and exemplars rather than abstract principles.

On this view, morality is less an affair of understanding and applying concepts and principles, and more one of recognizing the concretely specific modes of conduct relevant to one's particular community. The Socratic-Platonic vision is rational, while the tradition of the poets, physicians, and some historians is associated with the analogical mode of thinking.

In spite of his insistence upon abstract definition, Socrates remained skeptical of actually attaining knowledge. In fact, he claimed to know but three things: (1) that he did not know, (2) that knowledge and virtue are one, and (3) that he was an expert in love.[94] By rendering consistent these three claims, one divines the essential character of Socratic wisdom: Knowledge is the recognition of ignorance, which is the fundamental virtue leading to open enquiry. To recognize a lack of knowledge means that one acknowledges a desire (*eros*) for knowledge. If, as was true with Socrates, one spends a lifetime doggedly and systematically confronting one's ignorance, one might indeed become an expert in *eros*.

Because of the impact of the received Plato upon subsequent generations of thinkers, this commitment of Socrates to enquiry has often been suppressed. Nonetheless, belief in the erotic character of thinking as benignly skeptical and open-ended reflects the attitude that open-ended enquiry, not the creation of systems or the promulgation of doctrines, defines the philosophic task. The belief that the search for truth is valuable even if no systematically certain truths have yet been discovered, remains a continuing part of the philosophic tradition.

The essential themes of Plato's philosophy are well known. His dialogical understanding of philosophic thinking presented through his characterization of Socrates is shaped in the beginning by the presentation of Socrates as an open-minded thinker pursuing, but never grasping discursively, the wholeness of truth. In the dialogues of Plato's mature and later years this method seems to take on a more rigorous cast, and Plato has been interpreted as moving in the direction of a complete philosophic system.

The element of the received Plato which makes the dialectic a viable method involves positing eternal ideas or forms which exist as both the ground and goal of rational explanation. It is the aim of dialogue and the dialectic to arrive at these ideas and their systematic relationships. The idealism of the received Plato is an objective idealism in which the real is *ideal* in the sense of independently existent patterns, structures, or forms.

The presuppositions of such a system of objective idealism must include a principle of unity establishing the normative relationships among the forms. Plato's Principle of the Good serves this purpose. This principle is at the basis of Plato's intuition of the unity of all things. It is a consequence of his sense that order and value are related in such manner that the richest and most complex order manifests the greatest value. Thus Plato's unifying principle is interpreted as a normative principle.

Finally, the dynamic of Plato's philosophy is rendered in terms of *eros* as the desire for completeness of understanding. Predicated upon the lack of knowledge, this desire for knowledge is a sense of needing to complete oneself, to acquire what is necessary to make oneself whole. Without this dynamic, the ethical or normative aspect of Plato's philosophy, which comes to have such significance in Neoplatonism and Christianity, would be vitiated.

In his attempt to construct a coherent vision of the unity of things, the received Plato willed to subsequent generations of thinkers a number of persistent problems which have helped to define the character of philosophic speculation since. The distinctions between Being and Becoming, permanence and flux, reality and appearance, knowledge and opinion, and so forth, remain intransigent within our philosophic tradition. In large measure, of course, the problems are embarrassments inherited from Zeno.[95]

However valuable the influences of the received Plato have been, the most important elements of Plato's thinking for our purposes are two analogical matrices which not only constitute central foci of his own vision but which become highly important for much of subsequent philosophical speculation down to the present day. We refer to Plato's doctrines of the tripartite soul (*psyche ψυχή*) and of the Four Levels of the Clarity of Knowledge.

The forms of synthesis provided by Plato provide models for the development of conceptual matrices within which the subsequent history of strictly philosophic speculation has been couched. For our purposes what is most distinctive about the first great synthesizer of the Greek tradition is the manner in which he employs analogical devices in order (1) to fix the analogical relationships between the individual *psyche* and its social and cultural environs, and (2) to establish explanatory matrices which account for the character of right thinking on the one hand, while establishing metatheoretical criteria for the assessment of alternative philosophical visions on the other.

One of the most important consequences of reflections upon ancient cultures over the last generation or so has been the conclusion that self-consciousness is a historically contingent concept. In sympathy with this view, we would argue that the distinctive shape this notion took in the ancient Greek world was a consequence of the agencies of construal which may be associated, in the beginning, with the instantiations of *mythos* in the forms of epic, lyric, and tragic poetry.

There is a broad convergence of scholarly opinion to the effect that individuals in the Homeric period were in some important degree "selfless." Acccording to A. W. H. Adkins, "the early Greeks perceived the body as an aggregate, not as a unit,"[96] and, further, they "had not the conceptual framework to distinguish between a psychological function and an organ with physical location."[97] If this is so, neither the body/soul dualism nor the sense of identifying one's true self with the rational soul has any strict analogy in Homeric times. This view supports Snell's observation that:

> What we interpret as the soul, Homeric man splits up into three components each of which he defines by the analogy of physical organs. Our transcription of *psyche*, *noos* and *thymos* as "organs" of life, of perception and of (e)motion are merely in the nature of abbreviations.[98]

These three components, as we shall see, bear some analogy to the three functions of the soul in Plato, but it is important to stress, again in the words of Adkins, "Homeric man . . . has a psychology and physiology in which the parts are more in evidence than the whole."[99] It is left to Plato to provide a model for the unification of the soul and, thereby, of the self.

The problem of the *psyche* as Plato conceived it is construed in terms of a polar relation between the individual and society. The *locus classicus* for the consideration of the soul in these terms is Book 4 of the *Republic*, wherein Plato suggests an analogy between the state and the soul by demonstrating that those virtues in the state that are pre-requisites for the attainment of political justice—wisdom (*nous*[100] νοῦς), courage (*andreia* ανδρεία), and temperance (*sophrosyne* σωφρο-σύνη)—are the same as those we could find in a whole person pos-sessed of reasoning (λογιστικόν), spirit (θυμός), and appetite or desire (ἐπιθῦμία). In the whole person the rational element rules over both the spirit and the appetites. Justice in the soul is well-ordered har-mony of its three functions. Similarly, in the state, right decisions based on understanding and rational self-control must be the primary motivating factors in social and political life.

We must remember that Plato's aim in the *Republic* was to discover the meaning of justice in the individual *psyche*, not, primarily, to construct a just social organization. Thus, Plato was attempting a psychological analysis just as surely as he was developing a political theory. For the most part, subsequent generations have tended to be influenced by the narrowly political interpretation of Plato's *Republic* without consciously embracing his psychological views.

We have seriously denigrated the importance placed on the concept of justice as an individual virtue in our search for an adequate analysis of social and political meanings of justice. We may not, therefore, immediately recognize how much we have been influenced by Plato's vision of *psyche* and its analogy to the ideal polis. This has, in fact, turned out to be one of the most important of cultural and psycho-logical intuitions, for the analogy did not lose its effect simply because Plato's ideal *polis* was never founded; nor did its influence diminish with the collapse of the *polis* as a viable political entity.

It might well have been the case, however, that Plato's attempt to "write large" the human soul would have had far less influence within our cultural tradition if Aristotle had not employed that insight *mutatis mutandis* as one of the principles in accordance with which his diverse philosophic writings were organized. And as something like this organizational principle was used to construct the curricular patterns of the medieval and modern universities, it has become one of the principal foundations of intellectual culture in the West.

One of the significant effects of Plato's use of the *psyche/polis* analogy was to instantiate the distinction between theoretical and practical spheres. For Plato's *psyche* was divided in two manners—the tripartite structure itself was classified in terms of a binary relation in which reason was separated off from spirit and appetite. Thus, the effective distinction in the soul and the state was between the rational and nonrational elements of the soul which were reflected in the theory/practice distinction as fundamentally a class distinction.[101]

Book 6 of Plato's *Republic* considers the path from less to more adequate forms of knowledge. Plato's hierarchical understanding of the various approaches to knowledge is itself a way of coming to know the world. The first level of knowledge, according to Plato, is *eikasia* (εἰκασία), the perceptions of the world of passing fact. Primitive knowledge of this sort consists of the unmediated perceptions of fleeting experience, and the content of myths and stories. This is unstable or indirect knowledge whose epistemological status is that of "gossip," or second-hand opinion.

The second level, that of *pistis* (πίστις) involves belief or conviction of the sort we would call "know-how"—that is, technical knowledge without any grasp of the principles which justify that conviction. Its object is the ordinary world of experience construed in terms of relatively stable objects. *Pistis*, based upon past experience, permits the manipulation of these objects toward certain ends.

Knowing how to perform certain actions to achieve specific ends does not yet constitute true knowledge. Knowledge truly begins only with the stage of *dianoia* (διάνοια), understanding. One cannot know unless one grasps the principles justifying a knowledge claim. *Dianoia* permits one to construe a particular fact in terms of the general or universal idea it instances.

This sort of knowledge is only hypothetical, however, for the abstract understandings involved have not as yet been contextualized by a system of propositions whose coherence is established by the veracity of each of its fundamental principles. "Knowing that" something is the case contrasts with "knowing how" to perform certain practical operations. This names the contrast between *dianoia* and *pistis*.

Knowing the "why" of things is superior to the knowledge obtained through *dianoia*. The fourth level of knowledge, *noesis* (νόησις), is the stage at which we come to know why something is the case. *Dianoia* must remain content with deductions from hypothetical principles. *Noesis* strives to evaluate *dianoia* by creating an explanatory matrix accounting for the specialized data upon which the knowledge of *dianoia* is grounded.

Scientific knowledge, in the sense of the knowledge of the specialized scientists, is based upon *dianoia*. The special sciences attempt to confirm the implementation of hypotheses by appeal to a special body of rules. Philosophy, as the science of the general, criticizes these hypotheses by rendering them coherent with assumptions made by the other special sciences. *Noesis* envisions the forms of things themselves apart from their instantiations. The purest mode of *noesis* is what Plato terms "*dialectic*" (διαλεκτική). This is *a priori* reasoning.

The practitioner of dialectic is prepared for the final ascent to the principle of the unity of knowledge that provides the foundation of the cosmological order. This is the Principle of the Good which undergirds our understanding of both the unity of knowledge, and of the unity of the world as well.

Plato's doctrine of the Four Levels of the Clarity of Knowledge may be used as a means of classifying and criticizing his philosophic rivals. Because there had been no successful approach to the principle of principles uniting all theory and practice into a single cosmos, Platonists see the history of intellectual culture, from the Milesian Materialists to the Sophists, as constituted by seriously conflicting explanations of the nature of things.

Plato thought he had provided in his doctrine of the tripartite structure of the soul and his Divided Line a means of relating the thoughts, decisions, and appetites of the individual to the phases and functions of his social world, as well as offering a general theory which might account for the various extant ways of knowing. Homer's mythopoetic world may be construed in terms of *eikasia*. The Sophists with their emphasis on convention stress *pistis*, "know-how." By searching out the mathematical principles of things and employing them as means of classification, the Pythagoreans approached *dianoia*. Plato's teacher, Socrates, offered a *noetic* principle, "knowledge and virtue are one," upon which Plato modeled his interpretation of The Good as the principle uniting thought and things. In accordance with this principle, all preceding speculation may be incorporated in the final systematic explanatory scheme of Platonic thought.

Plato's analogical schemes of the tripartite structure of the *psyche* and the ladder of knowledge illustrate the same tendency toward the construal of chaos we have seen from the very beginnings of Western intellectual culture. And, as we shall immediately see, Plato's scheme will be incorporated *mutatis mutandis* into Aristotle's thinking, providing an alternative rendering of the metatheoretical problem.

——— **SEVENTH ANTICIPATION** ———

Socrates offered two apparently contradictory gifts to the development of the Western cultural sensibility. First, his concern for definition challenged that manner of thinking associated with giving accounts of things by appeal to instances or models exemplifying that which was to be understood. Socrates understood the definitional activity to consist in the search for what we now term *objective connotation*. This activity undergirded the belief in objective "essences" or "natural kinds," a belief which becomes central to the natural sciences. Henceforth, the rational understanding would shun subjective in favor of objective connotations, and reason would seek closure by searching out essential meanings through the act of definition.

Paradoxically, the same Socrates who provided such an impetus to the search for closure insisted upon the openness of rational speculation which would postpone any claims to finality until such was demonstrably achieved. Ramified by appeal to the Platonic "eros" as the desire for completeness of understanding, this refusal to accept unjustified dogmas offered a means of placing real limitations upon the authority of closed systems over open enquiry. One of the unfortunate developments in Western philosophy and science was that Plato's claim that rational knowledge existed only when contextualized by principles defining the most general system of ideas led later thinkers to make unjustified claims to knowledge based upon their belief in the universality of the systematic theories they constructed.

In China, as we shall see, the construction of objective definitions did not become important. Chinese thinkers remained content with the appeal to "examples" to provide explanatory accounts and, thus, were disinclined to search for "essences" or "natural kinds." There was no hard and fast distinction drawn between "objective" and "subjective" connotations. Closure was sought by appeals to the authoritative elements of the tradition, while openness was maintained by the tacit insistence upon connotative "vagueness" which permits the copresence in a single term of a variety of important meanings. The lack of emphasis upon connotative definition precluded the dependence upon rational systems or theories as the primary vehicles of ideas. In their place, ritual practices served as the primary media of cultural meanings and practices.

Plato's organization of the elements of the *psyche* into reason, spirit, and passion, later ramified by Aristotle and the Hebraic-Christian theological traditions, has served as an important determinant of the shape of Western intellectual culture. The absence in China of such a tripartite model and its analogies seriously qualifies the manner in which Western understandings of knowing, acting, and feeling are relevant to the interpretation of the Chinese sensibility and its institutional implications. [See chapter 3, sections 2, 4.1, 5.2, 5.3.]

---

8. ARISTOTLE: FOUR BEGINNINGS OF THOUGHT

Plato's tripartite division of the soul suggested to Aristotle his organization of the ways of knowing into thought, action, and passion. Similarly, Plato's Four Levels of the Clarity of Knowledge seems to have influenced the development of Aristotle's doctrine of the Four Causes. These analogical patterns provide a semantic context in which the diverse meanings of concepts and theories might be construed. One of the functions of a philosophical synthesis aimed at the coordination of a variety of significances is to account for contrast, conflict, and contradiction not only within the soul or among the various elements of society, but also among the variety of philosophic perspectives employed to interpret such fundamental cultural experiences.

According to Aristotle (384–322), "All thought is either practical (πρακτική) or productive (ποιητική) or theoretical (θεωρετική)."[102] These distinctions suggest influence by Plato's spirited, appetitive, and rational components of the *psyche*. Aristotle, however, is primarily concerned to organize the ways of knowing according to their subject matters and methods. Aristotle's division of thinking into theoretical, practical, and productive modalities provides the epistemological rationale for that organization.

Theoretical sciences consider "that sort of substance which has the principle of its movement and rest present in itself."[103] Thus, the theoretical or natural sciences treat of natural kinds of things. The practical disciplines concern the cultural world of *action* expressed primarily in terms of ethical and political activities. The productive sciences are distinguished from the practical, as *making* is distinguished from *doing*—that is to say, the productive sciences are sciences which involve the production and appreciation of cultural artifacts.

Political actions and artistic products must be understood on other than theoretical grounds since the subject matters do not admit of the same degree of perfection as do those of the natural sciences. For Aristotle, the practical sciences of ethics and politics must be separated from the theoretical sciences of metaphysics, physics, and biology as well as from the productive sciences of rhetoric and poetics.[104] Thanks to Aristotle, Plato's *psyche/polis* analogy has now been characterized in terms of a relation between the human mind and its cultural expressions. The educated mind is in fact *culture in microcosm* and reflects generic patterns of thinking, acting, and feeling as cultural expressions.

Philosophers since Aristotle have sustained the interest in this analogical relationship to the degree that it has come to shape a general interpretive construct of our intellectual history. A principal illustration is found in the thought of Immanuel Kant (1724–1804), whose three critiques articulated the nature and limitations of reason in its theoretical, practical, and productive modes. *The Critique of Pure Reason*, *The Critique of Practical Reason*, and *The Critique of Judgment* reflect the Aristotelian modalities of the ways of knowing.

As we have noted, Aristotle recognized that one of the functions of a philosophical synthesis is to account for contrast, conflict, and contradiction not only within the soul or among the various elements of society, but also among those who are attempting to characterize the data of intellectual culture from a variety of philosophic perspectives. His doctrine of the Four Causes can serve to perform precisely this task.

According to Aristotle, a responsible account of any item of experience must have recourse to a complete "causal" analysis. Aristotle defines four types of cause, or *aitia* (αἰτία), which are termed material, formal, final, and efficient. We shall see that these Four Causes or "reasons" bear analogies to the four levels of Plato's Divided Line.

The material cause names the stuff of which a thing is comprised. Formal cause designates its structure or pattern. The efficient cause is the agent or process which brings the object into being or maintains its existence. The final cause names the end for which an item exists or was made—its function or purpose.

Since the advent of the natural sciences in the seventeenth century, the efficient and material causes have all but dominated our discussion of causation. Moreover, appeals to final and formal causes still bear the mark of Aristotle's analysis. We seem unable to raise the topic of causation without at least tacitly celebrating Aristotle's doctrine of the Four Causes.

There is good reason to believe that our bondage to Aristotle is less a consequence of adherence to the notion of *aitia* and more a contingent fact of the filtering of that notion through the Latin language. The senses of *aitia* available by the turn of the millennium include (a) responsibility, guilt, blame, accusation; (b) cause, reason; (c) category under which something is classified; (d) occasion, motive; and (e) case in dispute.

Meanings of *aitia* related to human agency (responsibility and so on) and to analogical thinking (the activity of classification) dominate the meaning of the term in the beginning. The more sophisticated sense of "cause" (as in our post-scholastic understanding of Aristotle's "four causes") depends upon a later translation of the Greek *aitia* into the Latin term *causa*.

Causa is related to the same roots as the French *chose* or the Spanish *cosa*. The term originally designated "thingliness" apart from agency or motive force. By the beginning of the present millennium, it had come to possess the senses of "on account of," "pretext," "excuse," "a condition, state," "that by which, through which, or on account of which a thing is done." Its Latin synonyms included *fons*, *origo*, *principium*, *excusatio*, *negotium*, *judicium*. Not until the time of Cicero (106–42 B.C.E.) did the term have significant connotations associated with what we think of as efficient cause. The translation of *aitia* by *causa* and, finally, "cause" thus carries with it the senses of *physis* (*fons, origo*) and *logos* ("account"). The cluster of connotations associated with *aitia, physis*, and *logos* leads to the interpretation of cause in terms of source, origin, principle, account.

As we have noted, the meanings of *physis* include "origin," "the natural constitution of a thing as the result of growth," "Nature as an originating power," "principle of growth." The Latin *natura* used to translate *physis* is related to *nascor* ("birth"), and designates the natural order of things, the world or universe, the state or condition of a thing. The search for the *physis* of things leads to the positing of an origin, source, or ground which provides an account (*logos*) of the state at the end of the becoming of things. Thus *physis* serves as the primary analogate in terms of which accountings (*logoi*) are to be given.

It was in the combination of the search for *physis* on the part of those later to be termed "philosophers," and the presentation of *logoi* ("accounts") of the public events by those later called "historians," that causal language begins to be privileged. The combining of etiological explanation with the agencies of men and gods gradually weighted the search for *causes* in terms of what will later come to be called *efficient* causes.[105]

We cannot determine precisely Aristotle's sense of *aitia* by reference to etymological studies, of course. But such analysis can sensitize us to the difficulty of understanding the term *in situ*. In this instance, it is necessary to recognize that both the logical and the *ana*logical senses of cause are employed by Aristotle. Indeed, Demosthenes whose dates coincide exactly with Aristotle's, uses *aitia* primarily in its rhetorical, classificatory sense.

Aristotle's doctrine of the Four Causes is itself a classificatory scheme, of course, apparently born by analogy from Plato's Divided Line and from the sources employed by Plato himself—that is, the contrasts between rest (Being) and motion (Becoming), and between matter (body) and form (mind). Neither Plato nor Aristotle provided adequate logical arguments for the completeness of these distinctly analogical schemes.

Aristotle's philosophical scheme is most productively understood in terms of a primary analogate associated with the concept of biological organism. This suggests that Aristotle's causal scheme is less than value-neutral. The analysis of an organism yields the variables which ground the development of the specific causes employed in the four-cause scheme. But Aristotle begs the question of neutrality since his assumption of an organic metaphor as the ground of his philosophical system turns out to be an arbitrary choice vis-à-vis the alternative choices made by his peers. Is Plato's mathematical model (or Democritus' "atom," for that matter) any less or more viable than the concept of "organism" as a basis for a philosophical system?

Aristotle used his causal scheme to interpret the thinking of his predecessors. Thales, Anaximenes, and Anaximander were said to be materialists by virtue of their search for *physis*.[106] The Pythagoreans, who construed the world in terms of mathematical relations, primarily employed the formal cause. Empedocles' principles of Love and Strife exemplified the efficient cause. The doctrine of *Nous* associated with Anaxagoras constituted a final cause.

One of the most serious distortions in the history of Western philosophy consists in the presumption that Aristotle's Four Causes can be detached from the specific senses of "cause" established by his system. Indeed, the argument showing how a philosophy based on the metaphor of organism is grounded in a preference for final cause is a rather obvious one. Conceiving things by analogy to organisms requires that one analyze phenomena as "wholes," the "parts" of which functionally interrelate to realize a specific purpose. Here we see the ground of Aristotle's causal scheme: matter, structure, activity, and aim are rooted in his primary analogate.

We do well to avoid the standard Aristotelian interpretation of the development of Greek thought since it in effect begs the question of our enquiry. Aristotle supports in advance the Enlightenment *mythos* to *logos* interpretation. His view is that prior thinkers groaned and travailed in the attempt to reach the heights only he had attained.

Aristotle's view that the Presocratics, indeed Socrates and Plato as well, exemplified incomplete visions by virtue of their partial and differential applications of four causes omits the contrast between the "causal" and the "analogical" modes of thinking. Thus, when Aristotle finds that Thales and Empedocles and Anaxagoras and Plato stress but one among the possible four causes, and then produces in his own philosophy what he (incorrectly, we believe) takes to be a balanced consideration of the causes, he makes causal thinking the norm but without providing any analysis of the contrasting mode of thinking which he terms *mythopoetic* or (when he speaks strictly of *philosophoi* rather than *philomythoi*) simply describes as "vague":

All men seem to seek the causes named in the *Physics* [see Bk ii, 3, 7], and . . . we cannot name any beyond these; but they seek these vaguely; and though in a sense they have all been described before, in a sense they have not been described at all. For the earliest philosophy is, on all subjects, like one who lisps, since in its beginnings it is but a child.[107]

One may certainly take Aristotle seriously to the extent that there is an absence of sophisticated causal speculation among the Presocratics. But, in place of reading these thinkers projectively and programmatically as if they were doing badly what Aristotle will later perfect, we wish to recognize a persistent alternative tradition of analogical thinking which resists incorporation into the causal, rational mode. The coexistence of these two problematics in Greek culture permits us to recognize as quite articulate certain thinkers whom Aristotle believed to have been lispers.

Plato discovered inadequacies in alternative philosophies based on their various emphases upon less viable forms of knowledge. Aristotle sees inadequacy in terms of an unbalanced emphasis upon each of the four causes. In both Plato and Aristotle, we find a scheme of interpretation in accordance with which we can understand the nature of varying philosophic perspectives. Part of the cultural impact of the philosophic syntheses of Plato and Aristotle has been due, therefore, not only to their construction of the outlines of the human *psyche* and its relations to society and to intellectual culture, but also to their systematic explanations of conflict among various theories of the nature of things.

For all their vaunted differences, Plato and Aristotle share a significant number of dispositions that render their disputes family quarrels among the proponents of a common culture. Each believes in a single-ordered world. Both have faith in the efficacy of reason in searching out the laws which define the structure of that world and the relation of the human mind to that structure. And this faith leads each to defend the ideal of a philosophical system as a means of reflecting that structure and relationship.

Against the background of agreements such as these, their radically differing attitudes toward the importance of the phenomenal and of the priority of analysis or synthesis in philosophic thinking seem less dramatic. Though we cannot say of these two thinkers what Emerson said of Socrates and Plato—namely, that they constitute a "double star" which even the most refined lens could not separate,[108] nonetheless, it seems we must agree that Aristotle and *his* teacher are the closest of neighbors in a single solar system.

──────── EIGHTH ANTICIPATION ────────

With the emergence of the philosophical syntheses of Plato and Aristotle, Greek philosophy reached its culmination. Effectively, all of the major philosophical issues and problems which would influence subsequent speculation were now formulated. Of equal importance, the copresence of the Platonic and Aristotelian visions provided distinctive strategies for the resolution of the subsequent pluralism of ideas and beliefs which would pattern the Western tradition. At one level, the existence of the two broad traditions offered alternative manners of elaborating the distinct sensibilities owned by individuals. Coleridge's claim that "every man is born either a Platonist or an Aristotelian" suggests that these two systems are in some sense an elaboration of more primitive divergent sensibilities. At a second level, the taxonomic devices of the Divided Line and the Four Causes, employed by the Platonists and Aristotelians respectively as first-order epistemological tools, were soon to be recognized as metaphilosophical instruments for the organization and criticism of alternative philosophical positions.

If we recognize these two philosophical syntheses as contingent products of the peculiar history of Greek culture we have been narrating, then we shall exercise caution when approaching the Chinese: The broad traditions of Plato and Aristotle are unlikely to have any true counterparts in classical China. This means that not only should we avoid the temptation to look for Chinese versions of Plato and Aristotle, but we should be sensitive to the difficulties of employing the major theoretical categories drawn from either of these visions in interpreting Chinese thinkers. The Platonic and Aristotelian modes of organizing knowledge by recourse to their alternative schemes (the Divided Line and the Four Causes, along with the tripartite model of the *psyche*) are inconsistent with the Chinese modes of organization. Further, concepts such as Plato's *eidos* (εἶδος) and Aristotle's *ousia* (οὐσία) have no real equivalents among Chinese thinkers. And, most importantly, the understanding of "cause" originating in part in the Aristotelian *aitia* and filtered through the Latin *causa*—particularly the notion of "efficient cause" as it has come to constitute a basic element in the classical scientific models of explanation—is not a category which may be relevantly employed in interpreting Chinese thinkers. [See chapter 2, Sections 3.2, 3.3; and chapter 3, sections 5.2, 5.3.]

---

9. *HUMANITAS* AND THE *IMAGO DEI*

It would, perhaps, be convenient had the Platonic and Aristotelian syntheses culminated the development of the Western cultural paradigm, since, in that case, we would be able to close our account rather neatly with the end of the Hellenic period. But there was to be an additional, quite significant, development of our cultural matrix occasioned by the transformation of later Greek thought when filtered through Hebraic and Roman sensibilities.

One of the elements of Roman culture which will ultimately permit the extension of Greek rationality into the barbarian lands has little to do with Hellenic or Hebraic sources, but in many ways is strictly Roman. It is the theme of *humanitas*, championed by Cicero and elaborated in the *Aeneid* of Virgil (70–19).[109] This notion, along with the political concept of *imperium*, supports the sense of unity across ethnic and political boundaries. Neither the Greeks with their strong sense of provincialism vis-à-vis the barbarian world, nor the Jews with their sense of covenental relationship designating them as a "chosen people," could provide the practical social and political ideologies which would sustain the notion of *universal* human nature or *universal* natural laws.

Both Roman *imperium* and the more philosophic notion of *humanitas* suggest that psychological, social, political, and cultural orders define basic commonalities which are more important than putative differences. By the age of the Enlightenment, science, as the epitome of rational activity, will be added to these latter notions and will become an important factor promoting intercultural unification.

For our purposes in this context, however, it is not these very significant notions but the more philosophical concepts whose history we discussed up to the end of Greek culture that must be pursued. The best means of doing this is to select the figure who served Graeco-Roman-Hebraic culture, as Plato and Aristotle served the Greeks, as a synthesizer of many complex cultural trends. We refer, of course, to Augustine of Hippo (354–430).

In *The City of God*, Augustine cites three certain truths upon which the person of faith could ground his knowledge:

> For, as I know that I am, so I know this also, that I know. And when I love these two things, I add to them a certain third thing, namely, my love, which is of equal moment.[110]

These truths are *self-existence, knowledge of self-existence*, and *love both of the existence and of the knowledge*. Augustine understands these truths to underlie all action, knowledge, and feeling. Knowledge of one's existence grounds the knowledge of all other existents, and love of one's existence and knowledge is the fundamental subjective form of feeling from which all pure passions derive. Influenced by the Neoplatonic tradition, Augustine casts incorrigible claims to existence, knowledge, and love by implicit analogy to the Greek conception of the soul.

Augustine's grounding of this tripartite structure by reference to the *imago dei* provides a new account of the origin of *psyche*:

> We indeed recognize in ourselves the image of God, that is, of the supreme Trinity, an image which . . . is yet nearer to Him in nature than any of His works.[111]

As the "author of nature, the bestower of intelligence, and the kindler of love by which life becomes good and blessed,"[112] God insures that human existence, knowledge, and love are shaped in accordance with the uncreated essence of the Holy Trinity. Henceforth, many theologians and philosophers will feel justified in employing the elements of the Trinity—Father, Son, and Holy Spirit—as the analogical ground for the explanation of human action, reason, and passion.

Whether one sees the sorts of analogical relations that Augustine discerned is largely a function of the type of philosophical intuitions one owns. Augustine saw "the whole Trinity revealed to us in the creation"[113]—in the divisions of conscious certitude (of existence, knowledge, and delight in being[114]), in the tripartite division of philosophy (natural, rational, moral).[115] These are God's "footprints."[116] Such is Augustine's "natural theology."

When Augustine says "footprints" and "*imago dei*," he means that *God is reflected in nature*. If God is three-in-one, it is that image that is reflected in nature *insofar as we are able to discern it*. The fragmented understanding we have is a function of our fallen state. That is why we see the footprints and not the feet. The *imago dei* is not stamped on our foreheads but rather shapes our "personality."

Of course, the nature of Christian doctrine is such that it would be total heresy to split the trinity into separate and distinct faculties. It is possible, by virtue of man's fallen state, to note distinct faculties in the human soul. In the City of Man, one's soul is at war with itself. In the afterlife, when we achieve (qualified) immanence with the uncreated essence of the holy trinity,[117] enjoying the perpetual Sabbath that "knows no evening," the warring soul will be at peace, and will, presumably, have become harmonized to such a degree that it, too, will be "three–in–one." But a part of the imperfect representation of the *imago dei* in nature and human existence is that the trinity is "fragmented" in the fallen condition. The three parts of the trinity interpenetrate; not so with the three parts of the "soul at war." The undivided trinitarian elements may be identified with elements of the divided soul in its fallen state.

Thomas Aquinas (ca. 1224–74)—no stranger to natural theology per se—saw no such thing. Though he used the trinity as an organizing principle of his theological system, Aquinas thought it a truth revealed solely through scripture. Augustine's dialectical method drawn from the Neoplatonists allowed him to see the trinity as *imago dei*. Aquinas, more enamored by Aristotelian syllogistic thinking, had no direct means of deriving the doctrine. It is, as both Plato's and Hegel's methodologies demonstrate, the dialectical method which allows, or forces, one to see the tripartite structure of things.

The doctrine of the trinity is hardly resourced in scripture. The generation of the trinity comes as a result of the Platonic problem of mediation read in terms of the Christian Logos. Plato: How do the

Forms get in the facts? The Church Fathers: How does God become man? Thus the immediate impetus leading to the development of the doctrine of the trinity lay in the need for mediation between a transcendent and an immanent realm. God the Father, the Creative Power, was conceived as wholly other. Jesus Christ, the Son, was the Mediator—Very God and Very Man. The Holy Spirit was the immediate unity of the spirit of God and the spirit of human beings.

Importantly, Augustine's discussion of the trinity in relation to the *imago dei* suggests an alternative interpretation of Plato's *thymos* (θυμός) as "will" and brings a novel concept to bear upon the understanding of persons. There is now a sense in which the "I" suggestive of selfhood may refer not only to the intellect (*nous*, νοῦς; *logistikon*, λογιστικόν), as was the case in Plato and Aristotle, but to the active, decisional "will."[118] Augustine's reflection upon the Pauline dilemma ("The good that I would do I do not do"), particularly as it applied to his own desire for conversion, provides a paradigm instance of the manner in which the "I" of the volitional self is more personalized than the "I" of the intellect or rationality.

The movement toward the notion of a volitional self had profound consequences for our self-understanding. As Charles Kahn has said in discussing the Stoic contribution to the Augustinian notion of self:

> For Plato and Aristotle the "I" or true self was *nous*, the principle of reason most fully expressed in theoretical knowledge. . . . Theoretical reason is essentially impersonal, and the Platonic-Aristotelian identification of the person with his intellect offers no basis for a metaphysics of the self in any individual sense.[119]

The effect of identifying oneself with "the practical application of reason in selecting (one's) commitments . . . not extending (oneself) to goals and values that lie beyond (one's) control"[120] is to personalize and individualize the self.

One of the important reasons for bringing our consideration of the development of Western culture up to the period of Augustine is precisely seen here: The intersection of the Greek, Roman, and Hebraic sensibilities occasioned real transformations in the issues and vocabulary of the Greeks. Nowhere is this more dramatically illustrated than with Augustine's "invention" of the "will."

What Plato calls "the principle of high spirit" in the *Republic*[121] is certainly not to be directly identified with volition. Only if we understand volition as "the power of willing,"[122] can we see that the drive (*thymos*) which allies itself with reason against the appetites[123] suggests certain of the connotations of volition. It is this sort of association which Augustinian discussions of human and divine agency helps to further.[124]

Granted the contributions of the Stoics and others, until the Augustinian period the notion of a willing agent was vague at best. One would look hard and long for a notion of will as focus of agency and decision in the individual until this period. The primary importance of the attribution of volition to God is that it provided the means whereby the notion of human will was effectively invented. One can easily see how the concept of "will" would develop *pari passu* with the articulation of God as Creative Agent. "Self" comes into being by virtue of tensions with others. The volitional being is born through tension with the dynamic power of an omnipotent God.

As is the case with so many of the most important notions underlying our self-understandings, the Augustinian notion of "will" was clarified and ramified through the act of analogical projection in which the attribution is made first with respect to some element of the cosmological context and then later analogized downward to the human sphere. We saw this to be the case with notions of "cosmos" (*κόσμος*) and "justice" (*δίκη*), for example, which had their origins first in the human sphere but became clarified, and received transcendent ground, by the double analogical move which first projected them into a cosmological context, then presumed the mundane context to be a reflection of that transcendent realm.

By the time of Aquinas, who placed the capstone on discussions of "will" by integrating *voluntas* with the Aristotelian model of the soul, faculty psychologies are discussed at the most general level in terms of thinking, acting, and feeling (thought, action, passion). In discussions of these psychic elements, "action" is associated with will or decision.

After the Augustinian synthesis of Neoplatonism and Judaeo-Christianity, therefore, the analogical scheme relating soul, society, and culture has a transcendent ground in the trinitarian structure of the Divine life. In his *The City of God*, Augustine provides an analysis of the earthly and the heavenly cities by recourse to the relations of psychic, social, and spiritual structures.[125]

Augustine's *The City of God* is a latter-day *Republic*. In its provision of a paradigm that allows for cultural articulation and self-understanding, Augustine's *magnum opus* has been in many ways as influential as Plato's work. By writing the soul even larger, Augustine in effect completed the cultural synthesis begun by the Greeks a thousand years before.

The final victory over chaos was won when both the human and the divine ordering agencies were understood in terms of a tripartite structure serving as ground for the articulation of the objective conditions of natural, moral, and aesthetic experience. Concepts of reason, will, and passion as psychological factors analogized to the social relations of justice, power, and love may now be expressed in terms of their divine counterparts.

Before we leave Augustine, it will be well to see how he helps to provide final shape to the historical as well as the philosophic renderings of Greek culture. In his enquiry (*historia*), Herodotus had sought to provide accounts (*logoi*) which, like the thinkers of the Milesian schools, provided a sense of *logos* as *physis*. The historian, in other words, sought accounts which offered natural explanations whenever possible. Augustine's transmogrification of historiography consisted in the substitution of the Christian *logos* for that of the Greeks. Thus "Augustine opens the way for a philosophy of history in terms of the *logos* of Christ; that is, in terms of the trinity, recognized as the creative and moving principle."[126]

In Augustine's account of the City of God and the City of Man, the trinity is employed as an analogical pattern shaping the parallel events. The opposition between the citizens of the two cities establishes the basic dialectic of history which is now, in opposition to the naturalized historiography of the classical Greeks, neither the story of the compulsion of material forces nor the interplay of the material forces and archetypal patterns which repeat over time, but rather is to be seen as the struggle between the evil and good wills of human beings in their relationship with a transcendent God.

Justice, mediated by Christ and the Church, and power, manifest through the Will of God, undergird public relations in society and politics. Love, the desire for a reunion of the separated mediated by the Holy Spirit, gauges personal relationships. The unity of love, power, and justice provides a dynamic model for the unity of persons in both public and private existence.

The doctrines of sin and grace bring a moral and spiritual interpretation to history that was missing from the classical period. As

Plato before him, Augustine analogizes from the soul to the state, seeing the realization of the individual soul to consist in a proper relation to the body politic.

Yet how different is Augustine's view! There are now two distinct cities, driven apart by the prideful self-assertion of those who struggle against the Will of God. In the true *polis*, wherein salvation is offered through the gift of grace, the soul is seen only penultimately in terms of the state; it is the trinitarian virtues associated with the *imago dei* which are creative of the individuals and their historical destinies.

In spite of his insistence that the trinity was not revealed to reason, Thomas Aquinas used the trinitarian elements as the device for organizing the contents of his *Summa Theologica*. This work became a primary cultural resource insuring the perpetuation of the trinitarian structure as a principle of organization for social and cultural studies. The concepts of power and authority, law and sanctions, private and public existence, the nature of the state, and so on, contained in this and other Thomistic works have profoundly influenced subsequent philosophic constructions.

Beyond the middle period, the most influential theological synthesis was that of John Calvin's sixteenth-century work, *Institutes of the Christian Religion*. As influential on social and economic institutions as upon religious and theological speculations, the *Institutes*, like Thomas' *Summa*, employs the trinitarian elements as organizing principle.

Calvin affirms three separate functions within the economy of the one God:

> To the father is attributed the beginning of activity, and the fountain and wellspring of all things; to the son, wisdom, counsel, and the ordered disposition of all things; but to the spirit is assigned the power and efficacy of that activity.[127]

Despite the explicitly theological language, the importance of Calvinist thinking concerns the economic and social institutions as much as the theological. Weber's classic study, *The Protestant Ethic and the Spirit of Capitalism*, suggests something of the secular influence of Calvinism. Of equal importance is the effect of Calvin's affirmation of the need for institutional structures as means of rationalizing the will of God. "Institutes" and "institutions" are the proper mediators of God's purposes in the world. The development of schools, hospitals, and so on, as mediators of God's providence is a typical implication of Calvinist doctrine.

The early work of Hegel (1770–1831) in the philosophy of religion demonstrates how his reflections on the Christian doctrine of the trinity provided the basis for his development of the dialectic.[128] Certainly his *Phenomenology of Spirit* presents a rationalized version of the trinitarian elements, which he saw as "pictorial representations" (*vorstellungen*) of the dialectical structure of the absolute considered as immediacy, mediation, and reflexive unity—as *an sich, fur sich*, and *an-und-fur-sich*.

God the Father is presented as the bare notion of idea as immediate; the Son is self-existence as mediated for consciousness; the Holy Spirit is the expression of the unity achieved through the reflexive return to self as subject. This secularization of the trinitarian doctrine begun with Hegel continues in both idealist and materialist forms after Hegel.

For example, Ludwig Feuerbach (1804–1872) found in the concept of the trinity

> the highest mystery and the focal point of absolute philosophy and religion. . . . The secret of the trinity is the secret of communal and social life: it is the secret of the necessity of the "thou," for an "I"; it is the truth that no being—be it man, god, mind, or ego—is for itself alone a true, perfect, and absolute being, that truth and perfection are only the connection and unity of beings equal in their essence.[129]

Feuerbach's conception of religion was that it constitutes a projection of idealized aspects of man's natural existence. Theology is ultimately anthropology. Even in Marx's early version of the dialectic, with its discussions of alienation and estrangement, one can still discern the lineaments of the original theological notions which continue to color most dialectical philosophies.

Whether the doctrine of the trinity is seen as a revealed truth or, in its dialectical guise, a truth of rational philosophic speculation, it is an influential tool in the development of cultural awareness. The dialectical understanding of God allows an analysis of personal and social structures from a transcendent perspective.[130] The addition of this perspective in many respects added the capstone to the project of cultural self-articulation.

In the developments surrounding Augustine's elaboration of the trinitarian doctrine as a tool of cultural interpretation, we can see how the Christian *mythos* comes to subsume both *logos* and *historia*. The triadic relations of these disciplining agents which originated among the Greeks and which yielded the richest possible analogies in subsequent cultural developments have now been articulated in relation to a narrative of sin and salvation.

Literature, philosophy, and history, which form the core humanistic disciplines, are tinged with the salvation problematic. And though the modern reactions against religion will recast the theological syntheses of the Middle Period, the persistence of the transcendent, progressive, moralistic interpretations of history and culture which originated with Augustine's theological synthesis will yield strange fruit when science, the secularized religion of the Enlightenment, takes hold of Western culture.

NINTH ANTICIPATION

Though the thematics of Greek philosophy pointed toward universalism, the effective expression of this universalist impulse emerged in the Hellenistic and Roman Empires with the employment of notions such as *imperium* and *humanitas*, and of the Augustinian understanding of Divine transcendence. Augustine's articulation of the analogies between the tripartite *psyche* and the trinity in the development of his doctrine of the *imago dei* absolutized and universalized the meaning of the human being. Further, Augustine's "invention" of the will, modeled finally upon the notion of Divine Agency, and his articulation of the meaning of history as an interplay of sin and redemption added distinctive elements to the Greek cultural synthesis.

Chinese culture is not shaped by any appeal to universal categories defining human nature and establishing "the unity of mankind"; rather, the Chinese refer to themselves in more provincial locutions such as "the people of the central states" or "the people of the Han." Thus, neither in their articulations of the meaning of being human, nor in their understandings of culture and history, do classical

Chinese thinkers appeal to transcendent principles as the origin or certification of their visions. Exemplary models and cultural heroes from the past, such as the Sage Kings or Confucius, function in the place of transcendent structures such as the principle of Reason, or the trinitarian God, to provide the understanding of what it means to be human. Further, for the Chinese, history isn't seen as the unfolding of a narrative determined in advance by theological or philosophical principles. Historical movements are immanent, explicable by appeal to the relative success or failure of individuals to negotiate their particular circumstances in the most successful manner. [See chapter 3, sections 2, 5.1, 5.4.]

10. THE PERSISTENCE OF THE RATIONAL ETHOS

The narrative unfolded thus far contains a number of salient points which we ought now rehearse. Our first summary point is that the major characteristics of our contemporary intellectual culture are derived from the resources of the classical period which closes with St. Augustine. In this respect, much of what we have done in this long chapter is to justify the words of Whitehead quoted at the very beginning:

> There is reason to believe that human genius reached its culmination in the twelve hundred years preceding and including the initiation of the Christian Epoch. . . . Of course, since then there has been progress in knowledge and technique. But it has been along lines laid down by the activities of that golden age.[131]

The purpose of making such a claim is not to close the canon, or to reject the possibility of true novelty beyond the classical period; it is only to say that the narrative we have provided is one which tells of the invention of interpretive constructs that remain essential to the cultural self-consciousness of our late modern era.

Our second major conclusion is that the elements of our cultural sensibility, however they might finally be construed in detail, are contingent products of our peculiar historical development. Thus, in highlighting some of the important elements constituting our cultural sensibility, we shall, as we have insisted all along, be attempting to identify ideas, principles, and beliefs which, as historical products of our Western culture, may be employed in the interpretation of an alternative culture only with extreme caution. This is but to say that there is initially no strong reason to believe that the principal terms in our philosophic inventory—terms such as *nature, knowledge, freedom, law,* and so forth—have straightforward equivalents in alternative cultures. A fundamental reason for doubting such terminological equivalences lies in the conviction, which we shall be defending in chapter 3, that neither the sorts of theoretical constructs important to our culture, nor the means of accommodating the plurality of such constructs, serve the Chinese as principal media or means of cultural transmission.

Our insistence that we have provided a historicist treatment of the development of the Western cultural sensibility may seem paradoxical in the light of our endorsement of Whitehead's words just repeated, for Whitehead's historicism, if his views could be so characterized, was modeled on a cosmic scale. But we would contend that we have yielded none of our historicist method simply because we have chosen to highlight global features of Western culture as opposed to more specific ideas and practices. Tough-minded historicists are often disinclined to say anything about large-scale notions, finding it easier to do historicist analyses of this or that idea or institutional practice. But such a belief derives from those who seek to co-opt the term *historicism* for their own idiosyncratic ends.[132]

Precisely the same point is at issue in the discussion of putative wholes as for the consideration of any part. Claims about the "scheme of things entire" own the same historical contingency as does this or that particular doctrine or belief. Thus, we would claim that the interpretive constructs emergent from our tradition are no less contingent products of a peculiar set of historical circumstances than is any other idea, belief, or practice one might select.

Several strands of cultural development have comprised the threads of our narrative. Woven together, they form the fabric of our peculiar cultural sensibility. The first strand consists of the movement from Chaos to Cosmos, which sets the conceptual dominant for subsequent phases of Western culture. Cosmogonic myths as modes of construing Chaos either as emptiness, separation, or confusion set the pattern for future interpretations of reason as *rationalization*—that is, as a shaping, construing, controlling activity.

A second strand consists of Plato's construction of the tripartite model of the *psyche* which combined the three principal construing agencies of reason, appetite, and spirit, and the employment of that model to establish analogical relations among the components of the soul and the classes of society or the state. A consequence of this distinction was an endorsement of the division of the *polis* into the intellectual class and the laboring class of slaves, itself both cause and consequence of the theory/practice distinction that will persist through the history of Western culture.

A third strand involves Aristotle's use of the Platonic analogy to organize the primary cultural activities into theoretical, practical, and productive spheres. This model was used to articulate both "the ways of knowing" and "the body of the known." The organization of the disciplines derived from this set of distinctions served as a fundamental pedagogical model for the Middle period and beyond.[133]

The fourth strand of our cultural sensibility, one which makes an extremely important contribution to our cultural self-understanding, originates with Plato's and Aristotle's metatheoretical activities. The tools of the Divided Line and the doctrine of the Four Causes allowed the organization and interpretation of alternative philosophic viewpoints as expressions of four semantic contexts constituting perspectives from which to achieve cultural self-consciousness. It will facilitate the discussions of the next chapter if we pause here long enough to rehearse the nature of these primary semantic contexts before returning to our characterization of the remaining strands of our cultural paradigm.

The story of classical Western intellectual culture does not end with the victory of a single world view, but with the effective copresence of a number of visions of the way things are. In fact, as we well know, the large theoretical perspectives associated with Democritus, the Sophists, Plato, and Aristotle, along with a variety of more specialized stipulations of these traditions, persisted into contemporary Western culture. We need to say something about how this came to be so.

In our discussion of the resort to the formal definition of concepts which Plato and Socrates so effectively championed, we highlighted the distinction between two ways of responding to the question

"What is x?" After Plato, responding to this query by merely giving an example of x was generally thought to be inadequate. A more appropriate response would be to give a definition which provides an account of what we have come to call the denotative and connotative characters of x. After the instrumentalizing of scientific rationality in the modern period, such definitions may include generalized descriptions of operations with, upon, or by recourse to x. But, in whatever way we seek to stipulate the meanings of a concept, we always presuppose a context of alternative notions which promote the understanding of the concept being defined. In other words, a definition which places limits upon the sense and use of a given term presupposes a *definitional context* which itself sets limits upon the degrees of variability a stipulation may possess within that context. Another way of saying this is that, with the development of a number of alternative theories, any given term will grow to have a number of alternative definitions. We can't, of course, use them all at once without falling into the sorts of contradiction we generally regard as undesirable.

The persistence of a plurality of meanings associated with multiple definitional contexts is largely due to the general demand that responsible thinkers be able to provide a context of justification, or a specialized theory, which clarifies the principal terms they employ, and of the de facto irreducibility of these contexts one to the other. In the most general sense, the broad traditions of thought, along with the family of formalized contexts of justification belonging to each, provide the theoretical resources of Western culture.

Within broad traditions of thought—such as we term *materialism, idealism, existentialism,* and so on—we must allow for limits to the sort of accommodation possible among the meanings of terms. Meanings of *nature,* or *freedom,* or *power,* or *causality,* or *law,* or *God,* may be stipulated in a variety of ways within each of the dominant traditions. Thus, we have a variety of distinctive materialist interpretations, and an equally large variety of interpretations which belong to the family of idealist theories, and so on. One way of attempting to sort out the disagreements between, say, Democritus and Plato, or Freud and Jung, would be to note the distinctive meanings each pair gives to putatively common terms, if any, and then to contextualize these differences by recourse to the more general patterns of thought to which each implicitly or explicitly appeals.

Then we would not only be able to recognize that, on the whole, the understandings of Plato and Jung, and Democritus and Freud, respectively, are more compatible, but we could ourselves justify this recognition by appeal to the general traditions from which their more specialized contexts of justification are drawn.

We shall use the term *primary semantic contexts* to refer to those broad theoretical traditions which answer to terms such as *materialism* or *idealism*. As a consequence of the manner in which our theoretical problematics were historically shaped, these traditions have sorted themselves into four broad categories. A "semantic context" per se would then name a more specialized context of justification, a particular theory, which delineates the meanings of terms, along with their relations one to another within the given context, along with some plausible means of their application.

Of the many taxonomic schemes which are currently used to organize our theoretical perspectives,[134] the most prominent employs the Aristotelian causal categories as a means of constructing a primary philosophical type corresponding to each of four explanatory principles. Such an approach identifies four broad philosophic traditions which, as primary semantic contexts, have served as the source of the specialized theories of *materialism, formalism, organic naturalism,* and *volitionalism.*

The aim here is not to detail these visions, but merely to show that they are distinct enough to occasion radically different interpretations of any particular subject matter, and that as long as no objective or valuational consensus exists within or among the various theoretical interests, the irreducible plurality of perspectives will continue to serve as a repository of semantic contexts which shape the meanings of the terms employed in formal discourse within our culture, and thus provide the place from which we begin our intercultural conversations. It is, in fact, the primary semantic contexts which most efficiently house objective understandings that constitute the resources for our cultural self-consciousness.

Classically, the materialist vision answers the question "What kinds of things are there?" by saying something like: "There are only atoms and empty space." These atoms are extrinsically related one to the other in the sense that no single atom requires any other for its origin, existence, character, or significance. In this sense there are as many first principles as there are atoms. Here material cause is primary. We first ask after the material constitution of a thing. Efficient causes are then employed in conjunction with material causes to explain the organization and collocation of atoms by appeal to their essentially random motions.

On this view, all relations are extrinsic, and there is usually thought to be no room for human freedom.[135] Freedom is best understood as "freedom from responsibility." This psychological sense of freedom involves the recognition of the determinations of physical nature. These determinations, at the level of animal existence, involve the principles of pleasure and pain. We act, "by nature," to promote pleasure and avoid pain. Thus the primary analogate of this vision is *physical nature*, mechanically construed.

Materialism is a causal theory par excellence, since it is only by looking for determining causes that we are able to understand our world. Thus, in materialism, "the past" is the most important temporal mode. To understand is to construe the present and the future in terms of the past. Causal analysis is the primary philosophic method.

As we have noted, the classical Greek and Roman atomisms of Democritus and Lucretius were revived in the seventeenth and eighteenth centuries and made to serve as the basis for the newly developing physical and mathematical sciences (Galileo, Newton, Descartes), and the social sciences (Thomas Hobbes) as well. In recent times, the Freudian vision has employed the materialist paradigm as a means of interpreting the psychodynamics of human existence and behavior in terms of fundamental, unanalyzable drives or instincts. Freud's *Civilization and Its Discontents* provides a ready illustration of an interpretation of culture along materialist lines. Cultural artifacts, such as poetry and mathematical schemes, are sublimated products of repressed libidinal impulses. Civilization is a consequence of constraints placed upon behavior in accordance with the pleasure-pain principle.

Ludwig Wittgenstein's *Tractatus Logico-Philosophicus* became the bible of the positivist tradition by virtue of its analysis of language itself in terms of atomic facts, analogous to Humean simples, said to provide the means whereby we understand the world: "The World is all that is the case. . . . The world is the totality of facts, not of things."[136]

A second sort of philosophic vision is that of organic naturalism. Proponents of this view understand the kinds of things that exist to be analogues of organic phenomena. Here the metaphor of "biological organism" grounds the vision. Such organisms are whole things whose parts functionally interact to achieve an antecedent aim. The primary analogate here is "law" construed as the rule(s) determining the proper functioning of an organism. Just as in the case of atomism or materialism, the primary analogate of this system may be used to understand not only material phenomena and living things, but social and cosmological issues as well. Aristotle is, of course, the best known practitioner of this mode of philosophizing. His persistent use of final cause in his analyses of the variant organic complexes constituting the natural and social worlds well indicates his preference.

On the principles of organic naturalism, the fundamental entities are organic and, therefore, their elements are intrinsically related one to the other, though extrinsic relations may be asserted to exist among distinct organic entities. As final cause explanations are preferred, this vision looks to the future as the privileged temporal mode. Freedom, construed as "free choice amidst limiting circumstances," is characteristic of this view.

The persistence of Aristotelian naturalism throughout the Middle Ages makes of it one of the most important philosophical traditions in our history. This tradition remains viable not only as the basis for the theological, ethical, and political doctrines of Roman Catholicism, but in the pragmatism of individuals such as George Herbert Mead and John Dewey, as well as in many of the social psychologists.

The formalist vision sees the world as consisting of an unchanging set of patterns, relations, forms. This is a mathematical vision associated with the names of Pythagoras and Plato among the Greeks, and with idealists such as Spinoza and Hegel among the moderns. In formalist thinking, "knowledge," in the sense of the most general principles relating all things, is the primary analogate. Through a dialectical understanding of the particularities of the "world of becoming," one can discover a principle of relatedness which shows the cosmos, society, and human existence itself to be constituted by harmonious patterns.

All relations on this view are intrinsic: "No man is an island." And freedom comes from knowledge: "You shall know the truth, and the truth shall make you free." But the freedom of the knower is freedom referenced to the world of Being. Thus freedom is associated with the search for immortality beyond the world of becoming. The temporal mode of "eternity" dominates this view. The formalist vision persists into the modern age in all types of philosophical idealism, particularly Platonism, and in the psychologies of the sort represented by C. G. Jung, whose central notions of "symbol" and "archetype" suggest the ultimate reality of a world of forms.

The fourth vision is that of volitionalism. The volitional perspective affirms the dominance of efficient cause explanations associated with the actions of individual agents. To the question "What kinds of things are there?" the volitionalist answers, "There are persuasive actions," construed as expressive acts which presume the truth of Protagoras' slogan: "Man is the measure of all things." "Reality" is created by those individuals who influence their communities to accept their actions and constructions as models of understanding and action. Here one must accede to a "trickle down" theory of meaning and value.

The primary analogate of the volitionalist is "power." Thus all relations in the volitional world are power relations. Authentic individuals create themselves (and others) through persuasive expression. The power relations defining this world are both extrinsic and intrinsic, since the powerful do not need the weak, but the weak are dependent upon the powerful. Since persuasion is the goal of interaction, the volitionalist privileges present time, "the now." The Greek Sophists adumbrated this position; the modern movement of existentialism provided a variety of distinctive theories belonging to the volitionalist context.

The philosophic traditions emergent from these four distinct semantic contexts provide in a very general way the grounds for the variations in meanings of the important concepts of our intellectual inventory. "Nature," "knowledge," "power," "law," and so forth, are the notions which render possible full cultural self-understanding.

Now it seems obvious that, given the strong tendency of our tradition to seek the most comprehensive theoretical vision—the one that will ultimately be found "true"—attempts will be made to include the legitimate elements of the four semantic contexts in a more comprehensive and adequate theory. It is equally obvious, given the conflicting and often contradictory character of the terms stipulated within these semantic contexts, that there will be limits to the amount of accommodation that will be possible.

The effort to discover the truth of things through the construction of theoretical visions has led in two, rather distinct, directions: Some thinkers have attempted to conform to the demands of logical consistency and have produced theories which function reductively with respect to other points of view. Others have looked to the criterion of conceptual adequacy, and attempted to incorporate alternative viewpoints in a more comprehensive vision. The alternating dominance of the proponents of *consistency* and those of *adequacy* throughout our tradition advertises the futility of, once and for all, getting to the truth of things.

It is characteristic of late modern culture that we have become aware of the variety of responses philosophers are apt to give to any important question. These responses are rooted in the differences among schools or philosophic movements or differing professional communities. Such differences are accounted for rather informally by statements such as "She's a Platonist, or a Kantian, or an analytic philosopher." The intransigence of these schools, grounded as they are upon differing semantic contexts, leaves us with little to do but to chart the ways of thinking and to provide a guide to the assumptions of the philosophic schools.

One consequence of this development is certainly causal thinking gone bad. Some dogmatic metatheorists see as the end of philosophical thinking what Aristotle had taken to be its beginning—namely, the collection and organization of "the body of the known." The "body of the known," analyzed in terms of his four causes in *Metaphysics* Book Alpha, provided Aristotle the place to *begin* his investigations and speculations. Ironically, in late modern culture, metatheorists conspire to insure that, as far as philosophical knowledge is concerned, a variety of mutually irreducible semantic contexts, arrayed in an assortment of taxonomic schemes, is essentially all that remains at the *end* of thinking.

Two other strands of our cultural paradigm were adumbrated in the narrative of this chapter. The first consists of the concept of the trinitarian elements which express the nature of the divine life as a tripartite structure of Father, Son, and Spirit. The organization of "personality" foreshadowed in Homer's use of *psyche, thymos,* and *noos* to describe the human being, and rendered coherent in Plato's doctrine of the *psyche* as constituted by the faculties of *logistikon* (λογιστικόν) *thymoeides* (θυμοειδής), and *epithymetikon* (ἐπιθῦμε-τικόν), was likely an important source of the rational articulation of the trinitarian doctrine. As we suggested, the immediate impetus for the development of the doctrine of the trinity, however, lay in the need for mediation between a transcendent and an immanent realm.

These trinitarian elements, analogized from the *psyche*, become the ground of analogical procedures which led to the considerations of social relations as patterned by love, power, and justice. With this development, we are able to understand ourselves not only in terms of our internal psychic structure and its social analogue, but, as well, by reference to a transcendent realm paralleling our own.

A final strand of our cultural paradigm, though nascent in the Platonic and Aristotelian notion of the *psyche*, reached its full development only in the modern age. We refer to the articulation, beginning with Immanuel Kant, of the value spheres of art, morality, and science, and the consequent development of autonomous cultural disciplines grounded in these interests. The Aristotelian notions of theoretical, practical, and productive sciences, analogized from the tripartite *psyche*, served Kant in his articulation of the autonomous value spheres. Kant's three critiques (*The Critique of Pure Reason*, *The Critique of Practical Reason*, and *The Critique of Judgment*) establish the grounds for the autonomy of science, morality, and art. In attempting to win autonomy for the value spheres, Kant was also trying to win freedom for the individual as a thinking, acting, and feeling creature.

Kant was, of course, aware of a fourth value sphere which had laid claim to its autonomy with the emergence of the transcendent religions of Judaism and Christianity. Though Kant's Enlightenment sensibilities could not permit it full autonomy, religion was the subject of his *Religion Within The Limits of Reason Alone*. In Hegel's thought, which purports to carry through Kant's project, Kant's condemnation by faint praise is both doubled and undone through the sublation of religion into philosophy as the final avatar of the Hegelian system.

The consequence of the articulation of the value spheres in modern times is that five cultural interests have come to dominate the disciplinary activities of Western intellectual culture: science, morality, art, religion, and, finally, philosophy, which "takes survey of all the world." These are the interests with respect to which the modern sensibility is expressed. The specific values associated with morality, art, science, and religion were for the most part implicit in our culture for a long while. They became increasingly explicit with the need to incorporate a diversity of beliefs and customs in the sixteenth century and beyond. Those who would balk at the belief that all of the basic ideas that would form the sensibility of Western culture had been developed by the age of Augustine could certainly argue that at least one crucially important phenomenon had to wait the modern era for its emergence. For with the reflections of Kant and Hegel, *cultural self-consciousness*, which largely defines what we have come to mean by "modernity," is born.[137]

With the advent of cultural self-consciousness the content of social and cultural life is raised to the level of consciousness, and the ensuing recognition of conflict and relativity, issues into a process of abstraction, formalization, and generalization, which elides differences by suppressing content. The consequence is formal rationality. And the self itself receives formal articulation into reason, appetite, and will; or thought, passion, and action; or the scientific, aesthetic, and moral interests.

The value spheres of science, morality, art, and religion instantiated through Kant's three critiques and *Religion Within the Limits of Reason Alone*, and ramified in the works of subsequent philosophers from Hegel to Whitehead, now form the cultural importances which house and permit the expression of relatively autonomous values. After Kant, the cultural interest of philosophy assumed the role of articulating the nature and relationships of the autonomous value spheres. These cultural interests answer to the general qualities that define the human pursuit of value: truth, goodness, beauty, holiness, and importance. In very general ways these qualities have constituted the cultural aims that have defined and organized social activity and its products into the late modern period.

This completes our very broad sketch of the strands comprising our cultural paradigm. We have seen that the original attempt on the part of the early Greeks to construe a chaotic world has led to a set of alternative organizing matrices functioning in much the same manner as the cosmogonic myths which assumed the task of winning Cosmos from Chaos. Agencies of construal associated with myths and rituals whose task it was to bring order into a presumably chaotic world have been replaced by conceptual structures such as are expressed in theoretical traditions, and models of the human *psyche*, and so on, which serve to organize conceptions of self, society, and the formal interests of intellectual culture. With the emergence of cultural self-consciousness in the modern period, metatheoretical schemes have been devised to express the original cosmogonic motivation by seeking to organize the ways of organizing.

In the modern period, the complex relationships existing among the functions of the *psyche*, the persons of the trinity, the structures of society, and the interests of intellectual culture have formed a sensibility matrix which, when informed by the principal models of the organization of knowledge, and variously interpreted by recourse to the primary semantic contexts and their specialized permutations, have served as fundamental agencies of construal with which we, as the most recent representatives of second problematic thinking, have furthered the project of bringing order from out of chaos.

A culture such as ours, articulated in terms of second problematic thinking, is *theoretical* in a manner that a first problematic culture would not be. What this means, as we shall proceed to show in the following chapters, is that the meanings of ideas and doctrines are to be found by rendering them in semantic contexts which, as traditions and/or theories, serve as principal repositories of cultural significances. Further, in a theoretical culture, the accommodation of ideas and beliefs is achieved in large manner though the search for rational consensus which proceeds by appeal to dialectical interactions among proponents of alternative semantic contexts and their institutionalizations. As we shall soon see, the attempt to compare theoretical, second problematic thinking with that emergent from first problematic thought runs afoul of this serious problem: Both the means of envisioning the world and the manners of accommodating alternative visions are radically distinct among proponents of the two sorts of thinking.

In accordance with our general desire to remove the useless lumber that blocks the pathway to China, we shall be claiming that, in our interpretations of Chinese culture, attending to the semantic contexts dominating our culture will preclude the un-self-conscious employment of terms deriving both from the broad intellectual traditions represented by the four primary semantic contexts, and *a fortiori* from the specialized theories which specify these broad traditions.

For by raising to the level of consciousness both the general theoretical vocabulary of our own culture and the processes by which that vocabulary was developed, insofar as that is possible, we are better prepared to understand the degrees of sameness and of difference reigning in any particular intercultural conversation.

An important qualification is summed up by the phrase "insofar as that is possible." For, quite obviously, when we come to perform specific comparative exercises we shall be forced at least to begin with vocabularies drawn from our own tradition. Our comparative efforts will be successful, however, if we are able *in significant instances* to set aside any "transcendental pretense" when that serves the aims of intercultural communication. After all, the task of negotiating meanings across cultures is only in a matter of degree more difficult than are those same negotiations taking place within a culture.

What does all this finally come to? As heavy-handed as has been our exercise in delineating the general features of our cultural sensibility, the exercise will prove most valuable in the comparative task ahead. For, given the historicist assumptions underlying our work, our efforts should caution those of us in the West who would seek an understanding of an exotic cultural sensibility such as China's that it is illegitimate simply to assume the usefulness of interpretive constructs drawn from our own cultural milieu.

This would be a counsel of despair were it not for the fact that the content and organization of our cultural sensibility does not exhaust the inventory of interpretive constructs and methods available to us. Though the cultural dominant developed by appeal to the second problematic will not prove altogether useful in understanding the Chinese, there is an alternative impulse, that of first problematic thinking, which will serve us somewhat better. Of course, understanding is always a matter of negotiation on the part of all members of the conversation, and beginning with first problematic assumptions will not in itself solve our problem. It will, however, make it somewhat easier to appreciate the real contribution that the Chinese can make to cultural conversations with the West.

—— TENTH ANTICIPATION ——

Western philosophical speculation after the classical period is best articulated in terms of the employment of four primary semantic contexts as frameworks within which to articulate and refine the crucial vocabularies that have shaped philosophic speculation, and of the dialectical interactions among these contexts and their institutional manifestations. Of equal importance has been the manner in which the five principal cultural interests of art, morality, science, religion, and philosophy developed as important cultural determinants. The rational ethos we have outlined, though defined in the modern period as a search for truth and objectivity, may equally be seen as a consequence of the need to handle the intransigent ethnic, linguistic, and sociopolitical diversity of the tradition. The results of dialectical disputations among the various theoretical visions, as well as among the claims of the various value interests, shaped the character of the culture at any given time.

What is achieved in the West by dialectical accommodations of distinctive viewpoints is realized in China by institutionalized "vagueness." By refusing to stress the univocality of concepts or the hypothetico-deductive or axiomatic systematization of theories, and in the absence of a strict delineation of a variety of cultural interests, the Chinese have not so persistently raised to the level of consciousness the presence of distinctive semantic contexts, nor have they foregrounded to nearly the extent this has taken place in the West, the sorts of dialectical conflicts among opposing theoretical contexts. The greater homogeneity realized by the Confucian synthesis in the classical period allows, nonetheless, for the efficacy of rich and nuanced, albeit tacit, significances. Thus, it is important when interpreting the character of Chinese culture to pay attention not only to the contrasting inventory of ideas and practices, but equally to the manner in which these ideas and practices are fixed and transmitted.

The strands which, loosely woven together, establish the rational ethos of the Western tradition must be recognized as contingent historical products. If we approach the task of interpreting the various elements of Chinese culture with the tacit belief in the existence of a single-ordered world shaped by laws and principles transcendent with respect to that world, or with the presumption that the theoretical matrices which provide us the semantic contexts within which our terms receive their stipulated meanings are equally relevant to the translation and interpretation of Chinese sensibilities, or that the organization of our cultural interests into art, science, religion, and so on will somehow be mirrored in the culture of classical China, then we shall surely fail to understand the very different culture of the Chinese.[138] [See chapter 2, section 4.1; chapter 3, sections 3.1, 4.1, 4.2, 5 *passim*.]

11. COUNTERDISCOURSE: CHALLENGES TO THE RATIONAL ETHOS

The logo of the Western world, its pennant (eventually, we must assume, its epitaph), depicts Zeno's ever-fixed arrow and the futile trajectory of its unflown flight. All of the bemusements of rationality are rendered there: stasis, discreteness, objectivity, mensurability, facticity. Such are the determinants which compel us to suppress our most fundamental intuition: "All things flow."

Periodic reversions to the immediacy of experience on the part of seers, poets, and philosophers have occasioned the varieties of mystical, skeptical, and romantic visions comprising that institutionalized counterdiscourse which, by its loyal (and effete) opposition, has so long abetted the dominance of rationality. Indeed, no serious cracks appeared in the well-nigh monolithic culture of rationality until the nineteenth century. Appealing (against Hegel) to the radical temporality of experience, Kierkegaard responded to the Zenonian declaration, "It is impossible to think change," by asserting, "So much the worse for thinking." Employing an alternative stratagem, Friedrich Nietzsche assaulted the ultimacy of fact by uncovering the interpretative, multivalent, perspectival character of consciousness.

By the end of the nineteenth century, the cracks in the Enlightenment's foundation had become fissures and the structure had begun to shift. Today, the project of modernity has fallen prey to late modern critics who, in almost as many ways as there are critics, challenge the hegemony of objectivity. Broadly, however, these critics follow the paths set out for them by Kierkegaard and Nietzsche. Some attempt to rehabilitate the intuition of process and becoming, through a direct appeal to experience; others set out to uncover the paradoxes of consciousness and language which force us back into "the flux of passing circumstance."

Kierkegaard, Bergson, James, Dewey, and Whitehead follow the direct route. Nietzsche, Heidegger, the later Wittgenstein, Foucault, Derrida, and Rorty take the winding path. The vast differences among the members of each of these motley assemblages does not undermine their common mission: All challenge the ultimacy of fact and return to the language of the first problematic.

Philosophers no longer maintain a critical distance from the mythic and poetic elements in culture. On the contrary, since most of the critiques of modernity are motivated by a desire to unmask the metaphorical character of our putatively rational discourse, we are as apt to look to novelists and poets, shepherds of our mythopoetic resources, as to the philosopher or scientist for insight and understanding. Thus we have grown to have less faith that our story is one of the steady growth of reason, or that the movement away from the mythopoetic to the scientific mode of thought and activity is either apt to or ought to continue.

Most contemporary challenges to the ultimacy of fact are Nietzschean rather than Kierkegaardian. That is to say, the majority of critics begin with the failure of the language of literal fact, rather than with the immediate experience of becoming. For Heidegger, the language of Being cannot be strictly propositional. Truth expressed by such language cannot be seen as the correspondence between reality and appearance or as the coherence of propositions within a logically consistent context. Truth is *aletheia* (ἀλήθεια), "uncovering," "unconcealment"—a notion difficult to apply within an ontology of fact, but most appropriate to the attempt to "think the difference of Being and beings."

The later Wittgenstein challenged the belief that the analysis of language could yield univocity. There are an indefinite number of ways of sorting the relations between language and reality, on the one hand, and language and its logics, on the other. Recognizing family resemblances among concepts and uncovering overlapping rules among language games is the best we can (and should desire to) do.

Jacques Derrida's philosophy, which actually originated with a critique of Husserl's distinction between the indicative and expressive functions of the sign, could have begun almost anywhere since his fundamental insight involved the most general of philosophic discoveries: the reflexivity of reflection which entails the consequence that self-referential inconsistencies are always generated by the failure to recognize the complicity of an irreducible "other."

The press toward literal meaning which refuses the complicity of the figural—that is, the search for concepts which can be sundered from their metaphorical rooting in "the irreducibly other"—constipates the enterprise of thinking. The mutual grounding of concepts and metaphors, and the requirement that each (when made the focus of discourse) must transmogrify into its other is used deconstructively against all putatively rational ("logocentric") language.[139]

The common thread of these disparate critiques is the first problematic encounter with the analogical roots of language. A "language of presence" cannot tell us the difference between Being and beings. Other language must be sought. The absence of any final game for language to play renders the concept of "the literal" itself game-bound and, therefore, generally inadequate. Metaphors must be on hand to make and to dissolve appropriate connections. The *complicity* of concept and metaphor is necessary because of the *duplicity* of rational, causal language.

Since contemporary philosophers are more likely to focus upon language than upon the immediacies of experience, it is quite possible to overlook the affective consequence of contemporary assaults upon the ultimacy of fact: Without *objectivity*, objects dissolve into the flux and flow, the changefulness of our surround. A deobjectified, defactualized discourse is the language of process, and to speak and hear that language is to experience the flow of things.

Analogical language is the concrete language of the first problematic. Yet even so-called process philosophers often avoid such language, preferring the causally refined discourse of logistic and dialectical analysis and construction. For this reason, defenses of process which appeal directly to the flux of passing circumstance never seem to fare as well as those which employ *reductio* arguments against the language of substance and causality.[140] Perhaps first problematic thinking could be salvaged by expunging unnecessary resorts to causal explanation and by rehabilitating the constitutive role of analogical and metaphorical language.

One of the central beliefs of the Enlightenment is giving way. Late modern challenges to the project of modernity have rendered problematic the orthodox account of the *logos/mythos* relationship. Judging from our present cultural ferment, the *mythos*-to-*logos* model of cultural development tells only half the tale. The second half of our story promises to be a reversal of the first. Therefore, the appropriate model for cultural activity must combine both the progress and regress of rationality.

Culture, by analogy to our most popular cosmogonic model, may express itself in the rhythmic pulsation from origin to end followed by a return to the beginnings. Our story may well turn out to be one of expansion from an indefinitely compact mythopoetic stuff, followed by "a return of the dispersed" to its source. A Big Bang model of cultural development suitably accounts for our time of reversal, our movement from *logos* back to *mythos*, which effects the unconcealment of our origins and elicits a celebration of the chaos of sensibility prior to sense.

Our narrative of the development of the Western cultural sensibility in terms of the first and second problematics has provided a context within which to approach the task of intercultural conversation. For we are now able at least to begin to set aside the more intrusive of the second problematic assumptions and consider how the world might appear to one whose sense of things is informed by first problematic thinking. What this means is that if, as we shall now argue, the Chinese sensibility resonates with first problematic intuitions, we are in a better position to understand Chinese culture than are those who remain enthralled by the "transcendental pretense."

By recourse to the distinction of the two cultural problematics, we have tried to argue that any culture is more complex than the dominant problematic that shapes it. We shall now attempt to demonstrate that complexity by articulating in greater detail the contrasting cultural problematics that characterize classical Western culture as a means of understanding the contingency of our dominant mode of cultural expression. For recognizing this contingency will prevent us from assuming that classical China must be evaluated by appeal to the idiosyncrasies of our own cultural paradigm.

—— **ELEVENTH ANTICIPATION** ——

Having completed our task of identifying "the useless lumber blocking our highways of thought," we should be in a better position to gain a fresh understanding of the Chinese sensibility. What we have identified as useless lumber are those second problematic assumptions which require the acceptance of the sensibility matrix woven from the six strands of cultural development outlined above. The "likely story" we have been telling of the development of the Western cultural sensibility has been preparatory for entering into a dramatically different context that has developed within China. And it is certainly significant for our project that, at least since Nietzsche, the rational ethos defining the Western sensibility has been under serious attack. Today movements such as process philosophy, postmodernism, and the new pragmatism, by unearthing the analogical, correlative, roots of language, have begun to undermine the notion of objectivity as the principal aim of thinking. The priority of change and process, the intuition of manyness, and the plurality of orders these philosophies espouse, signal a return to first problematic thinking. If we begin to take our cues from those Western thinkers currently seeking alternatives to second problematic assumptions, we shall surely be better prepared to understand the Chinese. [See chapter 2, sections 2, 3.1, 4.2.]

CHAPTER TWO

The Contingency of
—— *Culture* ——

For reson can I non fynde, nor good ryme in your
mater.

John Skelton

Part of the force of Quine's and Davidson's attack
on the distinction between the conceptual and the
empirical is that the distinction between different
cultures does not differ in kind from the distinction
between different theories held by members of a
single culture.

Richard Rorty

Our ultimate purpose is to create a context within which mean-ingful comparisons of Chinese and Western cultures may be made. This requires that we rehearse in the broadest of manners the development and constitution of matrices of valuation which may be said to characterize the two cultural milieux. In the last chapter we discussed some of the principal elements of Western civilization which together comprise the cultural importances emergent from Hellenic, Latin, and Hebraic sensibilities. Before we perform the parallel operation with respect to the classical Chinese world, we have to prepare the way. It would be a futile exercise to delineate what we take to be the important elements of the two cultures if we are unwilling or unable to propose some plausible method of comparing the two traditions. For nothing is more evident in the field of comparative philosophy than the problematic character of the exercise of intercultural translation.

In the following pages, we shall be arguing that the complex fabric of Western cultural sensibilities we have tried to unravel is a *contingent* phenomenon. In the weaker sense, we mean to say by this that the particular character of our intellectual culture is significantly determined by the relative weight given at any particular epoch in our history to selected elements of our culture's "sensibility matrix" which we partially characterized in the preceding chapter. In the stronger sense we mean to say that the entire structure of valuations claimed to be characteristic of our Western cultural milieu, *including the first and second problematics as they developed within Western culture*, could have been significantly different. It is by no means an inevitable consequence of the human "mind" or "experience" or "language" that we, or the Chinese, came to build the cultures we in fact have built.

Since, however, we must begin intercultural translation with those tools at our disposal, we shall use the admittedly contingent contrast between the two cultural problematics to the extent that it serves us in making cultural comparisons. Our claim is that appeal to the contrasting modes of analogical and causal thinking as representations of the first and second problematics will provide us an initial means of bridging Western and Chinese cultures. For the Chinese tradition has (as contingently as the West) developed a culture grounded in *something like* what we have identified as the first problematic, analogical, mode of thinking. In the course of using the first problematic assumptions to understand elements of classical China, we shall find it necessary to adjust the senses of "analogy" familiar in our tradition to better suit the Chinese context.

1. THE FIRST AND SECOND PROBLEMATICS

Kant's call for a "History of Reason" at the end of his first critique expressed a desire for an accounting of the various roles transcendent reason has played in determining the shape of cultural milieux. In one sense Hegel tried to provide this in his presentation of intellectual history as the sharply cadenced dance of the Absolute. Contrary to these rational strategies, the weight of our remarks is to present a call for the *historicizing* of reason, for a presentation of the historical contingencies that have given birth to and nurtured those valuations and practices we have come to term "reason," "reasoning," and "rationality".

Anglo-European rationalism was born from the need to connect diverse ideas, beliefs, and practices. Our reason was the gift of the ancient city-states, spread from Italy to the Peloponnesus, spun through the shuttles of Hebraic Monotheism and Latin conceptions of *humanitas*, and variously refined in the competing furnaces of German, French, and English provincialisms. The early phases of this development, along with some of their more modern extensions, were detailed in the last chapter.

In cultures relatively closed to encounters with alternative ethnic and linguistic evidences, there is less necessity to articulate cultural interests and activities. Thus the values of a culture are made explicit only with the pressure to incorporate a diversity of beliefs and customs. This pressure became particularly great in Western societies after the sixteenth century. From that point rationalization is associated with secularization realized through the process of urbanization.

According to this essentially Weberian interpretation,[1] civilization is, as the term suggests, a process of "citification." The development of cities allowed for the institutionalization of plurality and diversity which both promoted and sustained a process of raising to consciousness the norms and principles of social and cultural life. The conflict among diverse norms was partially adjudicated through the process of abstract generalization which allows for the coexistence of differences by suppressing specific content. Formal rationality is the result. The rational self is itself a product of this process. To the necessity of harmonizing the internalized activities of thinking, acting, and feeling is added the cultural problem of harmonizing scientific, moral, and aesthetic interests interpreted from a variety of distinct theoretical perspectives.

Of course, as we shall have occasion to see in chapter 3, such a narrative of the interrelations of rationalization, secularization, and urbanization must be adjusted when telling the story of Chinese civilization. The tacit assumption that civilization is dependent upon rationalized urban centers is seriously called into question by the history of Chinese society. The historicizing of reason undermines the idea of rational agency as anything other than the result of appealing beyond the practical and ideological conflicts occasioned by ethnic and linguistic diversities to abstract principles or standards deemed objective with respect to the disputants. Thus, historicist readings deny rational method any status as universal and necessary, absolute or objective, by claiming that reason and rationality are contingent products of identifiable historical circumstances. Such readings argue against the overconfident use of strictly rationalistic methods beyond the specific context of their emergence.

Since the Enlightenment, two basic assumptions have undergirded our belief in the importance of reason: first, that there is an objective reality to which our words, concepts, and theoretical interpretations ultimately apply; and second, that a formal method shaped by observation and logical inquiry and identified as "scientific" provides the optimal means of understanding the nature of that objective reality.

Recent events both within and without Anglo-European culture have called this notion of rationality into question. From inside our culture, we have witnessed (1) the shift within both the biological and the physical sciences away from notions of absoluteness and certitude in response to the notion of the mutability of *species*,[2] the paradoxes of quantum theory, the incommensurability of quantum and relativistic conceptualizations, and the replacement in most instances of the notion of universal and necessary laws of nature, and of "natural kinds," with the probabilistic and statistical generalizations associated with this or that specialized science; (2) the failure of the rearguard action of the positivists to ground science and mathematics in incorrigible empirical and logical notions; (3) the presence of a vast plurality of theoretical constructs—analytic, metaphysical, hermeneutical, pragmatic—which stand stubbornly beside one another, unyielding to any attempts at reduction, sublation, or dialectical refutation; (4) the emergence of ethnic and gender-related movements, which challenge the objectivity of rational methods by claiming them to be ideologically grounded; and, finally, (5) the increased encounter with alternative cultures such as China, Japan, and Korea, which claim parity with our own culture but which operate on the basis of values and understandings sufficiently distinct from our own as to suggest the culture-specific character of our Enlightenment rationality.

In the last chapter we posited a narrative of the development of our cultural understanding which, to the extent that it is plausible, would challenge the universal and ahistorical character of our manner of understanding the world about us. We traced the motivations for the development of rationalism to the culture-specific assumption of the necessity to create Cosmos from Chaos.

Thus, rationality is both cause and consequence of an objective reality created by cosmogonic agency. Along with the transcendent reality, the soul or *psyche* as a tripartite construing structure, whose ordering mechanisms are constituted by thinking, acting, and feeling, is brought into being. Rationality, as we have come to employ it, is now vindicated as a means of controlling the passions and guiding activities in the sphere of praxis. When the "spirited activity" (*thymos*) of the Platonic *psyche* is reinterpreted by recourse to the Augustinian notion of "will" (*voluntas*), the rational *agent* would come into his own.

The so-called relativistic assaults upon Enlightenment rationality are, as we said above, often based upon the failure of reason to make good on its claims to objectivity, universality, and certitude. Thus, the failure of the positivists' program and the generation of a plurality of competing theories, each of which is as successful in making its case as are the others, can lead one to throw up one's hands and say, "So much the worse for reason!"

But there are also constructive motives for looking past the dogmatic claims made on behalf of science and rational method. Simple curiosity in the face of the "otherness" of an alternative culture, or reflection on whether the "other" gender in one's own culture has the potential for creating new ways of understanding, can lead to the qualification of claims to the omnicompetence of rationality.[3]

We have alluded to two principal problematics existing at the recorded origins of our culture. What we have termed the first problematic is acosmological in the sense that it does not presume a single-ordered world. By contrast, the second problematic, from which our mainstream culture actually arose, affirms the existence of but one, single-ordered cosmos.

In Greek culture, the first problematic is exemplified by the non-discursive myths and similes first employed by Homer, by the "many-worlds" views of thinkers such as Anaximander, and by the conventionalist perspective of the Sophists. Ironically enough, given the later employment of the atomistic paradigm in modern science, the thought of Democritus, insofar as it promoted the belief in the coexistence of many world-orders, manifested first problematic elements. One may add to these philosophic sources the practical spheres of medicine and technology, whose practitioners for the most part were analogical thinkers.[4]

The second problematic is that which dominates and has dominated the history of philosophic and scientific cosmology. It is the view that there is only one world-order, whose laws are relatively stable from the "beginning" to the "end" of the order. The second problematic is best illustrated by mature thinkers such as Plato and Aristotle, who attempted to provide contexts in which explanatory principles might be consistently invoked. But even with respect to these thinkers, analogy is at the root of their systematic theories. They both construct schemes which organize analogically the four kinds of causal explanation they employ.

The contrast between first and second problematic thinking is in fact a contrast between distinctive concepts of order, which we have elsewhere called "aesthetic" and "rational" order.[5] The rational understanding of order is associated with uniformity and pattern regularity. This type of "logical" ordering is an implication of the cosmological assumptions which characterize the *logos* of a cosmos in terms of causal laws and formal patterns.

The second type of ordering, the "aesthetic," is acosmological in the sense that the particularities defining the order are unique and irreplaceable items whose nonsubstitutability is essential to the order. No final unity is possible on this view since, were this so, the order of the whole would dominate the order of the parts, canceling the uniqueness of its constituent particulars.

Rational order instantiates a preexistent or presupposed structure or pattern. This sort of order is broadly quantitative and mathematical in the sense that the elements signalling the order are replaceable and substitutable. Aesthetic order is comprised by irreplaceable elements. Unlike the physical elements which may configure geometrical lines, planes, and solids, the elements of a given order are more than mere place-holders. Aesthetic ordering, at its extreme, is a consequence of certain specific particulars and no others. Rational ordering is such as to be realizable by recourse to an indefinite number of elements.

Reason and rationality presuppose both a single world-order and the indefinite substitutability of the elements comprising such a world.

It is simple enough to demonstrate that rational ordering is an anthropocentric notion, for the physiological, linguistic, and conceptual uniformities defining the human species determine in advance the sorts of ordering that will be anticipated with respect to one's understanding of the natural world. The sorts of beings we presume ourselves to be define the sorts of orders we may recognize and deem important. Alternative orders are considered unknowable since to know an order would mean that we were able to anticipate its pattern regularities, recognize its realized uniformities, and establish plausible grounds for causal sequences among the elements serving to instantiate those uniformities.

Aesthetic ordering presupposes an alternative method of knowing, one which has as yet received only marginal elaboration in our tradition. An order in which the ordering elements are insistently unique particulars cannot be discussed in terms of pattern concepts defining regularities or uniformities. Even the normal forms of metaphor which serve to extend the meaning of a literal term are of little use in characterizing such orders. In fact, one of the main burdens of contemporary speculative philosophy has been the need to discover a new language for philosophy which can accommodate aesthetic understandings.[6]

These two types of order are illustrated in the major kinds of abstractive procedure.[7] "Formal abstraction" yields logical patterns in which the actual characters of the constituents of the orders are ultimately irrelevant. "Selective abstraction" yields concrete correlations which constitute an order solely by virtue of the presence of the actual things comprising the order. Formal abstraction abstracts from actualities, such as are concrete particulars; selective abstraction abstracts from possibilities, such as are forms and pattern regularities. The reason for the inability to balance the activities of formal and selective abstractions lies in the fact that they proceed in opposite directions. The former moves toward the realm of purest possibility; the latter toward the sphere of unique particularity.

In our tradition, there is much lip service paid to the interdependence of the logical and the aesthetic aspects of experience. One of the romantic ideals of Western intellectual culture from Pythagoras to the present has been the discovery of a means whereby the conjoint appreciation of the two classes of value might be achieved. And we would certainly admit that such an appreciation is indeed possible to the extent that one does not foreground the sort of abstractive procedure presupposed in her approach to a given subject matter. But it is precisely this sort of foregrounding that is required by resort to rational or causal analyses. In a consciously rational culture, the conflict of the logical and the aesthetic is unlikely to be overcome.

First problematic thinking is acosmological and oriented toward the actual particulars whose various correlations are construable only in terms of constituent details. Second problematic thinking is cosmological in the sense that explanations are referenced to the pattern regularities associated with the overall context defining the order.

The distinction between "logical" and "aesthetic" order is related to a similar one made by F. S. C. Northrop. Northrop developed his comparative philosophy in terms of a distinction between "concepts by postulation" and "concepts by intuition." He claimed that the former dominated Western speculation while the latter was dominant in much of oriental culture:

> A concept by postulation is one the meaning of which in whole or part is designated by the postulates of the deductive theory in which it occurs . . . and a concept by intuition is one which denotes, and the complete meaning of which is given by, something which is immediately apprehended.[8]

We do not mean to endorse the subtleties of Northrop's argument, which in fact requires a quasi-Kantian search for a transcendental deduction of "possible concepts," but there are similarities between Northrop's approach and the one we have developed out of an analysis of types of order.[9]

In the foregoing chapter we have shown the joint emergence of two types of understanding—the rational and the analogical. Only by presuming a progressivist model of cultural development from *mythos* to *logos* may we be at all justified in refusing parity to the analogical mode. In fact, the argument of this entire book is that something like the analogical mode of thinking is most helpful in allowing us to understand the otherness of Chinese culture.

Presupposing the discussions of the principal types of order here and elsewhere,[10] we intend in the following paragraphs to further articulate the sense of first problematic thinking as a means of preparing for the argument that, in fact, such thinking has dominated classical Chinese culture. In chapter 3 we shall attempt to provide the concrete evidence for this claim by constructing a narrative of events in classical Chinese cultural history which presupposes such dominance. If, as we believe that it will, this narrative rings truer than those accounts of the Chinese sensibility which employ rational or causal assumptions, our claim will have been pragmatically justified.

——— TWELFTH ANTICIPATION ———

In this, our final "anticipation," it is important that we once again reinforce our overall intention in this work. We are employing a pragmatic method to remove some of the obstacles to understanding. These "obstacles" are, in fact, interpretive constructs which have real explanatory value when we seek to comprehend our own particular history, but only serve to obfuscate and embarrass our attempts to understand when we use them out of their cultural context. That we really have no choice but to use *some* of this lumber to build a bridge to China bespeaks the initial limitations placed upon intercultural conversations by the necessity of beginning from one's own provincial ethnos. There are large-scale systemic structures which we have come to recognize as reductionistic, and as having limited value in our attempt to understand Chinese culture. We must also proceed cautiously with more illuminating and liberating distinctions such as those between first and second problematic thinking, aesthetic and logical orders, and rational and correlative thinking. We have no choice but to start with the most fruitful interpretive categories at our disposal, but we must be conscious of the fact that we are speaking from our own tradition. When we begin a direct exposition of classical Chinese thinking, it will be necessary, to the extent possible, to adjust these categories and distinctions to better suit the Chinese context. As pragmatists we are perfectly sanguine about the fact that we shall never "get it right." Our task, certainly less grandiose but assuredly more fitting, is rather to "get on with it" in the most responsible manner possible. [See chapter 2, sections 2.2, 2.3, 3.1.]

2. CHINA AND THE FIRST PROBLEMATIC

2.1. New Approaches to China

Jacques Gernet's study of the seventeenth century in China uses diaries, journals, correspondence, and other such documents to put the Jesuit missionaries and the Chinese intelligentsia into conversation.[11] We must remember that the Jesuits did not take Christianity to China simply to persuade the Chinese to embrace a new religion. They were envoys dispatched by Rome to introduce a universal religion fortified by the best of Western classical and scholastic learning as part of a calculated strategy to alter China's fundamental conceptions about the world. The Rites Controversy, which raged for nearly a century, in which Rome had to decide whether the Chinese Christians could remain culturally Chinese, and the massive anti-Christian propaganda campaigns and pogroms that occurred in eighteenth and nineteenth century China, were natural expressions of this collision between civilizations.[12]

Gernet describes the role of philosophical thinking in this intercultural conflict in the following terms: The problem that Matteo Ricci and his colleagues faced was fundamental. In order to make Christianity understandable to the Chinese, the missionaries had first to teach the Chinese to think:

> Matteo Ricci . . . very well understood the necessity first to teach the Chinese to reason properly, that is, to distinguish between substance and accident, the spiritual soul from the material body, the creator and his creation, moral good and natural good. How else could the Christian truths be put across?[13]

Perhaps the most important contribution of Gernet's study is that it persuades us of the decidedly historicist character of two competing mental schemata, two very different ways of thinking. Gernet suggests that in the encounter, even logic was found to be culturally specific. For the Jesuits,

> logic was inseparable from the religious dogma and the Chinese appeared to lack logic. It probably never crossed the minds of the missionaries that what seemed to them to be Chinese inaptitude was in fact a sign not only of different intellectual traditions but also of different mental categories and modes of thought.[14]

According to Gernet, the Chinese intellectual elite of the seventeenth century found Christianity and the Western civilization which it communicated to be noise and nonsense which they could not intellectually entertain.

The historian Paul Cohen shares many of Gernet's insights and concerns. Cohen tracks the nineteenth-century ramifications of the China Mission in his *China and Christianity*, and tries to discover why the Chinese populace felt such violent antipathy toward the foreign religion.[15] In Cohen's more recent book, *Discovering History in China*, although his focus now is twentieth-century American historians rather than seventeenth-century missionaries, his critical concerns are still quite close to Gernet's.[16] Cohen begins his critique from the following premise:

> Among the several factors governing the evolution of any field of historical inquiry, the political, intellectual, and cultural milieu within which the historian lives and works is, in my view, primary; everything else is secondary. . . . The approaches followed, the basic questions asked, will still be principally shaped by the sociocultural environment of the historian.[17]

Cohen's chief worry is that distortions traceable to uncritical universalistic assumptions undermine the value of Western attempts to tell China's story.

By and large, Western historians have tended to read nineteenth- and twentieth-century Chinese history through the three dominant paradigms of impact/response, modernization, and imperialism:

> All three paradigms are . . . burdened by Western-inspired assumptions about how history *should* go and built-in questions— equally Western-inspired—about why it does or does not go as it should. Like all approaches of a highly teleological nature, they are fundamentally circular in that they end up finding in a vast and complex historical reality precisely what they set out to look for.[18]

How we categorize what we know—for example, how we structure our encyclopedias, how we define our academic disciplines, or how we periodize our history—is as direct an indication of our model of thinking as we can find. As Maureen Robertson observes with respect to the organization of historical events, periodization in any of its forms is one response to the necessity of recovering an intelligible pattern from what seriously threatens to remain formless and meaningless—the processes of change in time.[19]

Again, as we see it, the historian's obstacle to understanding China is of a piece with that of the Jesuit missionary. The problem is one of universalizing parochial assumptions. In the case of Cohen's critique, this involves universalizing the nature and significance of historical change.

How are we to resolve this problem? Cohen's recommendation is hermeneutical: We must resist insinuating into our perception of recent Chinese history our own historiographical assumptions, and instead must attempt a China-centered internal perspective which takes seriously culturally specific determinants and the vocabulary through which they are expressed. Perhaps the Chinese do think about, select out, and organize the welter of detail that constitutes their cultural superstructure in ways very different from our own. In order to appreciate an alternative set of cultural dynamics, we must try to get our own world view out of the way.

There is great value in the concerns that both Gernet and Cohen express over recovering an internal perspective, but, of course, the problem becomes increasingly complex as the boundaries of these previously resilient world views seem increasingly to become mixed and indeterminate.

In the past few years, three major studies of classical Chinese philosophy have appeared in English, all of them authored by leading names in the field after long and productive careers: Benjamin I. Schwartz's *The World of Thought in Ancient China* (1985), Angus Graham's *Disputers of the Tao* (1989), and Derk Bodde's *Chinese Thought, Society, and Science* (1991).[20]

We may ask whether, and to what extent, these three seminal studies have succeeded in addressing the legitimate concerns of Gernet and Cohen. It is our contention that the Schwartz and Bodde volumes, while extraordinarily successful on their own terms, still begin from uncritical assumptions about a shared humanity and a commonality in modes of thinking that partially delimits their descriptive and interpretive efforts.[21] Angus Graham's contribution takes a different tack. *Disputers of the Tao* is distinctive in that it seriously attempts to articulate what Graham perceives to be an alternative way of thinking unfamiliar to us in the post-Galilean West. Graham's break with the other doyens of the sinological world is reflected in his 1986 *Times Literary Supplement* review of Schwartz's *The World of Thought in Ancient China*:

> Some Western explorers of Chinese thought prefer to think of the Chinese as like ourselves, others do not. One tendency is to see in Chinese thought, behind all the divergences, an inquiry into universal problems, through ideas which transcend cultural and linguistic differences; the other is to uncover, behind all the resemblances, distinctions between key words which relate to culture-bound conceptual schemes and to structural differences between Chinese and the Indo-European languages. Benjamin I. Schwartz's *The World of Thought in Ancient China* is a very distinguished representative of the former point of view.

We would extend Graham's contrast here by saying some scholars are persuaded that the conversation is richest where there is the greatest degree of commensurability; others believe that behind the more obvious and uninteresting physiological and other apparently acultural similarities—one head, two ears, and so on—there may be profound differences that derive from culture-specific ways of thinking and living. Some believe that failing to regard the commonality as most important is to deny the Chinese their humanity; others believe that to assert such an essential commonality is to hobble the inquiry and, in so doing, to deny the Chinese their uniqueness.

2.2. Analogical or "Correlative" Thinking

In attempting to honor his commitment to difference, Graham explores certainly the most radical question raised by the work of Gernet and Cohen: Is it possible the Chinese might actually think differently from us, and if so, what might this mean? To respond to this question, Graham, in his later work, resorted to a contrast between "causal" and "correlative" thinking as alternative means by which philosophic discourse has been shaped in the modern Western and traditional Chinese cultural milieux.[22] In chapter 3 we shall provide illustrations of the employment of "correlative" thought in the Chinese tradition; in this present context we shall merely attempt to clarify the meaning of correlative, or analogical, thinking.

What has come to be called correlative thinking is effectively a nonlogical procedure in the sense that it is not based upon natural kinds, part-whole relations, an implicit or explicit theory of types, or upon causal implications or entailments of anything like the sort one finds in Aristotelian or modern Western logics. Correlative thinking employs analogical associations.

The relative indifference of correlative thinking to logical analysis means that the ambiguity, vagueness, and incoherence associable with images and metaphors are carried over into the more formal elements of thought. In contradistinction to the rational mode of thinking which privileges univocity, correlative thinking involves the association of elements into image clusters which guarantee to its constituents richly vague significance.

P. K. Feyerabend has alluded to this kind of thinking through his recognition of a distinction between classification and abstract definition in the history of Greek thought.[23] Giving examples, or making lists or classifications, is a consequence of correlative thinking, which Feyerabend terms "historical" or "empirical" in contrast to "theoretical" thinking. Though such thinking was surpassed among philosophers by causal thinking associated with formal or abstract definitions employed as class terms which organize along the lines of objective connotation, the older, first problematic, correlative mode continued in the arts, in religion, in medicine, and in technology. Correlations, such as those present in the humor theory of medicine, or illustrated by astrological charts, are not based upon dialectical principles of organization, nor is there any unified complex presumed whose analysis leads to the parsing out of these components. They consist of elements selected and correlated from the perspective of the correlator.

In place of a causally oriented science, those who think correlatively investigate the concrete items of immediate feeling, perception, and imagination related in aesthetic or mythopoetic terms. Correlative thinking is primarily "horizontal" in the sense that it involves the association of concrete experienceable items, usually without recourse to any supramundane realm.

From the perspective of correlative thinking, to explain an item or event is, first, to place it within a scheme organized in terms of analogical relations among the items selected for the scheme, and then to reflect, and act in terms of, the suggestiveness of these relations. Correlative thinking involves the association of image- or concept-clusters related by meaningful disposition rather than physical causation. Such thinking is a species of imagination grounded in necessarily informal and hence ad hoc analogical procedures presupposing both association and differentiation.

A simple illustration will clarify this point: In the most superficial understandings of totemic classifications, the association of a clan, family, or group with a particular animal or natural object is not based upon claims of a shared essence or upon an observed or inferred causal connection, but upon the assignment of a meaningful correlation. The meaning is *created* meaning in the sense that selected characteristics of the totem object elicit feelings and behaviors in the human beings associated with it which help to establish their character and import as individuals, as well as their patterns of communal association. Totemic classification establishes a field of meanings among those individuals represented by the various totems.

Likewise, in societies which place some importance on the act of naming, as well as upon the significance of the name given, name-giving may be seen as prospectively creating a world in which both the named person and those who identify her by name are called upon to instantiate in their relationships the harmonious patternings which characterize the system of names from which any given name is selected.

Angus Graham, among others, claims that in China the Han dynasty cosmologists employed a species of analogical thinking involving the correlation of significances into clustered images which, though they could by no means yield univocal definitions, could nonetheless be treated as meaning complexes ultimately unanalysable into any more basic components. The five directions (North, East, South, West, and Center), the five phases (Water, Fire, Wood, Metal, and Earth), the five smells, the five sounds, the five tastes, and so forth, associated with the so-called cosmologists of the Yinyang school, along with the eight trigrams and sixty-four hexagrams of the *Book of Changes*, are not organized by appeal to dialectical principles of organization, nor is there a unified cosmos presumed whose analysis leads to a resolution into these components.

Those who are suspicious of the explanatory force of these Han dynasty "pseudoscientific" schemata are so precisely because such schemes resist causal analysis. Correlative schemes must seem altogether arbitrary to the mind shaped by causal thinking. A rational individual is accustomed to assuming an objective ground that can underwrite standards of evidence, allowing claims to certitude or plausibility. But from the correlative perspective the quest for certainty is replaced by a search for significance and efficacy.

In his earlier work,[24] Angus Graham discussed such processes as those characterized above simply as analogical operations. His later treatment of this procedure, expressly with respect to the study of classical Chinese thought, appeals explicitly to the theory of correlativity developed by Claude Lévi-Strauss. Lévi-Strauss had formalized the sense of correlativity contained in Marcel Granet's *La pensée chinoise* by recourse to the work of Roman Jakobson who, in his studies of aphasia, had discovered what he took to be two distinct types of aphasic disorders—one which he termed "similarity disorders," the other "contiguity disorders."[25] The former were based upon an inability to recognize relations of similarity (metaphoric relations), while the latter concerned the inability to discern relations of part and whole, or of temporal connexity (metonymic relations). Jakobson speculated that metaphoric and metonymic operations underlay the processes of all language learning and use.

Jakobson's claim, as discussed by Graham, is simply that language is acquired through two sorts of pattern recognition. The first is that of the paradigmatic relation, which is one of similarity and contrast; the second, that of the syntagmatic, a relation of contiguity and remoteness. Words are selected from sets of words which share varying degrees of similarity, then combined in sequences to form sentences.

For example, consider the pairs "Day and Night" and "Light and Darkness":

    Day Light
    Night Darkness

Paradigmatic and syntagmatic relations may be understood in the following manner: Day/Night = Light/Darkness expresses a paradigmatic relation grounded in metaphor, while Day/Light = Night/Darkness expresses a syntagmatic relation based upon contiguity.

The acquisition and use of language is dependent upon both sorts of pattern generation and recognition. Both relations of similarity and

THE CONTINGENCY OF CULTURE

those of contiguity are conventionalized associations, so the learning of a language is a basic mode of socialization which "conventionalizes" the learner. Further, as Graham points out, learning these sorts of relations involves a great deal more than acquiring words and sentences:

Since the distinguishing of opposites is [often] guided by desire and aversion, which enchain the pairs with good and evil, someone thinking correlatively is satisfied not only of what to expect but of what to approve and disapprove.[26]

It is easy enough to see how difficulty in mastering a second language lies in part in the distinctive conventions associated with paradigmatic and syntagmatic relations. For example, the funereal color is black in the West, but white in China. It is difficult, though not impossible, to adjust one's emotional responses when confronting alien sets of relations associated with an alternative language.

Lévi-Strauss applies Jakobson's notions of similarity and contiguity relations to Marcel Granet's speculations concerning the "Chinese mind," surmising that what Granet had called correlative thinking could be formalized by recourse to the metaphor/metonym distinction. In his analysis of *la pensée sauvage*, Lévi-Strauss noted that totemic classifications could be considered fundamentally metaphoric, while rituals of sacrifice could be construed as metonymic. Thus, by viewing correlative cosmology as a "science of the concrete," he was led to suppose that the attempt to relate concrete phenomena to a nonexperienced domain, as in the case of the metonymic operations involved in sacrifice, is the foundation of religion.

With this insight, so Lévi-Strauss believed, the notion of correlativity gained clarity and rigor. Applying this insight to the Chinese employment of analogical thinking, it would be possible, for example, to understand the vast systems of classification associated with *yin-yang* cosmologies or the *Book of Changes* by appeal to these tropic devices.

We are inclined to believe that the attempt to formalize the analogical mode of thinking by appeal to Jakobson's speculations has in fact overly rationalized analogical, first problematic thinking and made it, while more precise and rigorous as a method, less applicable to the Chinese context. The burden of the following discussion will be to reinstitute the former, more naive understanding of analogical thought. To do this we must first say something more about the manner in which Graham develops the notion of "correlative" thinking by appeal to Lévi-Strauss and Jakobson.

Graham holds that correlative schematizing as a way of thinking is not distinctively Chinese:

> What Granet saw as the difference between Chinese and Western thought may nowadays be seen as a transcultural difference between proto-science and modern science. Correlative cosmos-building is most conveniently approached as merely an exotic example of the correlative thinking used by everyone, which underlies the operations of language itself.[27]

By acceding to the view that correlative thinking is grounded in the character of linguistic activity, Graham has followed Jakobson's belief that metaphoric and metonymic activities are essential to language acquisition and use.

Graham observes that within our own tradition, correlative thinking was the dominant mode of thought until Galileo and the revolution in thinking he introduced. As Graham suggests, until the development of modern science, there was really no alternative to a correlative cosmos.[28] Graham further argues for the primacy of correlative schematizing:

> One might put it this way: while explaining analytically, attention is diverted from the correlating of concepts in the background; but as long as analysis has nothing to put in front, correlative thinking is necessarily in the foreground.
>
> How does correlative thinking relate to analytic thinking? The common-sense thinking of daily life may be conceived as a stream of correlation redirected by analysis whenever we have occasion to doubt a comparison or connexion.[29]

The shift away from correlative to causal thinking takes place, if it does, because of a need to criticize correlations. This occurs when the presumed correlations are contradicted by experience. If, for example, in a sufficient number of influential instances one encounters darkness by day, one is then forced to analyse the syntagmatic relations critically and seek the precise, invariable and so causal connexion. A tension grows between the pressure of fact and the need for the security of remaining inside a fully comprehensible world. Causal relations begin to interlock, opening the prospect of another Cosmos, that of modern science, in which prediction is more accurate than ever before but there is nothing to tell us what to approve or disapprove.[30]

It is important to recognize that strictly analytic thinking is not the only sort that contrasts with the correlative mode. In the modern Western tradition, all the principal types of argument—analytic, dialectical, and analogical—have been rationalized. Analytic arguments require least units of analysis with respect to which objective claims may be made. The discovery of these units and the assessment of their causal interactions is the aim of rational analysis.

Dialectical arguments presume a putative whole in accordance with which claims of systematic coherence might be made. Without that assumption, syntheses would be ad hoc and local, with no guarantee that they could be generalized beyond a certain limited context. Further, as Plato argues in Book 10 of the *Laws*, without the guarantee of a guiding, ordering intelligence, the world would be left to its own immanent devices and order would be accidental.[31] Used as a rational mode of explanation, analogical arguments are determined by a primary analogate serving as the source and ground of the argument. "God" and "World" are the termini of an array of theological arguments. "Being qua Being," as well, serves in the capacity of primary analogate.

In a culture dominated by causal thinking, analysis, dialectic, and analogy may all be employed critically, for rational ends. In a culture heavily influenced by correlative thinking, all argumentative modes will take on a correlative cast. Correlative analysis would not presuppose discrete units objective with respect to any act of analysis, but would accept the relevant complex of correlations as the analysandum, and would not violate the integrity of the correlated items. Further, from the correlative perspective, dialectical arguments would take the form of forensic exercises guided by conventional norms rather than by the aims of systematic coherence. Such dialectical operations would involve the oppositional interplay of elements without the goal of contradiction, synthesis, or sublation. And, of course, analogical argumentation would be performed without the assumption of a primary analogate.

The difference between Western and Chinese attitudes toward correlative thinking is explicable in terms of the final dominance of modern science in Europe and the emergence of quantitative standards of evidence which exclude correlation as adequate explanation. According to Graham,

> The Chinese assumption seems to be that you can criticise correlations but you cannot dispense with them.
>
> The Western tradition, on the other hand, has long persisted in trying to detach the analytic completely from its background in the correlative, dismissing the latter as loose argument from analogy which we need in practical life but exclude from strict logic. It is only in the last half-century, with Ryle's exposure of the category mistake, Kuhn's proposal that all science assumes paradigms subverted not by demonstration but by correlative switches, Derrida's uncovering of chains of oppositions at the back of logocentric thought, that the West seems finally to be losing faith in its two-thousand-year-old enterprise.[32]

The explanation of the social, political, and cosmological processes in terms of the interaction of complementary contrasts is fundamental to the Chinese tradition.[33] This by no means indicates that the Chinese are somehow incapable of thinking in causal terms. The technological achievements in China are evidence enough that, with respect to issues of practical concern, the Chinese exercised that mode of thinking.

But when the question was one of the place of the human being in his or her broader social or cosmological context, there was among the Chinese a concern to relegate causal thinking to the sphere of everyday life, and to pursue the correlative mode of understanding with respect to the large issues of cultural life. As Graham has indicated, there is a real value in a correlative cosmos, since "those who live in it know not only what is but what should be."[34] Further,

> The primary social institution, language, is one . . . for which correlative thinking is perfectly adequate; although one may have

to analyse paradigms and syntagms in order to learn a language, one can speak it only when correlating them without analysis. Institutions in general require that for most of the time we adjust to pattern automatically, analysing only when faced with an occasion for choice.[35]

Here we find one reason why the Chinese may have had a stronger and more lasting commitment to correlative thinking than have we in the West. The plurality of beliefs and patterns of behavior, rooted in the interactions of distinct cultures and ethnicities presents us with too many "occasions for choice," pressing us toward causal analysis and away from the comforts of correlative associations.

It would appear that something like the causal and correlative modes of thought will persist alongside one another in all cultures. Comparing a rational culture such as ours with one shaped by correlative thinking involves primarily a recognition of alternative priorities with respect to the two modes of thought. It could be argued, however, that in any given culture the dominant mode of thinking might tend to inform and recast the recessive mode. For example, in modern Western cultures, the most recognizable illustration of a cultural artifact shaped by correlative thinking is that of astrology. Charting the positions of the sun, stars, and planets with respect to the times of the day, month, and year, and to one another, provides a complex array of correlated items. By recourse to conventional commentaries, individuals might obtain a series of advices assisting them in charting the course of their lives. When one actually reads the literature surrounding astrology, however, one discovers that much of the language is not correlative, but causal. Further, given the conventionalized common sense of the modern Westerner, the bias is toward a causal interpretation of even the more neutral language. One unconsciously filters discussions of "destiny" and "planetary influences" through the language of efficient cause. The fact that those who practice astrology often refer to it as "the science of astrology," while those ill-disposed to it call it a "pseudoscience," suggests that the scientific paradigm is a privileged criterion for what counts as respectable knowledge.

Something like the reverse of this situation may be said to exist in China. The primary examples of causal thinking in China, at least in the early period, are drawn from the technological realm. In the West, the scientific revolution eventually led to the rationalization of technological development involving the application of scientific principles to achieve technological results. This phenomenon was so significant that many think of technology, which developed for centuries independently of anything like formal science, simply as "applied science."

In China, up through modern times, the question of the integration of technological developments into the sphere of concrete social praxis has always been addressed in such a manner as to insure the continuance of that valuational matrix pervading the established correlative construction. In the West, "the objectivised world of modern science dissolves [the] primitive synthesis of fact and value, and in facilitating successful prediction leaves us to find our values elsewhere."[36] But in traditional China there is really nowhere else to go. As we shall see later on in this essay, there are a variety of reasons why the Chinese, even today, face a situation, confronted in the West until the seventeenth century, in which "the choice (is) between the cosmos of correlative system-building and no cosmos at all."[37]

The different priorities with respect to causal and correlative thinking in China and the West help to explain the contrasting genius of each society: Whereas the West's claim to fame is scientific rationality (a mode of causal thinking resulting in part from the press toward analytic thinking occasioned by having to confront ethnic and linguistic pluralism), China's claim is to a social and cultural stability persisting over two millennia. This stability is explicable in part as a consequence of the ability to maintain the spontaneous, automatic interactions based in correlative modes of organization associated with a focus upon language and social institutions.

Graham is explicitly aware of the importance of specifically analogical thinking in the works of the pre-Qin philosophers.[38] At the same time, he suggests that in China "throughout the classical period correlative schematising belongs only to professions such as diviners and physicians; the philosophers from Confucius to Han Fei do not engage in it at all."[39] Graham thus links correlative thinking to the process of unification and systematization which emerged at the end of the Zhou dynasty, thereby making an implicit distinction between structured correlation and ad hoc analogy as methods of argumentation. But, though the resort to complex schematising may be absent in Confucius and Han Fei, it does seem, as we shall detail in chapter 3, that something like correlative operations were employed at the beginning of the classical period in both the philosophical and political spheres. Not only was political unification achieved with the founding of empire and the unification of the Great Wall, but this process of standardization affected society at every level: laws, weights and measures, the written language, and so on. Extensive codes of laws and ritual practices were articulated, and the resurgence of Confucianism brought with it the establishment of canonical texts and exegetical schools. There was, at this juncture, the movement from what Karlgren has called the "free texts" of the Zhou era to the "systematizing" texts of the early Han, in which previously loose legends and protean heroes are drafted to serve as elements in formal classifications.[40] Previously disparate protocosmological fragments are integrated into something like systematic "cosmologies" during this transitional period, joining the social and political disciplines as an important area of philosophic concern.[41]

Graham's judgment that correlative thought is to be consigned to periods beyond the classical is based upon his acceptance of the metaphoric/metonymic distinction as an essential formalizing element in all correlative operations. We believe that this acceptance of Lévi-Strauss' Jakobsonian interpretation of Granet's initial insight leads him astray, finally causing him to fail to appreciate the extent to which first problematic assumptions shape the entire sweep of the Chinese cultural sensibility.

Our disagreement with Graham is not as serious as it may seem. We shall feel perfectly able to treat the activity of correlative thinking in the more formal manner that he, following Lévi-Strauss, chooses to do whenever that is relevant. We only insist that the more formal, rationalized interpretation not be treated as exhausting the meaning of this activity. In the following section we shall elaborate our more informal interpretation of correlative thinking. Our argument will be that we shall be able to employ the term "correlative thinking" as a synonym for the analogical procedures associated with first problematic thought without losing any of the relevant meanings that have come to be associated with the term when applied to the interpretation of Chinese culture.

2.3. Causality and Correlativity

Ultimately, all modes of causal analysis couched in terms of the rational dominant are based in the notion of logical order. Aesthetic, first problematic assumptions would lead us to characterize the way of things in a distinctly different manner. Causal language is the discourse of substances; correlative language characterizes processes. Whereas logical order is disclosed by pattern regularity indifferent to the actual content of the particulars constituting the order, aesthetic order discloses an ad hoc unity formed by irreplaceable items. The insistent particularity of these details is in tension with the harmony of the ad hoc unity, since the harmony cannot be appreciated except as a harmony of just those particulars. Logical order discloses pattern unity; aesthetic order discloses unique particulars.

In rational science, causal connections are sought in abstraction from the concern for human significance. For example, Charles Darwin, as scientist, could not concern himself about whether the revelation of putatively causal connections between human beings and animals advertised in *The Origin of Species* might decrease the sense of personal significance.[42] On the other hand, as we have already said, the correlative procedures of totemic classification attempt to establish meaningful, albeit acausal, connections between the human realm and the animal kingdom.

Employing the more formal sense of correlativity derived from Lévi-Strauss, it is plausible to surmise that what individuals in rational cultures generally recognize as correlative activity is primarily metaphoric (synchronic, spatial, based on similarity) and only secondarily metonymic (diachronic, temporal, based upon linear connections), since so many of what we perceive to be relevant connections shaped by temporal linearity have been accounted for in terms of the notion of efficient cause.

Such a conjecture has two extremely interesting consequences: First, this hypothesis suggests that rational thinking has more to do with metonymic operations associated with a putatively non-experienced domain, such as is exemplified in religion, than with the metaphoric operations of the science of the concrete. This in turn would offer yet another reason why quantitative science of the hypothetical deductive variety did not flourish in China, and would also give further credence to the view that Western science depended, at least at its origins, upon religious and theological under-standings. From the Western standpoint, therefore, the familiar claim that the roots of both objective science and transcendent religion are absent in indigenous Chinese culture makes perfect sense. Second, we have here a slightly oblique means of expressing Hume's stric-tures against the notion of causality: Cause-effect transactions are modes of correlation rooted in metonymic relations of temporal contiguity.[43]

The fact that one may argue for the grounding of causal relations in metonymic operations might suggest that we should adjust our ter-minology somewhat and claim that the distinction between the two problematics is best expressed as a contrast of metaphorical and metonymic thinking. That would, however, be a bit too simple. It does appear to be the case that metonymic operations have dominated in the West, expressed in the form of rational, causal, thinking. And we might opine that metaphoric activity has dominated the Chinese mode of correlativity. But the contrast between the two problematics is meant to point up the fact that the first problematic employs both metaphor and metonym in an informal, analogical manner while the second problematic formalizes both tropes.

We need to insist that though we believe the metaphoric/meto-nymic distinction to be quite helpful as a heuristic device allowing us to clarify correlative operations, there is no basis for claiming that it is in any sense an exhaustive pairing. It is certainly possible to employ this distinction to clarify this or that exercise of analogical thinking, even among the Chinese, but any claim of the sort that Jakobson and Lévi-Strauss would endorse, to the effect that these operations are essential to all language acquisition and use, is broadly beside the point in the interpretation of correlative thinking.[44]

Correlations are spontaneous in a sense that neither analytical nor dialectical procedures can be. The association of biological rhy-thms, or psychological attitudes, with times of the day, seasons of the year, or the character of one's surround are perfect illustrations of the correlative mode. An Age "grows old," a New Age is "born," and we all are potential victims of a "dark night of the soul." The same cor-relative procedures may be employed for certain "dehumanizing" purposes—as is the case with the development of Gregorian chant, which avoids rhythmic patterns as a means of pointing individuals away from the biological, and toward the spiritual, sphere.

Many would want to shy away from the claim that the informal analogies of correlative thinking lie at the basis of both analytic and dialectical thinking. However, the sudden insights upon which scientists ground their hypotheses result from spontaneous awareness of meaningful relationships which, though they may later be affirmed testable in their demetaphorized form, are not only unpredictable but highly implausible in their original guise.

Concepts based upon correlative thinking are image clusters in which complex semantic associations are allowed to reflect into one another in such way as to provide rich, indefinitely "vague" meaning.[45] Univocity is, therefore, impossible. Aesthetic associations dominate. Submerged by analysis and dialectic, metaphor and analogy persist as the ground of the language. Had we not contrived to forget that the principal terms of art in our philosophic and scientific lexicons had their origins in the metaphorical realm of human significances, and were spontaneously analogized to an alternative context, we should early on have suffered a failure of nerve (of the sort we are experiencing in contemporary philosophy) with respect to belief in literal, univocal significances.

One may justifiably claim that correlative thinking persists as the root of causal thought since, as seems to be the case, metaphors ground literal, scientific language. One of the surprising characteristics of causal thinking in Western science is the degree to which the masked metaphors underlying causal thinking have been taken uncritically to be literal, univocal terms.

The Aristotelian concept of *hyle* (ὑλή) provides a familiar illustration of this point. In Latin, *hyle* is translated *materia*. The English translation is "matter." Both *hyle* and *materia* mean something like "lumber"—that is, the sort of wood used in construction. This concept, originally used analogically by Aristotle, has persisted throughout our tradition. Construed in terms of the atomic or copuscularian hypothesis, the concept of "matter" yielded doctrines which were refined enough to own an aura of objectivity and facticity, though they were, of course, completely ad hoc and beyond the slightest comfort of empirical justification.

By the time these notions occasioned crisis, scientists were ready with another analogically grounded model—namely, the "planetary" model of the atom. The Bohr theory began as little more than a metaphorical emendation of a metaphor ("indivisible stuff," "corpuscles") which was itself a specification of the older metaphor (*hyle*, *materia*—"lumber").

A second example of the correlative ground of theoretical concepts concerns the notion of "cosmos." The presumption of a single-ordered world was unauthorized by empirical or logical generative criteria. The verb *kosmeo*, with its associations of housekeeping, military organization, or cosmetic adornment, was analogized, first, to Zeus Kosmetas and then applied to the external surround. These procedures were altogether correlative.

If we look at the notion of cultural problematics from the rational perspective, we have no choice but to find the first problematic to be a "prelogical" stage of thinking which must be surpassed. Viewing the two problematics from the correlative perspective, however, allows us to recognize the interdependence of the two modes. The rational, progressivist account of the development of our culture from out of *mythopoetic* beginnings has led to the construction of a variety of semantic contexts which cannot be reduced one to the others, and which carry richly diverse "rational" meanings of images and metaphors originating in the correlative mode.

The persistence into our contemporary period of the incompatible explanatory visions classified by Plato and Aristotle at the close of Athenian high culture argues against the rational assumptions of the second problematic and in favor of the correlative visions associated with the first problematic, for, ironically enough, the taxonomists have trouble defending the rationality of their schemes. For what could they mean by "rationality"? If a metaphilosopher claims that he is organizing not "the world" but "world-texts," it would seem that the rationality of his enterprise presupposes some rational means of organizing the very theories which have been shown to be incompatible. The mode of classification of such theories is not itself a theory, only a taxonomy. As long as we emphasize the application of this or that special theory, things go well. It is when we try to problematize the whole, asking after the status of the entire taxonomy of theories, that we discover the correlative character of the organization of our theoretical schemes.

Causal thinking comports well with substance views; correlative thinking best suits process understandings of the world. Thus, causal thinking supports the primacy of fact, while the acosmological, aesthetic, correlative, assumptions of the first problematic are better able to support the intuition that "all things flow."

Particularity—distinctiveness sliding toward the unique—is essential to process since the fewer particularities, the more *kinds* there will be. At the extreme, only one kind of thing might exist. In such a world, logical uniformities would not only be the *dominant* features, they would be the *only* features. Entertainment of the logical orders would have no reference to unique particulars. All items in this world would be replaceable by more of the same. There would be an absence of process, complete stasis. Logical order is a constraint against which particularity wages its battles.

If process is to be held primary, aesthetic order must be fundamental. And this means that, in appreciating any given event, inconsistency (nonsubstitutability) is prior to consistency, plurality to unity, disjunction to conjunction. Thus, all unities are ad hoc: There can be no cosmos in any final sense.[46]

The language of correlativity is the language of process, the only language which gets us close to the immediate sense that "all things flow." Metaphorical and imagistic language is grounded in correlativity. The language of correlativity is the result, the sign, and the reward of feeling the flux of passing circumstance. Such language is the ticket to a fresh, immediate feeling of the flow of things.

It is impossible to maintain the purity of process within the context of a tradition shaped by quantitative thinking, one which defines rationality in terms of causal analysis. For example, the irreversibility of linear causality, and the delineation of consequences in terms of those causal antecedents relevant only to strictly uniform metonymic relatedness, means that efficient cause is deleterious to process. Further, such analysis radically disjoins cause and effect, precluding any viable notion of self-creativity.

Material cause accounts destroy the sense of process by substituting static entities for transformative events. Process is then reduced either to the translation of matter through space or alterations in the material constitution of a complex. Morphological explanations ruin process by offering a pattern or patterns as determinative of isolatable factors or phases of a process. Insofar as the language of presence makes essence or Being present through beings (or becomings), it renders process stable, static, and devoid of vitality. Teleology frustrates process as well. Becoming defined in terms of an end is self-contradictory. If the end is present in the beginning as aim or goal, process is merely the rehearsal of a presumptive organic state. True process thinkers declare, along with Don Quixote, "The road ('way,' or '*dao*') is better than the inn."

Just as causal language ruins process, so substance language invites causal explanation. The modern appropriation of atomistic theory (the corpuscularian theory of Gassendi, Descartes, and so on) demonstrates quite well the fruitfulness of quantitative assumptions which permit causal explanations unclouded by qualitative considerations. Here there is the presumption that the world is composed of chunks of matter which arrange themselves in measurable ways—either as quantifiable entities with mass and volume, or in terms of causal relations open in principle to prediction and replication.

In Greek thought, the presumption of the priority of rest over motion led to the search for agencies productive of the movement of the entities forming the ontic realm. This search in turn led to the consideration of causal relations among the concrete individuals making up the congeries of the material world, and thence (as in Newton et al.) to the acceptance of a Divine Being as the agent responsible for the entire complex of events.

The copresence of alternative theoretical explanations sets the stage for the dialectical engagements that define the history of speculative theory. Analytic and analogical arguments were employed primarily within a given theoretical vision in order to generate and articulate the assumptions and conclusions of that system. Dialectical arguments were employed both intrasystematically and apologetically in order to establish the validity of one position vis-à-vis another. The agonistic form of intellectual engagement in terms of causal agencies took precedence over correlative operations which would realize harmony within a common tradition.

We have attempted to show that significant alternatives were available at the beginning of our cultural experience which could have led to a decidedly distinct set of orientations. The fact that the first problematic was effectively discarded in favor of the presumption of a single-ordered world; that substantialist notions took precedence over process views; that the appearance-reality, Being-Becoming, reason-experience, and mind-body dualisms were posited, insuring the necessity of radical transcendence and the development of a language of cause and effect, has in important measure determined the shape of our cultural self-understanding.

There is certainly nothing inevitable about the contours of our culture. Had we been subject to different historical contingencies we could have developed a quite different set of assumptions. There is no plausible reason why we should not believe in multiple world orders, why we should not have rejected both idealist and materialist ideologies, and rejected, as well, any final distinction between our sense experience of the world and our reasonings about it.

Something like this would in fact have been the case if we had adopted Heraclitus' process view of the world and Anaxagoras' notions of continuity; and if, above all, we had not felt constrained to take the mathematical mysticism of Pythagoras so seriously.

Our argument has been that we can save the term "correlative thinking" for the procedures we claim to be characteristic of Chinese intellectual culture only if, instead of acceding to the rationalized sense of the term, we provide something like an aesthetic, first problematic interpretation of the rational/correlative distinction. An aesthetic rather than a rationalistic version of the rational/correlative distinction entails an important consequence: Distinctions of the sort made by Jakobson, and acceded to by Graham, must be applied with extreme caution. All such distinctions, including the ones we have made, must be interpreted in accordance with the first problematic penchant for deuniversalizing all polarities.

Classical Chinese culture provides an excellent illustration of how one ought to treat distinctions of the sort we have discussed in this work. Perhaps the most identifiable philosophic feature of classical China is the seemingly ubiquitous distinction between *yin* and *yang*. As we shall argue in chapter 3,[47] the *yin/yang* polarity is no more than a convenient way of organizing "thises" and "thats." This is clearly a consequence of the nominalistic character of Chinese intellectual culture.

A. C. Graham's work on the absence of the copulative verb in the classical Chinese language, addressed earlier,[48] has a direct bearing on this point. Without recourse to the copula and the essentialism it entails, Chinese thinking does not presuppose the unity of Being behind beings, a One behind the Many. All you have in the Chinese world view is "the ten thousand things" as an ad hoc summing up of beings and events. Correlations among these "ten thousand things" are nonfoundational since they are only a matter of empirical experience and conventional interpretation.

Another consequence of an aesthetic interpretation of the rational/correlative distinction is to reinforce the radically historicist understanding of alternative cultural developments. Even if we were to allow that alternative cultures and epochs do engage in some similar patterns of correlative thinking, this concession would still amount to little in terms of narrowing the spectrum of cultural difference. The aesthetic version of the rational/correlative distinction is grounded in a sensitivity to and an appreciation of the insistent particularity of individual cultural sites and epochs.

A modality of thinking shapes and is shaped by the particular thoughts thought. Imagination has an important role to play in the process of thinking. It is the ongoing effort to configure particular images in anticipation of fruitful correlations. Hence, any conceptual or structural or theoretical comparisons of modes of thinking between China and the West, while interesting and important for the purposes of intercultural communication, cannot be formalized or overly rationalized without violating the very premise of aesthetic relatedness. When, instead of rationalizing alternative cultures by appealling to ethnocentric notions of "universal reason" or "objective principles," we engage them as artifacts, it is the profound contrast that emerges between their respective histories, ethnographies, biographies, and genealogies that requires explanation.

When all cultures are defined in terms of objective norms of rationality, significant differences among forms of life may be elided. On the other hand, the claim that all cultures engage in some kind of correlative thinking actually promotes the appreciation of differences. It is like claiming that different cultures are similar in having aesthetic sensibilities. Different cultures applying a supposedly acultural rationality would discover the same sciences; different cultures applying culturally grounded correlative schemata will produce radically different works of art.

3. COMPARING COMPARATIVE METHODS

In chapter 1 we argued that the character of Western culture is to a significant degree conditioned by the contingencies entailed by the dominance of second problematic assumptions. So far in this chapter we have attempted to further articulate the importance of the priority given to causal thinking in the West by contrasting it with the alternative first problematic mode of correlative thinking. We shall argue that Western interpretations of Chinese culture must learn to appreciate the correlative mode of thinking if they are adequately to orient themselves with respect to the Chinese world they are seeking to understand. In the remainder of this chapter we shall focus upon the manner in which a pragmatic approach to comparative activity allows us to do just this.

3.1. Transcendental and Pragmatic Approaches

The long shadow of Enlightenment rationalism has only just begun to recede from the contemporary scene. It was the influence of the Descartes-to-Hegel axis that led us to emphasize the metaphor of "mind" as the medium through which the world was to be accessed. Beginning with the existential critics of Hegel—principally, of course, Søren Kierkegaard—there was a shift away from "mind" to "experience" as the fundamental medium for world-access. This shift was rendered most effective among the Continental existentialists and the early American pragmatists.

In recent decades, primarily among Anglo-European thinkers, there has been a transition from "experience" to "language" as the principal metaphor by which to focus philosophical discussions. This shift in the philosophical dominant has provided Western philosophers with tools of analysis and construction that better serve comparative treatments of Chinese and Western thought. The Western focus upon issues of language and language use, is far less foreign to the Chinese than are the subjectivist treatments of either mind or experience, which inevitably lead to a concentration upon epistemological issues.

Philosophers who employ language analysis as the idiom through which questions of the nature of reality and the character of truth are considered have recently separated into those (from the logical positivists to the contemporary philosophers of mind) who model philosophical discourse along logical and scientific lines, and those (from the hermeneuticists to the new pragmatists) who appeal to literary and aesthetic models. The former movement provides us with examples of transcendental comparativists; the latter movement promotes a context for the sort of pragmatic method employed in this work.

There are, in fact, two major types of transcendental approach. In addition to the dialectical one which seeks to employ univocal concepts of logic and rationality in its interpretive projects, there is the perspective we shall term *transcendental pluralism* deriving from the metaphilosophical movements associated with recent developments in American philosophy. This perspective accedes to the fact of pluralism to the extent that it recognizes a small number of alternative perspectives generated by transcendental possibilities of interpretation.

Transcendental methods seek to provide a method of commensurating meanings drawn from alternative cultural contexts on the assumption that such commensuration is possible because of a common set of transcendental structures. In one case, there is but a single coherent set of possibilities, shaped by presumably univocal senses of "mind" and "logic." The aim of this method is to get at the truth of the matter. In the pluralist approach there are several theoretical alternatives, each with its own internal coherence.

We ourselves have appealed to what may look like transcendental pluralism in our analysis of the rise of the major theoretical paradigms in classical Western culture. But, as we shall try to demonstrate in our discussion of this position, our views are seriously at variance with those of the transcendental pluralist since we presume that the semantic contexts we choose to discuss are contingent, culture-specific products of the peculiar history of Western culture. Ours is, thus, a distinctly pragmatic, historicist approach. As pragmatists, therefore, we are interpretive pluralists. Before detailing what we intend by the term *interpretive pluralism*, it will be helpful to indicate in a more precise way what we mean by the term *pragmatic*.

At its very origins, the movement of American pragmatism rather sharply divided into Peircean ("scientific") and Jamesian ("literary") strains.[49] The rational, scientistic pragmatists still maintain some of the interests of the rational epistemologists. Among these concerns is that of the meaning/reference distinction, and the desire for consensual agreement on the truth of propositions. The Jamesian strand is focused upon the efficacy of beliefs in a pluralistic universe in which, according to James, "the word 'and' trails along after every sentence."[50]

As we shall demonstrate below, both of the principal transcendental approaches are evident within the scientistic strain of pragmatism. The difference between them involves the extent to which they take seriously the fact of theoretical pluralism. The dialectical type defends the "single best theory" approach. The pluralist, on the other hand, raises the ante and seeks "the single best *meta*-theory"—the one which best characterizes the transcendental possibilities of theory construction.

In contrast to transcendental approaches, literary pragmatists generally affirm a distinctly rhetorical theory of language which surrenders any attempt to provide a rational account of communication or intertheoretical discourse. In place of language as mediating between language user and a reference world, there is simply the more or less effective use of language as an instrument for performing desired tasks. Though we shall certainly not deny transcendentalists of the Peirceian persuasion the right to call themselves "pragmatists," in this work we intend to reserve the term for our distinctly literary, historicist, "Jamesian" form of pragmatism.

Our claim is that there are three principal methods of comparative analysis open to us. These we shall term *transcendental monism*, *transcendental pluralism*, and *interpretive pluralism*.[51] Those who appeal to the univocality of notions such as "mind" and "logic" are transcendental monists who believe that "Truth is one," and that the search for truth in alternative cultures follows essentially the same rules as in one's indigenous culture. What we are calling "transcendental pluralists" are illustrated by those who accede to the fact of pluralism, but do so only by allowing for a small number of alternative transcendental contexts. Finally, there is the new pragmatist, influenced by the literary and historicist strain of American pragmatism, who acts as an "interpretive pluralist." In this role one denies that there is any final truth to be attained or, for that matter, anything final about the interpretive tools one uses; nor does one even believe that there is a means of listing all the necessary tools.

There are, of course, comparativists, by far the majority, who remain uncritical with respect to the assumptions and predispositions of their intellectual work. One doesn't really expect commentators on international politics or economics, or intercultural aesthetics for that matter, to feel that they must articulate underlying assumptions of their inquiries. They simply believe themselves to be addressing particular issues or problems in as intelligent a manner as they are able. The argument of our work is that it is well-nigh impossible for such philosophically naive approaches to free themselves from methodological assumptions without first raising to consciousness the dominant sorts of ideological biases that have in fact operated in so many of the most influential comparative analyses. Therefore, presumably uncritical comparativists, no less than the more self-consciously theoretical ones, are likely to move discernibly in either the pragmatic or transcendental direction in their comparative work.

At the present time, the field of comparative philosophy provides an important testing ground for these three comparative approaches. If the transcendental monist, acting as a dialectical rationalist, can sustain the argument that there are universal meanings for reason and logic by recourse to alternative cultures—showing, for example, that only "primitive" cultures are nonrational and that any "developing" culture owes its genuine successes to the movement from *mythos* to *logos*—then the Enlightenment sensibility which has suffered the assaults of postmodernism at home will receive some renewed support abroad.

Alternatively, if by setting aside any strictly monistic claims the transcendental pluralist can argue successfully that an alternative culture illustrates types of philosophic thinking of the sorts that have developed in the West, and that, therefore, the same sets of semantic variables that organize and classify the various ways of thinking are equally applicable to the alternative culture, then we have made a large step in verifying the Enlightenment claim of the transcendental character of reason and rationality in its admittedly more modest, pluralistic form. If, however, as we believe, neither the first nor the second of these alternatives is likely to be sustained as a comparative method, then one should perhaps accede to the pragmatic and historicist attitudes of interpretive pluralism informing this present work.

Our pragmatic commitment is in large measure underwritten by the rather dramatic changes in the intellectual and political environments of the Anglo-European cultures. The transition from modern to postmodern perspectives is not merely a theoretical shift. It entails a vast network which has drawn together in a single mix movements as seemingly diverse as deconstruction, the new historicism, cultural studies, and feminist criticism—all of which at one level or another are rooted in the critique of the rationality of language. The presumption of a single coherent world that might serve as ground and goal of descriptive or interpretive endeavors, or of an essentialized mind or ego that might ground the thoughts, decisions, and actions of agents, as well as the very idea of a stable agent that could serve as the author of ideas or the terminus of ascriptions of responsibility with respect to actions and decisions, are no longer presupposed by the above named movements.

With the dissolution of "self" and "world," the remainder of the Enlightenment architectonic is undermined; for without an essential sense of world or self there is no longer any need to appeal to "essences" or "natural kinds." Language doesn't mediate between self and world, defining both polarities; instead, language constitutes these polarities in the vaguest of manners: Self is now characterizable in terms of "sentential attitudes," shifting patterns of desiring and believing, and "world" becomes but the vague background or ambiance of self—"a name for the objects that inquiry at the moment is leaving alone."[52]

3.2. Transcendental Monism

We have already alluded to examples of transcendental monism at the beginning of this chapter. One such example is that of the Jesuit missionaries to China who, of course, were armed with metaphysical and epistemological absolutes in addition to the specific dogmas of the Church. Though post-Enlightenment thinkers presume that it was the irrationality and paradoxical nature of the beliefs required of Chinese converts that presented the major difficulties for the Jesuits, it is clear that the categories associated with ontology and epistemology were equally decisive stones of stumbling.

In describing the largely failed encounter between the Jesuit missionaries and the Chinese intellectuals, Jacques Gernet ascribes the mutual misunderstanding to this contrast between externally imposed order assumed in our tradition, and the Chinese assumption that order is immanent in and inseparable from a spontaneously changing world:

> Believing that the universe possesses within itself its own orga-
> nisational principles and its own creative energy, the Chinese
> maintained something that was quite scandalous from the point
> of view of scholastic reason, namely that "matter" itself is intel-
> ligent—not, clearly enough, with a conscious and reflective

intelligence as we usually conceive it, but with a spontaneous intelligence which makes it possible for the *yin* and the *yang* to come together and guides the infinite combinations of these two opposite sources of energy.

Underlying this divergence is the basic difference assumed in relation to the priorities of permanence and process. Gernet notes that, "According to Aristotle, it is normal for all things to be at rest, whereas for the Chinese, in contrast, universal dynamism is the primary assumption."[53]

Were one to accept Gernet's account of the differences between the Chinese and their Jesuit visitors, then it would be easy to see how the Jesuits' belief in the correctness of their views would place a serious burden upon their Chinese communicants. The transcendental monism of the Jesuits led them to presume that the structures of logic and rationality, as they manifested themselves in the Western world, provided the norms for assessing the viability of Chinese intellectual culture.

Paul Cohen's criticisms of the use of Western historiography to provide accounts of modern China discussed at the beginning of this chapter are criticisms of such transcendental methods. Western historians beginning with a theory informed by the "impact/response" or "modernization" view are likely to have made two questionable assumptions: first, that the *sort* of theoretical language developed from out of the Anglo-European cultural sensibility is applicable to the interpretation of Chinese history; and second, that *the particular theory* espoused by the interpreter is the one which best suits the interpretive project.

Another illustration of transcendental monism is to be found in Lévi-Strauss' translation of Granet's *La pensée chinoise* into *La pensée sauvage*—an interpretation achieved by recourse to Jakobson's metaphoric/metonymic distinction. Lévi-Strauss' linguistic structuralism may provide for a distinction between the "primitive" and the "civilized" which avoids privileging the latter, but it does so in such a manner as to reduce human beings and cultures to media through which "myths think themselves."[54] Structuralism of this sort provides us with a perfect illustration of transcendental monism grounded in the assumption of universal mental structures shaped by linguistic and mythical categories.

Less pernicious examples of transcendental monism come from the work of individuals who are, for whatever reason, less self-consciously theoretical. For example, Benjamin Schwartz's *The World of Thought in Ancient China,* mentioned earlier, is a distinguished attempt to assay the classical Chinese "world of thought" without a heavy dependence upon a theoretical apparatus. But even if he does not explicitly appeal to philosophic assumptions to shore up his arguments, he is at least tacitly committed to a version of the transcendentalist position which affects his constructive efforts. In the introduction to his work Schwartz claims that

> The faith which must animate an enterprise such as this is the faith that comparative thought reaching across the barriers of language, history, and culture . . . is possible. It is a faith that assumes a common world of human experience.[55]

Schwartz believes that "what emerge from the common cultural orientations of . . . civilizations in the axial age are not univocal responses but rather shared problematiques."[56] Further, he agrees with the following words of Clifford Geertz on the development of human cultures generally: "The problems being existential are universal; their solutions being human are diverse."[57]

Schwartz reveals that his own interest in ancient Chinese thought was stimulated by "the type of 'world-historical' observations which we find in the chapter on the 'axial age' in Karl Jaspers' book, *The Origin and End of History*."[58] Schwartz notes that

> in this small volume Jaspers highlights the fact that in many of the high civilizations of the ancient world—the civilizations of the ancient Near East, Greece, India, and China—we witness over the period of our "first millenium B.C." the emergence of certain "creative minorities" who relate themselves in reflective, critical, and what one might even call "transcendental" ways to the civilizations from which they emerge.[59]

In spite of the rich ambiguities celebrated throughout his comparative enterprise, and the concreteness of his analyses, Schwartz's endorsement of the heuristic value of the notions of "the axial age," and of "shared problematiques," and of the universality of "existential problems," along with his faith in a "common world of human experience," nudge him into the community of transcendental monists.[60]

A more extreme example of transcendental monism is Chad Hansen's recent work, *A Daoist Interpretation of Chinese Thought*.[61] Because it is such an uninhibited example of "transcendental pretense"—and, thus, contrasts most radically with our own pragmatic approach—it will be helpful if we discuss this work in some detail.

Hansen offers his "Daoist interpretation" as an alternative to what he terms "the ruling theory" of Chinese thought. This ruling theory is in fact an ideal type formed by eliding "all the different interpretive theories with which [he is] familiar."[62] Among other things, this ruling theory, according to Hansen, (1) reads the history of Chinese thought from a Confucian perspective; (2) deemphasizes the dialectical interactions among various thinkers, thereby creating an "isolated schools" view of Chinese philosophy; and (3) "attribute[s] the conceptual structure of a Western theory of mind and language to Confucian writers," which "tempts us to view [Chinese] philosophical theories as straightforward counterparts of our own."[63]

The notion of a "ruling theory" serves Hansen as a dialectical foil over against which he articulates the lineaments of his own interpretation. Given his transcendental method, it is essential that he attack the first two elements of the "ruling theory." This is so because, in the first place, the Confucian perspective is not easily construed as amenable to a transcendentalist interpretation. Secondly, as a dialectical thinker, Hansen could hardly get his interpretive project off the ground if he acceded to the basically nondialectical character of the Chinese tradition. As for the third aspect of the ruling theory, Hansen is less worried about attributing Western views to the Chinese than he is with attributing the *wrong* Western views. His own interpretation provides a rather straightforward application of the dominant assumptions of Anglo-American analytic philosophy of mind to the interpretation of Chinese culture.

A closer look at the arguments of Hansen's work will illustrate the fact that, though in his discussions of Chinese philosophy he concentrates upon language as social practice rather than as a repository of essential meanings, he remains committed to the logical strand of Anglo-American philosophy. That is to say, logic and rationality provide the guiding criteria of his analysis and critique.

Hansen's dialectical transcendentalism leads him to hold that the history of Chinese intellectual culture has often been misconstrued by those who fail to apply appropriate standards of rational discourse to its interpretation, and that though the pragmatic functions of language are most important to the Chinese, they evidence sufficient interest in logical and syntactical issues to provide the resources for a rehabilitation of the realist and naturalistic aspects of Chinese philosophical culture.

Hansen construes the classical Chinese in terms of a theory of language and mind drawn from the analytic tradition of Anglo-American philosophy:

> Language is a social practice. Its basic function is guiding action. The smallest units of guiding discourse are *ming* [names]. We string *ming* [names] together in progressively larger units. The salient compositional linguistic structure is a *dao* [guiding discourse].[64]

It is important to recognize that Hansen's "Daoist theory of Chinese thought" employs this technical sense of *dao*. Hansen is not in any simple sense interpreting Chinese thought from the perspective of Daoist thinkers. He is assuming a theory of language which allows him to interpret *dao* as "guiding discourse." He uses this theory to interpret the Daoists, and then uses Daoism so interpreted as the perspective from which to view Chinese thought. We stress this since any who might come to Hansen's book armed with more traditional understandings of Daoism might wonder just what is Daoist in Hansen's interpretation.

By denying its strictly representational function, Hansen's theory of language promotes a theory of mind characterized in terms of dispositions rather than ideas and beliefs. Employing this theory of language and mind interpretively with respect to the scope of the classical Chinese tradition leads him to divide classical Chinese thought into four epochs: (1) a Confucius-Mohist period called the positive *dao* period, (2) the antilanguage period, (3) the analytic period, and (4) the authoritarian period.

The first epoch is shaped by the concern to find the right guiding discourse for society. Confucius found the language in those *li* 禮 (ritual actions) resourced in tradition, while the Mohists proposed to reform the language by appeal to principles of utility.

Hansen's dialectical approach urges him to stress the effectiveness of the early Mohist critics of Confucius to a degree that many texts have not done. In effect, Hansen believes that Mozi "set the philosophical agenda" for classical China—first, by beginning the process of reflective critique; and second, by focusing upon language as ethically guiding discourse. The response of subsequent Confucians to the Mohists sharpened the philosophical tools of the Confucian thinkers.

In the "antilanguage period," Mencius and the early Daoists rejected language as the resource for *dao* and appealed instead to natural and innate sources. Moreover, by reversing the priorities of morality and tradition, making the latter depend upon the former, Mencius perpetuated a "radical betrayal of the essence of early Confucianism."[65]

The rationalizing thrust of Hansen's transcendental monism leads him to assault vigorously the "accepted view of what Daoism is."[66] Impatient with the interpretation of Laozi as a metaphysical mystic, Hansen seeks to present Laozi's "antilanguage" perspective in a straightforward manner without appeal to any ultimate, and ineffable, reality:

> I understand *dao* in Daoism as I understand it in Confucianism, Mohism, and elsewhere. It is a guiding way. The distinctive Daoist skepticism comes from the fluidity of convention. It does not result in a theory that language cannot capture the *Dao*. The skeptical claim is merely that any prescriptive discourse—any *dao* that language can express [—] cannot be a constantly reliable guide to behavior.[67]

In the third epoch, which Hansen calls the "analytic period," the difficulties and paradoxes of the antilanguage position of Mencius and the early Daoists were uncovered by the later Mohists, the School of Names, and Zuangzi. It is here that Hansen's interests in logical analysis are most fully exemplified. Hansen's rationalism leads him to an analysis of the thought of Zhuangzi which some might see as a corrective to the romantic excesses to which many are given when contemplating that thinker. Hansen's Zhuangzi is no longer the muddled purveyor of paradoxes but is, above all, "conscious, direct and aware."[68]

Classical Chinese thinking closes with Xunzi and Han Feizi. Their "authoritarian reaction" was aimed at avoiding the political consequences of intellectual relativism spawned by the analytic period. Hansen contrasts the "conventionalist" Xunzi who gave priority to "tradition" over "morality" with the Xunzi who, like Mencius, reversed the priorities and held the heart-mind to be more important than conventions.

A most striking feature of transcendentalist approaches of the sort Hansen's work represents is the manner in which they must assume the existence of commonality among theoretical alternatives. Hansen's demonstration of this commonality is sustained by his employment of a "single thread" that secures the seams of his work. That thread, of course, is *dao* as guiding discourse. Perhaps the most interesting philosophical question raised by Hansen's transcendentalism is the usefulness of this assumption of thematic continuity.

Hansen's style of argumentation places him in the company of that presently diminishing number of philosophers who believe that there is "real philosophical progress" and that it depends upon dialectical engagements among alternative theories which aim at getting at the truth. Hansen's dialectical arguments promote intertheoretical engagement which can lead to adjustments of principles and arguments on either or both sides of the debate. These adjustments, insofar as they realize increased clarity and cogency, are thought to promise philosophical progress.

Hansen's work is perfectly consistent with the position of the transcendental monist in its rejection of the "isolated-schools approach" to Chinese philosophy. Such an approach involves a stress upon similarities within a school and a deemphasis upon influences among the schools. Hansen is not merely arguing that the schools interacted. There is more than enough evidence that they did so vigorously. He wants to make the more controversial claim that these interactions were, in the broadest sense, rational. In other words, as a transcendental monist, Hansen must believe that the interactions among the schools constituted instances of intertheoretical communication.

It is on this issue that the perspectives of the interpretive pluralist and the transcendental monist differ most profoundly. Most pragmatic thinkers have shifted away from the strictly epistemological to the hermeneutical strain of philosophical interpretation. This strain has received its latest expression in the work of individuals such as Thomas Kuhn, Donald Davidson, and Richard Rorty. The effect of this strain has been to move us away from questions of meaning disciplined by objects of reference to meaning as contextualized by discourses—narratives, theories, descriptive practices, and so forth. The hermeneuticist would hold that meanings are functions of linguistic usage and that two people mean the same thing by x only if they say, write, or act with respect to x in pretty much the same way.

The specter that haunts transcendental monism in all its forms is the specter of incommensurability. This involves the question whether in developing alternative theories, individuals are not creating discourses which so particularize the sense of terms as to render them untranslatable from one discourse to another. The linguistic and mythic structures of Lévi-Strauss, Schwartz's "common world of human experience" and "shared problematiques," as well as Hansen's *dao* all depend upon the assumption of a continuity of meaning from one theoretical discourse to another.

We find the most straightforward presentation of the issue of incommensurability in the Kuhnian distinction between "normal" and "abnormal" discourse. The former discourse is a complex of linguistic usages in which commensuration works since there are rules or conventions in place which would lead to an unforced consensus as to how disputes on the meaning or application of statements or principles might be reached. "Abnormal" discourse is realized when such conventions are no longer in place.

Transcendental monists want to suggest that logical rules constitute the primary conventions guaranteeing the commensuration of discourses. Thus the transcendental monist's assumption of meaning-continuity allows him to treat, for example, all the principal schools of classical China as if they were talking about the same thing whenever they employed the same locutions. Specifically, this allows him to understand terms such as *li* 禮 and *dao* 道 and *fa* 法 as suffering no profound alteration of meaning from, say, the beginning to the end of the classical period.

Clearly, the assumption of a continuity of meaning from one theory to another is a direct implication of transcendental monism. There would be little use in attempting to promote rational debate if it were assumed that the various schools so altered the meanings of the principal terms of their debates as to be talking past one another.

Over against this dialectical approach of the transcendental monist is the pragmatic approach, which accedes to the incommensurability of discourses whenever there is a lack of common conventions to which all parties to a dispute appeal in the attempt to adjudicate conflict. It is important to realize, of course, that the pragmatists' claim to the effect that we are unable to provide rational accounts of intertheoretical conversations does not mean that we must doubt that intertheoretical engagements lead to real changes either at the ideological level or within the more concrete realm of social praxis. The pragmatic approach only suggests that the nature and consequences of such interactions are seldom open to conscious articulation.

It was the recognition of the disharmonious consequences of interactions among the schools that led, for example, to the Confucian condemnation of the contentiousness of debating ideologues. The orthodox Chinese tendency to deemphasize dialectical debate in the quest for rational standards is quite likely based upon an implicit recognition of the problems of incommensurability. This recognition is a consequence of the belief, presumably grounded upon experience, that efforts at rational adjudication continually break down, and ideological conflicts threaten to continue indefinitely. This is a central theme in the Daoist literature as well: witness, *Zhuangzi 2.*

The pragmatic approach of the interpretive pluralist is less conditioned by the exclusive dialectic of "on the contrary" arguments and more by the inclusivity of the "on the other hand" style of argumentation. The pragmatist, by contrast with the transcendental monist, provides accounts which contextualize alternative arguments in such a manner as to foreground the consequences of their employment as interpretive devices. Our entire work, which began with a narrative of the development of classical Western culture, has consisted of such an act of contextualization.

One of the consequences of transcendental monism is that it quite often entails significant attempts to provide rational reconstructions of target cultures. Descriptive accounts of Chinese thought must buy into the dominant historiographical assumptions of the target culture if they are to present the character of intellectual culture in the most accurate light. On the other hand, rational reconstructions of the sort resulting from the presuppositions of the transcendental monist tend to be revisionist, not only with regard to the interpretation of this or that thinker or school, but with regard to the dominant historiographical assumptions as well.

Our pragmatic perspective allows us to accede, in at least a qualified manner, to such revisionist projects. Rational reconstructions, forwarded as self-consciously normative proposals, may be quite legitimate if they are presented without undue resort to "transcendental pretense." We may grant that whatever presently constitutes the dominant philosophical culture is a broadly political question. One has every right to propose what might seem better alternative constructions. The fault lies in claiming an undue generality for the provincial philosophical apparatus often employed in such projects. By importing substantial materials from their Western craft, transcendental monists effectively abandon the task of helping rebuild the Chinese vessel with its own planks.

If a Chinese thinker, for example, were to write a history of the classical period of Western philosophy—from, say, the pre-Sophistic thinkers to Aristotle—he would have a choice to make: Should he present the history in terms of the dominant internal trends of interpretation, which stress the rise of rationality—a transition from *mythos* to *logos* (from religion to philosophy and science)—or should he rather stress concerns emergent from his own cultural context, which might lead him to deplore such a transition as a movement from the aesthetic to the instrumental, from the imagistic to the conceptual, from the harmony of a ritual community to the organized chaos of conflicting opinions adjudicated by appeal to abstract principles and putatively transcendent laws?

If he chose the latter course, he might caution his readers that the dominant native interpretations of Western thought, as well as the Chinese interpretations that have bought into those native perspectives, constituted a dominant theory he has chosen to reject in favor of a more relevant approach (say, "A Heraclitean Interpretation of Western Thought") which will allow his Chinese readers to make sense of the Western tradition in a manner that could not have been possible before. Doubtless, Western readers who take their particular dominant interpretation for granted would find this Chinese interpretation rather quaint, and certainly skewed.[69]

Though there may indeed be pragmatic reasons for revisionist understandings of alternative cultures, it is essential that more descriptive constructions be retained.[70] We need first to understand how the mainstream Chinese might think of their intellectual history.

Only then may we responsibly move in the direction of revisionist reconstructions. Historical constructions keep revisionist theories from becoming narrative fantasies.

Pragmatists understand the consequences of meaning-change among theoretical orientations, and the attendant problem of incommensurability, in basically political terms. A thesis of many comparative treatments is that a chief difference between Chinese and Western cultures lies in the fact that, whereas the Chinese sought social harmony as a final value, we in the West pursued "Truth" as the ultimate goal. Surely, it makes more sense to acknowledge the fact that the chief goal of both Western and Chinese societies has been social harmony, though each society was encouraged to find harmony in its own peculiar way.

Logical, rational, objectivist discourse aimed at the discovery of Truth served the harmonious development of the Western world, beset as it was by a pluralism of languages and ethnicities. In pluralistic, highly individualistic societies, harmony cannot depend upon common myths, customs, and rituals. The achievement of harmony requires the ascent to the transcendental standard. It is here that one finds putative common ground among those of like minds. And that elusive capital T Truth, which stands above us all, serves as a cautionary standard preventing us, in spite of many lapses, from too easily sentencing the proponents of other doctrines to the stake.

Further, by separating theoretical discourse from its practical implementation, we in the West effectively tamed our ideological disputes by rejecting the notion that ideas are dispositions to act. Finally, by separating the private and public spheres we further guaranteed that the right of each individual to think as she or he pleases would not disrupt political stability and social harmony. Thus, the pragmatist would claim that our vaunted search for truth has been, first and foremost, a political stratagem for attaining social harmony.

It isn't very difficult to understand how the Chinese, characterized to a significantly greater degree than the Europeans by geographical and cultural isolation and, given the cultural impulse to identify with a specific locality, by a less severe linguistic and ethnic pluralism, should have found the secret of the socially harmonizing consequences of a guiding *dao* in the mitigation of theoretical activity and of stipulations aimed at the rejection of one theory in favor of another.

Most philosophers, no more or less arrogant than practitioners of other specialized pursuits, have tried to persuade themselves that their theories guide social and political practice rather than merely reflect it. A candid look at the real institutional differences between Chinese and Western "worlds" might teach us differently. Philosophers in both Chinese and Western societies are deeply implicated in, and serve as dependent variables of, the processes of political socialization. In China, where ideas, perceived as dispositions to act, have direct consequences upon the psychological, social, and political circumstances, the need to nurture, censor, discipline, and control ideological expression is far greater than in the West, where ideas, disjoined from dispositions and sundered from direct practical import, allow for a rather empty and inefficacious freedom of thought and expression.

There is every reason to believe that the "isolated schools" approach better served the aims of social harmony in China than would the "meaning-invariance hypothesis" of the transcendental monist. Nonetheless, it is perfectly possible for the pragmatic comparativist to give qualified support to transcendental monism. Though we are persuaded that, in general, we ought not export Western solutions to Chinese problems, it is clear that China is presently confronting modern liberal democratic societies in such a way that it must, willy-nilly, learn dialectical strategies. Revisionist histories of the sort produced by the transcendentalist highlight resources in China's past with which it may confront its international present. Isolation, whether at the cultural or theoretical level, may no longer be an option for China.

This is but to say that China is increasingly challenged to enter the modern world. And, not without some anxiety, China seems increasingly to welcome that challenge. Cultures as time-honored as is China's are indefinitely complex. There are resources in China's past to which the Chinese may appeal to make connections with the logic-abetted, scientistic, and technical West.

Thus, as pragmatists, we can affirm the value of both conservative (descriptive-interpretive) and revisionist (normative-interpretive) historiographies, each in their appropriate season. The latter without the former are (often) empty; the former without the latter are (sometimes) blind. While giving qualified praise to revisionist interpretations of Chinese thought, we should remain alert to the fact that one of the more jejune of the implications of transcendental monism carried to the extreme is that its practitioners somehow manage to believe that they understand their target cultures better than the members of those cultures understand themselves.

Our pragmatic, "on-the-other-hand" approach to the relations of Chinese and Western thought leads to this conclusion: We need attempts to construct the thought of China *in situ* as well as efforts to bring the Chinese into conversation with the world we occupy. There are pragmatic grounds for both sorts of account. On the one hand, China seems to need the modern world. If that is so, the Chinese require some assistance in discovering those resources within their own culture which resonate with the Enlightenment rationalism defining modernity. On the other hand, the new pragmatism, along with the new nominalism and historicism defining the postmodern sensibilities of many Anglo-European intellectuals, are strong signs of a shift in the intellectual dominant from the scientific to the literary model. This leads Western thinkers into closer proximity to the nominalist and historicist sensibilities of classical Chinese thought.

At the moment when China is entering the modern world, a large part of the West seems to be abandoning it. This means that there is real value in the (postmodern) West seeking comfort in the received traditions of a classical China with which it appears to resonate so well. On the other hand, the seeming inexorabilities of international economics and politics urge that a would-be modern China must learn the language of the Western Enlightenment. Thus, there is some real *pragmatic* value in transcendentalist reconstructions of Chinese thought which would help China confront the modern age.

3.3. Transcendental Pluralism

If we turn from the position of the transcendental monists to that of their pluralist counterparts, we shall again find that our pragmatic perspective will allow us to save much of what is presumed valuable in this position. We have already provided the beginnings of an account of the historical context from out of which the movement of transcendental pluralism arose in our discussions of the taxonomic implications of the Plato's Divided Line and Aristotle's doctrine of the Four Causes.

In recent decades, particularly in American philosophy, one of the chief philosophical problems has been that of pluralism, which requires that thinkers respond not only to issues of alternative beliefs and institutional practices but to the plurality of theoretical perspectives as well. The scientific-logical end of the spectrum leads to attempts to bring all elements of the culture under the protective rubric of the scientistic, if not the scientific, community. If pluralism is dealt with *dialectically*, the final aim is to achieve the "truth of the matter." The literary strain, on the other hand, has concerns closer to the sociopolitical commitments of a liberal democratic society. Here the aim is justifying the rights of others to hold beliefs other than one's own, rather than persuading others of the superiority of one's belief. In such a context we might surely expect that philosophy would have a pluralistic cast and that one principal activity might be that of accounting for the variety of philosophic opinions.

The movement we have identified as "transcendental pluralism" has developed from the speculations of two rather distinct philosophical programs. In his *World Hypotheses*, Stephen Pepper provided a set of semantic variables in the form of "root metaphors" ("similarity," "machines", "historic events," "organism") from which "world hypotheses could be discerned to have emerged."[71] Each of these hypotheses ("formism," "mechanism," "contextualism," "organicism") may be seen to ground a specific characterization of the world.

A second figure, Richard McKeon, employed concepts drawn from Aristotle's logical and rhetorical categories.[72] McKeon began his work with the isolation of variables analogized from Aristotle's doctrine of the Four Causes. These variables allow the articulation of semantic elements associated with any given theoretical orientation—"subject matters," "principles," "methods," and "interpretations." Further subtlety is achieved by distinguishing four types of subject matter, four sorts of principles, and so on. The exposition and analysis of these variables promotes an understanding of the distinctive contrasts among philosophical theories and provides, as well, some understanding of the variant consequences of these theories.

More recently, Robert Brumbaugh, a student of McKeon at the University of Chicago, worked out a subtle typology of philosophic visions employing Plato's Divided Line as the means of organization. Brumbaugh's Platonism provides an alternative to McKeon's Aristotelian perspective by offering a more metaphysically constructive proposal.[73]

No sooner had this movement been actualized, however, than a division occurred which advertised the tensions associated from the beginning with McKeon and Pepper's analyses. Is the activity of the metaphilosopher in fact but a raising of the ante with respect to the task of the search for truth? That is to say, should the taxonomic art seek to find a system which exhaustively incorporates all possible modes of speculation? The right-wing, transcendental pluralists believe just this. They seek a means of construing the possible ways of philosophizing, not only for this, but for all developed cultures. Left-wing, interpretive pluralists promote open-ended typologies and celebrate the plurality of interpretive perspectives to which philosophic thinking has given rise as pragmatically useful devices for handling intertheoretical and intercultural conversations.

A good example of transcendental pluralism employed as a comparative method is David Dilworth's *Philosophy in World Perspective—A Comparative Hermeneutic of the Major Theories*,[74] which is based upon the work of Dilworth's colleague, Walter Watson, himself heavily dependent on Richard McKeon's metaphilosophical project.[75] In his book, Dilworth considers the "universally esteemed works" of individuals such as Plato and Aristotle, Confucius and the Buddha, to be "products of greater minds" which "transcend the vicissitudes of time and circumstance [and] in the continuity of their influence . . . form the real bonds of our common humanity."[76]

Dilworth believes that since "philosophy has become global,"[77] the time is more than ripe for a characterization of the means of organizing and pointing up the relationships among the universally esteemed works produced by the geniuses of all major cultures. Dilworth's speculations take up the line of thought that began with the Enlightenment notion of "New Worlds," which energized "geographical explorations, scientific discoveries, and artistic and philosophic pursuits."[78] This line of thought extended through the principles of Nature in Newton and other Enlightenment thinkers, continued through Leibniz's search for "the principle of all principles" which would unite intellectual systems both synchronically and diachronically, and ended, finally, with Kant's promotion of philosophy to the rank of that foundational activity which was the only discipline capable of formulating concepts which are both universally significant and valid. Standing at the present terminus of this line,

Dilworth holds "that the time is ripe for constructing a theoretical framework that repossesses our premodern and modern, Eastern and Western, philosophical heritages."[79]

Dilworth claims that alternative cultural sensibilities give rise to the same basic fourfold family of theoretical orientations. Thus, though the histories of these alternative cultures are distinct, the forms of thought they produce belong to the same basic family of theories.

> Philosophies are intellectual products and processes of their own kind. The principle here seems to be that there are certain fundamental world views, occupying specific niches in the broader realm of discourse, that are reenacted in various philosophical configurations. This realm of discourse may develop historically along certain lines, but it is not necessarily historically generated. The forms of thought, rather, appear to represent eternal intellectual possibilities of the world.[80]

The various theories belonging to the basic fourfold family constitute *texts*. These texts are descriptive and/or interpretive of a "world" which is in some sense objective with respect to the various textual interpretations. According to Dilworth, "the world, which is not a text, appears in a philosophical text only in a particular ontological focus."[81] This Kantian claim concerning the manner in which the world transcends its interpretation is conjoined with the Aristotelian claim that there are four basic perspectives from which any subject may be viewed. The result of this conjunction is Dilworth's particular version of "transcendental pluralism."

The possibilities of theoretical interpretation offered by this type of transcendental pluralism are rooted in four "archic variables": (1) what is ultimately real; (2) the nature of concepts and their modes of association; (3) the theoretical, practical, and affective principles grounding the arguments of a text; and (4) the standpoint from which the text is constructed.

> Even when philosophers do not consciously make use of these four archic variables, they invoke them at an infrastructural and presuppositional level. A *sense of reality* and *its formal order*, together with an *authorizing perspective* and *grounding principles*, function as the transcendental conditions of every world-view.[82]

As is the case with McKeon's typological endeavors, each of these four variables—reality, method, perspective, and principle—is itself expressible in terms of four possible modes. For example, there are four methods: agonistic, logistic, dialectical, synoptic. Agonistic methods "obey the logic of contending forces, or of contrasting concepts, which cannot be reconciled through some higher agreement."[83] This is the Sophistic method associated with debate. Logistic method "reduce(s) complexes to simples,"[84] then proceeds by interrelating these simples—in the form of atoms, integers or elementary propositions, and so forth. This method is Democritean. Dialectical methods treat contrasting concepts or principles in such a manner as to subsume or reconcile them by appeal to a more coherent context. This was Plato's method. Synoptic method "converts a problem or subject matter into an analysis of generic and specific, relevant and irrelevant features. The whole and parts are seen together (hence synoptically) and treated as form and matter of the same holistic function."[85] Aristotle was a principal devotee of this method.

This version of McKeon's typology has 256 (4 × 4 × 4 × 4) permutations. One does not have to be a transcendentalist to see the value of this sort of metaphilosophy. Obviously we ourselves have taken taxonomic pluralism with some seriousness since, in the previous chapter, we went to some effort to demonstrate the manner in which the Platonic and Aristotelian fourfolds, as well as the elements of the tripartite structure of the *psyche*, have dominated the theoretical and practical activities of our cultural tradition almost from its beginnings.

The important differences between our treatment and that of Dilworth are, first, that we do not believe the fourfold has any transcendental status; these variables are, rather, historical products of philosophical speculation, which like the claims of univocal concepts of reason and logic in the dialectical perspective, have solely pragmatic value. Second, we believe that the pragmatic value of these interpretive perspectives with respect to the understanding of Chinese culture is extremely limited. Again, like the objectivist orientation presupposed by the dialectical perspective, the primary value of transcendental pluralism in comparative discussions is to alert the Chinese to the character of our intellectual culture. As for Westerners approaching the Chinese, such orientations as expressed by transcendental pluralists constitute relatively useless lumber which must be cleared away before we can move freely on Chinese highways of thought.

An example of how the McKeon approach, applied as incautiously as Dilworth applies it,[86] serves to strew the highway of comparative understanding with useless lumber is to be found in Dilworth's treatment of Confucian philosophy. According to Dilworth, Confucius' "archic profile" would be as follows:

Method:	Agonistic
Reality:	Essential
Principle:	Comprehensive
Perspective:	Diaphanic

Dilworth assumes that, in the absence of any overarching concepts or principles which might be used to synthesize the opposing propositions in a discussion, Confucius must be employing an "agonistic" method. He further assumes that appeals to the Way (*dao* 道) and the mandate of Heaven (*tian ming* 天命) illustrate Confucius' dependence upon a comprehensive principle and diaphanic perspective. *Dao* and *tian ming* are grounding principles which apply to each and every particular without exception—thus, they are *comprehensive*. Further, both *dao* and *tian ming* suggest that the authorizing perspective from which Confucius speaks is a transcendent one. Finally, Confucius' "essential" sense of reality is illustrated by claims made on his behalf that he embodied and transmitted the tradition. That is to say, the tradition is "essentialized" by Confucius.

In the first place, claiming that the Confucian "text" is coherent enough to serve as a "theory" requires the assumption that theory construction is a transcultural activity. We are not speaking here of an informal orientation or perspective, but of systematic vision interpretable in terms of variables associated with Aristotle's Four Causes. Our Western tradition has a long history of discussions that employ these variables, or analogies to them, such that we can coherently ask after a thinker's "method" or the nature of his "principles." The use of such language with regard to Confucius strains the matter overmuch.

Were we to treat the visions of the Chinese thinkers as theories in the sense of the term that we have come to employ, then we would have to presume the sort of dialogical or dialectical interactions among these visions familiar in our tradition as means of the mutual adjustment of views. This would lead us into the one of the fallacies of Chad Hansen's interpretation of Chinese thought alluded to above. Rejecting the "isolated schools" approach in favor of an interpretation of the growth of Chinese thought by recourse to dialectical engagements seriously misconstrues the actual manner in which the views of Chinese thinkers were adjusted one with respect to the other. Transcendental pluralism thus turns out to be a Trojan horse within which are hidden all sorts of agents capable of destabilizing, if not destroying, the indigenous balance of Chinese intellectual culture.

Further, comprehensive principles, diaphanic perspectives, and essential ontologies assume operative notions of transcendence. In functioning as both the comprehensive principle and diaphanic perspective,[87] the "mandate of Heaven" is presumed to be a transcendent principle and ground. But as we have argued in our work on Confucius,[88] notions of transcendence are inapplicable to the interpretation of Confucian thinking. Also, an essentialist ontology, which argues that essences are realized in nature,[89] precisely by its presumption of "essences" (the presumption, that is, that forms define the facts) separates form and fact. Again, this presumption leads to a misconstrual of the Confucian position.

It is not that we find the transcendental pluralist altogether unhelpful in comparative work. One might wish to begin with such an approach, using the categories as an interpretive pluralist might to see how far they seem to apply. This would involve, among other things, asking indigenous interpreters of Confucius if such an approach is helpful. In this present case, that question essentially reduces to "How do you like Confucius in a suit and tie?" It is true that some Chinese, especially those who wish to assist in the Westernization of China, might warm readily to this version of Confucius.

There is a certain pragmatic value to be realized in translating ideas from an exoteric culture into the standard idioms of one's own culture. But, if this is done in the absence of attempts to celebrate "the otherness of the other," more harm than good is likely to be done. It is important to recognize that one always begins with one's own ethnocentric context; it is equally important that one not accede to ending there.

4. INTERCULTURAL VAGUENESS

One of the surest signs that Enlightenment rationalism is losing its hold upon Anglo-European cultures is the changed attitude toward the lexicon. Dictionaries and encyclopedias, bulwarks of the Enlightenment, have been torn from their moorings. On the one hand, words are dissolving into their histories, their etymologies, while on the other, their meanings are ramified by myriad intertextual loci. As a consequence, dictionaries now serve primarily as compendia of ambiguities.

The collapse of the dictionary is symptomatic of our altered conception of thinking. Formerly we were accustomed to giving accounts, making sense, being *rational*, either by tracing the objective history of our subject or by analyzing its putatively logical structure. Our lexicons were created to serve as repositories of paradigmatic models of such accountings. Etymological accounts of a term tell the story of its semantic development while formal definitions characterize the properties common to the members of the class to which the item named by the term currently belongs.

Presently, however, neither genetic nor morphological accounts provide us much satisfaction. Few of us consult a dictionary any longer to certify a univocal sense of x. We are far more likely to try to uncover the unfamiliar senses of x that have been elided or ignored, the embarrassing denotations of x that undermine accepted usage, the diverse associations that constitute the almost always incoherent history of x. The more perverse among the lexical Luddites are particularly delighted to discover among the arcane advices of the Oxford English Dictionary that, once upon a time, x had the meaning "*not-x.*"

Continual challenges to this anarchic mentality on the part of the dogged remnant of the Enlightenment force us again and again into the fruitless dialectics of the relativity debates. The closed shop mentality of all parties to these debates—absolutists, relativists, and skeptics—ensures that nothing will be resolved.

We hope to avoid as much as possible the tedious idiom of relativism. If we are to do so, however, we must provide some plausible strategy justifying this luxury. For the pragmatic approach we have outlined would seem open to the antirelativist's critique since it denies that there are objective grounds for determining what an adequate orientation or hypothesis might be.[90] Our defense against the charge of any of the pernicious forms of theoretical and cultural relativism involves the reinterpretation of the meanings of both "theory" and "culture."

4.1. The Value of Vagueness

In the following paragraphs we intend to present a model of culture and intercultural conversation which entails a claim that at first will appear preposterous, but which, on reflection, might come to seem rather obvious. Our claim is that there is no plausible argument distinguishing, in any final sense, cultures and their languages. The conclusion we draw from this is that there is only one language (at most) and one culture (at most), and that many of the paradoxes involved in attempting to interpret across cultural boundaries are dissolved when one recognizes that there is but a single field of significances which serves as background from which individual cultures and languages are foregrounded. This conclusion makes intercultural conflict functionally equivalent to intertheoretical conflict extant within a single language or culture.

The paradoxical tone of this claim is intensified when we state that we are by no means arguing for anything like universalism. The universalist might hold there is finally but one culture because there is ultimately but one world which, with the help of logic and right reason, we shall one day be able to describe in a manner that yields consensus across cultural boundaries. That is *not* our argument. We shall urge, rather, that small-c cultures are but particular manners in which the vague field of principles and practices constituting capital-C Culture is variously focused. The recognition and cultivation of intertheoretical and intercultural vagueness would, we contend, offer a way around futile discussions of relativism.

We shall begin our argument with the simple notion of "vagueness." It is, of course, a term of art introduced by C. S. Peirce. We shall use it essentially as Peirce did, to refer to phenomena, concepts, or theories, which are open to rich and diverse interpretations. For our purposes we may delineate two senses of vagueness—*conceptual* and *historical*.

Unstipulated concepts are often vague in our sense of the term. We have shown this with respect to the diverse theoretical orientations that arose in classical Western culture. *Nature* thus can mean "atoms and space," or "teleogically interrelated organisms," or "mathematical patterns and relationships," or "the external surround as a conventional object of rhetorical definition." *History* can indicate the unfolding of ideas and movements, or accounts of physical causes for this or that set of events, or heroic chronicles focusing upon individual greatness, or narratives associated with the professionalized discourses of art, science, ethics, or religion. *Freedom* can mean "free choice amidst limiting circumstances," or "knowledge," or "the power of the will," or "the realization of determination." *Reason* can be identified with the discovery and manipulation of essences or logical finalities, or the discernment and coordination of ends in nature, or the discovery of efficient and material causes, or the employment of persuasive rhetoric. Each of these terms, until its meaning is successfully stipulated, is semantically vague.

Historical vagueness is a consequence of our ability to provide many interesting and, in their proper season, important narrative accounts, each of which includes some items and excludes others, renders some marginal and others central. Productive historical vagueness is realized to the extent that, first, we make every effort to save these accounts, banking them until the season of their relevance; and, second, we refuse in any final sense to privilege one account over others by cultivating tolerance in the active entertainment of alternative narratives.

The phenomenon of vagueness entails the consequence that whereas an idea may be in principle specifiable within a theoretical or narrative context, in the absence of such a context it lacks a univocal sense. Its practical meaning in demotic discourse, therefore, is vague with respect to any number of theories or narratives. It exists as an accreted cluster of associations. It is, therefore, a "cluster concept." Part of the thrust of this chapter is to suggest that the aim of intertheoretical conversations within a culture is the same as that of intercultural conversations: to protect the vagueness of the notions central to the interactions as a means of serving the pragmatic ends of conversation.

Vague notions as concept clusters lack semantic coherence. Their significance is tropic—imagistic, metaphorical, even oxymoronic.

Properly appreciated, the interwoven conceptual and narrative strands of significance form a diachronous web of interpretations. This is the web of culture itself. The privileging of a single narrative or conceptual element construes the whole as one of its parts. Thus, in an objectively vague culture the search for univocity is a special case of the employment of synecdoche.

Owning so many answers to so few questions inverts the priorities associated with the search for knowledge. That search now is most satisfying when we find ourselves moving away from sterile clarity, away from coherent understanding, into an increasingly richer muddle. One ought not really wish to move from darkness to light if our journey ends at a thousand points of light from which we are allowed to select only one. Properly understood, the world is vague and getting vaguer. *Per obscurum ad obscurius.*

Those victimized by hyperconsciousness suffer not only from an excess of history but equally from a surplus of stipulated meanings. Therefore, those who would avoid contemporary forms of the "anxiety of influence"[91] by recourse to vagueness must fray the boundaries of our sharply delineated concepts and fragment their polished surfaces in order to rewin the original richness of the language. Such a return to the origins of imaginative richness requires something like Nietzsche's program of "active forgetting." And since most of the important kinds of forgetting (repression, sublation, incorporation) are, in fact, acts of remembering, of dissolving and reconstituting the elements of imagination and sense, the production of vagueness achieves a principal aim of active forgetting—namely, a world in which the truth is the sum total of interpretations of its object.

With regard to our most important concepts, we should strive for vagueness by acceding to the Chan Buddhist dictum: "Avoid choosing by choosing both (or *all*)." Accepting terms as cluster concepts means accepting their meanings together in a single gestalt in which all meanings are potentially foregrounded. The consequence of this activity is that one is propelled from reason in the narrow sense to imagination and thus is forced to accede to the replacement of logical by aesthetic coherence.[92]

The appeal to vagueness does not preclude the stipulation of ideas or principles in certain contexts. Though never the sole aim of speculation and analysis, clarity is often of real pragmatic value. Nonetheless, with respect to such acts of stipulation, one never forgets the intransigent richness and ambiguity of the language.

Perhaps our view will appear less strange and paradoxical if we provide a simple illustration. Consider two sets of lovers, each of whom mutually pledge their devotion. Let us say that the members of one couple then proceed to articulate precisely what each means by the word "love." The other couple, however, remains content with the simple declaration. It is perfectly conceivable that the stipulations involved in the first instance can lead to real ideological conflict. Such conflict is less likely in the second case. What is the crucial difference? The second couple may marry and live in relative happiness for the rest of their lives even if, were the "truth" to be known, their unarticulated understandings of the word "love" are potentially quite divergent. The reason for this is that there is sufficient vagueness in one's actions and expressions to allow for a harmonious overlapping of practical import, as long as they do not receive conscious interpretation.

Should we really praise the intellectual integrity of the first couple, even though it were to lead directly to separation, and condemn the harmony of the second couple since it is based upon semantic ignorance?

We shall view intellectual culture as a vague field of significances open to articulation for this or that purpose, but existing primarily *in potentia*. The proponent of vagueness substitutes "and" for "or" in any listing of possible meanings, judging that any insistence upon the mutual exclusiveness of variant meanings must be motivated by what the postmodern critic and Chan master alike would claim to be a persistent but arbitrary dependence upon logical consistency and coherence. This persistence, both would assert, is far more a consequence of the desire for ego-stability and self-identity than of getting at any truth of the matter. A consequence of asserting *oxymoronically*, or of meaning *inconsistently*, can certainly be destabilization.

The ad hoc device of "defining our terms" or "getting our story straight" prior to the act of communication is unavoidably duplicitous. In our age of sophisticated metaconsciousness, this has much the same effect as a prosecutor listing for the jury those crimes committed by the defendant for which he is *not* on trial. We cannot help but mean more, or less, or differently, than we consciously intend. There is a surplus of meaning in every act of communication.

We do not wish to appear flippant. We take the condition of cultural vagueness to be an easily recognizable consequence of the collapse of the Enlightenment sensibility. Ideas yield themselves up to their opposites (Hegel); truth is the sum of mutually incoherent interpretations (Nietzsche); true words entail their opposites (Laozi); a cigar is never just a cigar (*pace* Freud).

4.2. Reason, Rhyme, and Relativity

Whatever one considers reason in its transcendental guise to be, it is hardly the sole or even the primary source of meaningfulness. The imaginative, often spontaneous, juxtapositions of events called "coincidence" or "correlation"; the juxtapositions of sense and sound associated with the parabolic, elliptical, and metaphorical language of the poet; the sharply focused trauma of mystical experience, often accompanied by the obscure language of oracles and revelations: these are all extra- or infrarational sources of the richest meaning.

In the search for meaningfulness, there is the vague notion of reason and its equally vague supplement—its *rhyme*. The rational thinker, at the end of reason's rope, reaches out to metaphor. The poet, exhausting rhyme, descends by that same rope. The strictly nonrational, the rhyme of reason, is associated with myth, poetry, and rhetoric. A richly vague notion of rationality, untutored by the transcendental impulse, contains both rhyme and reason. This broader sense of "reasonableness" allows for the parity of myth and rational narrative, of metaphor and logic.

Reason finds its rhyme in Plato's myth of Er, the imagery of the cave, the chariot, the analogies of the Sun and the Good. In a more extended sense, Plato is rhyme to Aristotle's reason, and vice versa. And Democritus the rhyme of both. Rhyme is reason's putatively meaningful other. A richly vague notion of rhyme or reason contains the senses of both. Together reason and rhyme offer the sum of meaningfulness and the tools for achieving it.

A vague concept of rationality, in both its conceptual and historical senses, must permit the rhyme of reason into its realm of associations. But productive vagueness is difficult to maintain in the face of the transcendental impulse. Obedience to criteria such as clarity, consistency, and coherence leads to exclusivist attempts to get at the true meaning or the correct narrative, even though among the educated in our highly self-conscious age there is an extensive awareness of most, if not all, of the principal meanings associable with a given term, or the alternative narrative accounts of any event.

Increasingly, survivors of the Enlightenment are disillusioned by the recognition that contemporary Western culture is decidedly *horizontal*. Poets and philosophers no longer offer a ladder of knowledge which may be used to arrive at significant values and understandings. Each of us is forced to move along the surface of a web with diverse strands, leading in multiple directions. This is intellectual culture: a complex network of strands of action and interpretation, each with its distinctive causes and conditions, anchorings and functionings, each individually understandable, but incomprehensible as a whole.

Confronted with such a mélange of values, interests, and ideologies, each of which defines its own conceptual and historical route of interpretation, individuals motivated by the transcendentalist impulse have but two choices—a provincial affirmation of dogmatic certitude with regard to one true theory, or the raising of rationality to the metalevel by constructing the one true theory of the sorts of possible theories. In the face of an intransigent parity of meanings and narratives, reason operating on exclusivist principles cannot but confound its own ends, either through a narrow, and thereby unpersuasive, dogmatism which yields the universality of reason, or through a taxonomic dogmatism which yields its unity.

The last desperate defense of the transcendentalist facing the inexorable pluralism of late-modern cultures is to level the charge of "relativism" against any who would abandon the Enlightenment project. But, truth be told, struggles over relativism are in fact family quarrels among the two sorts of transcendentalist. Taxonomists who defend a form of relativism which entails the irrefutability of one theory by another, thereby holding up the shield of Incommensurability, are confronted by the transcendental monist wielding the sword of Meaning-Invariance.

This is hardly a battle of the Titans. From the perspective of the pragmatist, it is rather like two gnats circling one another for the kill. Arguments about meaning-change or meaning-invariance, as they apply to issues of intertheoretical communication, are broadly irrelevant to the actual circumstances which define the sphere of praxis to which theories are meant to be applicable. After all, it is not how one theory translates into the language of another, but how each accounts for, translates into, or, better, *stimulates* practical endeavors that testifies to a theory's relative success or failure. It is only when theorists forget what their theories are for, that they can make such arcane issues as commensurability, or the lack thereof, central to their concerns. It is for this reason that those thinkers operating from the pragmatic perspective are somewhat bemused by being charged with relativism.

Richard Rorty presents in the clearest manner why pragmatists are immune to the charge of pernicious relativism. He does this by suggesting that we recognize a distinction responsible thinkers always make in practice—namely, the distinction between *real* theories and merely *philosophical* theories. Real theories are specific formulations relevant to the practical problems in politics, the sciences, and so forth. Philosophical theories are semantic contexts which contextualize more specialized theories.[93]

Transcendental pluralists organize alternative semantic systems which will relativize the meanings of intrasystematic terms. Further, these theories will be found formally incommensurable. Thus there will be no decision procedures permitting the selection of a best theory. *Enter the specter of relativism.* But when it comes to the question as to how alternative theories may be applied to solve specific problems, issues of incommensurability fade into the background. The merits of the alternative theoretical proposals will be decided through discussion, debate, and actual trial applications which will lead, in admittedly the most fallibilist of manners, to decision and action. *Exit the specter of relativism.*

The pragmatist's approach to the issue of relativism is simply to remind her accusers that the charge applies only to pure theorists, whose principal aim is the conceptual articulation and defense of propositional truth. The individual most guilty of relativism, therefore, is the transcendental monist who lays claim to truth only to be confronted by a member of his same claque making an alternative dogmatic claim. Neither finding himself to be either victor or vanquished in the logical *agon*, both hapless folk engage in relativism by default. It is this "default relativism" of transcendental thinkers, rather than the bugbear relativism attributed to the pragmatist, that provides the real import of the term.

It is good to recall here that even though the pragmatist eschews the two transcendentalist approaches, and thereby avoids the strictures of bugbear relativism, she remains committed to interpretive pluralism. The pragmatist celebrates the plurality of approaches to our central questions and problems on the practical grounds that the more tools we have at our disposal, the more likely are we to find the tool best suited for the task at hand.

The pluralism of theories presently indigenous to intellectual culture, though an obstacle for the seeker of objective truth, is a most useful building block for those engaged in the effort to relate principles and practice. Pragmatic philosophers, conscious of theoretical pluralism, become (nontranscendental) metaphilosophers. Under the sway of this "metamentality" we are able to entertain a variety of diverse, mutually incompatible ways of thinking. If this activity is employed as a means, not of seeking abstract truth, or ideational consensus, but for the promotion of a context within which communication and action are facilitated, then pluralism will have served us well.

The comparative philosopher, at least as much as the intracultural thinker, must be aware that the important questions do not so much involve the translation of a term from one semantic context to another, but its translation into (or from) practice. That is to say, in addition to questions such as "What do you mean by that?" we need to ask "Would you show me what you mean?" and "Why did you do that?" We must be at least as concerned with the rationalization of practices and their employment as illustrations of ideas and beliefs as we are with "defining our terms."

Thus, the sort of vagueness for which we are arguing is as useful at the level of practice as it is at the level of theory. There are many-to-one and one-to-many relations between ideas and practices. Many ideas may elicit or interpret a single practice, and many practices may be justified by a single idea. It is this fact that makes it unproductive to stress cognitive consensus in a democratic society. We need to depend upon vague notions such as "freedom" and "justice" and "equality" which may be specified in a variety of ad hoc manners and to which appeal may be made to justify a wide range of activities.

The genius of North American society from its beginnings has been its affirmation of pluralism. This pluralism has, philosophically, been couched in aesthetic rather than cognitive terms and thus has provided a distinctive approach to issues of intertheoretical and intercultural comparison.[94] In the absence of criteria for articulating one-to-one relations between ideas and their semantic content, and between ideas and actions, or actions and ideas, choices among theoretical principles may be made on grounds other than the strictly rational. These other grounds are *aesthetic*. The arguments of the antirelativists that work against a cognitively based epistemology are, as we shall now argue, broadly irrelevant to an aesthetically grounded orientation.[95]

Cultural relativism entails the view that meaningfulness is relative to specific cultures rather than determined by a priori structures of some Transcendental Ego, Laws of Logic, or Absolute Syntax. The apparently paradoxical character of such understanding is generated by the naive assumption that meaningfulness is encountered most unambiguously in the terms of natural languages.

The claim that meaning is relative to a specific culture or cultures has lately come to be expressed in something like this manner:[96] "Language S_1 relativizes concepts $T_{1...n}$ and Language S_1 relativizes concepts $R_{1...n}$." The problem is, of course, that the preceding English sentence entails the consequence that (assuming S_1 is the English language) S_1 relativizes both $T_{1...n}$ and $R_{1...n}$. Thus, the intent of the English sentence, "'Knowledge' and *zhi* (知) have quite distinctive conceptual contents" is compromised by the fact that the norms of the English language and culture determine the meanings of the sentence, including of course, the English meaning of the Chinese word *zhi*.

One really does not quite know what to make of the arguments that demonstrate the impossibility of radical translation. They have a certain logical cogency. But their persuasiveness is of the type possessed by arguments to the effect that bumble bees cannot fly. We do after all make the effort to communicate across cultures. And we do seem, on pragmatic grounds, to have greater or lesser success in these endeavors, at least in the sense that there are often useful consequences attending our efforts.

Our view has significant connections with analyses such as that of Michel Foucault, whose doctrine of culturally and historically grounded discursive formations which establish certain relations between power and knowledge does not in itself preclude productive comparisons of alternative discourses. Such views depend upon the notion of pragmatic import, which entails the view that meanings of terms have less to do with the syntax and semantics of the language and more to do with the practical import they have within the cultural milieu under consideration. It is the rhetorical force rather than the logical structure of a language that permits communication.

The paradoxes of intercultural translation depend upon a rather rigid sense of the centrality of logic and rationality. If we say "all claims to truth are relative," have we in fact committed a logical fallacy? That is, have we really claimed absoluteness for our statement? Such worries are only for the logically obsessive. Communication across cultural boundaries does not represent this sort of logical *agon*. We somehow get a feel for the expressions of one another and the proof of this is measured in terms of the effect of the communication. We can never know that we meant the same thing—that is, that we each referred to some common *tertium quid*—but so what? We can no more do that in personal communications between members of the putatively same conceptual and linguistic universe.

4.3. Is There More Than One Culture?

If we are finally to develop a context for intercultural conversation, we must confront the problematic status of the term *culture*. This can be done most straightforwardly by asking whether it is reasonable to assume there to be more than one culture? If this question is to be addressed in the popular idiom of Anglo-European philosophic discourse, we must speak not of "mind" or "experience" but of "language." Thus the question whether there is one culture or many entails the query, "Is there more than a single language?"

By attempting to define a natural language, one is already isolating, identifying, and characterizing elements presumed to be different among languages. But such an endeavor implies that translation has already taken place. Transformation rules, syntactical structures, semantic contextualizations, are common elements uncommonly applied within each language. The problem lies, of course, with the assumption that context demands coherence, and if logical coherence cannot be demonstrated, there must be alternative contexts in evidence. Thus, semantic, syntactical, or grammatical incoherence would suggest alternative structures and, therefore, alternative languages.

On these grounds, one could easily argue that there are as many languages as language users. Defense of this "idiolect view" would be couched in much the same terms as arguments concerning "other minds." If interpersonal communication is deemed problematic, it must be because the way one comes to be assured of the character of one's own self is not thought to be guaranteed with respect to the knowing of others. This is tantamount to the assumption that linguistic behavior of the sort that presumes a distinction between communicants is both semantically and referentially problematic. Whether there is synonymy is not decided by asking whether different verbal locutions have the same meaning, but whether two utterances of the putatively same locution carry the same sense.

Perhaps each of us owns his or her own language. These private languages then beg for translation each into the others. But, of course, no transformational rules or translation equivalents could be possible under such circumstances. This solipsism results from Cartesianism gone bad. The recognition that such a consequence is inevitable on the Cartesian model leads to behaviorist and instrumental models of language which presumably do not require that one look inside one's own or another's "mind" or "experience" for "meanings."

A second understanding of language would have it that in some important sense there is only one language, of which all putatively distinct languages are adumbrations and approximations. Whereas the idiolect view entails the consequence that communication is impossible because no one naturally means the same as another and that the act of translation cannot be successfully performed, defenders of a universal language would claim that the potentialities of communication are always greater than we believe, and that translation in the strictest of senses is unnecessary since there is no radically alternative language into which or from which translations could be made.

The universalist seeks both logical and grammatical constants. When such constants are discovered they are used as norms by which to construe the grammars of natural languages. The result of this approach is a syntactical and semantical rationalism which perpetuates the Enlightenment ideal of a universal language and logic.

Such an understanding of language is the motor of that cultural chauvinism associated with Modernity. It is not just an ideal language, but the culture of such a language as well, that serves as norm. For the moderns, that ideal culture is best approximated at this stage of history by the Western cultural milieu shaped by science and rational technologies.

Between these two extremes lies the conception of "language communities" within social or cultural contexts which are constituted by alternative rules. In the model Wittgenstein proposes, though there is never any final assurance that two people are playing precisely the same game, this must be the presumption in many cases. What makes two games similar is that they both have rules. The specificity of the rules of different games, however, militates against participation in both games at once. The context which contains mutually incoherent games without attempting reduction or sublation may be called "culture." Culture, therefore, cannot be defined by a coherence of ideals or principles, concepts or values.

Obviously the incoherence among many sets of rule-defined behaviors in the same culture does not per se make the culture incoherent. But an extremely high degree of professionalization could in principle lead to a situation in which, effectively, no ordinary uses of language remain. If there is no viable realm of demotic discourse, cultural incoherence is complete since the constitutive rules of alternative discourses exclude communication across rule-defined boundaries. We see an illustration of this phenomenon in the contrast of alternative axiomatic systems in terms of which anything like intertheoretical vagueness is consciously excluded.

Internal incoherence within a culture suggests the possibility of specialized cultures no longer emergent from, nor dependent upon, a single natural language. The coherence among the practices of physical scientists in America, France, Britain, Germany, Mexico, India, China, Japan, and so forth, indicates that the physical sciences may form a large segment of a scientific culture which is not meaningfully reducible to any particular natural language. Likewise, a transnational culture of literature, of religion, of art, of philosophy, defined by the professional interests of a plurality of countries, may presently exist in at least an adumbrated form.

Holistic or coherence-based interpretations of culture tend to be reductive in one of two manners: Either they reduce cultural significances to the formal rules of a single cultural interest, or they formalize a general theory of the interrelations of the natural and cultural sciences, and present this theory as the paradigmatic characterization of the culture.

Perhaps the best way to understand the vagueness of culture is to say that there is *at most* one language and *at most* one culture. The engagement between two cultures, then, is an articulation of alternative importances within a single (incoherent) complex. In this manner, one needs make no drastic distinction among different cultures or their languages.[97]

A productively vague model of cultures would construe them as local distortions of a general field which is itself without specifiable boundary conditions. This focus/field model contrasts readily with both positivist and idealist models by offering an alternative sense of abstraction. On the field/focus interpretation, culture is objectively vague in the sense discussed above. Any "part" abstracted from the whole adumbrates the whole. As a consequence, the partiality of the elements of a cultural field advertises the complexity of the field. In place of precise "locus," one employs vague "focus." The focus/field model suggests that culture is potentially, and almost always is in fact, a Chaos. Chaos is best construed as the sum of all orders which is itself not an order. It is Nietzsche's world wherein Truth is the sum of all interpretations.

Depending upon the degree of formalizability, the relatively stable distentions in the field of capital-C Culture, which we recognize as small-c cultures, are themselves incommensurable. Likewise the distentions within a small-c culture associated with the habits and institutions, the theoretical constructs, world-views, the cultural interests, the aims and activities, may themselves be to a significant degree incommensurable. Thus, as a complex aggregate of significances, Culture cannot be characterized by coherence.

Small-c cultures are indefinitely flexible. We must presume that each image, concept, proposition, or thematic extant in one culture might well be rendered in the language of another. The limits of this principle apply to the issues of *importance* only. We must presume that any x may be characterized in the idiom of an alternative discourse, but still thought trivial by the users of that discourse. If sufficiently trivialized, there is no plausible reason to believe that its meaning has been retained, and, from a pragmatic perspective, no reason to think of it as the same x.

Capital-C Culture refers to a vague complex of significances focused in accordance with a variety of interests. In Anglo-European cultures these interests are called aesthetic, ethical, scientific, religious. Within a single culture there are priorities of interest, which may of course change from time to time. The boundaries of these cultural interests are potentially as vague and permeable as are the boundaries of cultures and languages themselves. If the small-c culture which contextualizes intercultural conversations is that of a transcultural interest such as mathematics, physics, or biology, intercultural conversations may be enhanced by a high incidence of specialized discourse. However, most intercultural conversations, particularly those associated with aesthetic, moral, and religious interests, depend upon a sufficient degree of vagueness. Thus, intercultural communication may have little need to respond to the logical paradoxes of incommensurability except insofar as we are dealing with conversations presupposing alternative professionalized or axiomatized language.

Intercultural communication patterned by productive vagueness is not a strictly rational process, but a *reasonable* one. Such communication is not logical but *analogical*, a clumsy process of fits and starts which involves the juxtaposition of distinctive feelings and intentions, images and actions. To communicate is to articulate differences, and the procedures involved in such articulation are themselves not wholly open to articulation.

We shall now proceed to offer a narrative of the development of classical Chinese culture which will argue for the pragmatic relevance of the interpretation of culture as a vague field of significances assessed on aesthetic rather than logical grounds. In the course of this narrative, we shall attempt to clear a path leading to an understanding of the classical Chinese cultural sensibility. We shall be successful in this endeavor to the extent that we are able to avoid the imposition of those extraneous and potentially distorting concepts, categories, and methods which, appealing to the metaphor of "useless lumber," we have highlighted in our previous discussions.

CHAPTER THREE

Extending the
—— *Circle* ——

A path becomes a path by walking it.
A thing is made a thing by being so-called.
Why are things so?
They are so because they are so.
Why are they not something other than what they
    are?
They are not something else because they are not.

Zhuangzi

Might one say that the Chinese civilization, the
strength of which has always been in its sense of balance, has seen reason in its right proportions from the
beginning?

A. C. Graham

To this point we have tried to show there are among our cultural
resources unsown seeds and discarded scraps which, had they
been employed as dominant interpretive categories, would have led to
a significantly different cultural self-consciousness than that associated with what we have termed second problematic thinking. In
addition to noting, with respect to the shape of our cultural milieu,
that *it could all have been different*, we are now going to set out to
show that in classical China, things *were* quite different. For classical
China effectively resorted to something at least similar to those very
interpretations which were either rejected or left undeveloped within
our own culture.

In addition to promoting an understanding of Chinese process-thinking on its own terms, this essay might allow one to discover in the Chinese exercise of correlativity a suggestive resource for the development of languages of "difference," "otherness," and "plurality" currently sought by the postmodern critiques of "logocentrism" and "the language of presence," and by the movement of the new pragmatism toward a defense of philosophical and sociopolitical pluralism.

There is a difficulty which must be addressed right away: If we are correct in our (surely rather safe) assumption that the causal or rational mode of thinking is privileged in our tradition, then any difficulty in understanding some parts of what follows must largely derive from our readers construing our correlative language in terms of their causal language, thereby effecting a *reductio ad absurdum*.

As Richard Rorty has argued persuasively,[1] ethnocentrism is an unavoidable accompaniment of any responsible thinker's attempts to reach beyond his ken. This fact has been obscured among Western thinkers, since one of the strongest beliefs emerging from the Enlightenment is that of the universality of reason. The most profound expression of our own ethnocentrism, therefore, is to be found in the rejection of provincial beliefs tied to a particular ethnos in favor of the belief that science and rationality will eventually provide the standards for all humankind.

A paradoxical consequence of the peculiar content of Western ethnocentrism, involving as it does a belief in the universal nature of rationality, is a profound suspicion of ethnocentrism. But belief in the universality of reason is, on reflection, a provincial belief. We, no less than the confessedly provincial Chinese, are deeply ethnocentric. Moreover, since we mask our ethnocentrism with claims to universality, ours is doubtless the more pernicious form. No one is more provincial than he who insists that his own personal beliefs be held by everyone. The irony is hardly to be missed: We in the modern West are among the most dogmatically ethnocentric peoples who have ever walked the earth.

Fortunately, such ethnocentrism, once it is exposed, can yield itself up to the search for practicable ideas and programs beyond one's culture. The fluidity of the distinction between the intracultural and the intercultural, and the attendant fluidity of the distinction among languages, implies that our beliefs and desires, if not an unbroken web across cultures, can at least emerge as a quilt productively patched together from the fabrics of alternative sensibilities.

The phenomenon of intercultural vagueness ensures that our default ethnocentrism need have no pernicious consequences. For as we have argued, the coexistence in Western cultural beginnings of two fundamental problematics renders our culture productively vague in the sense that we have in our cultural inventory, illustrations of a sort of thinking analogous to that which dominated classical Chinese culture.

We are now to test the thesis that a strain of what has come to be called "correlative thinking," which has constituted the recessive modality of thought in our Western tradition, in fact dominated the development of classical Chinese culture, and moreover, persists as the most significant mode of thinking in the contemporary Chinese world.

1. ACOSMOTIC "BEGINNINGS"

The civilizations that share the Indo-European group of languages are certainly many and diverse, but by virtue of trade, travel, war, population movements, and the imperceptible dissemination of ideas entailed by such contact, they have over past millennia developed a cultural family resemblance. Moving exclusively among these cognate Indo-European languages can lull us into a sense of shared conceptual ground that is illusory when addressing truly exotic traditions.

As we saw with the discussion of the Western cosmogonic tradition, the particular understanding of "beginnings," whether they pertain to the cosmos as a whole or to the creatures that populate it, has a determinative influence over the way a culture comes to conceive of the nature and order of things. In fact, it is no exaggeration to say that "causal thinking" is rooted in a certain kind of cosmogonic speculation. In a cosmos the totality of things is necessarily ordered, and hence each thing is in principle explicable. The explanation is patterned after the causal agency responsible for the construal of cosmos from chaos.

We must pause here to clarify our terminology. It is embarrassing both to us and to the language we perforce must employ in this discussion to admit there is no word to describe the difference between the classical Chinese and Western traditions vis-à-vis the disposition toward the existence of a single-ordered world. Traditionally, we employ the term *cosmogony* to deal with questions of the origin of the cosmos and *cosmology* to deal with questions concerning the nature or order of the cosmos. It is possible to be "acosmogonic" in one's thinking, and yet still defend cosmological views. This would entail the claim that the order of the cosmos is without an initial origin or sustaining principle. It is also possible to be "acosmological." One would thus be denying that there is anything like a cosmos in the sense of a world ordered in any particular way. And, what amounts to the same thing, one would be asserting that there are many world orders (*kosmoi*).

It strains our vocabulary sufficiently if we try to pluralize cosmos. To have continual recourse to barbarisms such as *acosmogonical* and *acosmological* adds too much of a burden to the language. Possible associations with *acosmism* further discourage the use of these terms.[2] We propose, therefore, to employ the following neologism: The classical Chinese are primarily *acosmotic* thinkers. By "acosmotic" we shall mean that they do not depend in the majority of their speculations upon either the notion that the totality of things (*wan-wu* 萬物 or *wan-you* 萬有, "the ten thousand things") has a radical beginning, or that these things constitute a single-ordered world.[3]

The applicability of the very word *cosmology*, at least in its familiar classical Greek sense, is at issue. In Presocratic philosophy, the term *kosmos* is associated with a cluster of terms, including *arche* (origin, source, principle), *logos* (account, structure), *theoria* (contemplation), *nomos* (law), *nous* (mind, rational agency). However, this "cosmos" terminology is culturally specific. Indeed, in chapter 1 we argued that ancient Greek cosmological speculations were themselves culture-specific.

In classical Western metaphysics the equivocation between "unity" and "uniqueness" is resolved in favor of "unity." Thus in any of the various conceptions of a single-ordered universe assumed by the early systematic philosophers, the many phenomena comprising the world are defined in accordance with unifying principles which determine the essential reality of the things of the world. In classical Chinese reflections on world order, the equivocation between "unity" and "uniqueness" is resolved in favor of the unique. Hence, the nameless *dao* engenders an individual "one" which then proliferates.[4] The natural philosophy of classical China does not require a single-ordered cosmos, but invokes an understanding of a "world" constituted by the ten thousand things.

In ancient Greece, the preference for rest and permanence over process and becoming, entails the need for a causal agency accounting for change. The Chinese "world as such" is constituted by a "worlding" (*ziran* 自然), a process of spontaneous arising or "self-so-ing" which requires no external principle or agency to account for it.

This rather dramatic contrast in understandings of the origin and structure of the world suggests the inappropriateness of the term *cosmogony* as it occurs in the interpretive literature. There is an obvious tension in at once asserting that the world is "self-so-ing" (*ziran*) and that some initial creative act or categorial material principle brings the universe into "being."

Some scholars have noted that although cosmogonic myths were not an important feature of classical Chinese natural philosophy, something like them did begin to appear in China during the Han period.[5] John Major in his interpretation of the technical chapters of *Huainanzi* discusses in detail the various versions of "cosmogony" found in the *Huainanzi* as they are anticipated in texts such as the *Laozi*. The comparison of commentaries on a passage first presented in *Zhuangzi* 2, and repeated in *Huainanzi* 2,[6] is most illumining. Here we translate the *Huainanzi* 2 version:

> There is that which had a beginning.[7] There is that which never had "that which had a beginning." And there is that which never had "that which never had that which had a beginning." There is that which had something; there is that which had nothing. There is that which never had something or nothing. There is that which never had "that which never had something or nothing."[8]

The author of the original *Zhuangzi* passage wants to suggest that any notion of an initial beginning is problematic; the author of the *Huainanzi* version wants to describe the various stages in the emergence of the world *as we know it*. While the point made in these two passages is different, they share an important assumption that distinguishes both of them from what might be taken to be similar programs in classical Western cosmology. That is, there is an equivocation between two very different senses of the genesis of things. Clearly, both *Zhuangzi* and *Huainanzi*, as different as they are, come down on the same side. We must distinguish an unbounded world of ten thousand things that *emerges* genealogically from a sin-gle-ordered cosmos which is either brought into being by a trans-cendent agent or conforms to transcendent aims or principles. In a metaphysical cosmogony, the originative principle (the Judeo-Chris-tian God or Plato's *Demiourgos*) is independent of its creature and brings order to Chaos. Natural change is then driven by a linear teleology which takes us from creation to the realization of the given design.

As we have stated above, *dao* is not a superordinated principle, but the process of the world itself. This being the case, we must ask why *Huainanzi* "cosmologists" seem to posit a primordial process of cre-ation rather than simply assume as does the *Zhuangzi*, that the pro-cess has no initial beginning? The answer, we think, is *not* that they believed that some transcendent Agent, a Being behind the beings of the world, must be asserted in order to explain why things are, rather than aren't. Metaphysical cosmogony is very ambitious: The move is to trace the Many back to the ordering One, thus canceling con-tingency and rendering everything intelligible.

If, on the other hand, order is truly emergent rather than existing as an independent principle, then genealogical accounts must be far more modest. All aspects of this order—*yin* and *yang*, time and space, heaven and earth—must be historicized as a contingent vocabulary for the world order as we know it. These categories cannot stand as universal principles, as *necessary*, *a priori* conditions that give us a single-ordered world.[9] It is telling that the sense of "beginning" in these narratives is *shi* 始—a foetal beginning associated with foetus (*tai* 胎), to bequeath (*yi* 詒), to leave to (*yi* 貽). The language is per-vasively genealogical: ancestor (*zong* 宗), mother (*mu* 母), as well as "thearch" (*di* 帝) and *tian* 天.

Benjamin Schwartz, encouraged by the work of Akatsuka Kiyoshi and Chang Kwang-chih,[10] has in passing played with a similar thought:

Does the fact that in later Chinese high-cultural accounts of the origins of mankind or of the cosmos, the dominant metaphor is that of procreation or "giving birth" (*sheng*), rather than of fashioning or creating, have anything to do with the centrality of ancestor worship with its dominance of the biological met-aphor?[11]

What blunts Schwartz's insight in his interpretation of ancient China is his insistence that, although the worship of ancestors is everywhere in the tradition and even though early records state explicitly that both *di* 帝 and *tian* 天 "gave birth" to the Shang and Zhou dynasties,[12] these terms still denote transcendent Deity rather than ancestors:

> Most scholars now agree that Ti [Di] is not a deified ancestor, but the nonhuman high god who engendered the dynasty.... Whatever the origins of Ti, he remains awesome, transcendent, and supremely powerful.[13]

John Major contradicts Schwartz when he uses the translation "Thearch" for *di* with the following rationale:

> Thearch captures well the character of ancient Chinese thought wherein divinities might be (simultaneously and without internal contradiction) high gods, mythical/divine rulers, or deified royal ancestors: beings of enormous import, straddling the numinous and the mundane.[14]

We should recall another point made above: *Dao* has as much to do with the subjects of knowing and their quality of understanding as it does with the object of knowledge. That is, the genealogical narrative is also one which recounts an emerging understanding of world order and sets historical limits on that understanding. Our relatively clear understanding of our present situation cannot be universalized and relied upon to explain all situations. The genealogical account takes us back to an earlier set of conditions which cannot be explained by the application of our present philosophical vocabulary.

Without an originative principle, and the linear teleology that comes with it, the ten thousand things have no governing purpose, no preassigned design. And the alternative to some governing purpose is localized and temporalized self-sufficiency which enables one to achieve the greatest harmony (*he* 和) in any given situation.

On a more specific scale, the acosmotic character of ancient Chinese speculations has important consequences with respect to the understanding of the nature (Gk. *physis*, φύσις; L. *natura*) of things. Angus Graham takes issue with the simple identification of the classical Chinese concept of *xing* 性 with the familiar conception of nature as something "inborn and innate," something which contributes those qualities which a thing has to start with. Graham's insight is that the dynamic thrust of *xing* has not been adequately noticed.[15] In positing a revised interpretation of *xing*, Graham also makes a more general point. He suggests that many early Chinese concepts are not well served by their nearest English equivalents because the more dynamic connotations of the original Chinese are often lost.

Graham's discussion of *xing* underscores the hylozoism of the classical Chinese world view. His dynamic interpretation of *xing* calls into question not only the conventional translation, but further the appropriateness of common terminologies frequently used to explain it: *xing* is not reducible to what is innate (L. *in* + *nascor*: "to be born in"). Undoubtedly a contributing source of the tendency to reduce *xing* to what is "given" is the fact that, in the classical corpus, there are what seem to be numerous examples of *xing* being used as "starting conditions" when referring to "inanimate" things. But this again might be deceptive.

First, given the hylozoistic presuppositions that attend the notion of *qi* 氣, the continuous psychophysical sea of stuff that constitutes the ceaseless flow of existence, there is some question as to whether the animate/inanimate distinction has much currency in the earlier period. Certainly the application of *xing*, derived as it is from *sheng* 生 ("birth/life/growth"), to what we would consider to be inanimate phenomena suggests that *everything* in the classical Chinese world was considered to be "alive" and even "aware" in some degree. The absence of the animate/inanimate distinction generates an ambiguity. Certain things to which *xing* is applied, such as water and rocks, are not, over the course of their respective careers, marked by growth and cultivation, and hence it makes little sense to speak of them in terms of starting conditions and mature state.[16] The *xing* of such things remains relatively constant. However, the human being, as that phenomenon most given to cultivation and refinement, is a different case. In fact, it is precisely the indeterminate possibility for creative change that the contemporary philosopher, Tang Junyi, identifies as the most salient feature of the human *xing*. Tang says that while *xing* in reference to some things might denote fixed characteristics, properties, propensities or qualities,

from the perspective of the embodied ideal that we have of man
in relationship to his world, there is a real question as to whether
or not man has a fixed nature. This is because the world and the
ideal which man faces both entail limitless change. . . . The discussion of the human *xing* in Chinese thought has had as its one
common feature the reference to this locus for boundless change
in which it locates the special *xing* of man. This then is man's
spiritual *xing* which differs from the fixity and lack of spirituality
of the *xing* of other things.[17]

Hence, in the dynamic world of classical Chinese thought, the physical and psychical aspects of existence were construed as a continuum,
with the assumption that particular phenomena had varying degrees
of sensitivity or "awareness." Where a phenomenon is initiated by,
and dependent upon, a creative agent, and thus not self-generative
(*ziran* 自然), the creative contribution of that phenomenon to its
particular actualization is diminished.

Benjamin Schwartz supports the conventional interpretation of
xing as "a 'heavenly endowed' or 'heavenly ordained' tendency,
directionality, or potentiality of growth in the individual". He is
encouraged in doing so by what he perceives to be a "striking
resemblance" between *xing* and the Greek *phyo* (φύω "to grow") and
the Latin *nascor* ("to be born").[18] But the absence of cosmogonic
speculation in classical China in terms of which these presumed cog-
nates could be contextualized renders such resemblances deceptive.

In our understanding of *renxing* 人性, conventionally translated as
"human nature," we must avoid suggestions of the *physis/nomos*
dualism that arise as a consequence of dehistoricizing *xing*, making it
into a universal organizing principle identifying the "essence" of
human beings. *Xing* is not a superordinate and univocal principle that
inheres in all human beings at birth. While there is a givenness to *xing*
as an inherent organizing structure that persons in general develop
after conception, it also suggests the dynamic process of becoming
human.

In other words, in distinguishing the Han *genealogical* accounts
from cosmogonies of the classical West, and in distinguishing the
conceptions of human "nature" corollary to these accounts, we have
to find the "agency" of creative transformation within the process of

growth itself. Western cosmogonies entail a Creator/creature dualism, making the human being the product rather than the producer. Genealogical accounts such as we find in Han China, on the other hand, entail a foetal beginning which establishes important family resemblances but which also allows for complex transformations.

For Graham, the dynamic force of "human nature" (*renxing*) is evident in the metaphors the *Mencius* employs to characterize the concept: growing trees and animals, ripening grain, flowing water.[19] In extending the dynamic implications of nature to the human being, Graham is keen to correct his earlier understanding of *renxing* as "that which one starts with" in order to avoid the severe *physis/nomos* dualism entailed by innatist assumptions, thus revising his understanding of this expression to cover the entire career of a person's life. In the human context, then, the nature of the self denotes the entire process of being a particular person. Strictly speaking, a person is not a sort of *being*, but first and foremost a *doing* or *making*, and only derivatively and retrospectively, something done. Tang Junyi points out that, given the notion of creativity that *ziran* 自然 or "self-so-ing" presupposes, the inseparability of efficient and material cause is a pervasive characteristic of Chinese natural philosophy.[20] This means that in the creative project, there is no final separation between agency and object. For this reason, at least in reference to the human being, we must question the wisdom of translating *xing* as "nature," not only because it invokes unwanted associations with *physis* and *logos*,[21] but also because this translation fails to capture the sense that self is an ongoing process. We are persuaded that a more satisfactory rendering for *xing* needs to be found that factors into our understanding notions such as genealogy, culture, and history. For the human being at least, the *xing* of self seems to overlap with "character," "personality," or "constitution," as well as the initial conditions of one's birth.

A second caution that we need observe arises from the frequent use of "cultivation" in such a manner as to suggest the organic metaphor. "Cultivation" usually translates the character *xiu* 修, as in "cultivating oneself" (*xiuji* 修己)[22] or "cultivating one's person" (*xiushen* 修身).[23] The character *xiu*, translated "cultivate," is most commonly glossed as "effecting proper order" (*zhi* 治) in a sociopolitical rather than an organic sense. The point that we need to make is that the cultivation of self as a cultural product allows for a greater degree of creativity than the more restricted horticultural or husbanding metaphors might suggest, even though such metaphors are frequently encountered in the classical corpus.

Further, Aristotelian associations with this cultivation metaphor conjure forth a potentiality/actuality distinction that is not appropriate. Such a distinction is fundamentally progressive, entailing as it does an efficient, a formal, and a final cause that shape a given phenomenon. By contrast, there is a real question as to whether the classical Chinese notion of self can be most clearly understood by appeal to teleological models. The reason that teleology does not fit the Confucian model is that it introduces a goal that instrumentalizes the process by decontextualizing and dehistoricizing it. Progressionist theories suggest a steady advance toward a predetermined perfection. It is the degree to which this Confucian model of self is free of any specified goals that gives it its flexibility and creative range. In describing the emergent order that is self, one must employ *post hoc* generalizations rather than teleological explanations. The strictly physiological functions of the person can, perhaps, be discussed in terms of some teleonomic behavior-regulating program that controls a process and leads it toward a given end. But it is precisely the creativity of the human being, in contrast to such programmed behavior, that the early Confucians appeal to as being distinctively human. A self does not qualify as a self on the basis of its natural functions.

A common biological heritage, by defining the human life in terms of a familiar set of problems, sets constraints on the degree of difference evidenced by cultures and the semiotics that articulate them. But even at the biological level, there is good reason to proceed with caution when assuming the existence of unchanging conditions of origination. As Steven Collins observes,

> technological changes in biochemistry—notably in test tubes— might introduce novelty even here. Similarly, the use of speech for human communication, mutual identification and cooperation could perhaps also be construed as a basic predicament. But again, technological changes—in the past the transition from oral to written culture, in the future possible transformations of informational technology—might cause "categorial changes" in

language-using human organisms. . . . [We] should beware the too-easy identification of bio-social universals.[24]

The discussion of *renxing* in *Mencius* has had enormous influence in the tradition, and can be taken as a representative example to illustrate this discussion of "nature." If we allow for the radical malleability of the human being, we must take seriously the implications of passages such as *Mencius* 4B19, which states:

How the human being differs from birds and brutes of the field is ever so slight, and where common people lose it, the exemplary person preserves it.

Whereas the *initial* distinction between human and brute is exceedingly small, this slight difference can, through cultivation, be parlayed into moral, religious, cognitive, and aesthetic sensibilities that constitute a most significant difference. On the other hand, this passage and others like it say quite explicitly not only that some people *can* abandon that which distinguishes them from animals, but that they actually *do* abandon it. Humanity is neither inviolable nor universal. It is not the way that human beings have always been and always will be. For example, *Mencius* 6A10:

It is not the case that only those of superior character have this heart-and-mind (*xin* 心); all people have it. Those of superior character are simply able to avoid losing it.

This "preserve it or lose it" condition of humanity makes human givenness historical and contingent rather than ontological. One can let one's *xin* get away from one in the same way that one lets one's chickens and dogs get away.[25] Just as Mencius is quite ready to disqualify persons such as Zhou, the last ruler of the Shang, from being a "king," and to consider his overthrow the punishment of a thief rather than regicide, so Mencius is ready to call a brute a brute.[26] With cultivated *xing* rather than incipient *xin* being the primary defining character of humanity, and with the real possibility of "humans" who do not qualify as such, Mencius is a far cry from a recognizable liberal egalitarianism.

Mencius 6A15 states that the ability of the heart-and-mind to think and reflect is something that "*tian* 天 has given to me." In the same passage, *xin* is described as a bodily organ, just like the eyes and ears.

Once we appreciate the fundamentally familial import of *tian*,[27] to say that *tian* gave it to me is to say I inherited it from my parents and my ancestors, not that I have been given it by some transcendent power. *Tian* is the aggregate spirituality generated by a continuous culture. This ancestral sense of *tian* disambiguates passages such as 7A1:

> One who makes the most of one's heart-and-mind realizes *xing*, and if you realize *xing*, then you realize *tian*. Preserving your heart-and-mind and nourishing your *xing* is the way to serve *tian*.

The way that one contributes to one's lineage is through making the most of what one has inherited so that when one becomes an ancestor and thus an integral aspect of *tian*, one has made a contribution to an emerging humanity.

This specific historical process of shaping humanity is the substance of 7A30:

> Yao and Shun made it what humans are (that is, they "*xing*"-ed it); Tang and Wu embodied it in their persons; the Five Hegemons imitated it. Where persons imitate something resolutely over an extended period, who is to say that it is not theirs?[28]

As we find throughout the *Mencius*, it is really the heart-and-mind, *xin* 心, rather than *xing* that is the object of "preservation." For example, in 7A1, one "preserves" (*cun* 存) one's heart-and-mind, but one "nourishes, develops, cultivates, and grows" (*yang* 養) one's *xing*. The famous "Ox mountain" anecdote draws an analogy between the denuding of the mountain and the loss of the *liang xin* 良心, where continued degrading conduct, like the grazing of the cattle, finally denudes the mountain utterly. Such a degraded person is not far removed from being a beast. And when others see this bestiality, and conclude that this person never had any ability, how could this be the original circumstances of the person? The important point is that when incipient humanity is gone, it is gone, but that it didn't have to be this way.

In 4B28, when Mencius turns to "preserving" *xin*, we find that such preservation entails a dynamic process rather than simply maintaining the status quo:

> The way in which exemplary person's are different from other people is that they preserve their heart-and-minds.

How does one preserve one's incipient humanity? One preserves it through the *process* of becoming human:

Exemplary persons preserve their heart-and-minds by becoming human and by becoming ritualized.

That becoming human is a process is made clear in the grammar of 4B19:

Shun was discerning in all things, and was a careful student of human relations. His was a case of acting out of his humanity and his sense of what was appropriate, and was not simply doing what is humane and proper.

This is comparable to *Analects* 15/19, when Confucius says that it is the human being who extends *dao*, and not the other way around.

While we can generalize about *renxing*, we must also respect the site-specificity and particularity of *xing*, allowing that each person is embedded in a unique matrix of natural, social, and cultural circumstances that are constitutive of *xing*. Hence, we have to qualify a passage such as 4B32, which states:

How could I be different from others? Even Yao and Shun were the same as other people.

When Mencius uses "*tong* 同," he is not asserting an essential identity, but similarity. In 6A7, for example, when he insists that "the sage and I belong to the same category," he also says that "generally speaking, things which belong to the same category are similar to each other (*xiang si* 相似)." What Mencius is saying here is that *at the incipient stage*, those who become sages are "similar" to those who do not. But if we allow that what makes human beings truly human is the process originating with a set of initial conditions, what Mencius is saying ultimately is that persons who take these incipient conditions and act upon them so as to achieve sage-like conduct are sages. "Anyone who acts like a sage, is a sage."

The difference between the nature of a thing in a cosmogonic tradition and its *xing* in an acosmotic tradition is suggested by the kinds of questions asked within each culture. Cosmogonic concern ultimately leads to a search for an agent or agency that accounts for the beginnings of things. The thinker's role in the acosmotic tradition will not be so much to discover answers to the question of beginnings as to create a model of human beings and of society that is persuasive and evokes emulation.

A fundamental implication of acosmotic thought is the manner in which it renders unnecessary any recourse to notions such as "Being" or "essence." The things of the world do not require a hierarchy of beings or essences in accordance with which they may be said to form a coherent cosmos. And without the general recourse to "Being," the notion of "Not-being" likewise has little function. As we have already discussed,[29] Being and Not-being are fraught with the assumptions of an essentialist ontology. The Chinese *you*, by contrast, simply means "some things that are on hand," or "all of the things that are on hand." This latter expression may be translated *wan you* 萬有—"ten thousand haves." In the classical Chinese view, one deals not with the essences of things but with particular things themselves. Thus, whereas the vast majority of interpreters of Chinese classics have used "Being" and "Not-being" as equivalents for *you* 有 and *wu* 無 respectively, the more philosophically astute follow D. C. Lau, who has consistently opted for the nontechnical language of "something" and "nothing" instead.

In the strictest of senses, neither cosmological nor ontological speculations of the sort so important in the development of Western cultures have much relevance for the understanding of classical China. Metaphysical thinkers of the sort parodied by Gertrude Stein's "A rose is a rose . . ." would (mis)interpret that statement as a tacit expression of the difference between the "whatness" and the "that-ness" of a thing. Saying *what* a being is (a rose is a *rose*) answers a cosmological question; considering *that* it is (a rose *is*) is an ontological appreciation. A rose is an item interrelated in complex spatio-temporal, biochemical, and horticultural manners with the other items that constitute its ambiance. As such it is a cosmological entity. The specifically ontological character of the rose is expressed simply by its "is-ness."

Traditionally in the West, the ontological concern has dominated the cosmological. This is so in large measure because the second problematic has as its primary focus the assurance of order in the face of chaos. This order is realized by virtue of the presence of a common element binding the items constituting the cosmos. In Parmenidean terms it is the *Being* of the beings of the cosmos that serves as the fundamental guarantee of cosmic order.

It is only by believing that the ontological question is prior to the cosmological question that we are able to presume that both cosmology and ontology are concerned with order in some fundamental sense. The ontologist asks, "Why are there beings rather than no beings?" That is, "Why is there something rather than nothing at all?" The cosmologist asks, "What kinds of things are there?" By responding to the ontological question with a discussion of the *Being* of the beings of the world, the cosmogonic tradition in the Hellenic West has determined that subsequent cosmological speculation must involve the search for beings or principles which, as transcendent sources of order, account for the order(s) experienced or observed.

The tacit claim that the so-called ontological question is prior is a peculiar bias of those who privilege the Indo-European understandings of "Being." The concern for making Being present through the beings of the world is an expression of the preference of unity over plurality that undergirds second problematic thinking. Though it would be too much to say that such a preference is an accident of the linguistic disposition that leads us to interpret the verb *to be* in existential terms, there is some reason to believe that contrasting linguistic preferences furthered the dominance of alternative problematics in Chinese and Western cultures.

By virtue of the recent decline of "logocentric"[30] thinking, we in the West are better able to understand the character of the first problematic. And we are thereby better equipped to appreciate the thinking of classical China. Since Nietzsche, we have begun to unravel the radical implications of the cosmological concern. Many of us are now disposed to respond to the question, "What kinds of things are there?" by echoing the Nietzschean belief: There are only interpretations, perspectives, the sum of which is truth, the sum of which is chaos. First problematic, purely cosmological thinkers reject the ontological assumption that we must seek an ordered ground and ask about the character of things themselves, rather than the *type* or *kind* of things they represent. Such cosmologists, in so far as they are concerned with order in any sense, ask "How many and what kinds of *kosmoi* are there?" This leads to a reversal of the logocentric question of the ontologist, "Why cosmos rather than chaos?" The pure cosmologist, no longer burdened by the assumption of a single-ordered world, asks the first problematic question, "Why chaos (*kosmoi*) rather than cosmos?"

The historical movement in Western intellectual culture that began with Nietzsche's perspectivism, passed through Heidegger's "destruction of ontology," and culminated in the deconstructionist assault upon the logocentrism of a "language of presence" (Derrida), has led us again to the first problematic. By virtue of this fact we are far better prepared to understand the acosmotic character of classical Chinese culture.

2. ANALOGICAL DISCOURSE IN THE *CONFUCIAN ANALECTS*

The contemporary philosopher, Feng Qi, appeals to the *Analects* passage "as for my way (*dao* 道), there is a coherence which ties it together"[31] to argue that Confucius must be treated as a systematic philosopher.[32] But there is an ambiguity inherent in the term *yi* 一: "one" or "coherence." A distinction must be made between a "systematic" or "rational" coherence, and an "aesthetic" coherence.

A work of art can at once be unique and make claim to coherence. We would argue that Feng Qi's rationalization of Confucius privileges concept over image in a text which can most profitably be read as a sustained image of the road broadened by the historical Confucius.[33] This established image, including the detailed biographical portrait of Confucius in the central chapters, is the signature of the text. Insisting that Confucius is a systematic philosopher leads Feng Qi to overlook an important distinction between the conceptual edifice of systematic philosophy and an aesthetic coherence emergent from the process of bringing an image into focus. This distinction is, in large measure, a distinction between theory and narrative.

It is doubtful that Feng Qi would wish to import into his understanding of Confucius all the implications of the claim to "systematic coherence." For, as we saw in chapter 2 with respect to David Dilworth's interpretation of Confucius by appeal to "archic variables" drawn from Aristotelian philosophy, the presumption of theoretical coherence brings with it a whole host of misleading assumptions concerning the commitment to principles and methods.

We must be cautious, therefore, in using such freighted language to discuss Confucius' views. Rather than demanding moral *theory* or a *concept* of sagehood from the *Analects*, we might do better to limit our interpretation to moral examples from a particular lived experience, or one exemplary model of sagehood. Given the dependence of classical Chinese thinking on the conjuring of a particular image, we might have to allow that what provides order in the *Analects* is precisely that particular and nuanced portrait of Confucius emergent from those passages offering details recalled by those disciples who belonged to the conversation. This image of Confucius, as it came to attract an increasing number of adherents and to play a significant role in shaping their unique self-images, emerges as a model for appropriate conduct. This model may be seen as the functional equivalent of a concept or principle.

Authoritative images gradually lose their specificity and detail in the process of being appropriated from one concrete historical situation and applied analogously to another. It is not surprising that the same term *xiang* 象 is used to express both "image," and "model." Through analogizing, then, models come to do much of the work we expect from concepts by providing generalizations capable of organizing particular situations. There is, of course, no justification for assuming that generalized images organize particulars by appeal to some identical characteristic. As one would anticipate in the classical Confucian context, the relationship between "model" and "image" is appropriately described in a language of correlation between a historically available model and a particular situation, rather than by the subsumption of a particular under a universal category or principle.

In a recent publication, Angus Graham worries over the problem of "faithful" translation, contrasting translation with exposition:

> Granted that there can be different opinions about what counts as legitimate translation, it is reasonable to insist that a philosophical translator does his best to approximate to the key concepts of the original and to their logical relations, to follow the structure of the thought rather than to reprocess it; full success is unattainable of course, so to the extent that translation fails one supplements it by exposition.[34]

There might, however, be a contradiction in separating translation from exposition in a world that Graham himself allows has no transcendence.[35] Conceptual language, to the extent that it is dependent on univocal meanings, might be problematic. In rejecting transcendence as a meaningful category for understanding the Chinese tradition, Graham is denying the possibility of objective and, hence, univocal meanings. He is thus effectively eschewing conceptual language in any formal or technical sense.[36] In chapter 1,[37] we noted how the emphasis upon abstract definitions in ancient Greece, beginning with Socrates, served to ramify the divergence between rational and correlative thinking. The resistance of Chinese thinkers to such definitions is one of the strongest indications of the importance of the first problematic in determining the shape of Chinese culture.

The linguistic implication of abandoning transcendence—and with it, the foundations of objective certainty itself—is that literal language is not possible. If this is the case, Graham must allow that in the Chinese world view, the act of translation is not complete until readers themselves have read the text. This is but to say that the coherence of the Chinese order must take full account of context, including the biography of its readers. Thus translating *tian* as capital *H* "Heaven" for an audience residing within a culture imbued with Judeo-Christian theological beliefs leads to a distorted understanding.

In our *Thinking Through Confucius*, we underscored the importance of the Confucian notion of *shu* 恕 ("not imposing on others what you yourself do not desire") in Confucian moral reflection. D. C. Lau believes that references to *shu* in the *Analects* suggest an explicit methodology for determining appropriate conduct. This method involves "using oneself as a measure in gauging the wishes of others."[38] Lau's description of the place of analogical thinking in the *Analects* is worth citing at length here:

> Apart from reflecting on moral insights of the past, thinking also is important if we are to be able to see connections between phenomena that may seem unconnected at first sight. We have seen that this is important both in the sphere of literature and in the sphere of morals. In literature, we have seen that the *Odes* can stimulate the imagination so that we can see underlying similarities between disparate phenomena. In morals, it is by means of the method of *shu* that we can hope to be able to practice benevolence, and *shu* consists in using ourselves as analogy to find out about the likes and dislikes of other human beings.[39]

Confucius made much of the centrality of *shu* to moral conduct:

> Zigung asked, "Is there one expression that one can act on to the end of his days?"

The Master replied, "There is *shu*: do not impose on others what you yourself do not desire."⁴⁰

Herbert Fingarette distinguishes between the Kantian search for universal maxims and the Confucian pursuit of appropriate analogies in determining appropriate moral conduct:

> On key word here is *p'i* [*pi*] 譬, a word used with some frequency in the *Analects*. Although it is rendered in bilingual dictionaries by the English "to compare," the important features of its use in the *Analects* to which I would direct attention are these: First, *p'i* in the *Analects* is always a "comparison" of likenesses, not differences. Hence "analogy" is an appropriate term. Second, the comparison is expressed in terms of imagery, of persons, situations or activities, not in terms of abstract traits. Hence, *p'i* is in the *Analects* typically metaphorical. . . . The use of *p'i* is characteristic of Confucius' way of teaching. . . . It contrasts sharply with the method of abstract analysis, theory building, universalizing. *Shu*, in turn, is a specific kind of *p'i*. To be able from what is close—i.e., oneself—to grasp analogy with the other person, and in that light to treat him as you would be treated—that is *shu*.⁴¹

The commentarial tradition embraces a congeries of particular, disparate, and often contradictory readings, each relating to the others by favoring this school or elaborating that reading. As such, the tradition itself presents yet another example of analogical ordering in which the interpreted character of Confucius is presumed relevant to different places and times.

One recurring feature of the Chinese tradition which is certainly evident in the *Analects* is the degree to which it appeals to history rather than an established mythology as its primary resource for imagery. We might see in this phenomenon a suggestion of the irrelevance in the Chinese world of the Western distinction between *mythos* and *historia*. In China, myths generally have their origins in and are elaborations upon historical events, and hence are inseparable from them. Historical figures are euhemerized, ascending from the ranks of human beings to become local gods and cultural heroes. Thus *mythos* is a consequence of the gradual "mythologization" of history as a means of investing the historical record with additional authority. There is no assumption that the historical record, divested of its apocryphal accounts, has greater veracity than the mythological explanation, or even that there is some available standard for separating history and mythology. Thus, the need to distinguish biography from hagiography is not characteristic of early Chinese thought. Rather, mythological and hagiographic explanations are generally construed as fortified and more adequate historical explanations.

Confucius is a compelling example. By the time the Grand Historian, Sima Qian (ca. 145–86 B.C.E.), prepared his biographical account of Confucius in *Historical Records (Shiji)* 47, Confucius, in the available accounts of his life, had ascended from being a frustrated teacher, blocked from any real political influence, to police commissioner (*sikou* 司寇), then to upper ministerial rank as Minister of Public Works (*sikung* 司空), then to Minister of Justice (*da sikou* 大司寇), and finally, to the position of Prime Minister of Lu. During the reign of Emperor Wu (r. 140–86 B.C.E.) in the early Han dynasty, Confucius had come to be referred to as "the king incognito" or "the uncrowned king" (*su wang* 素王), meaning that although he never reigned as king, he had in fact received the mandate of Heaven (*tianming* 天命) to transform the world.

But Confucius' ascent was not merely secular. As Henri Maspero observes:

> Like all the gods of the official religion, Confucius climbed all the steps of the hierarchy one by one: he was duke in the first year A.D., king in 739, reduced for a while to the rank of duke in 1075, emperor in 1106. . . . On 4 December 1530, the Shih-tsung emperor stripped him of this status, giving him simply the title Perfect Sage Ancient Master (*Chih-sheng Hsien-shih*), which he has kept to our present day.[42]

Confucius had finally reached the top, being put on the same footing as Heaven, which also has had no hierarchical title.

Had Confucius become a god? Again, Maspero, in reflecting on Confucianism as the state ideology, worries about a Western interpretation which might be inclined to exclude this possibility:

> Insofar as our term "god" can be applied to the personages of Chinese mythology, it is thus clear that Confucius has been, at

least until quite recently, a god (not of individuals, but of the State), to whom one prayed and from whom one expected "happiness."[43]

The importance that Confucius has had in the tradition as a cultural model has meant that scholars and officials alike have, over the centuries since his death, sought a personal relationship with him by deferring to the record of his conduct, and by using him as a basis for their own analogical projections.

The place of analogical argument in the pre-Qin tradition cannot be exaggerated. D. C. Lau has taken some pains to defend the sophistication of Mencius in the application of this method, and appeals to the later Mohist canons to underscore the centrality of analogical argument as a means of bringing order to philosophical problems.[44] The prominent role played by analogical operations as a mode of philosophical argumentation in pre-Qin philosophy does not preclude the presence of more dialectical alternatives; nonetheless, it is the analogical, correlative mode of argument which is dominant.

3. EXPERIMENTS IN RATIONALISM

In the approximately one hundred years intervening between the death of Confucius and the birth of Mencius, a complex variety of philosophical schools emerged. In the overview of this period captured in the last chapter of the *Zhuangzi*, this growth in diversity is referred to as the period of the "Hundred Schools." Far from seeing in this a healthy pluralism of opinion, Mencius describes this phenomenon in the most negative of terms:

> Sage-kings have failed to arise. The feudal lords do whatever they want, scholars who are not employed in government are quite ready to pronounce on affairs, and the words of Yang Chu and Mo Di fill the empire. . . . I am deeply troubled by this. I protect the way of the former sages by taking a stand against Yang and Mo and by driving out their depraved views, so that those who would advocate heretical doctrines will not get the opportunity to do so.[45]

Mencius is not interested here in debating the opposition; he wants to eradicate it.

In the last chapter, we discussed at some length the reasons why the promotion of harmony over contentiousness served the Chinese desire for social stability in a manner not unlike the way in which the disciplining of plurality and difference by appeal to rational principles served the West. We will now attempt to provide some explanation of the fact that the Chinese responded in almost the opposite manner as did the West when they were faced by the generation of a plurality of dialectical conflicts among different schools of thought.

In spite of an underlying disaffection for contentiousness in the tradition, the period of the "Hundred Schools" began in earnest when Mo Di (ca. 479–381), the founder of Mohism, called Confucian ideas into question. Mohist thinking, often characterized as a kind of utilitarianism, constituted a significant challenge to the ritually grounded traditionalism of Confucius. Legalism, associated with Shang Yang (d. 338 B.C.E.) and Han Feizi (ca. 280–233), differed from both Confucianism and Mohism by beginning its social thinking not with the people but with positive laws and sanctions presumed to be external devices necessary to bring order to the turmoil of its day. With the Legalists came at least the adumbration of a rationalized political order. During the succeeding centuries leading up to the founding of the Han dynasty, a plethora of alternative schools emerged, and court-sponsored academies were established in different parts of the empire reminiscent of the great academies of classical Greece. The most famous representative of these academies during the fourth and early third centuries was Jixia at the Qi capital of Linzi, attracting over time a range of such notables as Zhuangzi, Song Xing, Shen Dao, Mencius, Gaozi, Xunzi, and Zou Yan.

In the beginning the competing schools engaged primarily in disputations (*bian* 辯) over doctrine, although they were also quite ready to offer commentary on the ever-changing political situation. Conservative Confucians who sought the meaning of life by appeal to family and social obligations were opposed by those Daoists who sought to attune the human world to the regular rhythms of nature.[46] There were fierce debates among the Confucians, Daoists, Mohists, Sophists, and Yangists (and many others) concerning the goodness or evil or neutrality of human nature. In due course, as the contest became increasingly complex, the debates took a procedural and logical turn. Thinkers such as Zhuangzi, Sophists such as Hui Shi and Gong-sun Longzi, and the later Mohist logicians, began to argue about the meaning of argument itself, and to worry over standards of evidence. Mohism and the School of Names developed a complex and technical vocabulary for disputation, and puzzled over the linguistic paradoxes which advertise the limits of language. Thus, as was the case in the history of early Greek thinking, resort to the second problematic was expressed as a means of adjudicating doctrinal conflict.

Many of our generation's most prominent sinologists, including Joseph Needham, Angus Graham, and Benjamin Schwartz have puzzled over the question: Why did these logical, rational, and proto-scientific sprouts that are in evidence in writings of the disputers in the late fourth and third centuries B.C.E. wither and ultimately disappear with hardly a trace remaining in the early years of the Han dynasty?[47] Explanations for this disappearance have generally been sociopolitical in nature, ranging from the basic distance of this unholy mixture of merchants, craftsmen, and displaced aristocrats from the enduring structures and institutions of classical Chinese bureaucracy, to the collapse of Mohism's formal organization under the pressures of a centralized empire. For some scholars, an easier inference is the "burning of the books" in 213 B.C.E.[48] Undoubtedly a complex of social and political factors conspired to shift the philosophic trajectory away from these positivistic beginnings. But perhaps one important player in the piece has not been properly noticed.[49]

A key figure in the emergence and, arguably, the ultimate decline of second problematic thinking in early China was the Confucian philosopher, Xunzi. Xunzi is often touted as the most rationalistic of the classical Confucians. But ironically, it is because his "rationalism" is grounded in history and culture without appeal to metaphysical determinants that he was instrumental in setting the tradition on a very different course from classical Greece. Rather than perpetuating the incipient second problematic thinking of the later Mohists and the School of Names into the Confucian program, he encouraged a return to its alternative: a first problematic form of nominalist historicism.

Mencius certainly was to emerge in the Chinese tradition as the most prominent of Confucius' interpreters, but he did not do so until relatively late in the tradition with the celebration of the *Mencius* among the medieval philosophers. In the formative years of Confucianism as a state ideology, it was Xunzi's ritual-centered Confucianism rather than the personal cultivation of Mencius that held sway. This was emphatically the case during the first century of the Han dynasty and the founding of empire.

The institutionalization of academic positions that the Han dynasty inherited from the Qin helped to perpetuate and galvanize the influence of Xunzi. Several of Xunzi's immediate students were responsible for the transmission of specific classics which comprised the Ru curriculum, including the *Guliang Commentary* to the *Spring and Autumn Annals* and the *Zuozhuan* historical narrative. Even the "Mao" orthodox version of the *Book of Songs* was named for a lineage of Xunzi disciples. In the preface to Xunzi's collected works written two hundred years after his death by the court bibliographer, Liu Xiang (79–8), it is reported that the region of Lanling, still under the influence of Xunzi, continues to produce fine scholars.

Perhaps Xunzi's greatest and most enduring influence came from the emphasis he placed on ritual practice as an instrument for socializing, enculturating, and humanizing the Chinese world. His description of the function of ritual in society is cited extensively in the histories and the many canons of ritual that were compiled during this period, and appears large in the syncretic philosophical literature that was to become the signature of the Han. The *Huainanzi*, for example, is by and large a text representing a variety of often conflicting philosophical positions, but the crown of this Han dynasty work is its final chapter, the "Greatest Clan (*taizu* 泰族)," which develops a philosophical position in many aspects reminiscent of Xunzi, especially with respect to the importance of ritual and learning.[50]

John Knoblock, in detailing the influence of Xunzi on the emerging Han dynasty, remarks: "Gradually the Ru tradition inherited from Xunzi was transformed into the state cult of Confucius."[51] Knoblock follows his well-documented and most persuasive demonstration of the importance of Xunzi by reporting on the sudden decline in his influence as the Han progressed: "By the time of Liu Xiang, his work had no fixed corpus, there was no tradition of scholarship associated with it, and there was no longer much interest in the attitudes he represented."[52]

This might be somewhat overstated. Knoblock himself reports on the esteem that Dong Zhongshu (ca. 179–104), the leading Confucian of the Western Han, had for Xunzi. Dong Zhongshu actually wrote a letter, referred to in Liu Xiang's "preface," specifically in praise of Xunzi. And Chen Chi-yun further identifies the strong influence of Xunzi on Wang Fu (ca. 90–165) and his *Qianfulun*, especially with respect to the social and political significance of prescribed norms, and the need for human effort in sustaining them.[53]

How then was Xunzi, a major force in the definition of Confucianism as a state ideology, responsible for undoing the second problematic thinking of the late Zhou dynasty?

In A. S. Cua's careful analysis of argumentation in Xunzi, he distinguishes Xunzi's "concrete" Confucian rationality from notions of abstract and impersonal reason familiar in classical Western metaphysical thinking. There is a marked consistency, and at the same time a fundamental difference, between Xunzi's rationality so described, and the peculiar kind of reasoning which grounds the *Canons* of the later Mohist thinkers. As Angus Graham has concluded, the "rationalism" apparently shared by Xunzi and the later Mohists is based upon their radical nominalism:

> Like Hsün-tzu [Xunzi] in his *Right use of names*, the only other pre-Han text which discusses the problem of common names, the Mohist has a radically nominalistic approach to naming ... for the later Mohists (as for Hsün-tzu in his *Right use of names* chapter) an object (*shih* [*shi*] 實) is a particular, and the function of common names is to be explained on purely nominalist principles. Indeed, if we are right in giving the particle combination *yeh che* [*ye zhe*] its full weight, a common name is treated as an abbreviation of "something which is like the object," the object being the particular for which the name is ordained.[54]

In fact, Graham identifies an almost total congruency between the later Mohists and Xunzi on the nature of language and logic, to the extent that Xunzi has no problem in utilizing most of the technical vocabulary of the Mohist disputers (*bian zhe* 辯者): relation (*he* 合), explanation (*shuo* 說), analogical projection (*tui lei* 推類), analogy (*bi lei* 比類), generic terms (*gong ming* 公名), specific terms (*bieh ming* 別名), and so on. Graham even suggests the possibility of a common source between Xunzi and the later Mohist *Canons*:

> The *Right use of names* is indeed so closely related to the summa and to *Names and objects* that one is strongly tempted to see it as

a digest of the techniques of Mohist disputation adapted to Confucian purposes. Hsün-tzu [Xunzi] may of course share with the Mohists common sources in the lost literature of the School of Names. . . . Although he is not the man to admit a debt to the enemies of Confucianism, we can hardly doubt that he owes most of his observations about names and objects to thinkers such as the Mohists who were interested in disputation for its own sake.[55]

Still, the fundamental distinction between Xunzi and the later Mohist thinkers lies in the importance invested in logical (and causal) necessity in the Mohists, and its total absence in Xunzi. For the Mohists, necessity (*bi* 必) is what is defined as "unending" (*bu yi ye* 不已也)—a condition of logical and scientific disputation which is invulnerable to time:

The Mohist has no metaphysic, but he does have a world-picture which unites his four disciplines; it is of a cosmos of concrete and particular objects, each of its mutually pervasive properties, located in space and changing through time, interconnected by necessary relations like the logical relations between their names.[56]

Graham argues that the two notions of "*a priori* (*xian* 先)" and "necessity (*bi* 必)" which introduce irrevocable linguistic determinants into Mohist thought are identifiably the philosophical discoveries of these later Mohists. "They discover in disputation a certainty (*pi* [*bi*] 必) invulnerable to time, the logical necessity which is eternal."[57]

In his analysis of argument in Xunzi, A. S. Cua is concerned that the central role of retrospective history in the reasoning process be fully appreciated, because it is this historicist appeal which makes the exercise of Confucian rationality both concrete and contingent. Cua states:

The Confucian emphasis on the role of historical knowledge, given the backward-looking character of analogical projection, is a useful reminder that any piece of ethical reasoning, if it is to claim interpersonal significance, though itself occasioned by a present perplexity, must have some contact with the cultural-historical experience of the people. It is in culture and history that an analogical projection finds its anchorage and not in rules and principles of *a priori* ratiocination. In this basic way, the prospective significance of analogical projection is rooted in retrospective ethical thinking.[58]

For Xunzi, the functional approximation of what we would regard as valid reasoning involves the discovery and articulation of appropriate and efficacious historical instances of reasonableness. "Reasoning" (*li* 理) and historical analogy are inseparable. On the one hand, *li*, which involves the mapping out of patterns, can only operate on the basis of assumed classifications (*lei* 類); at the same time, it is the mapping operation of *li*, including and excluding on the basis of perceived similarities and differences, that establishes classifications (*lei*) in the first place.[59]

We are now prepared to understand precisely why Xunzi's method of thinking is not a continuation or elaboration of the incipient rationalism of the later Mohists and the School of Names. The confusion concerning the nature of Xunzi's rationalism is a result of the failure to appreciate that there are two separate roots for nominalist thinking. In the West, in addition to the physicalist nominalism associated with atomistic assumptions, there is the tropic form of nominalism originating with the rhetorical tradition of the Greek Sophists. Nominalism of the rhetorical variety, as opposed to its logical or atomistic counterpart, is a much more informal way of thinking.

In Western theory, physicalist nominalism presupposes either that universals do not exist, or that there are no abstract entities and hence no such things as nonindividuals. Since all things are by nature individuated and particular, they are as such distinguishable. These beliefs are consistent with an atomistic nominalism grounded in causal assumptions, of the sort discussed in relation to Democritean atomism in chapter 1. Essentially the same assumptions serve to generate the sort of nominalism that some have identified with Mohist thinking.

Xunzi's linguistic or tropic nominalism is closer to the sophistic nominalisms of many of the early Greek rhetoricians. One appropriates an always-interpreted world through language acquisition and enculturation, and then continues the historical process of world-making. Distinctions, as ad hoc conventions, are always contingent and performative. Thus, as a distinctly historicist thinker, Xunzi makes no appeal to transcendent principles or necessary distinctions.

It can be argued that Xunzi, by co-opting the philosophic concerns of the early rationalists for the emerging Confucian program, made the formal continuation of these competing schools redundant. Said another way, the nascent second problematic thinking which was emerging in those individuals interested in logical argument was overwhelmed by the first problematic thinking of Xunzi and the large following he attracted in the early years of the Han as Confucianism was ascending to become the state ideology. Again, the Confucian sense of order that persists far beyond the temporal borders of the Han dynasty is typified by the *Xunzi*'s ritually constituted community involving a movement from contesting diversity to an inclusive harmony.

With the emergence of a Confucian orthodoxy in the Han dynasty based on the Xunzi branch of Confucianism, scholarly dispute was tempered by a fundamental commitment to mutual accommodation. There is a general distaste for contentiousness and an active cultivation of the art of accommodation—what Xunzi calls *jian shu* 兼術.[60] In the exercise of criticism, the ritual basis of order comes into play, since rituals serve as patterns of deference which accommodate and harmonize differences in desires, attitudes, and actions. Ideally, dispute is a cooperative exercise among responsible participants that leads to a search for alternatives upon which all can agree. There is a fundamental disesteem for coercion of any kind, since aggressiveness or violence threatens to disrupt rather than reinforce or improve upon the existing social order. After all, the goal of protest is not victory in contest, which is necessarily divisive, but the strengthening of communal harmony.

Contentiousness, by contrast, betrays a concern for personal advantage. The proper goal of criticism in the historical rationalism of imperial China, whether it be scholarly or social and political, is the strengthening of communal harmony. As Cua describes it, rituals are "schemes of mutual accommodation of differences in attitudes, belief, and values in social intercourse."[61] As we have seen, ritual practices are negotiated at the intersection of personal commitments and communally important values. In such a model, one important consideration, which must function as at once a constraint on self-assertive criticism and an encouragement for a consensual resolution, is that the protesters themselves are always implicated in the existing order, and hence any criticism of it is ultimately self-referential.

The interest in logic and rationality as tools of disputation that had emerged briefly in the pre-Qin days of the Hundred Schools, along with the analytical and dialectical modes of discourse attendant upon these methodologies, soon faded into the counter-current of Chinese intellectual culture. With the ascent of a Confucian ideology, China emerged as a culture grounded in the immanent aesthetic order of a ritually-constituted society, in large measure precluding the kind of dialectical conflicts familiar in the Western tradition. With the rising fortunes of Confucianism, there was a rapid decline in the importance of the Mohists, the Legalists, and the School of Names as distinct schools, and to the extent that they survived, they did so as eclectic alloys in the earliest amalgams of "neo-Confucianism." With the Han thinkers came the emergence of a fortified Confucian orthodoxy, complete with canon and commentary.

By the beginning of the first century B.C.E., Confucianism had become the clear victor over all contending voices. Its success was due in an important degree to its ability to accommodate within a ritually grounded society many of the profound elements of Daoism, Legalism, and Mohism, a pattern that would be repeated in Confucianism's gradual appropriation of Buddhist elements by its medieval adherents. That this continuing orthodoxy did not lead to the eradication of other important strains, principally those associated with the Legalists, Daoists, and Buddhists, is testimony to the inherent flexibility of an intellectual society that takes ritual harmony rather than rational certitude as its paradigm of order.

With the dominance of this fortified Confucian ideology came a new method of adjudicating doctrinal conflict. Beginning in the early Han, commentaries upon established "classics" would be produced and would vie for proximity to the center as the orthodox interpretations of the canon. The authors of these commentaries were not interested in overthrowing traditional authority in favor of their own ideas, but sought to enrich the authority of the classics by claiming to better interpret their original meaning. In fact, the profound vagueness of these texts provided ample leeway for literati to exercise their imaginations and devise truly creative elaborations upon the original language. A kind of "rhetorical skepticism" emerged which expressed itself in the affirmation of alternative interpretations. This strategy for maintaining a consensus served essentially the same function as the appeal to general principles in more rationalistic cultures.

Here we have a significant contrast with the dialectical means of adjudicating conflict in the Western philosophical tradition. There, the stipulation of terms within theoretical contexts led to the preference for clarity over vagueness, with the consequence that doctrinal differences were raised to the level of consciousness and had to be dealt with at that level.

In China, by contrast, critics of a particular doctrine depended, as did its proponents, upon a cultural repository of vaguely defined concepts. This is evidenced in the frequent canonical allusions employed to focus criticisms. The appeal to canonical authority is again a way of reinforcing a sense of shared community, and stands in sharp contrast to dialectical arguments undergirded by purportedly objective canons of reason or logic.

In the Western tradition, at least among those who have believed in the persuasive power of reason, it has been held possible, even desirable, to disagree with particular opinions while remaining respectful of the person or persons holding those opinions. This has given rise to notions of a "loyal opposition" in government, and to the kind of rational debate that fills academic and professional journals. This legacy has its beginnings in the celebration of dispassionate and impersonal reason. But in the Chinese tradition, there has not been the same discernible distance between one's belief or opinion and one's person. The assumption has been that good people write good books; good rulers promulgate good policies. One would not expect to read in the works of a classical Chinese scholar anything like Aristotle's statement, "I love my teacher, Plato, but I love truth more." Such a declaration would have been seen as indulgence in the sort of contentiousness and self-assertiveness which threatens social harmony. Instead, communication as constitutive of ritual community is effected through patterns of linguistic deference.

4. THE EMERGENCE OF HAN THINKING

4.1. Li 理 and Xiang 象: "Pattern" and "Image"

An implication of our discussions in the first two chapters is that the single greatest obstacle to understanding Chinese philosophy and culture has been the unannounced assumption that it is similar enough to our own tradition that we shall be able to employ inter-

pretive categories resourced in our tradition to understand the lineaments of that culture. This assumption often seems justified when, by
recourse to these categories, we seem to arrive at meanings strikingly
similar to our own. But this is often the case only because the application
of our most familiar interpretive concepts foreground certain content
while concealing what, to us, would be the more exotic meanings.

Any gross overlay of Western categories onto the Chinese world,
conscious or otherwise, must lead to distortion. The most productive
alternative to this kind of cultural reductionism is to import a vague
set of Chinese categories into the existing Western interpretive
vocabulary. If we are able to convey an understanding of the quality
of vagueness attaching to these categories as a synonym for "richly
complex," rather than "muddled" or "confused," then we shall be
able to employ these in a productive manner without having to provide strict definitions. If we succeed in this, our attempts to find a
perspective more internal to the Chinese experience will have been
significantly furthered.

When we turn to that particular cluster of terms used in the classical Chinese corpus to express "thinking," we find that we must begin
from two related terms, *li* 理, most frequently rendered into English
as "to reason" or "principle," and *xiang* 象, "to figure" or "image."
In what follows, we will complete this cluster with a consideration of
zhi 知—"to know," or "to realize."

We want to give an account of how the conventional translations of
li as either "reason" or "principle," while foregrounding our own
philosophical importances, pay the unacceptable penalty of concealing precisely those meanings which are most essential to an appreciation of its differences. Our concern then, is, through a reconstruction
of this cluster of terms, to lift to the surface those peculiar features of
classical Chinese thinking that are in danger of receding in our reading and interpretation of the texts.

In its earliest occurrences, *li* has both a nominal and verbal function
as "order," "pattern," or "markings," and "to order," "to pattern,"
or "to mark." Actually, in its earliest occurrence, *li* conjures up the
image of "dividing up land into cultivated fields *in a way consistent
with the natural topography.*"[62] It refers to the pathways that permit
access to the fields under cultivation.

The *Shuowen*, a Han dynasty Chinese lexicon, inspired perhaps
by the fact that *li* is classified under *yu* 玉, the "jade" signific, suggests

that "dressing or polishing jade" and the "veins or striations within the jade" are its most fundamental meanings.[63] Significantly, the dressing of jade requires craftsmen to conform their creative expression to those possibilities resident in the natural striations of the stone. In fact, the best lapidary is the one whose art maximizes the richest possibilities of the stone itself. As Tang Yi in his analysis of *li* observes, the process of dressing jade entails cutting and splitting the stone, as well as bringing out its luster through polishing.[64] There is an immediate analogy here with the manner in which language is perceived to "dress" the world, both cutting it up and arranging it.

The most familiar use of *li* in the classical literature is to indicate the inherent formal and structural patterns in things and events, and their intelligibility. In expressing this notion of coherence and intelligibility, no severe distinction is made between "natural" coherence (*tianli* 天理 or *daoli* 道理) and "cultural" coherence (*wenli* 文理 or *daoli* 道理). Just as nature and culture are embraced within the notion of *dao*, so each is integral to *li*. The expressions *dao*, *wen*, and *li* all overlap in evoking a sense of pattern and markings.

The most familiar uses of *li* in Western translations lie somewhere in the range of "reasoning" or "rationale" (Cua), "principle" (Chan), "organism" (Needham), and "coherence" (Peterson).[65] To focus the meaning of this term, we need, first, to assess the adequacy of each of these renderings.

Needham's use of the term "organism" is inappropriate if understood in the standard Aristotelian sense which defines the organic in terms of activity conditioned by specific ends. This characterization leads to a classification of ends or aims which would then undergird a taxonomic organization of "natural kinds."[66]

Li is the fabric of order and regularity immanent in the dynamic process of experience, and hence is frequently rendered "reason." However, *li* in defining order confounds the familiar distinction between rational faculty and the underlying principles it searches out. *Li* has neither an exclusively subjective nor objective reference. "Psychology" is translated into modern Chinese as *xinli xue* 心理學, "the study of the *li* of the heart-and-mind," but then "physics" is *wuli xue* 物理學, "the study of the *li* of things and events." *Li* does not entail the distinction between the intelligible and the sensible worlds which has had such prominence in the Western world after

Parmenides and Zeno. The absence of effective notions of transcendence suggests that there can be no efficacious appeal to objective reason. The *li* of both the heart-and-mind, and of things and events, are immanent in the phenomena themselves.

Another condition of *li* which separates it rather distinctly from our common understanding of "principle" is that *li* is both one and many. In his analysis of *li*, Allen Wittenborn notes:

> The problem . . . is whether *li* is a unity, or a multiplicity. It cannot be both. If it were then our entire way of thinking, our complete thought processes and forms of reasoning would have to be seriously reconsidered, and probably discarded.[67]

This is precisely the point. As Willard Peterson observes, *li* is the coherence of any "member of a set, all the members of a set, or the set as whole."[68] This description reflects both the uniqueness of each particular and the continuities that obtain among them.

A similar point is made by A. S. Cua, who has reservations about "principle" as a translation of *li* because principle

> is often used as a context-independent notion that can be employed as referring to a basis for justifying particular moral rules or notions. . . . For the Confucian, duty and obligation are tied to the roles and positions of persons in the community.[69]

Li establish the ethos of a given community. As such *li* may never be considered as independent of context. There are no transcendent *li*.

In the absence of teleological guidance, there is only an ongoing process of correlation and negotiation. One investigates *li* in order to uncover patterns which relate things, and to discover resonances between things that make correlations and categorization possible. The nature of classification (*lei* 類) in this world is juxtaposition through some presumed similarity. As Needham has pointed out, "things influence one another not by acts of mechanical causation, but by a kind of 'inductance.' "[70] Things are continuous with one another, and thus are interdependent conditions for each other. In a tradition which begins from the assumption that existence is a dynamic process, the causes of things are resident in themselves as their conditions, and the project of giving reasons for things or events requires a tracing or mapping out of the conditions that sponsor them.

Recalling the relevant discussions of chapter 1, we are able to understand one of the important implications of the fact that, contrary to the dominant strains of classical Western thought, the Chinese did not give priority to rest and permanence in their characterizations of the "ten thousand things." There is little impetus toward the development of notions of external agency in a world where change and process is deemed prior to rest. In such a world of changing things the most normal assumption is that things change themselves.

There is another important implication of this dynamism: Given the assumption of the primacy of change and becoming, coherence takes on quite a different meaning. Process entails uniqueness, and makes any notion of strict identity problematic. As such, coherent unities are characterized in terms of a relative continuity among unique particulars. And such continuity is open-ended rather than systematic; it is contingent rather than necessary; it is correlative rather than causal. Thus, it can include aspects which, if entertained simultaneously, would seem inconsistent or even contradictory, yet when entertained in process, are well within the boundaries of continuity.

To be in accord with *li* (*he li* 合理), an expression which in modern Chinese translates "to be rational" or "reasonable," entails an awareness of those constitutive relationships which condition each thing and which, through patterns of correlation, make its world meaningful and intelligible. All things evidence a degree of coherence as their claim to uniqueness and complexity, as well as their claim to continuity with the rest of their world.

Li constitutes an aesthetic coherence in the sense that it begins from the uniqueness of any particular as a condition of individuation, and is at the same time a basis for continuity through various forms of collaboration between the given particular and other particulars with which, by virtue of similarity or productivity or contiguity, it can be correlated. It is this collaboration which provides a ground for the various modes of analogical relationship that are the closest approximation to "reasoning" available in this tradition.[71]

In contrast to reasoning as the process of uncovering essences of which particulars are instances, *li* involves tracing out correlated details forming the pattern of relationships which obtain among things and events. Confucian thinking has as its goal a comprehensive and unobstructed awareness of interdependent conditions and their latent, vague possibilities, where the meaning and value of each element is a function of the particular network of relationships that constitute it.

Such "reasoning" permits noninferential access to concrete detail and nuance. For example, one may appeal to the categories of correlative "kinds" (*lei* 類) to organize and explain items in the world. The correlations one pursues among the welter of concrete details foregrounds similarities among them. Inclusion or exclusion in any particular "kind" is a function of analogical activities rather than logical operations dependent upon notions of identity or contradiction.[72] Such correlations are meant to provide a sense of continuity and regularity in the world, and are more or less effective as coherent orders to the extent that some juxtapositions tend to maximize difference, diversity, and opportunity, and hence are more productive of harmony than others.

Li is both descriptive and normative. It suggests how things ought to be. This prescriptive aspect of *li*, however, does not appeal to any order beyond that which is available by analogy to historical models. Ideals reside in history. In this sense, *li* is not "metaphysical" and must be distinguished from assertions about some a priori structure or transcendent aim.

A second term in the "thinking" cluster, *xiang* 象, is most frequently translated as "image." In the sense in which we shall be using the term, an image is a sensory (that is, visual, auditory, tactile, olfactory) presentation of a perceptual, imaginative, or recollected experience. The form of the perception, memory, or imagination may be distinct from the mode of its presentation. For example, the olfactory or visual experience of a rose may be imaged in the words of the poet. The word-picture as experienced by the celebrant of the poem, and not (necessarily) the private experience of the poet, constitutes the image as socially efficacious. The most productive manner of discussing images, therefore, is in terms of their communally experienceable character. Only such images have direct efficacy.[73]

The images associated with the hexagrams of the *Yijing* (*Zhouyi* or *Book of Changes*) are good examples of *xiang* since they are particularistic. That is, the image "fire" may be said to bring to mind particular experiences of the phenomenon of "fire" that are housed in the individual consulting the *Yijing* by virtue of his or her recourse to social memory and communal experiences (traditions, institutions, ritual practices, music, literature, and so on).

In epistemological discussions we may wish to distinguish between the image and the symbol in something like the following manner: An image is an object or event presented with arbitrary, ad hoc, or merely conventional associations. An image may become a symbol by accruing in the course of a particular narrative (a novel, a play, an historical account, an epic poem) a consistent set of significances. Nabokov's *Pale Fire* presents the image named in its title in such a manner that it gradually takes on interpretive "cash-value" in the course of its occurrence in a variety of contexts in the narrative. Privileging the clarity of univocally defined terms over the vagueness of metaphor and imagery in the more rationalistic West has made it difficult for poets and novelists to protect the richness of their imagery from the rationalizing interpretations of literary critics.

In the classical Chinese model, image is the presentation rather than re-presentation of a configured world at the concrete and historical levels. The constructed image assumes considerably more explanatory force than would a logical account.[74] Willard Peterson in fact argues that the term *xiang*, generally translated "image" or "model" in the *Yijing*, ought to be rendered "figure," in the sense of "to give or to bring into shape."[75] This is what is meant by the following words of the *Yijing*:

> The Sages, having the wherewithal to contemplate the complexity and diversity of the world, and to fathom in it[76] shapes and appearances, captured in their "images (*xiang*)" what is appropriate to things. For this reason, we call them "images (*xiang*)."[77]

There is a reported conversation in the *Yijing* between Confucius and his disciples that is an encouragement to read the *Analects* itself as a sustained image:

> The Master said: "The written word cannot do justice to speech, and speech cannot do justice to meaning."[78]
> "If this is the case, then is the meaning of the Sages beyond our grasp?"
> The Master replied: "The Sages constructed 'images (*xiang*)' to give a full account of their meaning, set up the hexagrams to give

a full account of what is natural and what is contrived, wrote their judgments on the images and hexagrams in order to say completely what they had to say, introduced the presumption of change and continuity as a way to take full advantage of any situation, and elaborated upon and embellished all this to do justice to its profundity."[79]

Although this passage describes the content and structure of the *Yijing*, it really has a much broader compass in the classical corpus. In the case of the *Analects*, for example, the central image around which the text is constructed is "Confucius treading a path." A careful reading of the *Analects* reveals that an extraordinary amount of the vocabulary used to present Confucius' philosophical insights is specific "way" imagery. This is a characteristic that our standard English translations have yet to reflect.[80] Much of the text is given over to the image of following the path that Confucius, having appropriated tradition as his own, has marked out for himself: extending the path, going out from it, going against it, quitting it, confusion over it, confronting obstructions along it, finding company upon it, taking one's place on it, dwelling or lodging along it, having the strength to continue the journey along it, driving a chariot on it, moving ahead on it, clearing and cultivating it, and so on. When Confucius modestly describes his own project, he says: "I follow along this way, I don't construct it."[81]

It would be an oversight, as well, not to appreciate the middle chapters of the *Analects* as an extended portrait of Confucius as a concrete image of this one particular human being, living an exemplary life. As the *Analects* quickly became canonical, this portrait of Confucius was culturally reinforced, and became an established image or symbol for the tradition.

The meaning resident in an established image is the reflexive act of creating, and recreating, the image itself. Contrary to naive expectations, what one finally sees in a work of art is the creative act that produced it. The creative process, not the object, is the repository of meaning. What is imaged is the process.

For example, the personal style of the calligraphy as contrasted with the text is nonreferential and nonrepresentational. Its reflexivity is, nonetheless, revelatory of the artist as a particular person. One's moods, one's times, one's joy and pain, one's place in the world—all are resident in the shaping of the Chinese character. In this sense, one's calligraphy is biographical. But in much the same way as Confucius the sage, one's biography is corporate and transmits not only one's own personal idiosyncracies and experiences, but the tradition as well.

This notion of art as self-expression is reiterated by Stephen Owen in the contrast he insists upon between "poem" as "made artifact" and *shi* 詩 (usually translated as "poem") as personal articulation:

> If we translate *shih* [*shi*] as "poem," it is merely for the sake of convenience. *Shih* is not a "poem"; *shih* is not a "thing made" like in the same way one makes a bed or a painting or a shoe. A *shih* can be worked on, polished, and crafted; but that has nothing to do with what a *shih* fundamentally "is." . . . *Shih* is not the "object" of its writer; it *is* the writer, the outside of an inside.[82]

The invention and ramification of metaphors is one of the fundamental ways through which a culture interprets its world.[83] A third-century statement of this insight is to be found in Wang Bi's commentary on the *Yijing*. In this discussion, there is an attempt to explain the relationship between image, word, and meaning. Wang Bi·begins by defining the role of word and image in constituting meaning:

> An image expresses meaning; words clarify the image. To do full justice to meaning, nothing is as good as an image; to do full justice to an image, nothing is as good as words. Because words arise from images, we can explore the words as a window on the image. And because the image arises from meaning, we can explore the image as a window on meaning. Meaning is given full account with an image, and the image is articulated in words. Hence, words are whereby we clarify the image. In getting the image, we forget the words. The image is whereby we hold onto meaning. In getting the meaning, we forget the image. It is like the snare serving to capture the rabbit; in snaring the rabbit, we forget the snare. Or like the fishtrap serving to catch the fish; in catching the fish, we forget the trap. As such, words are the "snare" for the image. And the image is the "trap" for meaning. For this reason, holding onto the words is not getting the image; holding onto the image is not getting the meaning.[84]

Wang Bi ends here by indicating the limitations of words and images. His point is to reject the notion of literal, referential language. Word and image in themselves are not repositories of meaning; in fact, if they are so interpreted, they can obstruct it.

Imaging involves analogy in the sense that it requires a movement between a generalized situation made intelligible in word and image, and the detail of one's own particular circumstances. And imaging has performative force. Meaning is not simply given; it is reflexively appropriated. It is "made one's own."

In the *Yijing*, the meaning of a general situation is captured in an image, and the image is explained in words. The words constitute the most abstract level of discourse and, as such, have the least degree of meaning for one's particular situation. Words, however, have the power to evoke an image, which in stirring one's imagination, enables one to focus the situation for oneself. What was general becomes increasingly particular. By virtue of its relative explicitness, the image displaces the words, and as the image is explored as a repository of significance for one's own circumstances, the lines of the image begin to fade. The image gives way to meaning. In being deepened and made more determinate, more meaningful for oneself, the image loses its more general character and becomes increasingly indistinct. The image retreats as the particular situation is inscribed. The important insight here is the circularity of the process and the absence of any foundational claims. There is an isomorphic relationship obtaining among these levels of discourse that allows us to privilege each level in turn.

Words and images in their stipulated forms are reasonably clear, but are equivocal in their application to particular situations. The meaning of a particular event, on the other hand, is clear as an immediate experience, and yet in its particular detail, is resistant to conceptual clarity. Hence, in moving from words to meaning, the impoverished vagueness of generality, which we often term "clarity," gives way to the rich vagueness of particularity.

Wang Bi's next step is to turn the circle in the alternative direction. Now, instead of images and words expressing meaning, they inscribe it. Meaning gives rise to images and words, which give rise to meaning:

> Given that an image arises from the meaning, in holding onto the image, what you are holding on to is not really the image. Given that words arise from the image, in holding on to the words, what

you are holding on to is not really the words. As such, to forget the image is to get the meaning; to forget the words is to get the image. Getting the meaning lies in forgetting the image; getting the image lies in forgetting the words.[85]

The intimacy of word, image, and meaning challenges any severe disjunction between reality and appearance, between reasoning and imagination. There is an unbroken line between meaning as what is real, image as the presentation and inscription of what is real, and words as the constitutive articulation of what is real. It is because this line is continuous that the interpretive vocabulary of the *Analects*, as well as classical Chinese philosophy more broadly conceived, is a language of tracing relationships by "unravelling" (*jie* 解), and "getting through" (*da* 達 or *tong* 通) without obstruction.

We can clarify Wang Bi's more theoretical commentary by looking at the way in which philosophy has generally been done in the Chinese tradition. Meaning is generated by "turning" productive images. For example, one of the more vivid images for "understanding" in the classical literature is a frequently encountered appeal to the chariot metaphor where, with varying degrees of facility and varying pedigrees of horses, one "makes one's way through" the world from one end to the other, partaking of its inexhaustible mysteries. The human being is the unraveller, the surefooted charioteer negotiating the contours and conditions of the terrain, dismounting in difficult patches to walk the horses across, and mounting again to course unobstructedly through the world:

Hence, the person of great stature:
    Being placidly free of all reflection
    And serenely without thoughts for the morrow,
    Has the heavens as his canopy,
    The earth as his carriage,
    The four seasons as his horses,
    And *yin* and *yang* as his charioteer.
    He mounts the clouds and soars over the skies,
    To be with the demiurge of change.
    Giving free reign to his heart's desire
    He gallops the great abode.
    As is appropriate, he walks his horses where they
        should be walked,

And as is appropriate, he runs them hard where they
   should be run.
He gets the god of rain to wet down the roads
And the god of wind to sweep away the dust.
With lightning as his whip
And thunder as his wheels,
Above he rambles in the lofty vastness
And goes out of the gates into boundlessness below.
   Having scanned all round and left nothing
      out,
He returns to watch over what is within to thereby
   remain whole.
He manages the four corners of the earth
Yet always returns to the pivot.
Thus, since the heavens are his canopy,
   Nothing is left unsheltered;
   Since the earth is his carriage,
   Nothing is left unsupported;
   Since the four seasons are his horses,
   There is nothing that is not at his beck and call;
   Since yin and yang are his charioteers,
   There is no contingency that is not amply provided for.
   Hence, he travels fast without pitching
   And travels far without fatigue.
   Without taxing his body
   And without straining his keenness of hearing and
      sight,
   He knows the lay and boundaries of the
   various divisions and quadrants of the
   world. How?
   It is because he has his hands on the control
   handles of dao and rambles in the realm of
   the inexhaustible.[86]

Words as articulations of the image do not identify and describe an independent reality, but both inscribe and participate in it. That which is known, and the act of knowing, come into being together. At the beginning of "The Great Ancestral Teacher" chapter in *Zhuangzi* 6, are these words: "There can only be authentic knowledge (*zhenzhi* 眞知) when there is the authentic person (*zhenren* 眞人)."[87] There is the natural "awakening to and manifesting" (*jue* 覺) of a reality to which one has immediate access as something between "within" and "without." And it is only by following the inscription (the image, the words, the path) that one comes to know the world.

The evocative concreteness of focusing an image is a familiar characteristic of the Chinese language, but it certainly is not peculiar to it. An important tropic feature the pre-Latinized Anglo-Saxon language owed to its Teutonic roots is kenning, which involves the construction of highly descriptive compounds or phrases by juxtaposing words and images.

For example, the ocean is the "whale's-bath," the "foaming-fields," or the "sea-street"; the boat is the "sea-wood," the "wave-courser." The king is the "leader-of-hosts," the "giver-of-rings," the "protector-of-earls," or the "heroes-treasure-keeper." These polynomial constructions do the work of abstraction by conjuring one image out of two or more. In the process of kenning, sound is not irrelevant. Often visual, imagistic clarity is sacrificed in some degree in order to achieve an aural effect. This capacity for creating richer meanings by juxtaposing and compounding concrete metaphors allows for the expression of qualitative generalizations while at the same time maintaining the vividness and vitality of the immediate image.

The etymological relationship between "kenning" and "knowledge" should not be lost, because it indicates that much was expected of this trope. Kenning was nothing less than a way of "knowing" the world. This capacity of Old English for kenning is reminiscent of the way in which the Chinese language has functioned late and soon to generate its abstractions, to maintain the focus of its concrete images, and to appropriate ideas from foreign sources. Most recently, the Chinese encounter with theoretically oriented Western cultures has been prosecuted through the largely Japanese invention of kenning-like abstractions: for example, *quanli* 權利, "to weigh up + advantages," for the modern notion, "human rights';' *gainian* 概念, "a piece of wood used to strike off grain in a measure + to think of," as an equivalent for "concept," and so on.[88]

In the classical Chinese world, the construction of human imagery (*xiang*) is perceived as an entirely natural phenomenon, pursued as a complement to and extension of the patterning of the heavens (*tianli* 天理) and the veins and relief of earth's topography (*dili* 地理).[89] The human enterprise of configuring the world takes the structures implicit in the heavens and the earth as models to inspire the imagination rather than as objects of imitation and replication. Further, where a continuum is assumed between subject and object, and the subject thus participates in the imagistic play which configures the world, images are necessarily multivalent.[90]

The method of expressing meaning through the process of imaging contrasts with the familiar classical Western notions of generating mental pictures which correspond to external realities. *Xin* 心, most appropriately rendered "heart-and-mind," is a correlative image which precludes any final separation between reasoning and imagination, reasoning and experience, reasoning and rhetoric, reasoning and feeling. This sort of correlativity has as one of its important implications a preempting of the move in our own classical tradition which separates ideation from emotion, and which, in so doing, gives us mental representations which are presumed distinct from both experience and practice. As we discussed in chapter 1, this move is primarily abetted by the mind/body dualism articulated from Pythagoras to Plato, and is ramified by the yawning gap that opened up between reason and experience after the challenge of Zeno. The assumed interdependence of the cognitive and affective aspects of thinking in the Chinese tradition thus precludes the "psychologization" of the person and the thought process. In this tradition, thoughts are, irrevocably, embodied actions.

For a work which places this understanding of embodied actions in context, one might consult Lisa Raphals' important comparative study, *Knowing Words—Wisdom and Cunning in the Classical Traditions of China and Greece*. While we share Raphals' interest in noting the distinctly practical orientation of Chinese modes of thought and deliberation, there are differences in our views with respect to the issue of the transcultural status of this or that aspect of Greek or Chinese cultures. We are less sanguine than she seems to be about the existence of real commonalities of form and content in the elements of the two cultures.

The dualistic consequences of the dominance of second problematic thinking in classical Greece expressed itself in a number of manners which should alert us to the difficulties of any straightforward attempts at the comparison of Chinese and Western cultures. In our previous discussions of the development in ancient Greece of epic, lyric, and tragic poetry, and the effect of this development upon self-articulation, we noted that both the shape of subsequent literature and the separation of philosophical and literary modes along the lines of a reason/affect disjunction effectively led to the judgment on the part of Western philosophers that literary pursuits were, for the most part, epistemologically irrelevant. The seeds of this kind of disjunction did not sprout in Chinese soil. As a result, the role played by literary discourse in China is significantly different from that which it has played in Western culture. That difference, briefly stated, is that it has played a more constitutive role in the development of the sort of thinking peculiar to the Chinese. The questions raised by this observation are complex, and we will not address them in this present context. At least this much should be said: The dualism of mind and body, or reason and affect, or theory and practice, in the Western tradition are all significantly shaped by the cosmogonic impulse of the second problematic, which in turn has in important measure determined the shape of the cultural interests which define and organize the thoughts, actions, and creations of our second problematic culture. Thus, attempts to find in the Chinese tradition counterparts of the epic or tragic poetry, for example, or to characterize the relations between literary and philosophic discourse, must proceed with the recognition that cosmogonic underpinnings of both philosophical and literary pursuits in the West may make such comparisons extremely difficult. Indeed, as we have already mentioned, our application of the term *philosophy* to a certain class of Chinese intellectuals may only be done in the most advised of manners.[91]

4.2. Daoism, Confucianism, and the Language of Deference

In consulting Chinese dictionaries, one might feel encouraged to believe that many, if not most, of the important categories of cultural interpretation have alternative meanings from which the translator, informed by the context, is required to select the most appropriate. Such an approach to the Chinese language signals precisely the problem to which we have repeatedly returned in our exploration of the Chinese world.

If we recall how important to the development of the specific shape of Western philosophy was the interest in univocal definitions, we shall perhaps be better prepared to recognize the unfamiliarity of a tradition such as that of the Chinese in which such a development never *effectively* took place.

Our interpretation of Chinese language and culture as "productively vague" forces us to stress that the appearance of any given term in a text introduces, with varying degrees of emphasis, a vast, seamless, range of meanings. And our project as "translators" in the broadest sense is to negotiate an understanding that is sensitive both to context and to this full semantic range. Any presumption to the effect that there are strictly *literal* meanings to be searched out would lead us astray.

It would be helpful here were we to reflect upon the contrasting meanings of the relevant uses of "context" in the Chinese and Western cultures. In chapter 1 we discussed at some length how divergent philosophic responses to the most basic questions led in the Greek tradition to dialectical engagements in which parties attempted to forge a superior theoretical position over against that of opposing perspectives. The result, as we have shown, was the development of a series of theoretical perspectives which served variously to contextualize key philosophic terms. These "primary semantic contexts" serve still as the principal means of providing the senses of our dominant terminologies. In a tradition less given to the development of theoretical contexts which provide stipulated senses for all principal terms, vocabularies remain richly vague.

In approaching the Chinese we must, therefore, learn not only to cope with vagueness, but to exploit it. In fact, it is this conscious effort to reconstitute the several meanings as an integrated whole, and to fathom how the term in question can carry what for us might well be a curious, often unexpected, and sometimes even incongruous combination of meanings, that leads us most directly to a recognition of difference.

As an example: we may wonder what the fact that the single term *shen* 神 can mean both "divinity" and "human spirituality" in the classical Chinese language reveals about Chinese religiousness. Or again, how can the term *yi* 義 carry with equal weight the senses of both "appropriateness" and "meaningfulness?" This combination of meanings underscores the place of correlative modalities of thinking within this tradition by suggesting that meaningfulness is the consequence of efficacious dispositioning which juxtaposes things in a mutually enhancing and fruitful manner.[92]

Recourse to the intimate correlation of alternative images as a way of expressing meaning is also in evidence in the tradition of textual glosses such as the *Erya*, which dates back to late Zhou times. These glosses suggest readings for problematic characters in a text. They begin by listing characters similar to the one at issue on the basis of meaningful correlation: Character *a* in this context suggests characters *x*, *y*, and *z* as useful for explanation—in part by overlapping, in part by extending the existing meaning. Of particular interest is the extent to which the present-day semantic content of the Chinese language is a function of the correlations made in these classical commentaries. That is to say, many of the binomial expressions that have come to constitute the modern Chinese language emerge out of what commentators took to be meaningful associations over the course of China's long history.

The manner in which the classical Chinese constructed and employed dictionaries has a great deal to say about the nature of the language. We can illustrate this fact by recalling once again the contrast between Chinese and Western interpretations of the locutions *you* 有, "being present," and the English copula, "to be."

The Chinese language is an aesthetic, correlative language to the extent that it privileges the classical meanings of *you* and *wu* 無.[93] This means, as we have already stressed, that *wu* does not indicate strict opposition or contradiction, but absence. In classical Chinese philosophical discourse, the distinction between "*not-p*" and "*non-p*" is understandably elided. Thus, the *wu/you* distinction suggests mere contrast in the sense of either the presence or absence of *x*, rather than an assertion of the existence or nonexistence of *x*.

The meanings of *you* and *wu* render problematic the resort to counterfactuals, dualistic categories, or claims to capital-*T* Truth. The correlative thinker may in fact wish to claim that so-called logical relationships are more appropriately understood in correlative terms. In the absence of a single-ordered world manifesting unity and coherence, the contrast familiar in our dualistic categories of Being/Not-being, truth/falsity, and so on, does not entail exhaustiveness or formal completeness.

The *you/wu* problematic yields a vague supplement not only to modern Western notions of reason but to the postmodern critique of reason as well. For there is no need to overcome the "logocentrism" of a "language of presence" grounded in "ontological difference" if no distinction between Being and beings is urged by the classical Chinese language. A Chinese "language of presence" is a language of "making present" the item itself, not its essence.[94]

We are not arguing that the Chinese experience provides the substitution of a language of difference for a language of presence. We propose, rather, that the Chinese tradition has given us a language of *deference*. In the Western experience, two sorts of language have dominated the tradition. The first, the language of ontological presence, is that against which the postmodern thinkers have revolted. Besides the language of presence, however, the Western tradition also allows the employment of language in a mystical or mythopoetic way. In this usage, language advertises the absence of the referent. This is the language of the mystical *via negativa* or the language of the poet who holds metaphor to be constitutive of discourse rather than merely parasitical upon a literal ground. We may call such discourse "the language of absence."

A language of presence is grounded upon the possibility of univocal or unambiguous propositional expressions. This possibility requires criteria for determining the literalness of a proposition. For this to be so, literal language must take precedence over figurative or metaphorical language. This means that in addition to richly vague sorts of language associated with images and metaphors, there must be concepts as candidates for univocal meaning.

Derrida's well-rehearsed notion of *différance* tells at least part of the story.[95] This neologism is meant to suggest that the differences investigated with respect to language have both an active and a passive dimension. Meaning is always deferred. It cannot be present in language as *structure*, when that is the focus, since that omits the meanings associated with the use of the language. But focusing upon language as *event*, language as constituted by speech acts, does not solve the problem either, because once more, the supplemental character of language (this time its structure) has been shifted to an inaccessible background.

An emendation of Derrida's notion of *différance* is necessary to closer approximate the tropic nominalism of the classical Chinese thinkers. If one introduces the homonymic "defer," meaning "to yield," then the resultant notion of difference, as connoting both active and passive senses of differing and of deferring, well suits classical Chinese thinking.

In China, the language of deference involves a yielding to the appropriate models of the received tradition and to the behaviors of those who resonate with those models. In the *Great Preface* to the *Book of Songs*, traditionally attributed to Confucius, we read:

> Poetry is the consequence of dispositions and is articulated in language as song. One's feelings stir within one's breast and take the form of words. When words are inadequate, they are voiced as sighs. When sighs are inadequate, they are chanted. When chants are inadequate, unconsciously, the hands and feet begin to dance them. One's feelings are expressed in sounds, and when sounds are refined, they are called musical notes.

Language is understood here after the analogy with music. Names are like notes. Harmony is a function of the particularity of names and notes and of their mutual resonances. Neither in Chinese music nor language is there the stress upon grammar and syntax one finds in the more rationalistic languages of the West.

The Chinese language is the bearer of tradition, and tradition, made available through ritualistic evocation, is the primary context of linguistic behavior. Text and discourse in such a world have the broadest possible cultural implications. The sage appeals to present praxis and to the repository of significances realized in the traditional past in such manner as to set up deferential relationships between himself, his communicants, and the authoritative texts invoked.

The Chinese sage is not prone to tie the significances of language to the norms of present praxis. He insists upon deferential access to the appropriate traditional models. If such models are not co-opted by an authoritarian government or a rigid bureaucratic elite, as indeed has been the case in the tawdrier periods of Chinese history, there is a rich and varied resource for the criticism of present praxis in spite of the fact that the language as a system lacks any transcendent reference.

The language of presence re-presents an otherwise absent object. The language of absence uses indirect discourse to advertise the existence of a nonpresentable subject. In either case there is a referent, real or putative, beyond the act of referencing. But the language of deference is based upon the recognition of mutual resonances among instances of communicative activity. There is no referencing beyond these acts of communication as they resonate with one another and with the entertained meanings of the models from the tradition.

One of the important consequences of objective discourse is that there must be real independence of a proposition from the state of affairs it characterizes. This entails dualistic relations of propositions and states of affairs. Without such independence, in the senses of dualism and transcendence, nothing like logical truth may be formulated.

In a correlative sensibility such as we find within the Chinese tradition, terms are clustered with opposing or complementary alterterms. Classical Chinese may be uncongenial to the development of univocal propositions for this reason. Without such propositions, semantic notions of truth are ultimately untenable. And without a capital-*T* Truth lurking behind our acts of communication, notions such as "logocentrism" and "presence" cannot serve as standards for philosophical discourse. Language becomes an undulating sea of suggestiveness.

A familiar anecdote in the *Zhuangzi*, by describing the positive contribution of "chaos," provides an ontological rendering of the characteristic of the Chinese sensibility we have just discussed in terms of language:

> The ruler of the North Sea was "Swift," the ruler of the South Sea was "Sudden," and the ruler of the Central Sea was Lord Hundun—"Chaos." Swift and Sudden had on several occasions encountered each other in the territory of Chaos, and Chaos had treated them with great hospitality. Swift and Sudden, devising a way to repay Chaos' generosity, said: "Human beings all have seven orifices through which they see, hear, eat and breathe. Chaos alone is without them." They then attempted to bore holes in Chaos, each day boring one hole. On the seventh day, Chaos died.[96]

Daoism is not a vision grounded upon order in the usual sense, but upon the spontaneity of the unordered. It is a vision in which harmony has a special kind of meaning associated with the breechless, faceless, orifice-free, Lord Hundun, and the hospitable way he interacts with his neighbors.

In this parable, the rule of Chaos is to be understood relationally, residing within the boundaries of north and south. Prior to Lord Hundun's demise by having order "suddenly" and "swiftly" imposed upon him, he makes his contribution by constantly renewing order from within. The locus of implicit "disorder" or "chaos" does not inhibit or subvert the self-ordering, self-organizing process; on the contrary, it stimulates it.

The expression *"hundun* 渾沌" (or *huntun*), here translated "Chaos," requires comment. Angus Graham in rendering this anecdote into English refuses to translate *hundun* at all, insisting it must not be confused with what we generally mean by "chaos:"

> Hun-t'un [Huntun] is the primal blob which first divided into heaven and earth and then differentiated as the myriad things. In Chinese cosmology the primordial is not a chaos reduced to order by imposed law, it is a blend of everything rolled up together; the word is a reduplicative of the type of English "hotchpotch" and "rolypoly," and diners in Chinese restaurants will have met it in the form "wuntun" as a kind of dumpling.[97]

Dollops of minced meat are enfolded into amorphous wrappers which are then immersed to cook in rapidly boiling water. This pot full of tasty "wuntuns" flapping about wildly in the roiling water, then, is the Chinese image of chaos.

This dynamic sense of order which, rather than separating what orders from what is ordered, locates the energy of change within chaos itself by insisting that order is always richly vague. As aesthetic, order is reflexive: it is self-organizing and self-renewing; it is "self-soing," *ziran*.[98] Naturalizing novelty problematizes any kind of causal reductionism or simple determinism. Freedom is guaranteed.

While the articulation and stabilizing regularity of any specific event anticipates the way in which it will continue to unfold, the chaotic aspect within the event itself precludes any notion of necessity or absolute predictability. The combination of pattern and uncertainty defeats the possibility of universal claims and renders precarious any globalizing generalizations. The notion of strict identity which guarantees a fundamental law of logic is inoperative because the proposition *"A = A"* does not report on the real world. All we can depend upon is the *relative* stability of site-specific and particular expressions of order, with constant attention to stochastic variables at every level which well might amplify into large scale changes. Order is thus always local.[99] And the achievement of these orders involves correlative activity. Further, the language which best articulates such a world is the richly vague language of deference.

Though grounded in spontaneity, correlative thinking is not an accidental procedure. There are distinctive methods which prepare one to perform correlative operations. These methods cannot, of course, be detailed in the manner we often purport to detail logical procedures. Nonetheless, it might be helpful to discuss the manner of experiencing which, in those cultures amenable to correlative thinking, leads to acts of signification independent of causal analysis.

Our subject is the sort of relatedness one experiences through immediate awareness in the acosmotic (correlative) mode. We shall treat the following lines from the *Zhuangzi*:

> Ziqi said, "Now, the Great Clod expels breath and we call it wind. At times it doesn't blow. But as soon as it begins the various apertures howl passionately. Have you alone not heard its distant wail? . . . A gentle breeze produces a soft chorus and the whirlwind a great symphony. As the fierce wind subsides the various apertures become empty. Have you alone not heard its tune, its melody?"
>
> Ziyou responded, "What you mean by 'earth's piping' is these various apertures; what you mean by 'man's piping' is a row of pitchpipes. Can I ask what you mean by 'heaven's piping'?"
>
> Ziqi replied, "The wind, blowing through myriad different things, causes these sounds to die out of their own accord. Together things each take on their own sounds, but who is behind it all? . . . Day and night alternate before our eyes, yet no one knows from whence they sprout. Never mind, never mind! Morning and evening we get whatever it is from out of which we live and grow."

> There is nothing which is not a "that," and nothing which is not a "this" . . .
> Where neither "this" nor "that" has an opposite
> Is called *dao*'s pivot,
> And once one has got the pivot at the circle's center,
> One can thereby respond endlessly:
>
> "This" is continuous and endless,
> And "not this" is also continuous and endless.
> Now *dao* has never had borders;
> Speaking has never been constant.
> It is only in indicating a "this" that a boundary is set.[100]

The "Great Clod" is an interesting metaphor. In the first place, it suggests eccentricity (Can a clod be the *center* of something?), indifference to analysis (A clod is not disassembled into its unit constituents; it *crumbles*.), the absence of dignity (Clods are hardly *majestic*.), acausality (What can a clod really *do*?), formlessness (What precisely *is* a clod's shape?), insubstantiality (How long does a clod *last*?), the absence of teleology (What in the world is a clod *becoming*? What is it *meant to be*?).

Angus Graham, in a note to his translations of these same passages, makes a point which is pertinent to our argument here:

> It may be noticed that Chuang-tzu [Zhuangzi] never does say that everything is one (except as one side of a paradox . . .), (he) always speaks subjunctively of the sage treating as one.[101]

The Daoist world, as Zhuangzi sees it, is a series of "self-choosings" and "self-endings" (in the language of Graham's translation) somehow related to the definitely nonassertive, noncompelling impulsions of the Great Clod. So complex and paradoxical a notion has been interpreted in myriad ways. Zhuangzi knows these ways to be but the pipings of humankind who in their declarations and assertions manifest their own self-choosings, which add yet more voices to the clamoring of the ten thousand things. In the following paragraphs, we will add yet one more note to the score.

The experience of *dao* is of something without borders. There is no sense of the unity of the world, no feeling that "all things are one." The fundamental sense of things is of "this" and "that." Only thises and thats exist as discriminable items. Where a Daoist celebrates her oneness with all things, the meaning of "oneness" is "continuity" with other things, not "identity."

Beyond the experience of "this" and "that," there is the complex experience of "this one" and "that one," in the sense of *this* unity and *that* unity. Oneness itself is a consequence of discrimination. One can discriminate a unity in the same manner as one discriminates a given item within a complex. This is accomplished by uttering, "That's it!"

Where neither "this" nor "that" have an object, there can be no discrimination. Discriminations either of items or totalities are consequent upon interrupting the process of existence to "tag" or "name" things as "this" or "that" thing, or "this" or "that" one. *Dao*'s "pivot," then, must be any unnamed instance of the process of becoming itself.

But Zhuangzi is no more interested in dividing the world into a many than he is in combining the things of the world into a one. The discriminating claim that asserts the world to be a complex Becoming-Itself must be understood finally to mean neither that becoming-itself names a pure, uncoordinated multiplicity of acts of becoming, nor a unified act of becoming one. The locution "becoming-itself" names the reflexive reference of processes without privileging either One or Many. Continuity makes *dao* one; difference makes *dao* myriad. For the Daoist, the question is that of the difference between an (ad hoc) whole and the part that construes it, the indiscriminate field and its particular focus.

In a radical processive *a*cosmology of the sort we claim Daoism represents, "Only becoming is. . . ." *Dao* may be construed as becoming-itself, the process of each instance of becoming. The boundless, boundary-less world of the "ten thousand things" is the subject of the mystical intuition underlying Daoist philosophy. What, more particularly, is the content of that intuition?

In Christian mysticism, the God-Soul identity state leads to the sense of union which then reflects into the things of the world, suggesting that they have a penultimate if not illusory status. Alternatively, an experience of the Nihil is the sense of the vanishing of all things into a disontological Void. One may experience the ultimate emptiness, the lack of own-being in the things of the world as they dissolve into their dependent, conditional, ultimately *indifferent* features.

The Daoist intuition is distinct from these. In the first place, the sense of "this" and "that" is a grasp of the insistent particularity of each of the ten thousand things. In a remarkable reversal of the dynamic of the philosophy of presence, where Being shines through each of the beings of the world, there is the shining through of the particularity of the ten thousand things in each thing. Thus, *beings* are "made present" through every putative being.

There is no Wholeness which can serve as the ultimate object of a mystical experience. Mystical experience involves no final order, boundary, definition, goal, or structure. Quite the contrary, the Daoist mode of mystical experience disqualifies wholeness and unity. This means that Zhuangzi's mystical intuition must be one of the processes of transformation (*wuhua* 物化) without any sense of overall unity or coherence. The insistent particularity possessed by each item—its *de* 德 (that is, its "particular focus"[102])—expresses itself in processes of self-creative events which construe worlds each in its own fashion through the utterance of "That's it!"

Such mysticism yields neither the sense of final oneness or many-ness, nor does it enjoin a sense of studied indifference toward one and many. The sage sees one and many layered into shifting patterns of *that* one and *those* many, which precludes one ever losing the weight of either experience.

The sage never tries to be objective, and thus is always open to harmonious engagement. The authenticity of this person means that one can never be indifferent to the ten thousand things surrounding one, and implicated in one. By encountering the particulars in their insistent particularity, the sage attains the disposition of always har-monious attachment and engagement in feeling, idea, or action.

This sort of *wuwei* 無為, or nonassertive, noncoercive engagement, is connected to the mode of correlative thinking. It is deferential engagement with the ten thousand things which establishes the motive for making correlations between this and that. This motivation derives from nonassertive engagement with the field of potential significances which serves as source of the correlated elements. The act of engage-ment which leads to meaningful correlations involves a compositional focusing of a field of significances.

It is important to realize that Daoism avoids anthropocentrism. The Confucian may be charged with such, of course, but the Daoist cannot but recognize other measures of things than human beings. When Zhuangzi says:

> If people sleep in damp places, they ache at the waist, and end up half paralyzed. But what of the mud loach?[103]

he means to compare two perspectivally construed worlds and thus to lead us into speculations about each of these worlds construed from the distinctive perspectives of the beings who create them.

It would be to miss the point to believe that the spontaneity of correlative thinking is *accidental*. Awareness is essential; preparation is crucial, and practice is indispensable. Impersonal thinkers insensi-tive to the insistent particularity of the items encountered in their ambiance, detached individuals seeking objectivity, believing above all in the ultimacy of fact, couldn't correlate their way out of a paper bag.

The acosmotic character of Daoism is based upon the affirmation rather than the negation of chaos. In the Anglo-European tradition, Chaos as emptiness, separation, or confusion is to be overcome. In Daoism, the chaotic aspect of things is to be left alone to contribute spontaneity to the processes of transformation. As Wang Bi in his commentary on the *Daodejing* says, "The myriad things manage and order themselves."[104]

Each particular element in the totality has its own intrinsic excellence and integrity. The Chinese term is *de* 德. This is the same character found in the title, *Daodejing*. We might thus translate the title of this text as the *Classic of Totality and Particularity*, or perhaps, the *Classic of Field and Focus*. Given the prescriptive and performative assumptions which attend expositions on order in the Chinese world (not only how the world is, but how it ought to be), *de* is understood not only as "this particular focus" but also as "the intrinsic excellence of this thing." The *de* of any phenomena is the means whereby it articulates the totality of things from its perspective, and thus "names" and creates a world.

An analogy might help here. Consider the value of any particular note in a symphony. The value of any one note can only be assayed by understanding its place in the entire piece of music and its performance. Any one note thus has implicated within it the entire score. The note thus has a holographic quality, bringing the field of relevant relationships into focus from one particular locus. Important here is that the field of relationships is not circumscribed or holistic, but an unbounded reservoir of particular detail that remains open and available for further inclusion. The field of relevant detail for the particular note can be extended to include a movement in another piece by the same composer, or his entire corpus, or the musical product of a particular era, and so on. As an increasing amount of detail is included, the focus becomes increasingly blurred.

The concepts of *dao* and *de* form a single notion, *daode* 道德, which is best understood in terms of the relationships of field (*dao*) and focus (*de*). In fact, as we have noticed elsewhere,[105] in the early historical literature, Daoism was known as *daodejia* 道德家—"the school (or "lineage") of *dao* and *de*" (rather than as the abbreviated *daojia* 道家—"the school of *dao*," as it is presently known). Just as in a holographic display each detail contains the whole in an adumbrated form; so each item of the totality focuses the totality in its entirety.

The particular focus of an item establishes its world, its environment. In addition, the totality as sum of all possible orders is adumbrated by each item.

Daoism is both "horizontal" and radically perspectival. Thus, there is true ontological parity. There are no hierarchies built upon implicit ontological claims. No "Great Chain of Being" or "Ladder of Perfection" exists in the Daoist thinking; only "the parity of all things" (*qiwu* 齊物), where each thing is at once insistently itself, and necessary for everything else to be what it is.[106]

The Daoist naturalized sense of becoming makes of the things that become, the final realities, though in their processive state they are not objectively, substantively, or in any sense *permanently* real. In fact, the character conventionally translated "real," *zhen* 眞, explicitly entails a processional understanding of reality. *Dao* as becoming-itself names the chaotic matrix of transformations which may be spoken of only in terms of their particular, concrete differences. Any attempt to make Being present through the beings of the world must perforce be rejected. Zhuangzi insists that "each thing comes into being from its own inner reflection and none can tell how it comes to be so."[107]

We are appealing to Daoism here to make the claim that order in the classical Chinese tradition, laced as it is with uncertainty, is always local and specific, constituting the coordination of "thises" and "thats." But we could as well make our case by reference to the classical Confucian corpus, where the qualitatively achieved person (*ren* 仁) is constituted ritually by personalizing (*yi* 義) formal patterns of conduct (*li* 禮). *Ren* is resolutely particular because the path that is walked is necessarily appropriated and personalized in the process of self-articulation. Hence, the general assertion that "it is the humanity that broadens the *dao*, not the *dao* that broadens humanity" is perhaps more appropriately rendered:

> It is this human being who broadens this *dao*, not this *dao* that broadens this human being. [108]

5. THE DOMINANCE OF HAN THINKING

We would now like to continue our exploration of the classical Chinese tradition by taking "Confucian thinking" as our primary focus. The relationship between "rationality" and "imagination" in configuring a Confucian world can serve to reinforce our claim that this vague, aesthetic sense of order is a pervasive feature of the Chinese world view.

The problems that have arisen for Western sinologists trying to make sense of the Chinese world view are numerous. First, we have to identify the fundamental commonalities and differences defining the relationships of our two civilizations; and then, we must attempt to exploit the linguistic resources of the Western tradition in such a manner as to reveal the similarities and differences in a balanced fashion. There are, of course, two major ways to err in this project. If we come to the tradition anticipating sameness, it is sameness we shall find. Likewise with the presupposition of difference.

The attitude of "Orientalism,"[109] which thrives upon the expectation of difference, moves between the extremes of romantic adulation and utter condescension. The universalist perspective, which expects sameness, has been more consistently expressed. The universalist recognizes differences in levels of attainment between China and Western liberal democracies in areas ranging from jurisprudence to technological sophistication. This position sees China on the same track as the West, only lagging far behind.

We would be naive were we to suggest that we have always succeeded in avoiding the *déformation professionelle* which threatens those nominalist and historicist approaches to alternative cultures that we endorse. Ours is the expectation of difference. But pragmatists such as we claim to be, can afford the smugness neither of romanticism nor of condescension. Our world, constituted by concreteness and particularity, is perforce patterned by difference. But differences, apart from the manner in which they may be exploited for practical purposes, are neither good nor bad. They sometimes are, however, most promising. To elide the differences is often to cancel important opportunities.

5.1. History and Historiography

The classical Chinese assumption is that personal, societal, and political order, as well as the order of the "ten thousand things," are coterminous and mutually entailing.[110] The assumption is, for example, that abnormal conduct within the human sphere will adversely affect the rhythm of the four seasons, and will ultimately result in natural climatic disorder.

The Chinese conception of aesthetic order, in contrast to the rational understanding of order, is characterized by the multiperspectival organization of particular details. Such order is not a function of "locus" (the placement of items in such a manner as to realize a formal pattern) but of "focus" (the construal of the particular elements in a field from the perspectives of focal centers).[111]

In our discussions of the tripartite *psyche* of Plato, and its permutations in figures such as Aristotle and Augustine, we attempted to show that this relational pattern was employed analogically to articulate the order not only of the human personality, but of the sociopolitical matrix, and of the Divine life, as well. This tripartite structure constituted a transcendental form which was thought to reveal the logical orderedness of the world in its psychological, social, and cosmological characters. We shall now see how very different was the Chinese approach to the question of order.

To illustrate the focus/field understanding of order in the classical Chinese world we will use the concrete historical example of the Han dynasty (206 B.C.E.–220 C.E.). The Han dynasty recommends itself for several reasons. First, it provides us with the first sufficiently detailed account of the dynamics of the classical Chinese world order. Secondly, there are clear indications of a far-ranging philosophic transformation in the conception of orderedness that marks the last centuries of the Zhou and the beginning of the Han dynasty. There seems to be a movement away from the particularistic and fragmented orders of Confucian aestheticism, and a marked shift in the direction of unity.

This movement can be sketched in the following terms. At a political level, the ascendancy of the Legalist thinkers and their ideas reinforced a movement toward federalism. Not only was political unification achieved, most graphically symbolized perhaps by the joining of the Great Wall, but a process of standardization affected society at every level: codification of laws, fixed weights and measures, formalization of the written language, the minting of coinage, and so on.

Angus Graham observes that whenever the frequently paired Shen Nong 神農 and Yellow Emperor (*Huangdi* 黃帝) are distinguished in the literature, Shen Nong is cast as the patriarch of a primitive and pastoral society, while the Yellow Emperor "stands as the founder in a new era of organized government."[112] According to the *Jingfa* 經法

treatise in the *Silk Manuscripts of the Yellow Emperor* (*Huangdi boshu* 黃帝帛書) (dated c. 179–168 B.C.E.), in fact, it is said that the Yellow Emperor "laid down the principles of government and became the 'ancestor of the empire'." Of course, it is this same Yellow Emperor as representative of systematic and regulatory government who is introduced into third century B.C.E. Daoism to constitute the popular Huang-Lao movement of the early Han.

Among the "Hundred Schools," the more analytically inclined philosophers (the later Mohist logicians, the School of Names, the Sophists) achieved a prominence that had previously eluded them. On the Confucian side, the more rationalistic wing represented by Xunzi—teacher of the Legalists, Han Fei and Li Si—led the Confucian tradition, at least temporarily, ever closer to Legalism. Extensive codes of ritual actions were articulated, and, following the Qin dynasty, the emergence of a Confucian state ideology brought with it the establishment of canonical texts and exegetical schools.

During this same period, there was a movement from what Karlgren has called the "free texts" of the Zhou era to the "systematizing" texts of the early Han, in which previously loose legends and heroes are drafted to serve as elements in set theoretical constructions.[113] There emerged a new genre of literature which, through a sometimes strained syncretism, pretended to a kind of encyclopedic comprehensiveness.[114] At the same time, in the movement to compile exhaustive histories, the philosophers are sorted and classified into sometimes unlikely schools on the basis of what are perceived to be overarching concerns.

"Systematic" natural philosophy dawns in China during this transition period, joining the social and the political disciplines as an important area of philosophic concern. In late Zhou, the Yinyang School, promoted by Zou Yan and other members of the Jixia academy, becomes a major force. In his work on early Chinese "cosmology," John Major reports on the gradual integration and coordination of previously disparate precosmological fragments into formal systems.[115] This increasingly overt sense of an order pervasive throughout the social, political and natural worlds, seemingly moving *in the direction* of what we have called "logical" order, is perhaps nowhere in greater evidence than in the emergence, finally, of explicit genealogical myths which function analogously to Western cosmogonies. For, as we have seen, cosmogonic speculation may very well entail a concern for the articulation of first principles and the single-ordered world they define.

But to suggest that during this period China moved from what we have called first problematic thinking, familiar in classical Confucianism, to the second problematic that we have associated with classical Western thought is to overstate the case. In fact, if we use the language often employed to characterize classical Greece, China in the transition from late Zhou to Han, far from moving from chaos to cosmos, from *mythos* to *logos*, from religion to philosophy, moved instead from a failed aesthetic order to an efficacious one, from a period of disunity and discord to the vague harmony of correlativity, from *interregnum* to dynasty. A pattern of unity followed by disunity emerged in this period that was to repeat itself many times throughout China's imperial history.

The first volume of the *Cambridge History of China* describes the career of the Han empire from its emergence under Liu Bang to its gradual disintegration three-and-a-half centuries later.[116] In this volume, Yü Ying-shih uses the "five zones" (*wufu* 五服) of submission as a device for describing the dynamics of the Han world order:

> According to this theory, China since the Hsia [Xia] dynasty had been divided into five concentric and hierarchical zones or areas. The central zone (*tien-fu* [*dianfu* 甸服]) was the royal domain, under the direct rule of the king. The royal domain was immediately surrounded by the Chinese states established by the king, known collectively as the lords' zone (*hou-fu* [侯服]). Beyond the *hou-fu* were Chinese states conquered by the reigning dynasty, which constituted the so-called pacified zone (*sui-fu* [綏服] or *pin-fu* [*binfu* 儐服], guest zone). The last two zones were reserved for the barbarians. The Man and I [Yi] barbarians lived outside the *sui-fu* or *pin-fu* in the controlled zone (*yao-fu* [要服]), which was so called because the Man and I were supposedly subject to Chinese control, albeit of a rather loose kind. Finally, beyond the controlled zone lay the Jung [Rung] and Ti [Di] barbarians, who were basically their own masters in the wild zone (*huang-fu* [荒服]) where the sinocentric world order reached its natural end.[117]

This hierarchical scheme also described the descending degree of tribute in the form of local products and services that was provided to

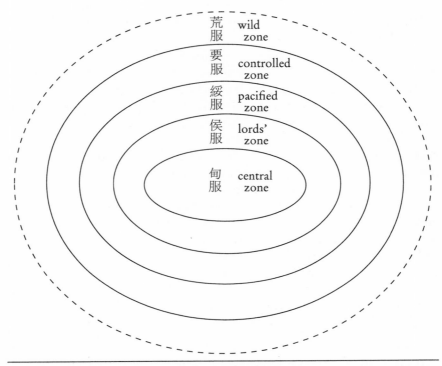

Figure 3.1. *The five-zone* (wufu 五服) *model of political order during the Han dynasty*

the court at the center. Although this five zone theory might seem more complex, it is really a focus/field distinction that defines the relative focus of an "inner-outer (*nei-wai* 內外)" circle:

> China was the inner region relative to the outer region of the barbarians, just as the royal domain was, relative to the outer lords' zone, an inner zone, and the controlled zone became the inner area relative to the wild zone on the periphery of Chinese civilization.[118]

This radial solar system seems to be a signature of the Chinese world order. It is a centripetal order articulated outward from a central axis through patterns of deference. These concrete patterns "con-*tribute*" in varying degrees, and are themselves constitutive of the authority at the center. They shape and bring into focus the standards and values of the social and political entity. This determinate, detailed, center-seeking focus fades into an increasingly indeterminate and untextured field. The magnetic attraction of the center is such that, with varying degrees of success, it draws into its field and suspends the disparate, diverse, and often mutually inconsistent centers that constitute its world.

Within the continent that was Warring States China, the full spectrum of peoples—some paying their allegiance to traditional hereditary houses, some ruled by locally powerful warlords, others organized around religious doctrines, yet others governed by clan or tribal regulation—were suspended in the Han harmony with each contributing in greater or lesser degree to the definition of Han culture. It was the effective correlation of these constitutive centers which determined the quality of the harmony of the field called "Han."

The Chinese sense of order is generally organized in the language of mutually defining and thus complementary opposites, such as "inner-outer," where history is construed as correlated events that move the process along this continuum.[119] Such oppositions are always more or less "inner," more or less "outer;" more or less "Chinese," more or less "barbarian." When the center is strong, tribute moves in to reinforce it, with the greatest degree of influence on the center being exerted from elements close to the center itself: the court officials, the aristocracy, the wealthy merchants, the military leaders, the population of the capital. As the center weakens, incidental elements which were on the periphery have the potential to exert an increasing amount of influence in the gradual process of reshaping, and in some instances subverting, the center. To the extent they do so, they move inward, and cease to be marginal.

This focus/field sense of order in which all of the diversity and difference characteristic of the multiple, competing political centers of the Warring States period are lifted into the deeply etched and powerful harmony of the Han dynasty has a ready analogy in its intellectual world. The intellectual geography of the Hundred Schools in the pre-Qin period gives way to a syncretic Confucian-centered doctrine which absorbs into itself and to some degree conceals the richness of what were competing elements, to articulate the philosophical and religious character of the period. Even where absorption has not been total, the lingering shadows of what were competing positions are themselves defined in terms of opposition to this Confucian center. This movement from disunity to unity is better expressed in the language of incorporation and accommodation than in terms of suppression and exclusion. The center sought is defined by and is definitive of that ethnicity from which most later Chinese will come to characterize themselves as "people of the Han."

As the centripetal core of the Han court weakens in the second century of the Common Era, and as the political order gradually dissolves into a period of disunity, the disparate centers precipitate out of the harmony to reassert themselves, and what had been their contribution to the harmonious diversity becomes the energy of contest among them. What was a tightening spire in the early Han becomes a gyre, disgorging itself of its disassociated contents. In the same period, there is a resurgence of competing philosophical schools and religious movements that reflect a disintegration of the centrally driven intellectual harmony.

It is important to acknowledge the importance of both the determinate and indeterminate aspects of this continuing process of world ordering. The locus of implicit "disorder" does not necessarily inhibit or subvert the self-ordering, self-organizing process; on the contrary, it can renew it. Changes in determinate orders are often irregular and unpredictable since seemingly minute fluctuations on the periphery can have dramatic effects. Periods of disunity in China, while often taking a toll in life and property, have also had a positive side. These interludes have been a source of revitalization, of creative transformation, of enrichment from what was the political and cultural margins. The relaxing of the strength which enforces a particular world order allows for the absorption of new and competing cultural and social forces, ideologies, and customs.

The familiar commentarial tradition in Chinese letters which begins in earnest during the Han dynasty is another illustration of this pervasive radial order. The commentarial tradition that attends Confucius, for example, is a sustained effort to clarify richly vague images. The *xungu* 訓詁 approach entails "*xun* 訓," the tracking down of a particular meaning at a particular place and time, and "*gu* 詁," the identification and explanation of old objects: plants, minerals, animals, and so on. This search for specific detail stands in obvious contrast to a more conceptual and theoretically oriented methodology.

Chinese historians have traditionally attracted respect for their compilations of a quite astounding variety of data, which, by virtue of the concreteness of their content, disclose the subtlety and detail of the historical terrain. On the other hand, they are relatively uncelebrated when it comes to the sweeping generalizations and grand methodological programs of the synoptic theorist.

The discrepancy between what the Confucian tradition has meant by historical understanding and what Western historians consider legitimate knowledge is evidenced in the willingness of the latter to critique the Chinese attempt to chronicle its own history by applying methodological and theoretical principles drawn from their rationalistic historiographies.[120]

Maureen Robertson, in her discussion of different historiographical models, demonstrates that the application of selective historical standards is an attempt to recover an intelligible pattern in the treatment of a large mass of data which otherwise remains formless and meaningless:

> When historians claim a close fit between their patterned or periodized accounts and actualities of the past, it is often easy to forget how highly selective a body of historical data is, how compelling the need to construct meanings is, and how processes of historical generalization and cultural coding work to shape that body.[121]

The periodizations familiar in the West

> have had a teleological character; movement is toward an anticipated end—the perfection of human reason, the Last Judgment, utopian social order, or the triumph of technology.[122]

By contrast, the model of irregular periodization that one would associate with the Chinese tradition

> claims strict dependence upon the configurations of the data studied, and does not, in its structure at least, display a belief that change obeys laws of regularity or directionality. . . . [T]he historian is likely to discover patterns he is culturally predisposed to see.[123]

That is, each heir to the tradition is responsible for ordering history's welter of "thises" and "thats" according to some site-specific and particular framework of correlations.

Although Robertson's distinction between Western and Chinese historiographical presuppositions has considerable merit, the contrast as stated might be too severe. It is possible to compare the Chinese organization of cultural experience with the manner we are inclined to periodize art. Our own conceptions of art history do not usually entail the theoretical assumptions which dominate other historical generalizations. Instead, a period or movement tends to be radial. It collects around and is defined by leading exemplars and their products, and by their lineages and schools. There is often only the most tentative sense of logical or causal relationships assumed in the movement from one period to the next. The assumption is that some periods stand out as having been richer and more compelling than others, and as such, may be judged qualitatively superior. Thus, the mode of Western historiography which resonates best with the methods of Chinese historians is that which characterizes most narratives of artistic activity.

5.2. The Correlative Circle of the "Leishu" 類書

One important method of exploring the sense of order dominant in a particular culture would be to examine the different structures under which knowledge itself is catalogued and organized. Liang Congjie 梁從誡, in his comparative work concerning the taxonomical structures employed in storing and organizing knowledge, provides us with a concrete way of envisioning the model of order pervasive in the Chinese tradition. Bringing this model into contrast with that of our own tradition alerts us to the provincial character of some of our presuppositions concerning order.[124]

We may recall that within the classical Western tradition, there was a distinctive concern with the organization and classification of both the ways of knowing and the body of the known. We have discussed in some detail the employment of taxonomies such as Plato's Divided Line and Aristotle's distinctions of theoretical, practical, and productive activities as means of organizing the ways in which the activity of knowing may be rationalized. We shall summarize and ramify

THE FORM OF THE GOOD

NOESIS (Reason) "Knowing Why"	Systems, General Principles
DIANOIA (Understanding) "Knowing That"	Specialized Theories, Abstractions
PISTIS (Belief) "Knowing How"	Conventional Objects, Techniques, Dogmas
EIKASIA (Imagination) "Guessing," "Feeling"	Fictions, Second-Hand Knowledge

Figure 3.2. *Plato's divided line*

those discussions before articulating the distinctive manner in which the Chinese came to approach the development of "encyclopaedias."

Plato's Divided Line organizes both the principal modes of knowing as well as the subject matter of each mode. The principle of organization in this Platonic scheme is that of abstract form. This principle serves to define both the subject matters of the various disciplines and the aim at formal unity of all the ways of knowing. We move from the world of sense experience to that of belief and thence to the realm of specialized theory grounded upon justified principles, and finally to the noetic realm in which mathematics and dialectic, the most formal of the disciplines, reside. The Principle of the Good exists beyond the confines of the classification, serving as the ultimate ground for the unity of the disciplines.

Aristotle's organization of the ways of knowing is horizontal in structure, as opposed to Plato's hierarchical taxonomy. Nonetheless, there is a clear hierarchy suggested by Aristotle's most prominent means of organizing the sciences. Recall the priority given to rest and permanence in the Greek tradition, and, in particular, Aristotle's claims (against Democritus) to the effect that motion must have an origin, and, therefore, requires an explanation. Aristotle carries this

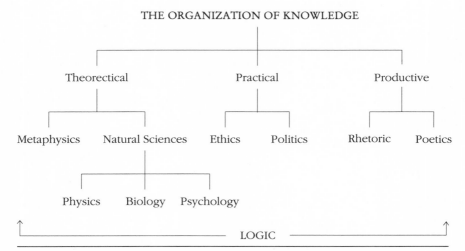

Figure 3.3.   *Aristotle's Organization of Knowledge*

belief into his understanding of the best manner of organizing the ways of knowing.[125]

Permanence is prior; motion secondary. But our world is characterized by types of motion. It is by recourse to principles of motion that we shape and organize our ways of knowing the world. There are four main sorts of investigations: First, we may enquire into those things which are unmoved; second, we may enquire into those things which move but have their principle of motion internal to them; third, we investigate those things which are characterized by both internal and external principles of motion; and fourth, we can ask after those items which are moved solely by external forces.

Alternatively, and these schemes are not inconsistent, Aristotle employs a structure analogous to Plato's tripartite psyche with its distinctive faculties of knowing, doing, and making to provide a basis for his organization of the disciplines. We move from "knowing," which at the highest level is a "thinking on thinking" (in which the mind rests in itself); through "doing" or "acting," which is shaped by both internal and external principles; to "making," which involves the production of artificial objects, such as speeches or plays (or shoes, for that matter), solely by recourse to external causes.

Further, just as with Plato's four levels of the clarity of knowledge, Aristotle presumed that there was a unity and coherence to the various ways of knowing. Whereas Plato found that unity in the dialectical organization of the most general principles finally realized in the Principle of the Good which resided beyond the four levels, so Aristotle employed the methods of logic as the basic means of articulating the pattern for discourse in all of the sciences. And, like the Principle of the Good, Aristotle's logic is not one among the various ways of knowing, but is the tool employed by all who would come to know.

In addition to attempts to classify the various disciplinary means of coming to know, there were the more "encyclopedic" efforts associated with the organization of the body of the known. The focus here is upon the objective description of the "knowable" in relation to the "known."

A familiar model for the organization of knowledge has been based on the "tree" metaphor employed by Aristotle. The assumption is that through analysis we can define certain underlying objective essences which enable us to divide that which is known into exclusive subcategories. We can thus use the branches of a "tree of knowledge" to assign a place to any species in the natural world, and to describe its place in the natural order of things.

Mary Tiles has discussed the Aristotelian genera/species mode of classification in some detail:

> The kind of rational structure which is given prominence in Aristotle's works is the structure of a classificatory system—a hierarchy of kinds of things organised successively by kinds (or genera) and forms of those kinds (or species). (In turn species become in effect genera to be divided into [sub]species and genera grouped into more comprehensive genera.) Definitions were not in the first instance thought to be accounts of words but of the "what-it-is-to-be" a thing of that kind, in other words accounts of essence. To define an object—give its name a precise or correct use—was to locate it in a classificatory system. Early in the Christian era this way of schematizing things was given its definitive icon in what is now known as the tree of Porphyry (after a neo-Platonist who lived c. 250 A.D.). On such a tree we can display for example the definition of *man*.[126]

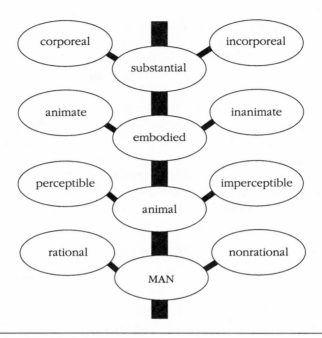

Figure 3.4.   A version of *Porphyry's Tree*

Commenting on the assumptions behind this method of classification, Tiles observes:

> This is a hierarchical order based on qualitative similarities and differences. A key assumption underlying such an order is that a thing cannot both have and lack a given quality—the requirement of non-contradiction. Non-contradiction is therefore fundamental to this kind of rational order. . . . Knowledge of definitions (or essences) coupled with the principle of non-contradiction can serve as the foundation for further, rationally demonstrable, knowledge.[127]

Turning again to Plato, we may further articulate the consequences of his manner of appealing to the principle of form. Plato finds that it is not the elements of a complex, but the relationships among those elements, which serve as the proper objects of knowledge. Our aim is not the analytic activity of articulating the parts; rather, knowledge is synthetic in the sense that it concerns how things fit together:

Harmony, ratios of numbers, rationality and accounts of how things ideally should be, all come to have close conceptional connections in Plato's thought. . . . Ratio and harmony are intrinsically relational concepts and rationality requires not merely distinguishing the distinct, but also observing the connections among the related.[128]

The implications of measuring one thing in terms of another for what we take to be our possible range of knowledge are enormous. For one thing, this means that reasoning is firmly rooted in "ratio" or "measurement":

Ratios can extend knowledge through the system of inter-relations to other things not directly knowable. . . . The ability to extend knowledge from the immediately known in this way indicates the power and hence the attractiveness of this conception of what we can know and how we can reason about it. . . . For inferences of this kind appear to confer on men the capacity to acquire a form of knowledge which transcends the limitations of human experience.[129]

The necessary logical relations that obtain among the categories of our knowledge coupled with teleological assumptions about an organic world-order enable us in principle to extend our purview and know the universe in all its parts. It is not surprising, then, that the Western tradition has so often tended to treat knowledge of the world as progressive, working on the assumption that more recent compilations supersede those that have gone before.

One of the most influential illustrations of hierarchical structure in the Western tradition is that associated with the belief in "The Chain of Being." This was the view, traced in Arthur Lovejoy's classic work *The Great Chain of Being*,[130] which assumed a continuous ladder of beings, "from the mushroom to the Angels"—in fact, from the emptiness of nonbeing to the fullness of being represented by the uncreated esssence of the Holy Trinity. No better illustration of the "squaring" of the cosmos may be found than that which establishes an absolute floor and ceiling for the cosmic edifice.

A most dramatic illustration of the enclosure of knowledge and being is to be found in a diagram from Robert Fludd's *Utriusque cosmi–historia* entitled "Nature and Art" (figure 3.5). Of course,

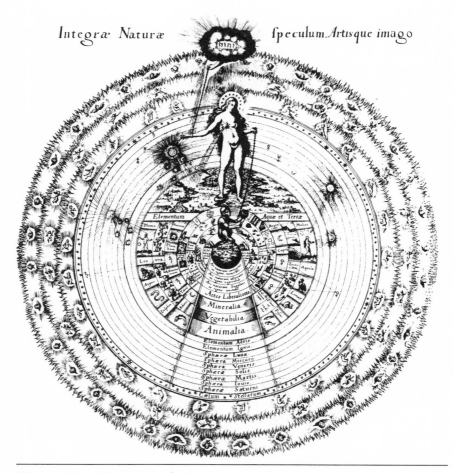

Figure 3.5. *Nature and Art*

Fludd is working within the magical and mystical traditions of medieval religion, but his presentation of the spheres of nature and art (the imitation of nature), reveal the affirmation of a link between knowledge and power which will soon be expressed in the rational science of the sixteenth century.

In this figure one can see the elemental world surrounding the central earth. This world is itself enclosed by the celestial world composed of the sun, moon, planets, and stars. The sun (the light of knowledge) is represented by a woman. The monkey seated on the earth symbolizes human art as the clever "aping" of nature. Beyond the fixed stars are three angelic spheres which enclose the elemental and celestial worlds. Finally, there is God, his Hebrew name written in the clouds, who is both creator and arbiter of the natural, celestial, and angelic spheres. The chains linking the monkey to the woman and the woman to the Deity represent the power of knowledge to manipulate nature through art and artifice. The total message is that the realms of nature and art are enclosed within the limits set by the Deity. The power of knowledge is to be expressed in accordance with those limits.

There is a stark contrast between these models of classification and the one characteristically found in the traditional "encyclopedic or classificatory works" (*leishu* 類書) of China. As we have noted above, Chinese "categories" (*lei* 類) are not understood by appeal to a shared essence or "natural kinds," but by a functional similarity or relationship that obtains among unique particulars.

At first blush, the organization of the Chinese encyclopedia seems elusive, if not truly Borgesian.[131] In the absence of what we would take to be logically defined relationships, there is not much to discipline what appears to be a welter of disparate detail. This is particularly true as one gets closer to the text and examines the individual entries. For here we encounter what for the enculturated Westerner is more than a little disconcerting: The Chinese don't seem to know what a definition is! Indeed, each time we have reason to expect the definition of a term, we are confronted only with the sort of vagueness we have presupposed throughout this work. Examples, yes. Models, certainly. Definitions, hardly.

The confusion is easy enough to overcome, however. Once we recognize that there is no basis for appeal to objective connotation in the sense that there can be no effort to characterize all of the essential properties common to the members of a class, then we shall understand that there can be no objective denotation in which, presupposing the connotative properties, we could point out all the members of a class. Once we understand this, we shall avoid demanding a definition and remain content with asking for concrete examples and models. If we stubbornly persist in our confusion and ask what the examples or models to which we have been directed are examples or models *of*, we shall be pointed, not toward abstract nouns, but in the direction of specific, paradigmatic instances celebrated, for this reason or that, by the tradition.

In a tradition that depends upon instances rather than formal definitions, and historical models rather than abstract principles, we should not expect the means of organizing knowledge to greatly resemble our logical classifications. For example, it is the earliest reference in the canons of classical literature, rather than principled explanation grounded in the canons of reason and logic, that holds the weight of authority.

In Chinese compendia, there is little interest in the objective description of natural phenomena. The concern is with analogical classification. And this concern, specifically, is with the relationship that the various contents of the world have to the social and cultural values which shape human experiences of it. As an example, Liang Congjie points out that "of the fifty-five sections (*bu* 部) that make up the *Taiping yulan* 太平卸覽, six of them—emperors, imperial relatives, officials, human affairs, ancestors, and ceremony—occupy thirty-five percent of the work."[132]

The Chinese *leishu* is hierarchical, though the hierarchy is not based upon distinctions such as genera/species or principles of abstract form. The human being is placed *self-consciously* at the center. However, "human being" here does not refer to a transcendental "humanity," but to the specific imperial Chinese person embedded within a particular set of historical circumstances.

The *leishu* illustrates what we should call an "ethical" or "aesthetic," rather than a "logical," principle of organization. Individual entries begin with the most "noble" and conclude with the most "base": animals begin with "lion" and "elephant" and finish with "rat" and "fox"; trees begin with "pine tree" and "cypress" and end with "thistles" and "brambles."

The world is not described in terms of objective essences but is divided, prescriptively, into natural and cultural elements which have an increasing influence upon the experience of the Chinese court as they stand in proximity to the center. An implication of the tropic nominalism which pervades this tradition is that the ruler, in "naming" (*ming* 名) his world, is "commanding" (*ming* 命) it to be a certain way.

Categories on the upper portion of the circle, by virtue of the benefits they provide the court, are more noble, while those on the lower half of the circle, by virtue of their possible noxious influences,

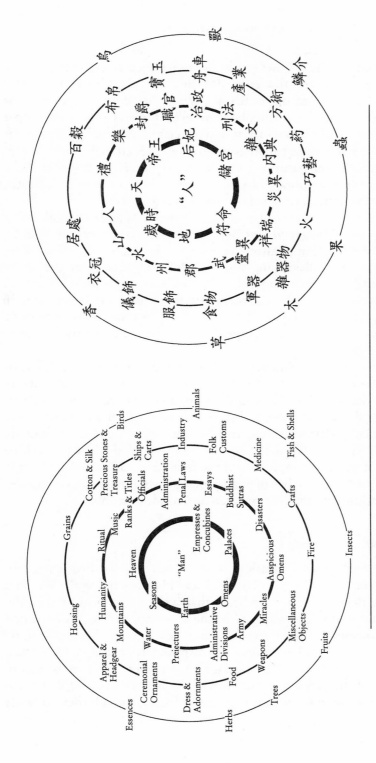

Figure 3.6. *The leishu circle of the* Yiwen leiju 藝文類聚 *(from Liang Congjie [1986])*

are more base. The Chinese cultural experience is embodied in the ruler at the center, and the *leishu* not only organizes his world in this particular way—it recommends it. When the court is strong, the centripetal harmony is maintained and everything is kept in its proper place; as the center inevitably weakens, elements which were on the periphery come to exert increasing influence. Seemingly insignificant abnormalities in the natural world, for example, reflect disorder at the court, and if not responded to in a timely way, can exert a dramatic, even transformative influence on the reigning center.

The limitations of this comparison between Western classification strategies and Chinese *leishu* arise when we consider the specific function of these compilations in each of the traditions. What were scholars doing in classifying their worlds? The fact that the *leishu* were generally commissioned by the court as a resource for indoctrinating an emerging bureaucracy has to be taken into account. In using the *leishu* to prepare for the official examinations, would-be officials were imbibing the Emperor's understanding of the world as it ought to be.

What are the consequences of taking the *leishu* notions of classification on their own terms? It relieves us of commitments to abstract essences, objective connotation, and class concepts. We surrender our devotion to internal and external principles of motion and mathematical relations, and revoke our pre-Darwinian faith in immutable species. We are, likewise, relieved of the onus of asking always, not for an example, but for a *definition*. In sum, we are ready to consult a Chinese dictionary or peruse a Chinese encyclopaedia, with an attitude neither of romance nor condescension.

5.3. Han "Cosmologies"

We proceed now to consider what is referred to throughout the literature on the early Han Dynasty as "Han cosmology". We have said more than enough to indicate that we are skeptical of the relevance of the term "cosmology" in the sense applied to Western natural philosophies. Western thinkers, reading of "cosmological" speculation in the Han, might be disposed to presume that these involved a consideration of the *logos* of the *cosmos*—that is, a consideration of the order and structure of the cosmos as a single-ordered world. We hope to show that Han cosmologies, though they certainly constitute formal and complex attempts to systematize and organize the things of the world, do not seem in any substantial manner to insist upon the comprehensive unity or singularity of the order determined to exist among the "ten thousand things." Thus, Han speculations did little to promote second problematic thinking among later Chinese philosophers. In fact, what we are calling first problematic, or correlative, thinking is perhaps most explicitly present in the so-called "cosmological" speculations of the early Han Dynasty. Indeed, as we have noted above, most discussions of correlative thinking in China share the view of Angus Graham rehearsed earlier to the effect that correlative thinking was not in evidence in the philosophers from Confucius to Han Fei.[133]

The identification of correlative thinking with the development of Han dynasty speculations has led many if not most scholars to associate correlativity with a phase of protoscientific thinking in China. And though its influence beyond the Han is well attested, earlier thinking, notably that of Confucius and his disciples as presented in the *Analects*, and even later thinkers, notably the philosophical Daoists, are often thought to employ something other than correlative thinking.

Our view, however, is that Marcel Granet was essentially correct in identifying what we are here calling correlative thinking with a fundamental commitment of the Chinese sensibility. This implies that even among those thinkers such as Confucius and the philosophical Daoists who were not so concerned with physical speculations, the mode of correlative thinking dominates. Our argument here is that Han exercises in correlative thinking are not anomalous, but are rather signal instances of correlative thinking in a tradition replete with such instances.

The primary evidence for this belief is that, as we have argued in our *Thinking Through Confucius*, the most influential strains of classical Chinese thought illustrate the primary characteristics of first problematic thinking—namely, the absence of belief in a single-ordered world and the employment of aesthetic over logical senses of order. Correlative thinking is an implication of these assumptions.

Han speculations led to the creation of vast and complex tables of correspondences that organized the psychological, physiological, social, and "natural" ambiance of human experience. Such classifications include body parts, psycho-physical and affective states, styles

	日	帝	神	虫	音	数	味	臭	祀	祭	方向	色	食	德
春	甲乙	太皞	句芒	鳞	角	八	酸	膻	户	脾	东	青	麦羊	木
夏	丙丁	炎帝	祝融	羽	征	七	苦	焦	灶	肺	南	赤	菽鸡	火
秋	庚辛	少皞	蓐收	毛	商	九	辛	腥	门	肝	西	白	麻犬	金
冬	壬癸	颛顼	玄冥	介	羽	六	咸	朽	行	肾	北	黑	黍彘	水

Table 3.1. Lushi chunqiu *"Mengchunji" Uses the Four Seasons as its Framework*[135]

五行	方位	时序	五气	生化	脏	腑	窍	体	志	色	味	音	声
木	东	春	风	生	肝	胆	目	筋	怒	青	酸	角	呼
火	南	夏	暑	长	心	小肠	舌	脉	喜	赤	苦	征	笑
土	中	长夏	湿	化	脾	胃	口	肉	思	黄	甘	宫	歌
金	西	秋	燥	收	肺	大肠	鼻	皮毛	忧	白	辛	商	哭
水	北	冬	寒	藏	肾	膀胱	耳	骨	恐	黑	咸	羽	呻

Table 3.2. Huangdi neijing *Uses the "Five Phases" as its Framework*[136]

of government, weather, tastes, domestic animals, technological instruments, heavenly bodies, and much more, depending on the main subject under scrutiny.[134] The active (*yang* 陽) and more passive (*yin* 陰) dynamics are employed in conjunction with these correspondences to organize and to articulate the transformations and interrelations of the elements within the system.

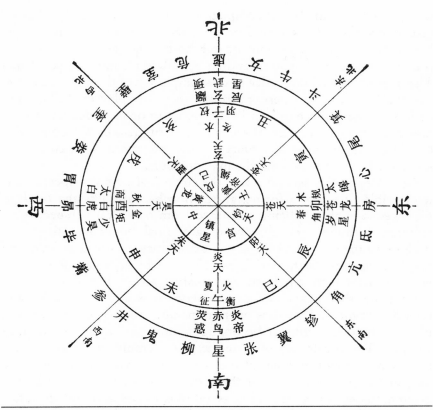

Figure 3.7. *A Reconstruction of the* "Tianwen *(astronomy)*" *treatise of the* Huainanzi *which reflects one correlative schema*[137]

There are several points to make in reflecting on these correlative schemata. First, the correlations entail a radial center around which they are arrayed: one of the cardinal points, for example, is itself designated "the center," which in turn is correlated with yellow, earth, the capital, the inner court, and so on. What constitutes the center and the specific framework is a function of expressed interest. In a medical text, it would likely be the heart, while in a treatise on the heavens, it would be a particular sky.

Secondly, the pattern of correlations constitute an ad hoc framework. There is no disciplining "system," in the rigorous sense of the term, which would assume completion and closure. To rationalize or essentialize the pattern would be to violate its premises. The schema has to be in some important degree both contingent and vague in order to invite participation and to stimulate imaginative construal. The images selected do justice to the complexity of the world, and the pattern of order that emerges through their interplay might be more or less relevant, more or less inclusive, more or less adequate to the task of shaping a moment. There is a regularity (*chang* 常), continuity (*jing* 經), and even predictability (*qi* 期), but there is no correct or incorrect manner of making the juxtapositions.

Corollary to this second point, the circle is always site-specific and irreversible. It is not a formal abstraction because, like the *Book of Changes*, it is always being consulted from one focal perspective or another. Although the absence of any final boundary suggests a declining range of relevance at the extremities, it also anticipates an ongoing tension with peripheral forces which, when the center weakens, have increasingly strong transformative influences.

Fourthly, the images used to articulate the world are dynamic and interdependent, and are thus open to manipulation. They are seasons, phases, processes: summer-becoming-autumn, and spring-becoming-summer. The vocabulary of *qi* and *yin-yang* emphasizes acoustic resonance and response. Each of the contrastive images stands in some dynamic opposition to all of the rest, and thus its meaning at any given moment can be traced out as a matrix of constitutive attributes-becoming-their-opposites: cold-becoming-hot, dark-becoming-light.

Finally, in discussing these correlations, the use of the word "image" is deliberate. The correlative phases are not representational. They are focused "emblems" which mediate the intellectual and the sensible in a richly vague manner in order to both construct and interpret our worlds.[138] Thus, in the naming of a world, we are commanding a world to be read and to be valued in a certain way.

The correlative nature of these organizations may be clarified if we recall that there can be no strict analogy between the logical "*p*" and "*non-p*" on the one hand, and the contrast of *yin* and *yang* on the other—either in the sense that one excludes the other, in the sense that one logically entails the other, or in the sense that together (as in the "*p*" and "*non-p*" contrast) they logically entail self-containment, completeness, or totality. *Yin* and *yang* are elements of a correlative pairing which are pragmatically useful in sorting out "this" and "that." *Yin* and *yang* are not, as often claimed, dualistic principles of light and dark, male and female, action and passivity, where light and dark exclude each other, logically entail each other, and in their complementarity constitute a totality. Rather *yin* and *yang* are, first and foremost, a vocabulary of qualitative contrasts which are applicable to specific situations, and which enable us to make specific distinctions.

For a proposition to have a univocal sense, terms must be strictly delimitable. A polar sensibility precludes such delimitation in any but the grossest terms. Thus, the classical Chinese understanding of *yin* and *yang* as contrastive concepts cannot coherently lead to dualistic translations or interpretations. *Yin* is a becoming-*yang*; *yang* is a becoming-*yin*.

Yin and *yang* always describe the relationships of unique particulars. Originally these terms designated the shady side and the sunny side of a hill, and gradually came to suggest the way in which one thing "overshadows" another in some particular aspect of their relationship. The nature of the opposition captured in this pairing expresses the mutuality, interdependence, diversity, and creative efficacy of the dynamic relationships that are deemed immanent in and valorize the world. The full range of difference in the world is deemed explicable through this pairing. In sum: *yin* and *yang* are ad hoc explanatory categories that report on interactions among immediate concrete things of the world.

For example, in a given relationship, *this* older woman might by virtue of her wisdom be regarded as *yang* in contrast to *that* younger woman who is *yin*. But if we were to focus on their fecundity, the correlation would likely be the opposite. And since no one thing is *yang* in all respects, there is always some basis for complementarity.

Yin and *yang*, as characterizations of particular relationships, invariably entail a perception from some particular perspective that enables one to unravel patterns of relatedness and to interpret specific circumstances. They provide a vocabulary for sorting out the relationships among things as they come together and constitute themselves in unique compositions. It is only through a process of generalization that feminine and male gender traits are construed as predominantly *yin* and *yang* respectively, and vocabulary such as vaginal orifice (*yin men* 陰門) and virility (*yang dao* 陽道) emerges to "essentialize" the *yin* and *yang* contrast.

Important here is the primacy of particular difference and the absence of any assumed sameness or strict identity. Things are not purported to be the same because they own identical essences, but are deemed to have resemblances based upon analogous roles or functions. Hence, describing any particular phenomenon involves an unravelling of the relationships and conditions of the phenomenon's context, and its multiple correlations. And each phenomenon, in suggesting other similar phenomena, has the vagueness of a poetic image.[139]

"*Yin-yang* thinking" is, then, another name for "correlative thinking." Both involve "the art of contextualization." In the postface of the *Huainanzi*, very possibly written by Liu An himself, the immediate comparison drawn between this text and the traditional corpus is with the *Book of Changes*. This association reflects the perception that both texts have recourse to the application of correlative categories in exploring and understanding the world:

> Now, the "*qian*" and "*kun*" contrast in the *Book of Changes* is enough to exhaust *dao* and give a full account of its meaning, and the eight trigrams can be used to recognize what is auspicious and inauspicious, and to anticipate good fortune and calamity. But the reason the Fu Xi introduced the sixty-four changes and the House of Zhou (King Wen) increased the trigram to six lines was to fathom utterly the marvelous *dao* and to seek out the forbearers of the myriad things.[140]

There have been at least two ways of interpreting this "Han" correlative thinking in its relationship with conceptual thinking. One way is to rationalize it. Hellmut Wilhelm, echoing the *prelogical* and *logical* categories of the French sociologists such as Marcel Mauss and Lucien Lévy-Bruhl, gives a qualified endorsement of this kind of thinking as preparatory to higher modalities of thought:

> What we observe here is apparently an attempt to create and formulate concepts for specific purposes, if not to define them. We stand witness here to the first manifestation of a new stage in the self-realization of the human mind in which the faculty of judgment is first exercised and leads to abstractions distinct from images. . . . It would be a fallacy, however, to reduce these con-

cepts entirely to their image antecedents and to deny to the authors of these early texts the faculty of abstraction that is reflected in these terms. It is a different mental faculty, newly awakened, than the one that contemplates and represents images. A realization of this faculty only renders to the hexagrams their tension, their clarity, and their authority.[141]

In Wilhelm's discussion of the polarity in the human mind between the "contemplated" image and the "reflective" concept, the reduction of the dynamic and performative act of "imaging" to passive contemplation privileges conceptual thinking which occasions the awakening of some hitherto unstimulated faculty. What Wilhelm fails to see is that the "com-positioning" of particulars in the process of imaging might serve as a functional equivalent of conceptual judgments, but it is not the same thing.

Jacques Gernet analyzes the relationship between the Chinese language and correlative thinking in a surer manner. Even though he believes this correlative world of classical China contrasts so starkly with our own that we find ourselves "in the presence of a different kind of humanity," he demonstrates sensitivity by resisting Wilhelm's reductionist tendencies. He thereby expresses a significantly stronger endorsement of this modality of thinking:

> The lack of those mental categories which we take to be constitutive of all rational thought does not imply an essential inferiority, but rather different modalities of thought, the strength and flexibility of which may, on further consideration, be seen as advantages. In the manipulation of the Chinese language, the mental mechanisms and aptitudes that are at work are different from those which have been favored in the West.[142]

One way of making Gernet's argument is to try and take the Han dynasty tables of correlations seriously. Han correlations are most often organized around the contrast between *yin* 陰 and *yang* 陽, and "the five phases" (*wuxing* 五行). These types of organization came to be almost pervasive in the literature, regardless of particular lineage or doctrine. When we look at a chart of correlations from the Han dynasty, the welter of associations seems at first random, even bizarre. The correlated items include things (trees), actions (sounds), attributes (colors), and modalities (flavors), as well as time (seasons), space (directions), and matter (five phases) (see tables 3.3 and 3.4).[143]

These kinds of tables correlate the five phases (wood, fire, earth, metal, water), the five directions (north, east, south, west, center), the five colors (green, red, yellow, white, black), the five notes, and so forth. In addition, they are extendable to become vast and complex tables of correlations that include the eight trigrams, the four seasons, the twelve months, the twelve pitches, the twenty-eight constellations, the ten heavenly stems and the twelve earthly branches, and much more.

How would someone have to think about the world for these correlations to have explanatory force? Or put another way, how can we set aside our own worldview in order to entertain the Han dynasty worldview on its own terms? After all, such lists offend against our most basic categories, mixing together things, actions, attributes, and modalities, and conflating time, space, and matter.[144]

The first consideration would be to take account of different understandings of causal relations. These correlated categories are apt to appear simply as "pseudoscience" to individuals who subscribe to a linear notion of causality. That is, the assumption of classical Chinese philosophy that each phenomenon is embedded in a context, and that its explanation is a function of mapping all of its associated environing conditions, and tracing out their relative degrees of causal influence, makes the kind of correlative thinking represented by these charts complex and inclusive. At the same time, a notion of linear causality would, from this perspective, appear to be simple, and randomly exclusionary.

A second consideration that would add a degree of coherence to the charts would be to appreciate the specific value of each category in terms of its suggestiveness. The items in these correlations are mutually ramifying; each one will be seen to reflect into, allude to, and thereby enrich the others, depending upon the degree to which one has mastered the tradition that contextualizes these items.

A related consideration would be to take account of differing grammatical expectations. The parts of speech inherent in our Western language—nouns, verbs, adjectives, and adverbs—encourage us to divide up the world in a culturally specific manner. Under the influence of these grammatical determinants, we are inclined to separate things from actions, attributes from modalities, where from when, and when from what.

Table 3.3. Earthly-Branch Correlates in Huainanzi 5

Month	Branch	Dawn-Culminating Asterism	Dusk-Culminating Asterism	Pitch Pipe	Room of Mingtang	Office	Tree
1	yin	Array	Tail	Great Budding	NE Corner	Master of Works[e]	Willow[f]
2	mao	Bow[a]	Establishing Stars[b]	Pinched Bell	Eastern Chamber	Granary	Almond
3	chen	Seven Stars	Ox-Leader	Maiden Purity	SE Corner	Villages	Pear
4	si	Wings	Widow[c]	Median Regulator	SE Corner	Tilled Fields	Peach
5	wu	Neck	Rooftop	Luxuriant	Southern Chamber	Functionaries	Elm
6	wei	Heart	Stride	Hundred Bell[d]	Central Palace	Lesser Ingathering	Hazel
7	shen	Dipper	Net	Tranquil Pattern	SW Corner	Armory	Tung-tree
8	you	Ox-Leader	Turtle-Beak	Southern Regulator	Western Chamber	Military Officers	Cudrania
9	xu	Emptiness	Willow	Tireless	NW Corner	Archer-Lords	Sophora
10	hai	Rooftop	Seven Stars	Responsive Bell	NW Corner	Master of Horses	Sandalwood
11	zi	Eastern Wall	Chariot Platform	Yellow Bell	Northern Chamber	Metropolitan Guards	Jujube
12	chou	Bond	Root	Great Regulator	NE Corner	Prisons	Chestnut

a. Bow (*hu*) is a constellation south of the Lunar Lodge Spirit-Bearer.

b. Establishing stars (*jian xing*) is a constellation of six stars north of the Lunar Lodge Dipper.

c. Widow (*wunu*) is a constellation north of the Lunar Lodge Serving-Maid.

d. Hundred Bell = Forest Bell.

e. The monthly offices (or, more broadly, functions of government) are not terribly systematic, but tend to derive in a general way from the content of each month's ordinances.

f. The monthly trees generally follow a natural seasonal progression, from the early-greening willow and early-blooming almond of spring to the jujube (the fruit of which is usually eaten dried) and the long-keeping chestnut of winter.

Table 3.4. *Five Phase Correlations in Huainanzi 5*

Season	Direction	Heavenly Stem	Phase	Class of Beast	Note	No.
spring	east	*jia, yi*	wood	scaly	*jue*	8
summer	south	*ping, ding*	fire	feathers	*zhi*	7
midsummer	center	*wu, ji*	earth	naked	*gong*	5
autumn	west	*geng, xin*	metal	hairy	*shang*	9
winter	north	*ren, gui*	water	armored	*yu*	6

Flavor	Smell	God	Organ First Offered in Sacrifice	Son of Heaven's Food	Ritual Fuel
sour	musty	door	spleen	wheat, mutton	fern stalks
bitter	burnt	stove	lungs	legumes, chicken	Cudrania branches
sweet	fragrant	drain	heart	millet, beef	Cudrania branches
pungent	rank	door	liver	hempseed, dog meat	Cudrania branches
salty	putrid	well	kidneys	millet, pork	pine branches

Color	Music	Weapon	Animal	Thearch	Assistant
bluegreen	strings	spear	goat	Tai Hao	Gou Mang
vermilion	pipes	glaive	chicken	Chi Di	Zhu Rong
yellow	[none]	sword	bovine	Huang Di	Hou Tu
white	bells	halberd	dog	Shao Hao	Ru Shou
black	chimes	partisan	pig	Zhuan Xu	Xuan Ming

Of course these grammatical determinants are rooted in the fundamental "categories" which have shaped our modes of thinking from
the beginnings of Western speculation. Aristotle's categories—substance, quantity, place, time, relation, and so forth—dealt with the
structure of thinking as suggestd by the Greek language. When filtered through the Latin thinkers, and ramified by subsequent modern
philosophers, notably Immanuel Kant, such categorial schemes have
expressed the structure of Western thinking in its dominant modes.
Were we to ask after the relevance of our traditional categories for the
interpretation of the structure of Chinese thinking, we would, not
surprisingly, find that they are quite often of very little use.

Given the fluidity between time, space, and matter in classical
Chinese speculations, these categories do not govern the way in
which the world is divided up. The categories used to define a

Chinese world must be seen as crossing the borders of time, space, and matter. *Dao*, for example, is both "what is" (things and their attributes) and "how things are" (actions and their modalities). *Dao* has as much to do with the subjects of knowing and their quality of understanding as it does with the object of knowledge. We have to resist the temptation encouraged by the grammatical and syntactical features of our languages to draw clear lines between things and events, thus entifying "the Way" as a *what* rather than "Way" as *how*.[145]

Generally speaking, our environing conditions provide a pattern of productive regularity and, occasionally, a memorable experience of what happens when these patterns, for whatever reason, break down. Hence, these correlative tables that structure Han dynasty speculations not only *describe* the expectations one has of natural regularities, they *prescribe* the world by announcing the way the world ought to organize itself. When winter overwhelms spring, there are floods, frost, crop damage, famine, and death, and such a situation is bad.

As mentioned above, the absence of a basis for making objective statements about the world makes fact and value interdependent and mutually entailing, and thus make definition and simple description problematic. The values of the observer are always implicated in the observation. The line, then, that divides science from art, alchemy from chemistry, astronomy from astrology, geology from geomancy, and psychology from physiognomy is always tenuous.

If we are able to read a Han dynasty chart of correlations in relative innocence, we discover a real coherence obtaining among its various categories. When we can find a perspective internal to the everyday ways of living and thinking in Han China, the motivation behind these specific correlations and their resonances becomes increasingly apparent. John Major has provided precisely this kind of linkage in his commentary on the fifth fascicle of *Huainanzi*, "The Seasonal Rules (*shize* 時則)."[146] Taking just a random sample of the *Huainanzi* text itself:

Section X: Tenth Month
In the first month of winter, *zhaoyao* points to *hai*.
(The Lunar Lodge) Rooftop culminates at dusk; (the Lodge) Seven Stars culminates at dawn.
(Winter) occupies the north. Its days are *ren* and *gui*.

The fullness of power is in Water.
Its beasts are (those of the) armored (class).
Its (pentatonic) note is *yu*.
The pitchpipe of (of the tenth month) is Responsive Bell.
The number (of winter) is six.
Its flavor is salty.
Its smell is putrid.
Its sacrifices are made to the well-god.
From the body of the sacrificial victim, the kidneys are
    offered first.[147]

Major's commentary illumines this laconic passage by offering rich
allusions to the everyday life of Han China:

> The rapidly shortening days betoken a closing down of the year,
> and the ruler responds by repairing gates and fortifications, and
> prohibiting people from leaving their places of residence. Winter
> definitively ushers in the season of death. Punishments are car-
> ried out with increasing severity. The meritorious dead are also
> attended to, as their widows and orphans are put under govern-
> ment protection; regulations are issued concerning mourning
> rituals and the design of graves. Apparently in recognition of
> winter as a season of cosmological danger, attention is paid to the
> rites and implements of divination. The tree of the tenth month is
> the sandalwood, presumably because it was used in making
> incense used in connection with such rites. . . . The farmers rest
> from their labors, and officials turn their attention to the pro-
> ducts of artisans, from whom levies of goods are collected and
> inspected, and to the secondary products of the countryside—
> the rushes and reeds, fish and tortoises, and other products of
> hunting and gathering.[148]

5.4. Ritual, Role, and Family: The Confucian Synthesis

The continuity between humanity and the world in Chinese natural
philosophy leads to the assumption that there is no final distinction
between nature and human culture. The same vocabulary is used to
articulate the order which inheres in nature and the order which is
inscribed in the world as the contribution of the human spirit: *dao* 道,
wen 文, *li* 理, *xiang* 象, *xing* 性, and so on.[149]

This continuity between humanity and the world also leads to the singular importance of certain metaphors in the definition of relational order within a Chinese world. One model frequently cited in explanation of the Confucian order is that involving the Western metaphor of "organism." This model is influential in some measure because of Joseph Needham's employment of it.[150] But Needham's use of the term *organicism* is a peculiar one, discussed most fully by reference to Leibniz's theory of monads and Whitehead's philosophy of organism. Additionally, Needham brings in the organismic theories of Plato and Aristotle with analogies of microcosm and macrocosm, as well as the analogical relationship between the individual and the state. For Needham, the paradigm illustration of organicist thinking among the Chinese is the twelfth-century Neo-Confucian, Zhu Xi.

Although there is certainly some explanatory force in appealing to the organic metaphor, Needham's position becomes somewhat ambiguous to the extent that he attempts to dissociate the Chinese form of organicist thinking from important elements of its Western counterpart. According to Needham, in the West

> the animal organism might be projected onto the universe, but belief in a personal god or gods meant that it always had to have a "guiding principle." This was a path the Chinese definitely did *not* take. To them . . . cooperation of the component parts was spontaneous, even involuntary, and this alone was sufficient.[151]

This is an unusual understanding of "organism," at least from a Western perspective. This term is most generally associated with living things conceived as complex arrangements of parts functioning with respect to some end or aim. Indeed, the most general understanding of organism (this is the sense Aristotelian naturalism employs) is as a whole with parts which functionally interrelate to achieve an inherent purpose. The Aristotelian language of potentiality and actuality is frequently appropriated to articulate this notion. The acorn is *potentially*, and may *actually* become, an oak tree.

This biological sense of organism is pervasive in both our sciences and our broader intellectual culture. Aristotle used the organic metaphor as a fundamental tool in constructing his entire philosophical system. The search for the purpose or function of any subject matter under investigation, from the human being to the state, to the cosmos as a whole, was basic to the Aristotelian method of coming to know.

It is this that signals the dominance of final causes in Aristotle's philosophy.

It is, of course, the essential connection between final cause and the notion of organism that Needham wishes to challenge in using organism to interpret Chinese culture. Let it be said, however, that if we take away from organismic philosophies the notion of final cause as the determinant of the process of organismic functioning, there is little left of that notion, at least as it has served Western intellectual culture.

Take, for example, the two thinkers to whom Needham appeals most as models of organicist thinking which harmonizes with that of China—namely, Leibniz and Whitehead. Leibniz's notion of "possible worlds" from which God selects that which is best, and his doctrine of "preestablished harmony" which guarantees harmonious interactions among myriads of "windowless monads," place the final cause of the totality of things squarely in the Mind of God. And Whitehead's "primordial nature of God" is a repository of those possibilities which serve as "initial aims" for the "actual occasions" constituting the world of things, evoking the best harmony possible from the results of the world's processive activity. Again, the unity and harmony of things is dependent upon the coordination of final causes.

Even with modern Western forms of organicist thinking represented by Whitehead, there is a significant distance from the sort of thinking Needham recognizes as characteristic of the Chinese. We would argue that the Chinese mode of correlative thinking really bears little resemblance to anything like organismic theories as we in the West have developed them. Thus, very little is to be gained by resort to the model of organism, either in its strictly biological sense, or in the extended applications made of it within our Western tradition. In fact, one can expect real confusions to result from any such resort.

There is reason to believe that the abuse of the notion of organism in attempts to understand the Chinese sensibility is a consequence of eliding the significant differences between biological "organism" and bureaucratic "organization." It is the latter which more closely approximates the model to which the Chinese appeal in understanding the world about them.

Indeed, Needham himself seems to believe that the organicist understanding of the Chinese world developed out of the bureaucratic, "administrative approach" to natural phenomena. Commenting upon the *Book of Changes* as a "cosmic filing system," Needham asks whether the "compelling power which it had in Chinese civilization [was] due to the fact that it was a view of the world basically congruent with the bureaucratic social order?"[152]

> Perhaps the entire system of correlative organismic thinking was in one sense the mirror image of Chinese bureaucratic society. Not only the tremendous filing system of the *I Ching* [*Yijing*], but also the symbolic correlations in the stratified matrix world might be so described. Both human society and the picture of Nature involved a system of coordinates, a tabulation framework, a stratified matrix in which everything had its position, connected by the "proper channels" with everything else.[153]

Benjamin Schwartz cites approvingly both Joseph Needham's claim that the "cosmic filing system" of the *Book of Changes* was strongly influenced by the "bureaucratic sense of order" and Donald Munro's suggestion that familial order is the fundamental Chinese paradigm.[154] Schwartz's conclusion is that "one might say that the 'state analogy' may be much more important as a paradigm of Chinese holism and organicism than the biological organism."[155]

The bureaucratic metaphor is an appealing candidate for understanding "Chinese thinking." It certainly is consistent with correlative operations as they are manifested in a variety of ways in the Chinese organization of cultural significances. At the level of physical nature, thinking of space in terms of the five directions, and time in terms of the seasons, and the coordination of space and time (*yuzhou* 宇宙) through paired correspondences, and the connections of the divisions of space and time with a vast complex of other similarly divided elements, certainly offers a recognizably "bureaucratic" scheme.

This use of the "state analogy" is hardly as odd as it might seem. As we have noted on several occasions, in the West, the term *cosmos* had its original uses in terms of everyday associations of order, adornment, and arrangement relative to the household, the military, and social organization, long before it came to be applied—presumably by resort to the "state analogy"—to the external surround. There is every reason to believe that analogical projection was initially made from the familiar to the unfamiliar. Believing that the order of society is patterned on cosmic order may very well have resulted from nature first having been idealized by appeal to sociopolitical metaphors, and then being used as a model for society.

One implication of a distinction between a cosmogonic and an acosmotic worldview is that, in the absence of some overarching *arche* (or "beginning") as an explanation of the creative process, and under conditions which are thus "an-archic" in the philosophic sense of this term, although "nature" might indeed refer to "kinds," such categories would be no more than generalizations made by analogizing among similar phenomena. Difference is prior to identified similarities.

For example, as Mencius states explicitly, what distinguishes a person from a human beast is not some inviolate natural endowment, but a tentative and always particular cultural refinement.[156] Even Confucius, who insists that he cannot gather with the birds and beasts because he is, after all, a human being, still makes it abundantly clear that he will only associate with *some* human beings—namely, those who have worked at becoming human.[157]

The continuity between humanity and the world leads to the singular importance of the family metaphor in the definition of relational order within Chinese culture. As we have noted, Benjamin Schwartz follows Donald Munro in challenging the suitability of Joseph Needham's use of the organic metaphor, preferring the family metaphor—ancestor, mother, womb, and so on—that is so pervasive throughout classical Chinese speculations.[158]

Our focus/field model of order is to be understood as fundamentally a "familial" model, one which could easily be extended into the bureaucratic, administrative approach to understanding the way of things which appears fundamental to Chinese conceptualizations.

Whereas the Latin term *locus* means simply "place," the term *focus* means "place of convergence or divergence." Originally, the term meant "hearth" or "fireplace." It came to mean "burning point"—identifying the place at which the sun's rays pass through a lens to converge with intensified heat. Kepler was apparently the first to use the term in its geometrical sense as focal point of a curve. We mention this bit of etymology only to point out something of the richness of the word *focus*, which has its original association with hearth and home. This humanizing sense of focus ought to be factored into our extension of the term to characterize the Chinese sense of family and society.

Field likewise has original domestic associations which we do not wish to abandon, though we shall be using the term in the sense of "sphere of influence." By sphere of influence we shall indicate the area within which the influences of and upon an agent may be discernibly experienced and perceived.

The means of characterizing a correlative ordering in terms of the relationship of field and focus is rather straightforwardly expressed, though in practice it will constitute an always vague and incomplete process. At any given moment, items in a correlative scheme are characterizable in terms of the focal point from and to which lines of divergence and convergence attributable to them move, and the field from which and to which those lines proceed. With respect to historical figures, particularly paradigmatic persons such as Confucius, these lines of convergence and divergence are thought to move throughout the entire field of the Chinese cultural tradition.

It is important to recall that fields and foci are never finally fixed or determinant. Fields are unbounded, pulsating in some vague manner from and to their various transient foci. This notion of field readily contrasts with the one-many and part-whole models. The relations of human beings to their communities, for example, are not established by the presumption of "essences" or "natural kinds" defining membership in a set of such kinds, nor by the presumption of the contextually defined mereological sets wherein the parts constitute the wholes in an additive or summative manner. There is neither "one" (in the sense of an essential unity) nor "many" (in the sense of many instances of one essential kind). Nor are there "parts" which add up to "wholes" which are no greater than their sum. Instead, there is a vague, unbounded field, both constituting and constituted by its discernible foci. Alternatively, there are a variety of shifting foci, the influences upon which and from which are resourced in a vague unbounded field. Thus, our model is neither one-many, nor is it a nominalized version of the part-whole model. The focus/field perspective employs a "this-that" model.

Our focus/field model must be understood in terms of the general vision of *ars contextualis*.[159] It is the "art of contextualization" that is most characteristic of Chinese intellectual endeavors. The variety of specific contexts defined by particular family relations or sociopolitical orders constitute the "fields" focused by individuals who are in turn shaped by the field of influences they focus. *Ars contextualis*, as a practical endeavor, names that peculiar art of contextualization which allows focal individuals to seek out the viable contexts which they help to constitute and which in turn will partially constitute them.

Rudolf Arnheim in his reflections on the visual arts provides us with a useful vocabulary for exploring this classical Chinese conception of *ars contexualis*. Arnheim is persuaded that the nature of composition in the visual arts reflects an underlying cosmological tendency:

> Cosmically, we find that matter organizes around centers, which are often marked by a dominant mass. Such systems come about whenever their neighbors allow them sufficient freedom.[160]

This phenomenon, observes Arnheim, is true of both the vast astronomical space and the microscopic realm. The center that is so constituted is "the center of a field of forces, a focus from which forces issue and towards which forces converge."[161] These centers, then, relate to each other as a calculus of centers which, from their interplay, produce a balancing centripetal center which tends to distribute the forces of its field symmetrically around its own center:

> Overcoming the egocentric view amounts to realizing that a center is not always in the middle. . . . More often, the environment is dominated by other centers, which force the self into a subordinate position. . . . Speaking generally, one can assert that every visual field comprises a number of centers, each of which attempts to draw the others into subservience. The self as viewer is just one of these centers. . . . The overall balance of all these competing aspirations determines the structure of the whole, and that total structure is organized around what I will call the balancing center.[162]

The notion of composition that Arnheim is elaborating here can be be helpful in understanding correlative schemes. In the predominantly "anarchic" tradition of classical China, which invested little interest in metaphysical questions, the appeal can only be to historical and cultural analogies, and as such, any claims based upon these analogies are necessarily site-specific and provisional.

The classical Chinese assumption is that personal, societal, political, and natural orders are immanental, coterminous, and mutually entailing. Thus, to the extent we understand order in any one aspect of the human experience, we have a direct insight into other areas of experience as well. In characterizing an item as focal, we are indicating that it inheres in its immediate context in such a manner as to shape and be shaped by that context as field. The focus/field model results from understanding an item's relation to the world to be constituted by acts of contextualization. Thus the concepts of *focus and field* and *ars contextualis* are useful in underscoring certain of the basic features of this sense of order.

First, as we have said, *ars contextualis* suggests a "this-that" rather than a "one-many" model, where, in the absence of any metaphysical assumptions about the One behind the many or Being behind beings, order emerges from the coordination of so many "thises" and "thats" as various foci and the fields they focus. The art of contextualization involves appreciation of harmonious correlations of the myriad unique details (*wan wu* 萬物 or *wan yu* 萬有) which make up the world.

Reflection, we believe, would persuade one that the focus/field notion of order, although well illustrated by the Han synthesis detailed above, is not peculiar to it. It is precisely that order captured in the Confucian notion of ritually constituted family and community which is central to all of Chinese culture. Constitutive rituals (*li* 禮) and roles (*lun* 倫), defined at the center by the authority of the tradition, not only demand personalization and participation, but further, are always reflective of the quality and the uniqueness of their participants. In fact, in the language of this tradition, the meaning of ritually ordered community itself is made literal from the image of "a deferential assembly gathering around the sacred pole erected in the center of the community" (*shehui* 社會). Nishijima Sadao tells us:

> Such community life, based on the hamlet, had its religious center in the altar (*she* 社) where the local deity was enshrined. In the same way there was an altar for the state community (*kuo-she* [*guoshe*] 國社), and each county and district also had its own altar. The religious festivals which took place at the hamlet altar (*li-she* 里社), at which meat was distributed to the participants, helped to strengthen the community spirit.[163]

Above we have employed the Han court analogy as a means of illustrating the classical Chinese conception of world order, but we must acknowledge that this same court analogy expresses a level of political discourse which is itself derived from the ritual- and role-constituted family model. The family, as the correlation of relationships, is a basic variation on this notion of a graduated, centripetal harmony. The sociologist Ambrose King argues persuasively that, in the Chinese world, all relationships are familial:

> Among the five cardinal relations, three belong to the kinship realm. The remaining two, though not family relationships, are conceived in terms of the family. The relationship between the ruler and the ruled is conceived of in terms of father (*chün-fu* [*junfu*]君父) and son (*tzu-min* [*zimin*]子民), and the relationship between friend and friend is stated in terms of elder brother (*wu-hsiung* [*wuxiung*] 吾兄) and younger brother (*wu-ti* [*wudi*] 吾弟).[164]

The family as the "in-group," is determinate and focused at the center, but becomes increasingly vague as it stretches out both diachronically in the direction of one's lineage, and synchronically as a society full of "uncles" and "aunts." It is articulated in terms of roles (*lun* 倫), a ritual "wheel (*lun* 輪)" of social relations that "ripple out (*lun* 淪)" in a field of discourse (*lun* 論) to define any one person as a network of persons, a field of selves.

King's critique of this model of family order is most insightful. He observes:

> What must be emphasized here is that while Confucian ethics teach how the individual should be related to other particular roles through the proper *lun*, the issue of how the individual should be related to the "group" is not closely examined. In other words, the individual's behavior is supposed to be *lun*-oriented; the *lun*-oriented role relations, however, are seen as personal, concrete, and particularistic in nature.[165]

While King's insistence that the Confucian model of personal, social, political, and natural order is constructed in concrete, particular, and differentiated relationships between "self" and "other" is certainly on the mark, this parochial order is certainly not devoid of a sense of community. The concreteness and immediacy of one's own definition is, like graduated love, necessitated by the unwillingness in this tradition to disengage the theoretical from the experiential.

However, King might be going too far in suggesting that the vagueness of a person's sense of community precludes the possibility of a broader civil ethic. He states:

> It seems to me that Confucian social ethics has failed to provide a "viable linkage" between the individual and *ch'ün* [*qun*] 羣, the nonfamilistic group. The root of the Confucian *Problematik* lies in the fact that the boundary between the self and the group has not been conceptually articulated.[166]

King, in failing to identify the link, echoes Bertrand Russell's reservations about the weight given to family relations in the Chinese world:

> Filial piety, and the strength of the family generally, are perhaps the weakest point in Confucian ethics, the only point where the system departs seriously from common sense. Family feeling has militated against public spirit, and the authority of the old has increased the tyranny of ancient custom. . . . In this respect, as in certain others, what is peculiar to China is the preservation of the old custom after a very high level of civilization had been attained.[167]

The link that both King and Russell are missing here is that although the family, the community, the state, and even the tradition itself, as the extended "group" or "field," is each ambiguous *as a group or field*, the vagueness of the more general nexus is a virtue rather than a defect since it may be focused and made immediate in the embodiment of the group or field by the particular father, the social exemplar, the ruler, and the historical model.

The meaning of the group is made present in *my* particular father, teacher, *my* Mao Zedong and Confucius. Each *lun* as the focus and articulation of a vague field of roles is holographic in that it adumbrates its own field. Although the concreteness and immediacy of the centripetal center is contextualized by the vague sense of "Chineseness," this notion comes alive *to each of us* in the image of a Zeng Guofan or a Yang Youwei. The totality is itself nothing more than the full range of particular foci, each defining itself and its own particular field.[168]

In the immediately human world of the Confucian, these compositions are reflected in an irreducibly social conception of person, families, and communities, where the social grammar is always constituted by personalized ritual practices and social roles. It is because of the immanence and uniqueness of an order so defined that Confucius, rather than appealing to transcendent principles, can describe the process of learning in terms of "starting from what is most basic and immediate, and penetrating through to what is most elevated."[169] The Confucian assumption traditionally has been that personal, familial, societal, political, and natural order are coterminous and mutually entailing, and further, from the personal perspective, are emergent in the process of one's own self-cultivation and articulation. From the perspective of any person, order begins *here* and extends *there*.

6. A CLOSING ANTICIPATION

The danger of overstatement cannot itself be overstated. By denying primary importance to causal thinking in classical China, we are neither claiming that such thinking was wholly absent among Chinese scholars, nor are we suggesting that the Chinese were any less subject to the causal rigors of brute circumstance. At the same time, the importance of the Chinese employment of the correlative mode in constructing their world order should not be understated. Our argument has been that, relative to the contrast of Chinese and Western sensibilities, we are able to assume there to be these two distinguishable modalities of thinking—the aesthetic and the logical, or the correlative and the causal—and that an emphasis upon one mode in a given context leads to an attenuation *in that context* of the other mode. The overall dominance of the correlative mode in classical China is well attested by the attenuated influence of schools of thought that experimented with causal thinking, such as Mohism and Legalism.

In the Chinese worldview, order is not imposed from without, but is inherent in the process of existence itself, as are the rings of this tree trunk, the veins in this particular piece of the stone, the cadence of Kailua's ocean on this Sunday morning, the constitutive roles and relationships within the Robert Neville household, and so on. "Causes" are not external; "that which causes" and "that which is caused" are not finally distinguishable.

In a sequel volume we shall attempt to demonstrate the persistence of correlative thinking in China through a discussion of three problems that have shaped many of the comparisons of Chinese and Western thinking in recent years. Although our topics—"Self," "Truth," and "Transcendence"—are obviously drawn from the inventory of Western philosophic speculations, they will provide us with concrete cultural contrasts between the two traditions necessary to make our case.

One of the most fundamental distinguishing characteristics of the Chinese philosophic tradition available to the comparative philosopher as a point of reference is the notion of human agency. It is because "person" is a touchstone for registering cultural differences that in recent years there has been such a proliferation of research on this specific subject among comparativists.[170] Presuppositions concerning the meaning of "self" in the Chinese tradition make the available Western models and vocabularies of self-cultivation inappropriate. Even the appeal to language as apparently neutral as "mind," "body," and "will" threatens to conceal more about Chinese conceptions of person than it discloses. Our argument is that "Han thinking" provides a model of order which, when applied to the articulation of one's person and its emerging character, defines one as a "focal self": a social center of relevant roles and ritually constituted relationships.

There are, of course, many subthemes involved in exploring human agency. For example, the correlative categories characteristic of Han thinking can be of service in interrogating traditional Chinese society on gender construction, and in laying bare a particularly pernicious albeit peculiarly Chinese brand of sexism. We shall explore these issues in our forthcoming volume.

We shall also investigate another theme central to comparative studies of China and the West: the issue of "truth." The relative unconcern of Chinese thinkers with what in our tradition we term semantic theories of truth provides direct evidence for the ubiquity of correlative thinking. For semantic truth theories are implicated in analytical, dialectical, and strict analogical modes of argumentation. The undervaluing of speculations concerning truth or falsity in any rigorous sense in classical China is a consequence of correlative thinking which does not invite rational objectivity.

Without the logical means of assessing propositional truth, it is unlikely that causal language could be deemed of much importance beyond the specific rigors of the everyday. Characterizations of physical causation in formal theories require the logic of entailment. Alternatively said, without the concern for delineated relations among events in terms of efficient causation, a logic of entailment might not have much application.

Finally, the absence of strict transcendence in the tradition has profound implications for religious and sociopolitical experience within the Chinese culture. The entire vocabulary of Western religious life—God, creation, sin, grace, eternality, soul, and so on—proves inappropriate for describing the nontheistic spirituality at the core of Chinese religion. Religious themes such as mysticism and divine creativity have to be rethought in light of Han ways of thinking and living. This we shall attempt to do.

Building upon our discussion of the focal self as a model of persons in the Chinese tradition, we turn in the subsequent volume to the implications of Han thinking for social and political life constructed without appeal to transcendent principles. To test our hypothesis, we shall visit such contemporary issues as the Chinese response to the notion of human rights, China's constitutional experience, and the Chinese reconfiguration of Marxism.

* * *

We shall close this present work with two important points: First, in advocating the centrality of Han thinking in the Chinese experience, our claims, though they may doubtless appear rather grandiose, are meant to be modest. We are suggesting that in seeking to understand some specific aspects of contemporary Chinese culture, our reflections on the presuppositions which have given Han thinking its peculiar character have relevance as a resource for guaranteeing the Chinese tradition a full measure of difference.

Second, in our treatment of the classical period of China we have perforce omitted consideration of a possibly significant transformative agency in post-Han China. We refer, of course, to the Buddhist incursions which began just after the turn of the millenium. Many have suggested that neo-Confucian philosophy, influenced in important ways by Buddhist doctrines and sensibilities, dramatically changed the intellectual landscape of China. If this were the case, an argument could be made that what we have been describing as Han thinking was, in some degree, suspended during this medieval period, and an interlude reminiscent of the "experiments in rationalism" that we identified as being a feature of late Zhou China occurred within neo-Confucian circles. These are complex claims, and we are simply not ready to speculate on them.

We would, however, point to the sustained attack on the speculative rationalism of Song-Ming "*dao-xue* 道學" by the evidential research (*kao-zheng* 考證) literati of the seventeenth- and particularly eighteenth-century Qing dynasty detailed in the recent scholarship of scholars such as K. C. Liu, Rich Smith, Ben Elman, and John Henderson.[171] This assault on speculative philosophy and the return to culture, artifact, and historical record (*xungu* 訓詁) as standards of evidence by the Qing scholars has to be factored into any attempt to assay the explanatory force of Han thinking as a persistent feature in defining contemporary Chinese culture.

In any case, we are satisfied that the claims we have made in this work, and shall make in our subsequent volume, for the persistence of Han thinking are demonstrably valid. If we produce a work beyond the volume which follows this one, we may be inclined to examine, in greater detail than we have until now, the shape and cultural importances of neo-Confucian China.

Notes

INTRODUCTION

1. Jaspers (1949).

2. See Solomon (1993). Our readers would certainly benefit if they came to our work after exposure to Solomon's account of the noble and the base consequences of our modern Western world's sustained resort to the transcendental pretense. For contemporary heirs of the Enlightenment continue to evangelize other cultures in the name of rational objectivity and universal science. This fact more than any other has prevented our understanding of exoteric cultural sensibilities.

3. A corollary of this claim is: The fact of the unimportance of an idea or doctrine in a particular cultural context is more interesting if it can be shown that the conditions for its development were present but that it was rejected in favor of an alternative notion or notions.

4. Hall and Ames (1987).

5. This work presently bears the title *Thinking From the Han: Self, Truth, and Transcendence in China and the West.*

6. For a discussion of this distinction as it is relevant to the interpretation of the Western cultural tradition, see Hall (1982b:*passim*).

7. See Cornford (1957).

8. See Hall and Ames (1987) and Hall (1994).

9. The city plan of Beijing provides an illustration of the use of nested squares. The "nesting" of the Forbidden City within the Imperial City which is itself nested in the Inner City stresses the concentration of power and majesty at the center. The Outer City constitutes a "beyond" which further softens the permeable boundedness of the nested squares.

CHAPTER ONE: SQUARING THE CIRCLE

1. For an extensive analysis of the characteristics of "modernity," see Hall (1994), chapter 1, "Holding One's Time In Thought."

2. Robert Frost (1963:145), "In the Home Stretch."

3. Aetius 2.1.1 (DK 14, 21) in Robinson (1968:77). Note: We have taken most of the material from the Presocratics from two readily accessible English language sources: Kirk and Raven (1964) and Robinson (1968). The abbreviations of the original sources are consistent with those used in these two works. In most cases we have been able to include from these two sources (in parentheses after the original citation) the reference to the standard comprehensive source—H. Diels and W. Kranz, *Die Fragmente der Vorsokratiker*, Berlin (abbreviated as DK).

4. Simplicius *Phys.* 24.13 (DK 12 A 9) in Kirk and Raven (1964):106–107.

5. Many cosmological concepts were applied to the natural world by analogy from the social and political context. See Frankfort et al. (1967), Cornford (1957), and Lloyd (1966) for illustrations of this analogical process. There is nothing surprising about this fact. Abstract thinking of the sort associated with general philosophical or theoretical concepts more than likely involves the process of progressive generalization and refinement which leads from the specific and familiar to more general contexts.

6. Though we are by no means able to deal with issues beyond the formative period, we should note that the analogical "invention" of the cosmos is not itself an isolated instance of the employment of rhetoric and poetics in the understanding of the "universe." See, for example, Hallyn (1990:117–118), for a discussion of the tropic procedures of Copernicus and Kepler in their transitions away from the Ptolemaic models:

> Copernicus' enthusiasm for the sun's centrality reveals his desire to protect created space from the homogeneity of Euclidean space where all locations are like all others.... For Copernicus the sun's location is eminently *suitable*: It is not located at a random point in infinite space but at the predominant place within created space.

7. Diogenes Laertius 9.19 (DK 21 A 1) in Robinson (1968:54).

8. Augustine *Civitas Dei.* 8.2 (DK 12 A 17) in Robinson (1968:39).

9. Hippolytus *ref.* 1.13.2 (DK 68 A 40) in Kirk and Raven (1964:411).

10. This view is still present in the modern period. No less a figure than Isaac Newton, doubtless for reasons not unlike those of Democritus, accepted the possibility of a plurality of worlds, though he balked at the notion on theological grounds. See Newton (1952:543). Likewise, A. N. Whitehead's notion of "cosmic epochs"—world-orders which succeed one another over vast expanses of time—is a version of the many-worlds view. See Whitehead (1978:91–92, 96–98, 197–199).

11. Plato (1961): *Philebus* 28d–29a.

12. Plato (1961): *Timaeus* 31b.

13. According to Kirk and Raven (1964:412), Leucippus and Democritus "are the first to whom we can attribute with absolute certainty the odd concept of innumerable worlds [co-existing in space]." It is likely that Kirk and Raven insist upon this statement precisely because they believe the view of Leucippus and Democritus to be "odd." But this belief is only odd to those of us long-tutored by the vision of the importance of rational thinking and the understanding of reason as an ordering principle and of order as presupposing unity and coherence. For a discussion of the prevalence of this "odd concept" among the early Greek thinkers, see Vlastos (1975:23–25).

14. See Plato (1961): *Laws* 903b–909d.

15. Genesis 1:1.

16. The extent to which "chaos" as *tohu wa bohu* and as "yawning gap," "gaping void," is to be interpreted as "nonbeing" is unclear. When the Greek language becomes the medium through which this concept is passed, serious complications arise by virtue of the fact that explicit uses of "being" and "nonbeing" in Greek philosophy exploit the fact that the existential "be" overlaps the copula "is," "exists." There are languages, Chinese is the most relevant example, in which the copula is not expressed by "being" (in Chinese, *you* 有). The senses of the Nihil, of the negativity of nonbeing, are harder to come by. Chaos—the Chinese equivalent is usually taken to be *hundun* 渾沌—originally does not seem to have a negative connotation since "not-being" has the connotations of "there is not present, " that is, "not being around," "not ready to hand."

17. This interpretation seems most consistent with the character of the myth though, like most interpretations of cosmogonic myths, it is controversial . We cannot expect mythopoetic language either to follow or to be predicated upon the demands of either causal or narrative rationality. For a fuller discussion of the problems of interpreting Hesiod's myth, see Kirk and Raven (1964:24–32). We contend that any of the relevant readings of the myth will make our point.

18. Plato (1957): *Timaeus* 30a, 48a.

19. See Jonas (1966:219ff).

20. Jaeger (1967:13–14).

21. See Aristotle (1984): *Physics* 208b31–32.

22. See Aristotle (1984): *Metaphysics* 5.1 for a discussion of the various meanings of *arche*.

23. Ovid (1955), *Metamorphoses* 1.5–9.

24. Milton (1962:55), 2.910–911.

25. Milton (1962:55) 2.907–909.

26. P. B. Shelley (1965:394), *Adonais*, 29.

27. Alexander Pope (1965:181), *Dunciad* 1.653.

28. See Eliade (1961:95–104 and *passim*).

29. Snell (1960:205).

30. Sappho Poem (137). Quoted in Snell (1960:53).

31. According to Martha Nussbaum (1986:51), "The *Antigone* is a play about practical reason and the ways in which practical reason orders or sees the world."

32. Snell (1960:112).

33. The later division of labor which led to history having the "past" as its subject matter, while philosophy was to concern itself with eternal or rational-nontemporal factors, was a result of the Platonic and Aristotelian attempts to organize the dominant cultural interests.

34. See Nussbaum (1986:20).

35. *Ibid.*

36. Nussbaum's work, along with that of Bernard Williams' *Shame and Necessity* (1993), and more recently Lisa Raphals' *Knowing Words—Wisdom and Cunning in the Classical Traditions of China and Greece* (1992), continues a line of thought that begins, perhaps, with Nietzsche and Rohde in the nineteenth century and includes such works as Bruno Snell's *The Discovery of the Mind* (1960), E. R. Dodds' *The Greeks and the Irrational* (1951), and Adkins' *From the Many to the One* (1970), among others. These works, as various as they may be in their specific foci, constitute a significant counterdiscourse to the rationalistic interpretations of Greek culture exemplified by works such as John Burnet's *Greek Philosophy* (1964) and F. M. Cornford's *From Religion to Philosophy* (1957). (Cornford significantly modified his understanding of the origins of Greek intellectual culture in his posthumously published *Principium Sapientiae* (1952).) But it is doubtful whether any of these, with the possible exception of Nietzsche, and then only with respect to his more general philosophical writings, escapes the strictures of the second problematic. Indeed, it is equally doubtful that, again with the same exception noted, any of these individuals wishes to do anything more than to add significant depth and nuance to second problematic thinking.

37. Aristotle (1984): *Metaphysics* 985b23–34.

38. See Kirk and Raven (1964:269–273) for a detailed discussion of the Parmenidean fragments interpretable in terms of the identity of being and thinking.

39. Simplicius *Phys.* 145.27 (DK 28 8, lines 34–36) in Robinson (1968: 115).

40. Simplicius *Phys.* 146.15 (DK 28 B 8, lines 42–49) in Robinson (1968: 115).

41. See Brumbaugh (1985:59–67) for a discussion of Zeno's paradoxes employing this sort of analysis.

42. Epiphanius *Adv. haer.* 3.11, in Robinson (1968:134).

43. This argument is often presented as a simple illustration of relative motion, which offers no great paradox. On the more subtle interpretation, however, the paradox presents difficulties that still plague interpretations of quantum phenomena. See Kirk and Raven (1964:295–297) for a discussion of this more subtle understanding.

44. Simplicius frag. 8 *de caelo* 558.21 in Kirk and Raven (1964:304).

45. It is scandalous just how many histories of ancient Greek philosophy one can read which treat the arguments of Zeno as so many curious sophistic anomalies, with little real influence. But the evidence is overwhelming that the influence of Zeno and Parmenides was perhaps greater than any others' in shaping the character of subsequent theory until the time of Plato. For texts and commentary supporting this view see Kirk and Raven (1964:323–324, 370–373, 404–405); Kerferd (1981:91, 96, 109); Brumbaugh (1985:70–73, 78–82, 100–103).

46. Salmon (1970:54).

47. See Salmon (1970:45–58) for this essay by Russell. Other essays in this volume are equally fascinating. The testimony of this entire collection is of the continued influence of Zeno upon our scientific and philosophic culture.

48. James (1911), quoted in Whitehead (1978:68).

49. Whitehead (1978:68–69).

50. Whitehead (1978:69).

51. Salmon (1970:43–44).

52. Hippolytus Frag. 64 *Ref.* 9.10.6 (DK 22 B 64) in Kirk and Raven (1964:199).

53. Diogenes Laertius 9.8 (DK 22 A 1) in Robinson (1968:89).

54. Hippolytus Frag. 53 *Ref.* 9.9.4 (DK 22 B 53) in Kirk and Raven (1964:195).

55. Hippolytus Frag. 60 *Ref.* 9.10.4 (DK 22 B 60) in Kirk and Raven (1964:189).

56. Stobaeus *Florilegium* 1.180a (DK 22 B 115) in Robinson (1968:100).

57. Plotinus *Enneads* 4.8.1 (DK 22 B 84a) in Robinson (1968:97).

58. Whitehead (1978:208). A few lines from these, Whitehead continues:

Without doubt, if we are to go back to that ultimate, integral experience, unwrapped by the sophistications of theory, that experience whose elucidation is the final aim of philosophy, the flux of things is the one generalization around which we must weave our philosophical system.

59. Brumbaugh (1964:47–48) compares Heraclitus to the Zen Buddhist poet Bashō. These individuals, according to Brumbaugh, "share a funda-

mental sense of paradox and the belief that philosophy, if it is to be true, must not be taught indirectly and abstractly; it must be expressed directly."

60. [Aristotle] frag. 10 de mundo 5.396b20 in Kirk and Raven (1964:191). The reference is to a pseudo-Aristotelian source.

61. Clement frag. 30 Strom. 5.104.1 in Kirk and Raven (1964:199).

62. See Vlastos (1975:3–6).

63. See Kirk (1954).

64. Aetius 1.3.4 (DK 13 B 2) in Kirk and Raven (1964:158).

65. Clement Frag. 15 Strom. 110 (DK 21 B 15) in Kirk and Raven (1964:169).

66. Clement Frag. 23 Strom. 5.109 (DK 21 B 23) in Kirk and Raven (1964:169).

67. "But without toil [this god] sets all things in motion by the thought of his mind." Simplicius Phys. 23.19 (DK 21 B 25) in Robinson (1968:53).

68. Sextus Frag. 24 adv. math. 9.144 in Kirk and Raven (1964:170).

69. Iliad 5.190.

70. Iliad 5.902.

71. Frag. 103/84 in Inwood (1992:249).

72. Frag. 27/23 in Inwood (1992:219).

73. Quine (1963:44).

74. See Hall (1987) for a discussion of the inveterate anthropocentrism of the most general and abstract speculation.

75. When we have occasion to discuss philosophical Daoism in chapter 3, we shall see resorts to notions of anthropocentrism and anthropomorphism seriously qualified. The Daoist enjoins taking up the perspective of the subject of one's interest. The important point, however, is that such an approach is diametrically opposed, as is anthropocentrism, to notions of rational objectivity.

76. See Kerferd (1981:59–60) for a discussion of Zeno's contribution to dialectical argumentation.

77. Sextus frag. 3.1.9 adv. math. 7.125 in Kirk and Raven (1964:325).

78. Simplicius frag. 17.1.6 Phys. 158.6 in Kirk and Raven (1964:324).

79. Aristotle (1984): On the Heavens 300b9–16.

80. Censorinus De die natali 4.9 (DK 68 A 139); Lactantius Inst. div. 7.7.9 (DK 68 A 139) in Robinson (1968:216).

81. Lucretius influenced Enlightenment thinkers though his long poem, De Rerum Natura (The Nature of Things). The poem was apparently a rather faithful expression of the atomism of the Greek, Epicurus (341–270), who had modified Democritean atomism in a manner which permitted an account of human freedom, thus allowing for a fuller exposition of the ethical implications of atomism. However, relatively little of Epicurus'

writings remain. It is for this reason—and, doubtless, also because of the power of Lucretius' poetic expression—that the name of Lucretius, rather than that of Epicurus, is most often associated with the renewal of atomistic thinking.

82. Russell (1918): chapter 8, "The Relation of Sense Data to Physics."

83. See Aristotle (1984): *Metaphysics* 982b12–20.

84. Kirk and Raven (1964):404.

85. See the *Theatetus*, Plato (1961:152ff). For a detailed summary of the various interpretations of this statement see Guthrie (1971:*passim*)

86. Vlastos (1975:18–19).

87. Democritus Frag. 9 Sextus Empiricus *Adv. Math.* 7.135 (DK 68 B 9) in Kirk and Raven (1964:422).

88. Diodorus Siculus 1.8 (DK 68 B 5) in Robinson (1968:217–218) C. H. Oldfather (trans.).

89. See "Solidarity or Objectivity?" in Rorty (1991a:21–34).

90. Hippocrates (1923:41).

91. Hippocrates (1923:53).

92. Hippocrates (1923:53, 55).

93. For more balanced treatments of the Sophists, see Guthrie (1971) and Kerferd (1981).

94. The first two of these claims are persistent themes throughout the early dialogues. For illustrations of the third claim see Plato (1961): *Lysis* 204c, *Symposium* 177d and *passim*.

95. Plato, who treated Parmenides with great respect, effectively dismissed the arguments of Zeno by characterizing them as a form of *antilogike* (ἀντιλογική). In the *Phaedrus* 261c–261e (Plato [1961]), Plato discusses "antilogical" arguments of the sort Zeno gave in much the same manner as he treated those of the Sophists. In the *Parmenides* 135c–166b (Plato [1961]), Plato uses Zeno's "antilogical" method to parody the Parmenidean principle, "The Real is One." Plato's use of Zeno's methods against Parmenides resulted in a sort of metaphysical stand-off. The serious point is that Plato did not engage the Zenonian arguments in such a manner as to demonstrate their impact upon his constructive speculations. Of equal importance, Aristotle's treatment of the arguments (see Aristotle [1984], *Physics* Bk. 6), generally acknowledged by moderns to be most inadequate, carried much weight by virtue his unquestioned authority throughout most of the Middle Ages. This fact, too, served effectively to mask the effects of these arguments upon all subsequent thought. The ineliminable pluralism of later Western thought will be motored by the unyielding bifurcations generated by the dichotomy of reason and experience which has its firmest historical foundation in Parmenides and Zeno.

96. Adkins (1970:17). See also Snell (1960) and Dodds (1951) for discussions of the "Homeric view of man" which characterize the "fragmentation" of personality in the early Greek world.

97. Adkins (1970:21).

98. Snell (1960:15).

99. Adkins (1970:26).

100. We are here using *nous* as a general category to name the element of reason in order to associate it with *noesis*—the activity defining "fourth level" thinking in the *Republic*. There are all sorts of complexities that need be addressed with regard to other terms Plato applied throughout his corpus (the use of *logistikon* as the faculty of reasoning in the discussion of *psyche*, for example). We would hold, however, that when the dust cleared, we finally would be left with *noesis*, *dianoia*, and *pistis* as the correlates of the reasonable, ambitious, and appetitive (ruler, soldier, and producer) classes in the *Republic*. See, for example, Brumbaugh (1985:165–171). The problem of the meaning of *psyche* in Plato is, indeed, a challenging one. For a summary of some of the complexities, see Adkins (1970).

In any case, in this present work, our concern to trace the development of dominant cultural sensibilities in terms of the subsequent use of taxonomic models such as the Divided Line and the tripartite structure of the *psyche* is a descriptive one. We are not endorsing the manner in which such uses have oversimplified the very real complexities internal to the Platonic corpus; we are merely reporting on their evolution and their influence in providing the vocabularies that shape our cultural self-consciousness. As philosophers of culture, we must be attentive to philosophical or cultural *importances* rather than interpretive veracity. We are concerned, therefore, with the manner in which "important" texts have been read rather than with the manner in which we believe they should have been read. The story of intellectual culture is, after all, largely a tale of the "strong misreadings" of texts.

101. John Dewey, of course, makes this point at the beginning of his *Quest for Certainty*. See Dewey (1960).

102. Aristotle (1984): *Metaphysics* 1025b25–26.

103. Aristotle (1984): *Metaphysics* 1025a20–21.

104. See the comparisons of Chinese and Western models of the organization of knowledge in chapter 3 for further elaboration on Plato's and Aristotle's classifications of the ways of knowing and of the body of the known.

105. The later step, taken in the first instance by Augustine, was to connect the sense of source, origin, and principle with Divine Agency. See Augustine's causal arguments in Augustine (1950): Book 9.

106. This judgment (which would be severely criticized by any who believe that the Milesians took seriously the senses of *physis* involving

"growth" or "originating power") all but determined the subsequent inter-pretation of these thinkers until well into the twentieth century.

107. Aristotle (1984): *Metaphysics* 1.9. The primary sources for Aristotle's discussion of the four causes are *Physics* 2.3.7 and *Metaphysics* 1.

108. See Emerson (1968:589).

109. Cicero and Virgil are convenient names to associate with a commit-ment to the idea of "humanity." The movement toward the recognition of a common humanity had its Western origins, arguably, with Homer. But the efficacy of such Greek concepts as *philanthropia* (φιλανθρωπία), "sympathy for one's fellow human being," and *oikomene* (οικομένε), "inhabited world," was hardly significant in overcoming the invidious distinctions between Greek and barbarian, free man and slave, or man and woman, until the Hellenistic and Roman periods, which advertised a reasonably successful political unification of diverse peoples and cultures. The *Pax Romana* pro-vided a context within which a form of the *societas generis humani* could be realized. For discussions of the growth of the idea of the "unity of man-kind," from the Greeks onward, see Baldry (1965:*passim*) and Snell (1960:246–63).

110. Augustine (1950:370–371).

111. Augustine (1950:370).

112. Augustine (1950:369).

113. Augustine (1950:369)

114. Augustine (1950:370).

115. Augustine (1950:369).

116. Augustine (1950:373).

117. See Augustine (1950:374–375).

118. Albrecht Dihle finds Augustine's discovery of volition to be part of the dynamic associated with the moral problematic of Augustine's *Confes-sions*. See Dihle (1982:*passim*).

For an elaboration and qualification of Dihle's argument, which stresses the ecclecticism involved in Augustine's and Aquinas' development of the notion of "will," see Kahn (1988). Kahn stresses the manner in which Augustine and Aquinas develop the notion of human will in terms of the exercise of obedience to Divine Will. Kahn stresses, as well, the principally nontheological sources in Stoicism of reflection upon the notion of will.

For a discussion of the consequences of Augustine's construction of the concept of "willing" for moral theory, see MacIntyre (1988:146–163).

119. Kahn (1988:253).

120. Kahn (1988:253).

121. See Plato (1961): *Republic* 439a–440d.

122. See the *Oxford English Dictionary* entry on "Volition."

123. See Plato (1961): *Republic* 440b.

124. Thus Paul Friedländer (1958:193), perhaps, provides a somewhat anachronistic interpretation when, discussing Plato's figure of the soul as chariot and charioteer, he claims:

The two horses are of different kinds, the one being desire (*epithymia*), the other will, drive (*thymos*). Either the mind bridles the two in balance or they drag it with the charioteer into the abyss.

125. See Augustine (1950): Book 19 and *passim*.

126. See Cochrane (1957:480, 399–455). One should not undervalue the effects of Augustine's use of the Johanine notion of *Logos* as the Christ, which helped to provide sophistication and nuance to the original sense of *logos* as "causal account."

127. Calvin (1960): 1.13.18.

128. See Hegel (1961).

129. Feuerbach (1966:72).

130. An example of such usage drawn from the contemporary period is that of Paul Tillich's theological writing. Tillich (1954) makes the analogies explicit. Tillich (1951, 1957, 1963) elaborates the trinitarian analogies in every conceivable direction—from psychic to social relations—in the development of his systematic theology.

131. Whitehead (1968:65–66).

132. For a discussion of the complex issues involved in laying claim to a historicist method, see Hall (1994:53–64).

133. We shall be comparing Aristotle's organization of knowledge with Chinese "encyclopedic" models in chapter 3.

134. For a discussion of the metaphilosophical schools prominent in contemporary philosophy and a list of bibliographical references, see section 3 of the following chapter, entitled "Comparing Comparative Methods."

135. Some materialists attempt to account for freedom by recourse to a variety of ad hoc devices. But the fact that the materialist paradigm has been applied most often to the subjects of scientific inquiry has mitigated any concern to account for freedom from this perspective.

136. See Wittgenstein (1961:7).

137. For a discussion of the importance of the Kantian and Hegelian treatments of the value spheres to the development of our understanding of modernity, see Hall (1994:29–33).

138. For example, we have used the term *philosophy* in an advised manner to apply to certain modes of Chinese thinking. As we shall see in chapter 3, when applied to Chinese thinking, the term fails to overlap in significant ways its principal senses in the West.

139. See the early essay by Derrida (1982) entitled "White Mythology." One might also consult Rorty (1979). Rorty holds that metaphors such as

"mirror" and "glassy essence" are far more than rhetorical decorations for epistemological assumptions; rather, they (or something very like them) were the *generative* ground for the association between "mind" and "reality" that set the program for much of traditional Western philosophy.

140. A. N. Whitehead presents the most poignant illustration of this generalization. His rigorous assault upon the primacy of fact focused directly upon the flux of things as the fundamental datum of which philosophy must give an account. Yet, effectively, his work fell dead-born from the press.

This fate was not inevitable. Whitehead was a victim of his disciples. His thought was seriously compromised by its immediate degeneration into a doctrinaire scholasticism occasioned by a failure of nerve on the part of those who, embarrassed by his constitutive employment of metaphorical language, conspired to purge the poetry from the system.

Whitehead's philosophical remains have since been picked over by Learned Doctors of Morphology, who either cull and rummage, hunting an as yet unsung *analysandum* to import into their own philosophical inventories, or who fiddle, tinker, and refine in an effort to achieve the most precise calibration of the One True System. In either case, the consequence has been the presentation of Whitehead's defense of the intuition of flux, more often than not, as an argument for the ultimacy of fact.

CHAPTER TWO: THE CONTINGENCY OF CULTURE

1. Weber (1958) discusses secularization as a movement from traditional to rational societies. For a more complete discussion of this trend in relation to the development of Western concepts of modernity, see Hall (1994:34–37).

2. See Dewey (1969–72), "The Influence of Darwin on Philosophy."

3. An advantage of applying this correlative method in approaching Chinese culture is that it permits a construal of the gender issue in a way which supports the claims of some Western feminists that reason and rationality are ideologically grounded. In our forthcoming work, *Thinking from the Han—Self, Truth, and Transcendence in China and the West*, we shall discuss in some detail the gender issue in comparative perspective.

4. There are, of course, contemporary spokespersons for the first problematic. The most subtle of these, perhaps, is A. N. Whitehead, whose doctrines of the immanence of law and of "cosmic epochs" (contexts within which general laws of nature may be presumed relatively stable but between and among which there may obtain vastly different types of order) promote the notion of a plurality of world-orders. Likewise, decontructionists (where they still may be found) and proponents of the new pragmatism are first problematic thinkers.

5. See Hall (1982b) and Hall and Ames (1987).

6. One could construe the deconstructionists and Richard Rorty's new pragmatism as such attempts. A relatively novel project, one which we shall be drawing upon in this work, is that of Angus Graham. Graham (1985) develops an understanding of the valuational process underlying all thinking which is peculiarly apropos for the consideration of the relations of causal and correlative thinking.

7. A. N. Whitehead (1968), chapter 3, "Understanding," is the primary source for our construal of abstraction in terms formal and selective modes. See Hall (1982b) for a discussion of these modes.

8. Northrop (1947:83).

9. See Hall (1982a:183–95 and 283) for a critique of Northrop's comparative taxonomy.

10. See Hall (1982b), Hall and Ames (1987), and Hall (1987:*passim*) for detailed discussions and applications of the distinction between logical and aesthetic order.

11. Gernet (1985).

12. The ultimate failure of the accommodationist position in the Rites Controversy is fair demonstration that Rome was not ready to tolerate alternative world views. For a description of anti-Christian sentiment among the general Chinese populace, see Cohen (1963).

13. Gernet (1985:3).

14. Gernet (1985:3).

15. Cohen (1963).

16. Cohen (1984). See also Cohen (1987). We are aware of Cohen's expressed reservations about the position Gernet takes, but hope that our discussion here will encourage a more sympathetic reading of Gernet. It is certainly our argument that cultural incommensurability and linguistic determinism do not follow from identifying and respecting fundamental differences between Chinese and Western philosophical presuppositions.

17. Cohen (1984:xv–xvi).

18. Cohen (1984:5).

19. Robertson (1983:5).

20. We shall be discussing another recent publication, Chad Hansen's *A Daoist Theory of Chinese Thought* (1992), in section 3.2 of this chapter.

21. Schwartz, for example, is concerned about "sameness" as a basis for comparisons: he argues that Confucius in his proportioning of the "religious" and the "this-worldly" is not so very different from Moses, Plato, and the *Upanishads*. He is attracted to comparisons between Mozi and Hobbes, who both describe the state of nature as a war of each against all. Later on in this chapter we shall detail other ways in which Schwartz presumes China and the West to share common projects.

22. It is not clear where the notion of correlative thinking originates. Perhaps it may be traced to Marcel Granet's *La pensée chinoise* (1950), written in 1934, wherein correlativity is taken to be a characteristic of the "Chinese Mind." In the preface to *The View From Afar*, Claude Lévi-Strauss (1985) tells how, upon reading Marcel Granet's *La pensée chinoise*, he was immediately drawn to the characterization of the "Chinese Mind" in terms of correlative thinking. He was, however, frustrated by the vagueness and imprecision of the notion as discussed by Granet. As we shall explore, Lévi-Strauss found in Jakobson's work on aphasia a means of rationalizing the analogical procedures Granet had associated with correlative thinking. Lévi-Strauss (1966) uses the notion of "correlative thinking" to characterize "*la pensée sauvage*." Cassirer (1955) discusses, without using the term, the method of correlative thinking associated with mythopoetic thought. Needham (1956:253–345 *passim*), also influenced by Granet, discusses "correlative thinking" in general and the specific "symbolic correlations" associated with the Chinese cosmologists. Chang Tung-sun (1959:299–324) contrasts a Western "logic of identity" with a Chinese "'logic of correlation' which is neither monistic, nor dualistic, nor reductionistic." John B. Henderson (1984) provides an extensive treatment of correlative "cosmologies." Benjamin Schwartz (1985) devotes a chapter to this subject.

An enlightening work which employs correlative thinking with reference primarily to Western thought is P. K. Feyerabend (1987). What we are calling "correlative thinking" Feyerabend simply designates "empirical thinking." G. E. R. Lloyd (1966 and 1979) describes the correlative mode of thinking in the history of classical Greek thought. An excellent example of the employment of this mode of speculation in the Late Middle Period of European culture is provided by Fernand Hallyn (1990).

By far the most sophisticated philosophical treatment of correlative thinking, as we shall attempt to demonstrate, is provided by Angus Graham, first in *Reason and Spontaneity* (1985:57–60 and section 1.5 *passim*). In this work the term "analogical thinking" is used to describe what are later termed correlative procedures. In *Yin-Yang and the Nature of Correlative Thinking* (1986a) Graham adopts Lévi-Strauss's structuralist approach to correlativity. The substance of this discussion is included in *Disputers of the Tao* (1989:315–370).

23. See Feyerabend (1987:104–127), "Knowledge and the Role of Theories," for a discussion of Socratic definition.

24. See Graham (1985).

25. For the history of this development, see note 22 above.

26. Graham (1989:321–322).

27. Graham (1989:320).

28. See Graham (1989:318, 322).

29. Graham (1989:322).
30. Graham (1989:322).
31. See Plato (1961): *Laws* 889–890. See also Vlastos (1975:23–25) for a discussion of Plato's arguments against the *physiologoi*.
32. Graham (1989:323).
33. See Wilhelm (1977:35–40).
34. Graham (1989:350).
35. Graham (1989:350).
36. Graham (1989:350).
37. Graham (1989:322).
38. Graham (1989:81, 119–123, 155, 420).
39. Graham (1989:319).
40. Karlgren (1948).
41. See Major (1984).
42. In fact, Darwin was most concerned with this eventuality, as the rather tortured apologetics of his "Conclusion" to *The Origin of Species* attests.
43. For a contemporary analysis of causality that allows one to discern its roots in correlative thinking, see Hanson (1965).
44. It would be well to reflect upon the fact that it is a characteristic of the rational intellect to make hard and fast distinctions. For example, the right brain/left brain distinction (which is often forwarded ostensibly in order to support the significance of an aesthetic "right brain") is a distinction a so-called "right-brained" intellect would likely never think to make. We in the West must be mindful of the way in which the distinctions we perforce must make tend to misdirect our understanding of at least one of the distinguished functions.

In saying this we have certainly not forgotten that our own distinctions between logical and aesthetic order, and between first and second problematics, are distinctions made from out of a cultural context dominated by rational, causal assumptions.
45. For our technical discussion of the notion of "vagueness," see section 2.4 below.
46. Whitehead's notion of "cosmic epochs" both testifies to and is entailed by his sense of the primacy of aesthetic order.
47. See chapter 3 for a discussion of the interpretations of *yin* and *yang* along essentialist, universalist lines. For a consideration of the way in which the dualisms that are often purported to underlie metaphysical thinking in the West may be nominalized and rendered relatively harmless, see chapter 5 of Hall (1994).
48. See chapter 1 above, p. 24, and Graham (1990a).
49. For a more complete narrative of the development of these two strains of pragmatism see Hall (1994:65–128).
50. James (1977:145).

51. In a special issue of *Monist* on the subject of metaphilosophy, a distinction is made between "systematic" and "interpretive" pluralism. The former term refers to what we are calling "transcendental pluralism." Our use of the latter term derives from the discussions in this issue. See vol. 73, no. 3 (July, 1990).

52. Rorty (1982:15).

53. Gernet (1985:210).

54. See Lévi-Strauss (1960:56).

55. Schwartz (1985:13).

56. Schwartz (1985:14).

57. Quoted in Schwartz (1985:8).

58. Jaspers (1949): chapter 1, "Die Achsenzeit."

59. Schwartz (1985:2–3).

60. In spite of our criticism of transcendental approaches, we have obviously benefitted from them. We would be remiss if we did not confess that we are seriously indebted to studies such as those of Benjamin Schwartz—as are most students engaged in Chinese-Western comparisons. In urging sympathy for a more pragmatic approach to comparative treatments of Chinese culture, we are merely trying to move closer to an understanding of China and its people that respects its own presuppositions.

61. Hansen (1992).

62. Hansen (1992:5).

63. Hansen (1992:7). Without lending credence to the notion of a "ruling theory" so defined, one would have to say that Hansen exaggerates the extent to which these characterizations of commentators on China are fair. Philosophically sophisticated interpreters of Chinese thought such as A. C. Graham, Herbert Fingarette, and Jacques Gernet certainly do not in any relevant sense attribute a Western theory of language and mind to the Chinese, nor do they view Chinese philosophical theories as straightforward counterparts of our own. And, certainly, the thrust of our own comparative work is in precisely the opposite direction. Further, with regard to the philosophical interpretations that have attempted a balanced assessment of the entire sweep of classical Chinese thought (such as Graham's *Disputers of the Tao*), the "pro-Confucian" interpretation of Chinese thought rather objectively reflects the historiographical assumptions of the received interpretations without endorsing those assumptions.

64. Hansen (1992:3–4).

65. Hansen (1992:163). Unfortunately, Hansen's discussion of Mencius is seriously marred by indulgence in the most gratuitous of rhetorical excesses. Criticizing Mencius' mode of analogical argumentation and D. C. Lau's explication of that method, Hansen provides an embarrassing demonstration of the fact that our affirmations are more often correct than are our (vehement) denials. After the smoke of his disputation clears, one remains

unconvinced that it was Mencius, rather than his would-be verbal assassin, that was the "(ana)logical simpleton" (see p. 189).

Hansen's profound discomfort with Mencius raises a general point about the rationalist bias of the transcendental monist. The occupational hazard of the dialectician is that, sometimes, his impatience with his own lack of understanding of, or appreciation for, a text or argument may lead him (as William Blake said of the rationalists—those seduced by "single-vision and Newton's sleep") to "throw the sand against the wind, which only throws it back again." In Hansen's case, this sometimes leads to *ad hominem* assaults in which he unwittingly manages to toss sand into his own eyes. Quite apart from the irrelevance of these harangues, anyone who champions the cause of logic and rationality as does Hansen should not fail to recognize how resorts to *argumentum ad hominem* will necessarily effuse an aura of self-reference.

66. Hansen (1992:227).

67. Hansen (1992:229).

68. Hansen (1992:303).

69. There is good evidence of this kind of appropriation in two recent collections edited by Graham Parkes, *Heidegger and Asian Thought* (1987) and *Nietzsche and Asian Thought* (1991). The real value of these anthologies lies in an appreciation of how Chinese and Japanese thinkers have come to revision prominent Western philosophers in service to their own cultural contexts. A colleague, John Rothfork, has pointed out to us that Sarvepalli Radhakrishnan's *Eastern Religions and Western Thought* offers a rather novel conceptualization of Western intellectual history from an Indian, specifically Hindu, perspective.

70. Of the type, for example, represented by Graham (1989).

71. See Pepper (1942). This taxonomy was worked out over many years, concluding with his *Concept and Quality: A World Hypothesis* (1967).

72. The best introduction to McKeon's philosophical methodology is found in "Philosophic Semantics and Philosophic Inquiry" in McKeon (1990:242–256). Though this essay was first published in the above cited volume, it was delivered in the form of a paper in 1966. The arguments of the essay had long served as the basis of McKeon's lectures in the "Ideas and Methods" program at the University of Chicago. See also Plochman (1990).

This present work is informed by the taxonomic operations of McKeon and his Platonic avatar, Robert Brumbaugh. As further discussions will demonstrate, however, we provide a distinctly pragmatic interpretation of these notions, and we are not at all convinced that the semantic analyses which are so helpful in understanding the pluralism of Western philosophical culture are relevant to the interpretation of cultures informed by different histories, such as the Chinese. In fact, it should be said that McKeon's own metaphilosophical work leans very far in the pragmatic, culture-specific direction we have taken in this work. McKeon's pragmatism may be attributed to his perhaps most influential teacher, John Dewey.

73. See Brumbaugh (1992). Philosophers such as Pepper, McKeon, and Brumbaugh have taken seriously the pluralism of philosophic theories that besets contemporary thought. In so doing they have continued the tradition of metaphilosophy that originated with Plato's Divided Line and Aristotle's Four Causes. As we noted in the previous chapter, the former was self-consciously used as a means of classifying types of thinking in terms of levels of clarity, while the latter were employed as a means of assessing the adequacy of previous opinions.

74. Dilworth (1989).

75. See Watson (1993), originally published in 1985. In the new edition of his work, Watson discusses his dependence upon his studies with McKeon, a fact that had not been as generously noted in the first edition.

76. Dilworth (1989:1).

77. Dilworth (1989:3).

78. Dilworth (1989:4).

79. Dilworth (1989:6).

80. Dilworth (1989:22).

81. Dilworth (1989:23).

82. Dilworth (1989:23, italics added).

83. Dilworth (1989:29).

84. Dilworth (1989:29).

85. Dilworth (1989:30).

86. We know of no evidence that McKeon presumed the transcultural validity of his schema. That is to say, it is by no means certain that McKeon himself was a transcendentalist, as opposed to a more pragmatically inclined interpretive pluralist.

87. See Dilworth (1989:71).

88. See Hall and Ames (1987).

89. See Dilworth (1989:29).

90. Rescher (1985:173–201) defends a form of pluralism similar to that we have espoused against the self-defeating consequences of a pernicious relativism. Rorty (1982:167–169), in an essay entitled "Pragmatism, Relativism, Irrationalism," defends his pragmatic position against the charge that it entails relativism. The following defense is similar to that employed by these two thinkers.

91. The term is Harold Bloom's.

92. See chapter 3 for a discussion of Chinese terms as constituting concept- or image-clusters. The heavily connotative character of the Chinese language insures that all principal meanings of a term cling to every use of the term.

93. See Rorty (1982:167–169).

94. For a discussion of the axis of "aesthetic pluralism" in American thought from Jonathan Edwards to the present, see Hall (1994:66–80).

95. See Barbara Herrnstein Smith (1988).

96. We believe that this is Donald Davidson's formulation.

97. See Davidson (1986:157–174). Basing his analysis on that of W. V. O. Quine and Donald Davidson, Richard Rorty (1991a:26) draws the same conclusions as we have just drawn with respect to the relations of the intracultural and the intercultural:

> The same Quinean arguments which dispose of the positivists' distinction between analytic and synthetic truth dispose of the anthropologists' distinction between the intercultural and the intracultural.

CHAPTER THREE: EXTENDING THE CIRCLE

1. See "On Ethnocentrism: Reply to Clifford Geertz," in Rorty (1991a: 203–210).

2. This may mean either the denial of the universe or the denial that the universe is distinct from God. See the OED entry for "Acosmism."

3. One advantage of this terminology is that it frees us to use *cosmological* in the one important sense that indeed does have relevance for the comparison of classical Western and Chinese thought—that is, as opposed to *ontological*. As we shall be using these two terms in relation to Chinese speculations, cosmological issues concern the things of the world; ontological issues concern the *being* of the things of the world.

4. See *Laozi* 42:

> *Dao* engenders one,
> One engenders two,
> Two engenders three,
> And three engenders the myriad things.
> The myriad things shoulder *yin qi* and embrace *yang*,
> And mix them to achieve harmony.

5. See, for example, M. Loewe (1982:63), Schipper (1978:3, 4, 371), Hall (1982b:246–249), and Tu Wei-ming (1976:118–119). A. C. Graham, in *Disputers of the Tao* (1989:12), states:

> The past to which Confucius looks back is not the beginning of things; there is no cosmogonic myth in pre-Han literature, merely a blank of pre-history before the first Emperors....

6. See Major (1993:326–327).

7. Note that the phrase which precedes is always embedded in the phrase which follows. The character *you* 有 is added to the first phrase.

8. Cf. *Zhuangzi* 5/2/49. All of the texts except the *Sibu congkan* have this last phrase.

9. In the *Yijing* there is a passage which makes the contingent nature of *yin-yang* clear:

What *yin* and *yang* cannot be used to fathom is called the inscrutable.

10. See Akatsuka Kiyoshi (1977) and Kwang-chih Chang (1980).

11. Schwartz (1985:26).

12. For example, see *Book of Songs* 253.

13. Schwartz (1985:30).

14. Major (1993:18).

15. See Graham (1990a:8).

16. Examples of *xing* being used for inanimate things in the classical corpus abound. In the single text *Huainanzi*, *xing* is used for water (2/16/6, 20/216/12), metal/gold (11/95/27), silk (11/95/28), and for all of the five phases (metal, wood, water, fire, and earth) (20/213/2).

17. Tang Junyi (1968:6). See also Mou Zongsan (1963).

18. Schwartz (1985:175).

19. Graham (1990a:43).

20. Tang Junyi (1988:114–117).

21. See the discussions of the relations of *physis* and *nomos* in chapter 1, pp. 58–65.

22. *Analects* 14/42.

23. *Mencius* 7A/1, 7A/9, and 7B/32.

24. See Collins (1985:73). See also Hall (1982a:353–411) for a discussion of the transformative consequences of contemporary technologies.

25. Mencius 6A11.

26. See 1B8, 4A1, 4A9, 5A5, 589, 7A31.

27. We shall discuss the importance of the familial metaphor later in this chapter.

28. See also 3A/1.

29. See chapter 1, pp. 21–24.

30. The term belongs to Jacques Derrida.

31. The expression "there is a coherence which ties it together" *yi yi guan zhi* 一以貫之 occurs twice in the *Analects*: see 4/15 and particularly 15/3. The 15/3 passage reads:

"Do you, Si, take me to be one who learns a great deal and then remembers it all by heart?"

"Yes, indeed I do. Is this not the case?"

"It is not. Rather, there is a coherence which ties it together."

32. See Feng Qi (1983:84).

33. See *Analects* 15/29.

34. See A. C. Graham (1990b:288).

35. Graham (1989:30, and 1990b:287).

36. I. A. Richards (1932:87) recognizes the possibility that "concept" might be a culturally specific instrument:

> The problem seems to grow still more formidable as we realize that it concerns not only incommensurable concepts but also comparisons between concepts and items which may not be concepts at all.

37. See pp. 66–75.

38. This is the interpretation of *shu* by Lau (1983). See his note on the translation of *Analects* 15/24.

39. Lau (1983:xiv).

40. *Analects* 15/24.

41. Fingarette (1979:382–383).

42. Maspero (1981:136).

43. Maspero (1981:137).

44. See D. C. Lau's essay "On Mencius' Use of the Method of Analogy in Argument" (1984), which is included as Appendix 5, and also "Some Logical Problems in Ancient China" (1952–53).

As we have noted, in his *A Daoist Theory of Chinese Thought*, Hansen (1992) excoriates Mencius' resort to analogical argumentation along with D. C. Lau's defense of Mencius. Suspicion of any sort of analogical operation which is not disciplined by a primary analogate is, of course, a direct consequence of Hansen's transcendental monism. Those, such as Hansen, who promote rational reconstructions of Chinese thought have always been frustrated, nonplussed, and indignant in the face of Chinese uses of correlativity and analogy. Part of the argument of the last chapter is that the Western dialectical rationalist as transcendental monist fails to understand nonrationalized analogical operations, and so fails to understand analogy or correlativity as an autonomous mode of thinking. This is a serious failing for any who would claim to approach Chinese culture descriptively rather than through the medium of a rational reconstruction.

45. *Mencius* 3B/9.

46. Daoism is a complex movement in early China. There were certainly Daoists in late Qin and early Han, advocates of Huang-Lao precepts, who combined Legalistic designs with Daoist techniques as a strategy for participating effectively in the political order. There are several essays in the *Hanfeizi* that reflect this manipulative spirit.

47. See Needham (1956:182), Graham (1978:10), and Schwartz (1985: 168–172).

48. Lloyd (1990:110).

49. Graham (1978) cites an article by Fukui Shigemasa (1970) that suggests a relationship between Xunzi and the disappearance of Mohism.

50. Xu Fuguan (1975:150–151) discusses the meaning of the title of this chapter. He takes this one fascicle to be a grand summary of the entire text, and following historical commentators from Xu Shen of the Han dynasty to Zeng Guofan of the Qing, suggests that it means "The Great Gathering" or "The Greatest Category." Xu Fuguan insists upon the centrality of this chapter in bringing together the Confucian ideas found in several of the other chapters, notably "Miucheng xun," "Fanlun xun," "Quanyan xun," and "Renjian xun." The summary postface was probably written by someone with Daoist sympathies, so this point is not widely appreciated.

51. See Knoblock (1988:36–49), "The Influence of Xunzi's Thought."

52. Knoblock (1988:49).

53. Chen Chi-yun (1986:790–792).

54. Graham (1978:32 and 325).

55. Graham (1978:63–64).

56. Graham (1978:53).

57. Graham (1978:62 and 22).

58. Cua (1985:96–97; also 56–61).

59. Cua (1985:54).

60. Cua (1985) provides a detailed analysis of the "style" of argumentative engagement in late Zhou China. See especially pp. 6–12.

61. Cua (1985:11).

62. See *Book of Songs* 210.

63. There are several good discussions of the origins of this important philosophical notion. See Graham (1958), Chan (1964:124–129), Needham (1956:472–475), Wittenborn (1981:32–48), and Peterson (1986:13–31).

64. See Tang Yi (1988:1–27).

65. Cua (1985) in his discussion of the *Xunzi* highlights the philosophic importance of *li*. For the neo-Confucian extension of this term, see the arguments of Peterson (1982). Peterson, having reflected on the import of this term in the texts of Song neo-Confucianism, arrives at a set of propositions from which we borrow freely in defining the classical sensibility. The major difference between the classical and medieval interpretation of *li* lies in Peterson's attribution of a kind of transcendentalism to the texts of neo-Confucianism.

66. See the critique of the organic vocabulary in Ames et al. (1994:198–201).

67. Wittenborn (1981:42).

68. Peterson (1986:18).

69. Cua (1985:22–23).

70. See Needham (1956:280).

71. See Cua (1985) for a discussion of the various modes of analogical thinking associated with *li*.

72. Cua is sensitive to this basic meaning of *lei* when he states that "a *lei* is formed by way of comparison or analogy between similarities and differences" (1985:55). He further qualifies his usage of *lei* when he states: "In this essay, I have used 'sort,' 'kind,' and 'class' interchangeably without implying that *lei* is a set-theoretical notion. So also, my occasional use of 'category' must not be construed as an ascription of a general doctrine of categories to Hsün Tzu [Xunzi]" (1985:178–179).

73. It is perhaps significant that the basic meaning of *xiang*, the term used for "image," is "elephant." Although we have archaeological evidence that elephants once existed in northern China and that ivory carving as a Chinese artform was already highly developed as far back as the Shang dynasty, an analysis of this evidence suggests that the elephant, like the whale and the rhinoceros, were rare species imported from outside of China, which, because of their novelty, were used primarily for display. Thus a creature known but rarely seen came to be used to denote the presentational act of "conjuring" or "imaging." See Norman and Mei (1976:274–301).

74. In fact, just as *cosmos* in its classical Greek usage means an elegant as well as an ordered world, so *logos* means *oratio* as well as *ratio*, the rhetorical as well as the rational, the "word" itself as well as the reasoned explanation. That is, the aesthetic and rhetorical side of cosmology tends to go unnoticed in the rationalistic interpretations of the classical Greek tradition that have dominated Western philosophy.

75. See Peterson (1982:67–116, especially 80–81).

76. Note that *ni* 擬 means "to calculate" or "to estimate" or "to fathom," as well as "to imitate." "To imitate" makes the exercise too passive.

77. See *Yijing* [*Chou-i*] 41/*xi shang*/6. Cf. Peterson (1982:114).

78. The character *yi* 意 is translated variously as "concept" (Owen), "thought/s" (Wilhelm-Baynes, Yu, Peterson), and "ideas" (Hellmut Wilhelm, Graham, Schwartz). *Yi* is glossed in the *Shuowen* lexicon as "intended meaning, purpose" (*zhi* 志), reflecting its performative connotation. It is in this sense of "design" that we understand it.

79. See the *Yijing* [*Chou-i*] 44/*xi shang*/12. Cf. Richard Wilhelm (1967:322).

80. The degree to which the *Analects* is constructed out of a concrete "path" vocabulary has not been fairly noticed. Consider the number of key terms that focus this image: "to go against, to deviate from" (*wei* 違); "to go out from, follow" (*you* 由); "(to line shoulder to shoulder =) to order" (*qi* 齊); "gate" (*men* 門); "to reach" (*zhi* 之 or *ji* 及); "to dwell or abide" (*ju* 居 or *chu* 處); "to look out over" (*lin* 臨); "to err by overstepping" (*guo* 過); "to get through (= to understand thoroughly)" (*da* 達); "to go straight" (*zhi* 直); "to pass" (*shi* 逝); "to ford a stream (= to help)" (*ji* 濟); "to follow the proper way" (*shu* 述); "to repair, construct, clear" (*xiu* 修); "to be at a dis-

tance" (*yuan* 遠); "to be near at hand" (*jin* 近); "to leave behind" (*yi* 遺); "to leave tracks" (*ji* 迹); "to move ahead" (*jin* 進); "to retire" (*tui* 退); "followers (= disciples)" (*tu* 徒); "a roundabout way, astray" (*yu* 迂); "to move to" (*xi* 徙); and so on.

In addition to the "path" imagery, there are others: "archery" (*she* 射), "the vessel" (*qi* 器), "design" (*wen* 文), and so on.

81. *Analects* 7/1. The primary meaning of *shu* 述 is "to follow along the path." By extension, it means "to record," "to transmit"—hence, the more familiar translation, "I transmit but do not innovate." See Lau (1983).

82. Owen (1992:27). The only problem with Owen's reflection on *shi* is his seeming inclination to limit this insight to poetry as opposed to other art forms. We would want to include Chinese art broadly under this characterization.

83. For discussions of the importance of metaphor in this way, see Lakoff and Johnson (1980), and more recently, Lakoff (1987). See also Pepper's (1942) classic treatment of metaphors underlying our metaphysical traditions, and his later extension of this work (1967). For accounts of metaphor associated with post-analytic pragmatism, see Donald Davidson's 'What Metaphors Mean" (1984) and "A Nice Derangement of Epitaphs" (1986).

84. See Wang Bi (1965:10b–11b).

85. Wang Bi (1965:11b).

86. *Huainanzi* SBCK 1/4b–5a, draft translation in collaboration with D. C. Lau.

87. Zhang Dainian's (1982:497) position is that it is not until Buddhism enters China that what is known becomes inextricably bound to the knower, but authentication in action seems to be a premise found not only in Daoism, but throughout the early indigenous corpus. Confucius in defining "knowing" (*zhi* 知) as dynamic and performative clearly represents this relationship.

88. The introduction of Buddhism into China is, in an important degree, an exception to this kenning analogy. Often the new vocabulary would be transliterated—*nieban* 涅盤 for *nirvana*—accumulating a set of characters identified for this particular purpose. Even so, this claim cannot be pressed too hard, since the "scrutinizing the meaning" (*geyi* 格義) method of translating technical Sanskrit terms by equivalents taken from the Chinese corpus—*wuwei* 無爲 for *nirvana*, for example—was a continuing challenge to the more philologically sophisticated translators who worried about conceptual equivocation, and who insisted upon transliteration as one guarantee of accuracy.

89. Hellmut Wilhelm (1977: especially pp. 198–199), in his discussion of imagery in the *Yijing*, collects passages from the text that connect the formulation of human imagery with the patterning of heaven and earth.

90. For a discussion of the function of image in Chinese thought, see Pauline Yu (1987), especially the first chapter, "Setting the Terms." See also Owen (1985), especially the first chapter, "Omen of the World: Meaning in the Chinese Lyric."

91. Thus, when Raphals makes the tentative and heuristic claim that "the Chinese counterpart of the Greek epic is the Chinese novel and its antecedents" (1992:189), a number of important issues are elided. Not the least of these issues involves the need for a comparison of the role of *mythos* in the generation of literary genres in the West with the equivalent dynamic in classical China. Raphals is singularly equipped to address issues such as these. We would all benefit were she to do so.

92. If we were to find fault with A. S. Cua's (1985) otherwise exemplary treatment of *li* 理 in the *Xunzi*, we would question his willingness to separate out instances of *li* under the headings of purportedly different meanings. See pp. 21–22.

93. And, of course, it could be, or become, rational discourse to the extent that it adopts the Indo-European meanings of "not" and "non".

94. Language which does not lead one to posit ontological difference between Being and beings, but only a difference between one being and another, suggests a decentered world whose centers and circumferences are always defined in an ad hoc manner. The mass of classical Chinese philosophical discourse, then, is already deconstructed. Or better said: the *you/wu* problematic does not urge the creation of texts which can be victimized by the deconstructor.

95. See Derrida (1978:*passim*).

96. This is the last passage in *Zhuangzi* 7. Cf. Graham (1981:98).

97. Graham (1981:98–99).

98. Interpreters with less pride than we have might find a pun in "self-so-ing," suggesting as it does "self-sowing" and "self-sewing."

99. This vocabulary will be familiar to the reader from contemporary chaos theory discussions; see especially the work of Katherine Hayles (1990 and 1991).

100. These three passages are all excerpted from *Zhuangzi*, chapter 2. Cf. Graham (1981:48–57). Both Needham (1956) and Schwartz (1985) claim that philosophical Taoism is holistic, and look for the meanings of things in "the ineffable Tao." Graham seems to prefer, as do we, a more phenomenalist interpretation of *Zhuangzi* that precludes the assumption that everything is one.

101. See Graham (1981:56).

102. For a discussion of the concept *de*—conventionally translated "power" or "virtue"—as "particular focus," see Hall and Ames (1987:216–226).

103. *Zhuangzi*, chapter 2. Cf. Graham (1981:58).

104. See Rump (1979:17).

105. See Ames (1989).

106. "A Discussion of Parity among Things" is the title of the second chapter of the *Zhuangzi*.

107. The translation—admittedly a controversial rendering of an obscure segment of *Zhuangzi*, chapter 8—is cited from Chang Chung-yuan (1963:66).

108. *Analects* 15/29.

109. See Said (1978).

110. The *locus classicus* that expresses this interdependence among dimensions of order is the opening passage of the *Great Learning (daxue)*.

111. We introduced this focus/field model briefly at the end of the last chapter.

112. Graham (1979:86).

113. Karlgren (1948).

114. The *Lushi chunqiu* and *Huainanzi* are perhaps the two most notable examples of this new genre.

115. See Major (1984).

116. Twitchett and Loewe (1986).

117. Yü Ying-shih (1986:379–380).

118. Yü Ying-shih (1986:382).

119. The fact that this sense of history continues even today can be illustrated by examining contemporary Chinese thinkers. When Mao Zedong, for example, defines the relationship between any single event and the course of history in his 1937 essay, "On Contradictions," he is articulating a classic example of Chinese historiography rather than translating Marxist-Leninist dialectics into Chinese. See Mao Zedong (1951).

120. In the *TLS* review of *The Cambridge History of China*, vol. 1, Roger T. Ames (1988) was critical of Derk Bodde's contribution in precisely these terms. Bodde rehearses the recorded events leading up to the founding of the Qin dynasty and those which describe its brief tenure, only to then dismiss them for questionable historicity. Rather than reducing Chinese history to what Napoleon called "agreed upon lies," it would have been much more informative and important for Bodde, given his enormous familiarity with this period, to explore the ritual and participatory meaning of these events.

121. Robertson (1983:4).

122. Robertson (1983:4).

123. Robertson (1983:3–4).

124. See Liang Congjie (1986).

125. This diagram is elaborated from a number of discussions in the Aristotelian corpus. We have drawn primarily upon Aristotle (1984): *Metaphysics*, *Physics* and *Nichomachaen Ethics*.

126. Mary Tiles (n.d.:5–6). A revised version is available in Tiles (1992). See also Mary and James Tiles (1993).

127. Tiles (1992:7–8).

128. Tiles (n.d.:8).

129. Tiles (n.d.:8).

130. Lovejoy (1962).

131. We can't resist citing in full the "Chinese Encyclopedia" entry of Borges. In this present context one can appreciate how, from the Western perspective, Borges' "entry" would not seem very much more fantastic than would those in the authentic encyclopedias of China. In "The Analytical Language of John Wilkins" [Borges (1981:140–143)], Borges refers to

> a certain encyclopedia entitled *Celestial Emporium of Benevolent Knowledge*. On those remote pages it is written that animals are divided into (a) those that belong to the emperor, (b) embalmed ones, (c) those that are trained, (d) suckling pigs, (e) mermaids, (f) fabulous ones, (g) stray dogs, (h) those that are included in this classification, (i) those that tremble as if they were mad, (j) innumerable ones, (k) those drawn with a very fine camel's hair brush, (l) others, (m) those that had just broken the flower vase, (n) those that resemble flies from a distance.

132. Liang Congjie (1986:40). We have also consulted the draft translation of this essay by Lynette Shi.

133. Graham (1989:319).

134. A rather extensive table of one version of these correspondences is contained in Needham (1956:262–263). Needham's note on the tables of correspondences is revealing of a Western distinction that has little relevance for a Chinese world constructed on the basis of fruitful correlations: "We have already noticed that certain gods and spirits, of which little is known, were connected with the five elements. I omit them as lacking scientific interest."

135. From Zhou Guidian (1989:47).

136. From Zhou Guidian (1989:48).

137. From Zhou Guidian (1989:51).

138. See Tiles (n.d.: 10–11) for a discussion of the use of "emblems" in the hermetic tradition.

139. For an elaboration on this point see the discussion of the "*li/xiang*" relationships above, pp. 211–225.

140. *Huainanzi* SBCK 21/5b.

141. Hellmut Wilhelm (1977:200–201).

142. Gernet (1985:242).

143. These tables are taken from John Major (1993:222–223).

144. A parallel kind of problem is announced by Nietzsche (1977) in his

reflections on how languages such as French and German came to be gendered, "la table" and "le soliel:"

> When man gave all things a sex he thought, not that he was playing, but that he had gained a profound insight . . .

145. See the discussion in "Relating Categories to Question Forms in Pre-Han Chinese Thought" in Graham (1990a:360–411), where Graham concludes:

> the sentence structure of Classical Chinese places us in a world of process about which we ask "What is it like?" (*ho jo*), centered in things which we distinguished by the question "Which?" (*shu*), with location and direction on the Tao for which we ask with a "Where/whence/whither?" (*wu-hu*), and further categorized by "At what time?" (*ho shih*) and the rest of the question forms. But on the outskirts of this clear-cut world are water, fire, breath, air, [*sic* and earth] which in varying degrees resist being categorised even as thing or process, and which Chinese philosophy classes not as things (*wu*) but the *ch'i* 氣 out of which things condense and into which they dissolve. In the realm of *ch'i* the question "which?" carries us, beyond the Five Phases (*wu hsing* 五行) to the ultimate dichotomy, of Yin and Yang. Beyond that is the primordial *ch'i*, of which one can still ask "Whence?" and also, since it is moving, "At what time?"

146. We would prefer the more provisional "patterns or model" instead of "rules" for *ze* 則.

147. Major (1993:249).

148. Major (1993:251–252).

149. See Major (1993:11), who insists that the "cosmos is a unity" (we would, of course, prefer the language of "continuity" to that of "unity") in the sense that "there is no distinction between the affairs of nature and the affairs of humans—and their ruler." Illustrations of this continuity are:

> *Yijing* 3/1 言:
> The great person in virtue is continuous with the heavens and the earth, in brightness is continuous with the sun and moon, in fortune is continuous with the ghosts and spirits.
> *Zhuangzi* 2:
> The heavens and the earth were born together with me; the myriad things are continuous with me.

150. Needham (1956:18–26).

151. Ronan (1978:170). See Needham (1956:302).

152. Needham (1956:337).

153. Needham (1956:338).

154. Schwartz (1985:373).

155. Schwartz (1985:373).

156. See *Mencius* 4B/19.

157. See *Analects* 18/6, which needs to be qualified with 5/10, 4/25, 4/3, and so on.

158. See Munro (1985:*passim*) and Schwartz (1985:200, 416–418).

159. See Hall (1987), Hall and Ames (1987), and Hall (1994) for discussions of *ars contextualis*.

160. Arnheim (1982:vii).

161. Arnheim (1982:2).

162. Arnheim (1982:5).

163. Nishijima Sadao (1986:522).

164. King (1985:58).

165. King (1985:62).

166. King (1985:62).

167. Russell (1922:40).

168. This model of centripetal harmony is pervasive in the defining literature of the Chinese tradition. It explains Mencius' point in claiming that "all of the myriad things are complete here in me" and "one who applies exhaustively his heart-and-mind realizes his character, and in thus realizing his character, he realizes *tian* 天" (*Mencius* 7A/4 and 7A/1). Again, it describes the relationship between the fields (*dao* 道) and foci (*de* 德) that we are familiar with from the Daoist cosmology. It is also the vision of the Hua-yan notion of *shi shi wu ai* 事事無礙—a field of interpenetrating particulars in which each construes its own whole.

169. *Analects* 14/35.

170. See Deutsch (1992), Kasulis et al. (1993), Ames et al. (1994), and Carrithers et al. (1964).

171. See Liu (1990), Smith (1983 and 1991), Elman (1984), and Henderson (1984).

Bibliography of Works Cited

Adkins, A. W. H. (1970). *From the Many to the One*. Ithaca: Cornell University Press.

Akatsuka Kiyoshi (1977). *Chūgoku kodai no shūkyō to bunka*. Tokyo: Kadokawa Shoten.

Ames, Roger T. (1989). "Putting the *te* Back in Taoism." In *Nature in Asian Traditions of Thought*, J. Baird Callicott and Roger T. Ames (eds.). Albany: State University of New York Press.

———. (1988). Review of *The Cambridge History of China*, vol. 1 (Denis Twitchet and Michael Loewe, eds.). *Times Higher Education Supplement*, 22 January.

Ames, Roger T., W. Dissanayake, and Thomas Kasulis (eds.) (1994). *Self as Person in Asian Theory and Practice*. Albany: State University of New York Press.

Analects (Lun-yü) (1940). Peking: Harvard-Yenching Institute Sinological Index Series, Supplement 16.

Aristotle (1984). *The Complete Works of Aristotle*. 2 vols. Jonathan Barnes (ed.). Princeton: Princeton University Press.

Arnheim, Rudolf (1982). *The Power of the Center: A Study in the Visual Arts*. Berkeley and Los Angles: University of California Press.

Augustine (Saint) (1950). *The City of God*. Marcus Dodds (trans.). New York: Modern Library.

Book of Changes. See *Chou-yi*.

Baldrey, H. C. (1965). *The Unity of Mankind in Greek Thought*. Cambridge: Cambridge University Press.

Borges, Jorge Luis (1981). *Borges: A Reader*. Emir Rodriguez and Alasdair Reid (eds.) New York: E. P. Dutton.

Brumbaugh, Robert (1992). *Western Philosophic Systems and Their Cyclic Transformations*. Carbondale: Southern Illinois University Press.

———. (1985). *Philosophers of Greece*. Albany: State University of New York Press.

Burnet, John (1964). *Greek Philosophy—Thales to Plato*. New York: St. Martin's Press.

Calvin, John (1960). *Institutes of the Christian Religion*. John T. McNeill (ed.), Ford Lewis Battles (trans.). Philadelphia: Westminster Press.

Carrithers, Michael, Steven Collins, and Steven Lukes (eds.) (1985). *The Category of the Person*. Cambridge: Cambridge University Press.

Cassirer, Ernst (1955). *Philosophy of Symbolic Forms*. New Haven: Yale University Press.

Chan, W. T. (1964). "The Evolution of the Neo-Confucian Concept *Li* as Principle." *Tsing Hua Journal of Chinese Studies*, n.s., 4.2 (February): 123–148.

Chang Chung-yuan (1963). *Creativity and Taoism*. New York: Harper and Row.

Chang Kwang-chih (1980). *Shang Civilization*. New Haven: Yale University Press.

Chang Tung-sun. (1959). "A Chinese Philosopher's Theory of Knowledge." In *Our Language and Our World*, S. I. Hayakawa (ed.). New York: Harper. This article appeared originally in Chinese in the *Sociological World* 10 (June 1938) under the title, "Thought, Language and Culture." It was translated by Li Anzhe, and published in English in the *Yenching Journal of Social Studies* 1, no. 2 (1939).

Chen Chi-yun (1986). "Confucian, Legalist, and Taoist Thought in Later Han" In *The Cambridge History of China Volume I: The Ch'in and Han Empires 221 B.C.–A.D. 220*, Denis Twitchett and Michael Loewe (eds.). Cambridge: Cambridge University Press.

Chou-i (1935). Peking: Harvard-Yenching Institute Sinological Index Series, Supplement 10.

Chuang Tzu (1947). Peking: Harvard-Yenching Institute Sinological Index Series, Supplement 20.

Cochrane, Charles Norris (1957). *Christianity and Classical Culture: A Study of Thought and Action From Augustus to Augustine*. New York: Oxford University Press.

Cohen, Paul A. (1987). Review of *China and the Christian Impact: A Conflict of Cultures* by Jacques Gernet, trans. Janet Lloyd (Cambridge: Cambridge University Press, 1985) in *Harvard Journal of Asiatic Studies* 47:2 (December, 1987): 674–683.

———. (1984). *Discovering History in China: American Historical Writing on the Recent Chinese Past*. New York: Columbia University Press.

———. (1963). *China and Christianity: The Missionary Movement and the Growth of Anti-foreignism, 1860–1870*. Cambridge: Harvard University Press.

Collins, Steven (1985). See Michael Carrithers.

Cornford, Francis M. (1957). *From Religion to Philosophy: A Study in the Origins of Western Speculation*. New York: Harper and Row.

———. (1952). *Principium Sapientiae*. New York: Harper and Row.

Cua, A. S. (1985). *Ethical Argumentation: A Study in Hsün Tzu's Moral Epistemology*. Honolulu: University of Hawaii Press.

Davidson, Donald (1986). "A Nice Derangement of Epitaphs." In *Philosophical Grounds for Rationality: Intentions, Categories, Ends*, Richard Granely and Richard Warner (eds.). Oxford: Clarendon Press.

———. (1984). "What Metaphors Mean." In *Inquiries into Truth and Interpretation*. Oxford: Clarendon Press.

Derrida, Jacques (1982). "White Mythology." Reprinted in *Margins of Philosophy*, Alan Bass (trans.). Chicago: University of Chicago Press.

———. (1978). *Writing and Difference*. Alan Bass (trans.). Chicago: The University of Chicago Press.

Deutsch, Eliot (1992). *Creative Being: The Crafting of Person in the World*. Honolulu: University of Hawaii Press.

Dewey, John (1969–72). *John Dewey, The Early Works, 1882–1898*, vol. 4. Jo Ann Boydston (ed.). Carbondale: Southern Illinois University Press.

———. (1960). *Quest for Certainty*. New York: G. P. Putnam's Sons.

Diels, H., and W. Kranz (1962). *Fragmente der Vorsokratiker*. 10th ed. Berlin.

Dihle, Albrecht (1982). *The Theory of Will in Classical Antiquity*. Berkeley: University of California Press.

Dilworth, David (1989). *Philosophy in World Perspective—A Comparative Hermeneutic of the Major Theories*. New Haven: Yale University Press.

Dodds, E. R. (1951). *The Greeks and The Irrational.* Berkeley: University of California Press.

Eliade, Mircea (1961). *Myths, Dreams, and Mysteries: The Encounter between Contemporary Faiths and Archaic Realities.* New York: Harper and Row.

Elman, Benjamin A. (1984). *From Philosophy to Philology: Intellectual and Social Aspects of Change in Late Imperial China.* Cambridge: Council on East Asian Studies, Harvard University.

Emerson, Ralph Waldo (1968). "Plato." In *Ralph Waldo Emerson: Essays and Journals,* Lewis Mumford (ed.). Garden City, NY: International Collectors Library.

Feng Qi (1983). *Zhongguo gudai zhexue de luoji fazhan* [The logical development of ancient Chinese philosophy]. Vol. 1. Shanghai: Shanghai Peoples' Press.

Feuerbach, Ludwig (1966). *Principles of the Philosophy of the Future.* Manfred Vogel (trans.). New York: Bobbs-Merrill.

Feyerabend, P. K. (1987). *Farewell to Reason.* New York: Verso Press.

Fingarette, Herbert A. (1979). "Following the 'One Thread' of the *Analects.*" *Journal of the American Academy of Religion,* Thematic Issue 47, no. 3S:373–406.

Frankfort, H. and H. A., Wilson, John and Jacobson, Thorkild. (1967). *Before Philosophy: An Essay in Speculative Thought in the Ancient Near East.* Baltimore: Penguin Books. Original edition 1946.

Friedländer, Paul (1958). *Plato: An Introduction.* New York: Harper and Row.

Frost Robert (1963). *Complete Poems of Robert Frost.* New York: Holt, Rinehart and Winston.

Fukui Shigemasa (1970). "The resuscitation of Mo-chia in the former Han dynasty." *Tōhōgaku* 39:1–18.

Gernet, Jacques (1985). *China and the Christian Impact: A Conflict of Cultures.* Janet Lloyd (trans.). Cambridge: Cambridge University Press. Originally published in 1982 as *Chine et christianisme* (Paris: Editions Gallimard).

Graham, A. C. (1990a). *Studies in Chinese Philosophy and Philosophical Literature.* Albany: State University of New York Press.

———. (1990b). "Reflections and Replies." In *Chinese Texts & Philosophical Contexts: Essays Dedicated to Angus C. Graham,* Henry Rosemont, Jr. (ed.). Peru, IL: Open Court.

———. (1989). *Disputers of the Tao.* La Salle, IL: Open Court.

———. (1986a). *Yin-Yang and the Nature of Correlative Thinking*. Singapore: Institute of East Asian Philosophies.

———. (1986b). Review of Benjamin J. Schwartz's *The World of Thought in Ancient China*. *Times Literary Supplement*, 18 July.

———. (1985). *Reason and Sponteneity*. London: Curzon Press.

———. (trans.) (1981). *Chuang-tzu: The Inner Chapters*. London: George Allen & Unwin.

———. (1979). "The *Nung-chia* 'School of the Tillers' and the Origins of Peasant Utopianism in China." *Bulletin of the School of Oriental and African Studies* 42, part 1.

———. (1978). *Later Mohist Logic, Ethics and Science*. Hong Kong: The Chinese University Press.

———. (1958). *Two Chinese Philosophers*. London: Lund Humpheries.

Granet, Marcel (1950). *La pensée chinoise*. Paris: Editions Albin Michel.

Guthrie, W. K. C. (1971). *The Sophists*. Cambridge: Cambridge University Press, 1971. Originally published as volume 3 of his *History of Greek Philosophy* (Cambridge: Cambridge University Press, 1969), part I, "The World of The Sophists."

Hall, David L. (1994). *Richard Rorty: Prophet and Poet of the New Pragmatism*. Albany: State University of New York Press.

———. (1987). "Logos, Mythos, Chaos: Metaphysics as the Quest For Diversity." In *New Essays in Metaphysics*, Robert C. Neville (ed.). Albany: State University of New York Press.

———. (1982a). *The Uncertain Phoenix: Adventures Toward a Post-Cultural Sensibility*. New York: Fordham University Press.

———. (1982b). *Eros and Irony: A Prelude to Philosophical Anarchism*. Albany: State University of New York Press.

Hall, David L., and Roger T. Ames (1987). *Thinking Through Confucius*. Albany: State University of New York Press.

Hallyn, Fernand (1990). *The Poetic Structure of the World—Copernicus and Kepler*. New York: Zone Books.

Hansen, Chad (1992). *A Daoist Theory of Chinese Thought*. Oxford: Oxford University Press.

Hanson, N. R. (1965). *Patterns of Discovery*. Cambridge: Cambridge University Press.

Hayles, N. Katherine (ed.) (1991). *Chaos and Order: Complex Dynamics in Literature and Science*. Chicago: University of Chicago Press.

———. (1990). *Chaos Bound: Orderly Disorder in Contemporary Literature and Science*. Ithaca: Cornell University Press.

Hegel, G. W. F. (1961). *On Christianity: Early Theological Writings*. T. M. Knox (ed.). New York: Harper Torchbooks.

Henderson, John B. (1984). *The Development and Decline of Chinese Cosmology*. New York: Columbia University Press.

Homer. (1955). *The Iliad*. E. V. Rieu (trans.). New York: Penguin Books.

Huainanzi. (1920–22). Sibu congkan edition. See D. C. Lau and Chen Fong Ching (eds.).

Inwood, Brad (trans.) (1992). *The Poem of Empedocles*. Toronto: University of Toronto Press.

Jaeger, Werner (1967). *Humanism and Theology*. Milwaukee: Marquette University Press.

James, William (1977). *A Pluralistic Universe*. Cambridge: Harvard University Press.

———. (1958). *Varieties of Religious Experience*. New York: New American Library.

———. (1911). *Some Problems of Philosophy*. New York: Longmans, Green, and Co.

Jaspers, Karl (1949). *Vom Ursprung und Ziel der Geschichte*. Munich: R. Piper and Co. Verlag.

Jonas, Hans (1966). *The Phenomenon of Life*. New York: Harper and Row.

Kahn, Charles (1988). "Discovering the Will: From Aristotle to Augustine." In *The Question of Ecclecticism*, J. M. Dillon and A. A. Long (eds.). Berkeley: University of California Press.

Kasulis, Thomas P., Roger T. Ames, and W. Dissanayake, (eds.) (1993). *Self as Body in Asian Theory and Practice*. Albany: State University of New York Press.

Karlgren, B. (1948). "Legends and Cults in Ancient China." *Bulletin of the Museum of Far Eastern Antiquities* 18.

Kerferd, G. B. (1981). *The Sophistic Movement*. Cambridge: Cambridge University Press.

King, Ambrose (1985). "The Individual and Group in Confucianism: A Relational Perspective." In *Individualism and Holism: Studies in Confucian and Taoist Values*, Donald Munro (ed.). Ann Arbor: University of Michigan Press.

Kirk, G. S. (1954). *Heraclitus, The Cosmic Fragments*. Cambridge: Cambridge University Press.

Kirk, G. S., and J. E. Raven (1964). *The Presocratic Philosophers*. Cambridge: Cambridge University Press.

Knoblock, John (1988). *Xunzi: A Translation and Study of the Complete Works*. Volume 1, books 1–6. Stanford: Stanford University Press.

Lakoff, George (1987). *Women, Fire, and Dangerous Things*. Chicago: University of Chicago Press, 1987.

Lakoff, George, and Mark Johnson (1980). *Metaphors We Live By*. Chicago: University of Chicago Press.

Lau, D. C. (1952–53). "Some Logical Problems in Ancient China." *Proceedings of the Aristotelian Society* 53:189–204.

———. (trans.) (1983). *Confucius: The Analects*. Hong Kong: Chinese University Press.

———. (trans.) (1984). *Mencius*. Hong Kong: Chinese University Press.

Lau, D. C., and Chen Fong Ching (eds.) (1992). *A Concordance to the Huainanzi*. ICS Ancient Chinese Text Concordance Series. Hong Kong: Commercial Press.

Lévi-Strauss, Claude (1985). *The View From Afar*. New York: Basic Books.

———. (1966). *The Savage Mind*. Chicago: University of Chicago Press.

———. (1960). "Overture to 'le Cru et le cruit.'" In *Structuralism*, Jacques Ehrmann (ed.). New Haven: Yale French Studies, no. 36.

Liang Congjie (1986). "Non-congruent Circles: The Organization of Encyclopedic Knowledge in Chinese and Western Cultures." Originally published in Chinese as "Bu chunghe de quan—cong baike quanshu kan zhongxi wenhua," in *Towards the Future* No. 2 (1986), with a draft translation made by Lynette Shi.

Lloyd, G. E. R. (1990). *Demystifying Mentalities*. Cambridge: Cambridge University Press.

———. (1979). *Magic, Reason and Experience: Studies in the Origin and Development of Greek Science*. Cambridge University Press.

———. (1966). *Polarity and Analogy: Two Types of Argumentation in Early Greek Thought*. Cambridge: Cambridge University Press. Reprinted by Bristol Classical Press, 1987.

Liu, Kwang-Ching (ed.) (1990). *Orthodoxy in Late Imperial China*. Berkeley: University of California Press.

Loewe, Michael (1982). *Chinese Ideas of Life and Death: Faith, Myth, and Reason in the Han period (202BC–AD220)*. London: George Allen and Unwin.

Lovejoy, Arthur O. (1962). *The Great Chain of Being—A Study of the History of an Idea*. New York: Harper and Row.

Lucretius (1946). *On the Nature of Things*. Charles E. Bennett. (trans.) Roselyn, NY: Walter J. Black.

MacIntyre, Alasdair (1988). *Whose Justice? Which Rationality?* Notre Dame: Notre Dame University Press.

Major, John S. (1993). *Heaven and Earth in Early Han Thought: Chapters Three, Four, and Five of the Huainanzi*. Albany: State University of New York Press.

———. (1984). "The Five Phases, Magic Squares, and Schematic Cosmography." In *Explorations in Early Chinese Cosmology*, Henry Rosemont, Jr. (ed.). Chico, CA: Scholars Press.

Mao Zedong (1951). "Maodunlun (On Contradictions)." In *Mao Zedong Xuanji (Selected Works of Mao Tse-tung)*, vol. 1. Peking: Peoples Press.

Maspero, Henri (1981). *Taoism and Chinese Religion*. F. Kierman, Jr. (trans.). Amherst: University of Massachusetts Press.

McKeon, Richard (1990). "Philosophic Semantics and Philosophic Inquiry." In *Freedom and History and Other Essays: An Introduction to the Thought of Richard McKeon*. Chicago: University of Chicago Press.

McNeill, John T. (ed.) (1960). *Institutes of the Christian Religion*. Ford Lewis Battles (trans.). Philadelphia: The Westminster Press.

Mencius (Meng Tzu) (1941). Peking: Harvard-Yenching Institute Sinological Index Series, Supplement 17.

Milton, John (1962). *Paradise Lost*. Merritt Y. Hughes (ed.). New York: The Odyssey Press.

Mou Zongsan (1963). *Zhongguo zhexue de tezhi*. Taibei: Xuesheng shuju.

Munro, Donald J. (1985). "The Family Network, the Stream of Water, and the Plant." In *Individualism and Holism: Studies in Confucian and Taoist Values*. Ann Arbor: University of Michigan Press.

Needham, Joseph (1956). *Science and Civilisation in China*, vol. 2. Cambridge: Cambridge University Press.

Newton, Isaac (1952). *Optics*. Robert Maynard Hutchins (ed.). *Great Books of the Western World*, vol. 34. Chicago: Encyclopaedia Britannica Inc.

Nietzsche, Friedrich Wilhelm (1977). *Daybreak* 3. In *A Nietzsche Reader*, R. J. Hollingdale (trans.). Middlesex, UK: Penguin.

Nishijima Sadao (1986). "The Economic and Social History of Former Han." In *The Ch'in and Han Empires 221 B.C.–A.D. 220*. Vol. 1 of *The Cambridge History of China*, Denis Twitchett and Michael Loewe (eds.). Cambridge: Cambridge University Press.

Norman, Jerry, and Tsu-lin Mei. (1976). "The Austroasiatics in Ancient South China: Some Lexical Evidence." *Monumenta Serica* 23:274–301.

Northrop, F. S. C. (1947). "The Possible Concepts by Intuition and Concepts by Postulation as a Basic Terminology for Comparative Philosophy." In *The Logic of the Sciences and The Humanities*. New York: World Publishing Co.

Nussbaum, Martha C. (1986) *The Fragility of Goodness: Luck and Ethics in Greek Tragedy and Philosophy*. London: Cambridge University Press.

Owen, Stephen (1992). *Readings in Chinese Literary Thought*. Cambridge: Council on East Asian Studies, Harvard University.

———. (1985). *Traditional Chinese Poetry and Poetics*. Madison: University of Wisconsin Press.

Ovid. (1955). *Metamorphoses*. Rolfe Humphries (trans.). Bloomington: Indiana University Press.

Parkes, Graham (ed.) (1991). *Nietzsche and Asian Thought*. Chicago: Chicago University Press.

———. (ed.) (1987). *Heidegger and Asian Thought*. Honolulu: University of Hawaii Press.

Pepper, Stephen (1967). *Concept and Quality: A World Hypothesis*. La Salle, IL: Open Court Press.

———. (1942). *World Hypotheses*. Berkeley: University of California Press.

Peterson, Willard J. (1986). "Another Look at *Li*." *The Bulletin of Sung-Yuan Studies* (1986):13–31.

———. (1982). "Making Connections: 'Commentary on the Attached Verbalizations' of the *Book of Changes*. *Harvard Journal of Asiatic Studies* 42(1):67–116.

Plato (1961). *The Collected Dialogues of Plato*. Edith Hamilton and Huntington Cairns (eds.). Princeton: Princeton University Press.

———. (1957). *Plato's Cosmology*. Francis MacDonald Cornford (trans.). New York: The Liberal Arts Press.

Pope, Alexander (1965). *Alexander Pope's Collected Poems*. Bonamy Dobreé (ed.), New York: Dutton.

Plochman, George (1990). *Richard McKeon—A Study*. Chicago: University of Chicago Press.

Putnam, Hilary (1990). *Realism with a Human Face*. Cambridge: Harvard University Press.

Quine, W. V. O. (1963). *From a Logical Point of View*. New York: Harper and Row.

Raphals, Lisa (1992). *Knowing Words—Wisdom and Cunning in the Classical Traditions of China and Greece.* Ithaca: Cornell University Press.

Rescher, Nicholas (1985). *Strife of Systems—An Essay on the Grounds and Implications of Philosophical Diversity.* Pittsburgh: University of Pittsburgh Press.

Richards, I. A. (1932). *Mencius On the Mind.* New York: Harcourt, Brace and Co.

Robertson, Maureen (1983). "Periodization in the Arts and Patterns of Change in Traditional Chinese Literary History." In *Theories of the Arts in China,* Susan Bush and Christian Murck (eds.). Princeton: Princeton University Press.

Robinson, John M. (1968). *Introduction to Early Greek Philosophy: The Chief Fragments and Ancient Testimony, with Connecting Commentary.* Boston: Houghton Mifflin.

Ronan, Colin (1978). *The Shorter Science and Civilisation in China—An Abridgment of Needham's Original Text,* Vol. 1. Cambridge: Cambridge University Press.

Rorty, Richard (1993). "Putnam and the Relativist Menace." *The Journal of Philosophy* 90(9):443–461.

———. (1991a). *Objectivity, Relativism, and Truth. Philosophical Papers,* vol. 1. Cambridge: Cambridge University Press.

———. (1991b). *Essays on Heidegger and Others. Philosophical Papers,* vol. 2. Cambridge: Cambridge University Press.

———. (1982). "The World Well Lost." In *Consequences of Pragmatism.* Minneapolis: University of Minnesota Press.

———. (1979). *Philosophy and the Mirror of Nature.* Princeton, N.J.: Princeton University Press.

Rump, Arrienne, in collaboration with Wing-tsit Chan (trans.) (1979). *Wang Pi's Commentary on the Lao tzu.* Society for Asian and Comparative Philosophy, Monograph no. 6. Honolulu: University Press of Hawaii.

Russell, Bertrand (1922). *The Problem of China.* London: George Allen & Unwin.

——— (1918). *Mysticism and Logic.* London: Longmans, Green.

Said, Edward (1978). *Orientalism.* New York: Random House.

Salmon, Wesley (1970) *Zeno's Paradoxes.* Library of Liberal Arts. New York: Bobbs-Merrill Company, Inc.

Schipper, Kristofer (1978). "The Taoist Body." In *History of Religions* 17, nos. 3–4:355–386.

Schwartz, Benjamin I. (1985). *The World of Thought in Ancient China*. Cambridge: Harvard University Press.

Shelley, Percy Bysshe (1965). *The Works of Percy Bysshe Shelley*. Vol. 2. Roger Ingpen and Walter E. Reck (eds.). New York: Gordian Press.

Smith, Barbara Herrnstein (1988). *Contingencies of Value: Alternative Perspectives for Critical Theory*. Cambridge: Harvard University Press.

Smith, Richard J. (1991). *Fortune-Tellers & Philosophers: Divination in Traditional Chinese Society*. Boulder, CO: Westview Press.

———. (1983). *China's Cultural Heritage: The Ch'ing Dynasty, 1644–1912*. Boulder, CO: Westview Press.

Snell, B_____ *The Discovery of the Mind—The Greek Origins of* ___ght. New York: Harper and Row.

___1993). *The Bully Culture: Enlightenment, Romanti-* ___ranscendental Pretense 1750–1850*. Lanham, MD: ___tlefield.

___ongxi zhexue sixiang zhi bijiao lunwenji*. Taipei:

___uo zhexue yuanlun: Yuanxing pian*. Hong Kong:

___gguo wenhua zhong de lixing siwei" (Rational ___se culture). *Wenhua: Zhongguo yu shijie* (Culture: ___rld) 5, Beijing: Xinhua shudian:1–27.

___es of Reason in Western Culture." In *Alternative* ___ Deutsch (ed.). Honolulu: Society for Asian and ___ophy.

___the Market Place—Knowledge and Language,"

___les (1993). *An Introduction to Historical Epis-* ___rity of Knowledge*. Oxford: Blackwells.

___ *Power, Justice*. New York: Oxford University

___ *Systematic Theology*, 3 vols. Chicago: The Uni- ___ess.

___lity and Commonality: An Essay on Chung-* ___ersity of Hawaii Press.

___el Loewe (eds.) (1986). *The Ch'in and Han* ___ 220*. Vol. 1 of *The Cambridge History of* ___mbridge University Press.

Vlastos, Gregory (1975). *Plato's Universe*. Seattle: University of Washington Press.

Wang Bi (1965). "Ming Xiang" [Elucidating the Image]. In *Zhouyi lueli* [A Summary Introduction to the *Book of Changes*] in the *Baibu Congshu jicheng*.

Watson, Walter (1993). *The Architectonics of Meaning: Foundations of the New Pluralism*. Chicago: University of Chicago Press. Originally published in 1985 by the State University of New York Press.

Weber, Max (1958). *The Protestant Ethic and the Spirit of Capitalism*. New York: Scribners.

Wendel, Francois (1963). *Calvin—Origins and Development of his Religious Thought*. Philip Mairet (trans.). New York: Harper and Row.

Whitehead, A. N. (1978). *Process and Reality*. Corrected Edition. David Ray Griffin and Donald W. Sherburne (eds.). New York: The Free Press.

———. (1968). *Modes of Thought*. Reprint. New York: Free Press.

Wilhelm, Hellmut (1977). *Heaven, Earth, and Man in the Book of Changes*. Seattle: University of Washington Press.

Wilhelm, Richard (trans.) (1967). *The I Ching or Book of Changes*. 3d ed. Translated into English by Cary F. Baynes. Princeton: Princeton University Press.

Williams, Bernard (1993). *Shame and Necessity*. Berkeley: University of California Press.

Wittenborn, Allen (1981). "*Li* Revisited and Other Explorations." *The Bulletin of Sung-Yuan Studies* 17:32–48.

Wittgenstein, Ludwig (1961). *Tractatus Logico-Philosophicus*. D. F. Pears and B. F. McGuinness (trans.). New York: The Humanities Press.

Xu Fuguan (1975). *Liang Han sixiangshi*. Hong Kong: Chinese University of Hong Kong Press.

Yijing. See *Chou-i*.

Yu, Pauline. (1987). *The Reading of Imagery in the Chinese Poetic Tradition*. Princeton: Princeton University Press.

Yü Ying-shih (1986). "Han Foreign Relations." In *The Ch'in and Han Empires 221 B.C.–A.D. 220*. Vol. 1 of *The Cambridge History of China*, Denis Twitchett and Michael Loewe (eds.). Cambridge: Cambridge University Press.

Zhang Dainian (1982). *Zhongguo zhexue dagang*. Peking: Chinese Academy of Social Sciences Press.

Zhou Guidian (1989). *Dongxue tanwei*. Peking: Peking Normal University Press.

Index

science, and transcendental religion, 134–135
second problematic thinking, xvii–xviii, 2, 11–13, 25, 31, 54, 64, 102–103, 108–109, 112–119, 137, 181, 196, 204, 209, 241, 257
  in China, 202–211
  and culture, 17
  and definition, 39
  and dualism, 224
self, ix
  in Aristotle, 85–86
  in Augustine, 85–87
  "focal," 279
  in Plato, 85
  Homeric, 70
self-consciousness, 181
Shang, Yang, 203
shangdi 上帝 ("ancestoral lord"), xvi
shen 神 ("divinity, spirituality"), 226
Shen, Dao, 203
Shen, Nong, 239
shi 詩 ("poetry") distinguished from "poetry," 219
shu 恕 ("taking oneself as analogy"), 199–200
Shuowen, 212
Sima, Qian, 201
Skelton, John, 111
skepticism, 165, 210
Skinner, B. F., 52
Smith, Richard, 281
Snell, Bruno, 70
Socrates, 5, 29, 31, 62–63, 73–74, 79, 93, 199
  and definition, 66, 68
solipsism, 176
Solomon, Robert, xiv, 283
Song, Xing, 203
Sophists, 28, 56–66, 73, 93, 98, 116
  as a counterdiscourse, 56–66
  as pragmatic thinkers, 64
Spinoza, Baruch, 97
square, xxi–xxii, 283
Stadium paradox, 27
Stein, Gertrude, 195

stochastic variables, 231
Stoics, 85–86
structuralism, 147
subjectivity, xiii
Summa Theologica, 88
syllogistic thinking, 84
symbol, 217
Symposium, 7

T
Taiping yulan, 254
Tang, Junyi, 188–190
Tang, Yi, 213
teleology, 53, 186–187, 191–192, 245, 251
  the absence of, 233
  and process, 138–139
"ten thousand things," 11, 55, 140, 184, 215, 234–235, 238, 257
Thales, 4, 18–19, 79
Theogony, 7–8
theory, 136, 172
  metaphorical ground of, 135–141
  and *theoria*, 49–55
Thinking Through Confucius, xvi, 199, 257
"this" and "that" model of order, 232–237, 246, 273
Thrasymachus, 60–61
Thucydides, 15
thymos, 85–86
tian 天 ("Heaven/nature"), xvi, 186–187, 192, 199
tianli 天理 ("natural coherence"), 213, 223
Tiles, Mary, 248
Tillich, Paul, 292
Timaeus, 5, 7
totemic classifications, 125, 127, 134
tragedies, Greek, 14
transcendence, xiii–xv, 2, 36, 85–86, 89, 100, 105, 115, 139, 143, 155, 186, 193, 198, 214, 229–230, 239, 279, 283
  and concept-formation, 39
  and methodology, 142–165